**INTERNATIONAL
BUSINESS
STRATEGY AND
CROSS-CULTURAL
MANAGEMENT**

INTERNATIONAL BUSINESS STRATEGY AND CROSS-CULTURAL MANAGEMENT

AN APPLIED APPROACH

NICOLE FRANZISKA RICHTER
Associate Professor of International Business, Department of Business and Management, University of Southern Denmark, Denmark

JESPER STRANDSKOV
Professor Emeritus of International Business, Department of Business and Management, University of Southern Denmark, Denmark,

SVEN HAUFF
Professor of Human Resource Management, Department of Humanities and Social Sciences, Helmut Schmidt University, Hamburg, Germany

VASYL TARAS
Associate Professor of International Business, University of North Carolina at Greensboro, USA

Cheltenham, UK • Northampton, MA, USA

© Nicole Franziska Richter, Jesper Strandskov,
Sven Hauff and Vasyl Taras 2022

All rights reserved. No part of this publication
may be reproduced, stored in a retrieval system
or transmitted in any form or by any means,
electronic, mechanical or photocopying,
recording, or otherwise without the prior
permission of the publisher.

Published by
Edward Elgar Publishing Limited
The Lypiatts
15 Lansdown Road
Cheltenham
Glos GL50 2JA
UK

Edward Elgar Publishing, Inc.
William Pratt House
9 Dewey Court
Northampton
Massachusetts 01060
USA

Companion website material can be found at
https://www.e-elgar.com/textbooks/richter

A catalogue record for this book
is available from the British Library

Library of Congress Control Number:
2022931150

Printed on elemental chlorine free (ECF)
recycled paper containing 30% Post-Consumer Waste

ISBN 978 1 83910 862 4 (cased)
ISBN 978 1 83910 863 1 (eBook)
ISBN 978 1 83910 864 8 (paperback)

Printed and bound in the USA

CONTENTS IN BRIEF

Full contents		vii
Preface		xi
How to approach a case challenge		xiv
1	Analyzing international markets	1
2	Selecting international markets	26
3	Analyzing and selecting modes to enter, operate in and exit international markets	59
4	Entering markets with a partner	96
5	Developing strategy and strategic positioning in international markets	129
6	Designing global value chains	174
7	Designing the MNE organization	199
8	Navigating intercultural interactions	231
9	Leading and motivating people in an international environment	257
10	Building an effective international workforce	290
Index		319

FULL CONTENTS

Preface	xi
How to approach a case challenge	xiv

1 Analyzing international markets — 1
- 1.1 Analyzing the formal context — 2
  - 1.1.1 The economic context — 2
  - 1.1.2 The political and regulatory context — 6
  - 1.1.3 A standard framework to assess the formal context — 9
- 1.2 Analyzing the informal context — 11
  - 1.2.1 Country cultures — 11
  - 1.2.2 Clustering national cultures — 16
  - 1.2.3 Cultural archetypes and individual cultural value patterns — 17
- Chapter review questions — 20
- Magic Juice: A disruptor in the business of juice bars — 22

2 Selecting international markets — 26
- 2.1 A top-down or restricted international market selection — 26
  - 2.1.1 Internationalization motives — 26
  - 2.1.2 Portfolio analyses — 28
- 2.2 A bottom-up or expansive international market selection — 35
  - 2.2.1 Liabilities of foreignness — 35
  - 2.2.2 Managing distance — 37
- 2.3 The international market selection at Metro Group — 42
- 2.4 An international market selection toolset — 45
- Chapter review questions — 49
- Market selection at Magic Juice — 52

3 Analyzing and selecting modes to enter, operate in and exit international markets — 59
- 3.1 Complexity of the entry mode decision — 60
- 3.2 Non-equity modes — 63
  - 3.2.1 Export modes — 63
  - 3.2.2 Contracting modes — 65
- 3.3 Equity modes — 69
  - 3.3.1 Ownership modes: Wholly owned subsidiaries versus joint ventures/strategic alliances — 70

		3.3.2	Establishment modes: Greenfield investments versus acquisitions	75
	3.4	\	An analytical framework to guide the entry mode decision	77
		3.4.1	Internal firm factors	79
		3.4.2	Home-country factors	83
		3.4.3	Host-country factors	83
	3.5		Entry mode changes over time and foreign market exit	87
	3.6		Entry modes in fashion retailing, with a focus on Bestseller	89
	Chapter review questions			92
	Magic Juice: Which entry mode(s) to choose?			95
4	**Entering markets with a partner**			**96**
	4.1		Selecting the right partner	97
	4.2		Paying the right price	101
		4.2.1	Valuation methods	101
		4.2.2	Form of payment	106
	4.3		Negotiations	108
	4.4		Integration approaches	111
	4.5		Cultural integration	113
	4.6		Best practices to integrate the partners	116
	4.7		Adidas and Reebok: What went wrong?	118
	Chapter review questions			122
	Magic Juice: Entering a partnership?			124
5	**Developing strategy and strategic positioning in international markets**			**129**
	5.1		Crafting a strategy	130
		5.1.1	Strategy statements	130
		5.1.2	Strategic analyses	134
	5.2		Developing a global or local positioning	140
		5.2.1	Identifying customer needs and viable segments	140
		5.2.2	Developing value propositions	144
		5.2.3	Integrating value propositions or not	146
	5.3		Monitoring strategic success	153
	5.4		Strategic positioning and strategy at IKEA	161
	Chapter review questions			164
	Magic Juice: Strategy and positioning			167

6	**Designing global value chains**		**174**
	6.1 Understanding global value chains		174
		6.1.1 Elements of the value chain and value added	174
		6.1.2 The rise of the global value chain and the "smiling curve"	178
	6.2 Value chain strategies		182
		6.2.1 Value chain configurations and their determinants	182
		6.2.2 Strategic options to configure the value chain	186
	6.3 Global value chain design at ECCO A/S versus competitors		191
	Chapter review questions		194
	Magic Juice: Expanding the value chain?		196
7	**Designing the MNE organization**		**199**
	7.1 Hierarchical models (traditional structures)		200
	7.2 Heterarchical models: Networks and transnationals		206
	7.3 Organizational coordination mechanisms: Centralization, formalization and socialization		209
	7.4 Subsidiary roles and mandates		212
	7.5 Power and conflicts within the MNE organization		217
	7.6 Procter & Gamble: Organizational transformation		221
	Chapter review questions		226
	Magic Juice–Zumo Saludable: How to organize the combination?		229
8	**Navigating intercultural interactions**		**231**
	8.1 The culture map		232
		8.1.1 The dimensions of the culture map	232
		8.1.2 The culture map in action	236
	8.2 Intercultural competence		241
		8.2.1 The dimensions of intercultural competence	241
		8.2.2 Intercultural competence in action	248
	8.3 Intercultural competence development at the Bosch Group		250
	Chapter review questions		252
	Intercultural communications at Magic Juice: Difficulties ahead?		255
9	**Leading and motivating people in an international environment**		**257**
	9.1 Leadership in international environments		258
		9.1.1 Global leadership dimensions and attributes	258
		9.1.2 Cultural values and clusters as predictors of leadership expectations	263
		9.1.3 Keys for successful leadership in international environments: Expectation-behavior fit	264

	9.2	Leadership in global virtual teams	267
		9.2.1 The challenge of leading global virtual teams	267
		9.2.2 Keys for successful leadership in global virtual teams	268
	9.3	Motivation in an international environment	271
		9.3.1 Theories to understand motivation: Maslow, McClelland and equity theory	271
		9.3.2 Work centrality and work values around the globe	277
		9.3.3 Determinants of job satisfaction across cultures	279
	9.4	Employee engagement at a marketing consultancy	282
	Chapter review questions		284
	Magic Juice: Towards self-management?		287
10	**Building an effective international workforce**		**290**
	10.1	Recruitment and selection	290
		10.1.1 Recruitment approaches	290
		10.1.2 Selection tools	292
		10.1.3 Selection criteria for international assignments	296
	10.2	Training and development	298
	10.3	Compensation	302
		10.3.1 Compensation components in an international context	302
		10.3.2 Approaches for compensating international employees	304
		10.3.3 International assignment policy at Bosch	306
	10.4	Performance management	306
		10.4.1 Cross-cultural perspectives on performance management	306
		10.4.2 High-performance work practices	308
	10.5	Integration of international migrants	310
	Chapter review questions		314
	Magic Juice: Towards an HRM strategy		318
Index			319

PREFACE

THE APPROACH OF THE BOOK

Teaching international business (and related courses) with a focus on cross-cultural aspects for several years or even decades, we have identified a need for a new textbook that satisfies the following requirements: First, we need a textbook that provides a more advanced and applied approach to international business. Hence, the textbook should include conceptual frameworks and analytical toolsets with the relevant level of depth to ultimately perform evaluations in real practical settings. Second, and related to the first aspect, we need a textbook that more strongly connects theoretical foundations with case work. In our perspective, it is essential to pay attention towards applying theory to cases, as this will enable the reader to work on a diversity of case challenges. There is a clear relation between theory and toolsets that needs to be understood in order to develop convincing applications. Third, we need a more balanced approach between more traditional strategic management or international business topics with aspects of cross-cultural management. Most textbooks focus on one of these topics; thus, students sometimes do not fully experience the connection between the topics, and lecturers are required to recommend more than one textbook. Fourth, we need a textbook that sheds specific light on current trends and challenges in international business and cross-cultural management – such as research on cultural intelligence, migration or digitalization – and integrates these new aspects with the traditional elements. Finally, we perceived a need for accompanying materials that are ready and easy to use and that reflect the current (electronic) realities of readers.

With *International Business Strategy and Cross-Cultural Management: An Applied Approach* we aim to meet these requirements. For each of the covered topics, we strongly build on theory without over-simplification. Thus, readers will be able to fully capture theoretical details and advancements. Whenever possible, we provide toolsets that will help students and practitioners to translate the contents into real practical settings. In addition, we always demonstrate how theory corresponds to real life using practical examples from multinational firms, often headquartered in a European setting yet active around the globe. In order to further strengthen the reader's ability to apply theory to practice, we have developed the Magic Juice case that goes throughout the book and covers the key topics of each chapter. Overall, our ambition was to integrate international business and cross-cultural management areas and shed light on the current trends and challenges in these areas. Therefore, the book provides a comprehensive overview of key international business and cross-cultural management topics that always integrates current developments. Last but not least, we have put a lot of effort into preparing contemporary materials that are available on the book's website (see below).

FOR WHOM THIS BOOK IS WRITTEN

With this book we address several target groups. First, the book addresses postgraduate, master-level students in international business and management, cross-cultural studies, international human resources management or other studies with an international perspective. In particular, we provide a key source for lecturers and students involved in the X-Culture project (www.x-culture.org), an international online business collaboration project in which students are working in international virtual teams in order to develop solutions to an international business challenge. Second, the book can be a valuable source for business practitioners. With our applied approach, and especially with the toolsets that are outlined in every chapter, we offer multiple insights and guidelines that can support leaders and managers in facing the challenges of a global world. Third, we also address researchers in international business and cross-cultural management. We provide a comprehensive overview of classic and contemporary theories and illustrate various research approaches related to the different topics, which can support future studies.

THE STRUCTURE OF THE BOOK

The book contains 10 chapters. In Chapter 1 we give an overview on ways to analyze international markets, differentiating between the formal and the informal context. Building on that, Chapter 2 focuses on the selection of future markets in which to do business. Chapter 3 deals with the choice of an appropriate entry mode, and the questions of how to operate in an international market and how to exit it if necessary. In Chapter 4 we shed specific light on issues related to entry modes that involve a strategic partnership, like selecting the right partner, negotiating the terms of the deal, paying the right price and integrating the partners. In Chapter 5 we introduce theoretical backgrounds and conceptual frameworks related to the development of a strong strategic positioning of multinational enterprises (MNEs) in different international markets and integrating this into an international strategy framework. Chapter 6 explains the relevant concepts and frameworks related to the analysis of global value chains. Chapter 7 discusses the various organizational designs used by MNEs, and headquarter and subsidiary roles that fit different environmental needs. In Chapter 8 we introduce and discuss two concepts that can be used to navigate intercultural interactions: the culture map and the concept of cultural intelligence. Chapter 9 describes the influence of international culture on the behavior of leaders, and the preferences for leadership styles and motivation of employees. Finally, Chapter 10 provides insights into the key instruments of international human resource management.

THE BOOK'S WEBSITE AND ACCOMPANYING MATERIALS

The book's website can be accessed via https://www.e-elgar.com/textbooks/richter. On the website you will find multiple materials customized to lecturers and readers. We provide further data and links to relevant data providers (for instance, to retrieve relevant indicators on the international environment). We offer various toolsets in the form of, for instance, Excel templates that come with cases or provide input to practical challenges. We offer a compilation of links to video materials that accompany the book's contents, in the form of providing either thematical overviews, practical insights or reflections of theoretical concepts by their inventors.

For lecturers, we provide slides for each chapter that go beyond simple copies of the chapter figures and are ready to be used in class. In addition, we provide further cases/exercises, recommended further readings for each chapter and student best practices in solving specific case challenges of the book. For our case study, we offer a teaching note that assists in using the case in courses. Finally, we provide a test bank of multiple-choice questions for each chapter.

ACKNOWLEDGMENTS

We would like to take this opportunity to thank our friends and colleagues for their ideas and support, as well as numerous corporate practitioners for their in-depth insights. We thank Prof. Dr. Christopher Schlägel for providing comments on the book proposal. We thank all X-Culture members who shared their insights in our survey on relevant book contents, and hope that we managed to meet your requirements. We thank Jennifer Schleusener, who helped to prepare the materials included in this book and on its website. We would also like to thank Fiona Briden and Francine O'Sullivan and the whole Edward Elgar team for their careful and helpful support in the realization of the book.

Nicole Franziska Richter
Jesper Strandskov
Sven Hauff
Vasyl Taras

HOW TO APPROACH A CASE CHALLENGE

Reading this book, you will be familiarized with the concepts, theories and toolsets of relevance in international business and cross-cultural management.[1] Yet, to develop relevant skills you will need to practice and learn by doing. To help you do that, we have integrated various cases in our book and more comprehensively developed the fictional Magic Juice case. Cases discuss a specific dilemma or situation of a (real or fictional) firm. The idea of a case is that it offers an opportunity to apply knowledge and develop managerial skills. There are no real-life consequences if you make mistakes; hence, feel free to experiment with different toolsets to identify which works best with you.

A case provides a description of the challenge(s) to be addressed and offers additional information to assist you in performing relevant analyses. Cases often also integrate information that may not be of use, and on the other hand lack relevant information. In a real management situation, you will face the same dilemma: Information may be incomplete and may be secondary and not customized to the problem that you are analyzing. In real situations, you will search for further (external) information, and request information from relevant stakeholders; for some cases, you are invited to do the same. Yet, it may also suffice to make assumptions on information gaps.

Cases often put you into the position of a top manager having responsibility for the performance of an entire organization. While you may currently not be an active member of a top management team, having the ability to understand the bigger picture will increase your value as an employee, and improves your chances of getting to the top – if you desire. Cases may relate to a current situation or a past situation; while readers often prefer current examples, the recentness of a case is not decisive. Many challenges that firms face are timeless in nature; for instance, how to adapt to a changing environment, to best compete in a certain market and to expand to other markets. It matters more that you practice to analyze a problem and to propose solutions that fit a certain situation (may it be current or past). Finally, fictive cases are often useful as everybody has access to the same information, and such cases enable students to practice specific skills of relevance.

STEP 1: ANALYZE THE STRATEGIC SITUATION AND DIAGNOSE

The first step in analyzing a case is to identify the basic or key facts. Reading the case for the first time, we recommend that you note down the following key information:

1. What firm(s) is the case about?
2. Who are the relevant actors in the case?
3. What are the key events that happened, and when and where? Here it may be of use to create a timeline of events. In most case challenges, you will need to re-read the case in more detail to better define the challenge.
4. Which aspects are relevant, and why?

5. What is going well, and what is going wrong? At this stage you identify the symptoms to decide on further toolsets to run in order to diagnose the main problem or challenge.

Be careful that you do not jump too quickly into proposing solutions – do a thorough analysis first and carefully select a toolset that will be of relevance to truly understand the problem and potential solutions. Truly understanding the problem(s) faced and therewith also the opportunities for the firm are key parts of solving a practical challenge. The frameworks and toolsets to be used depend on the challenge you face. For example, if the case challenge relates to the strategic set-up of the firm, it is useful to analyze the firm's external environment with a focus on its industry and competitive situation (for example, see the toolsets in Chapter 5, such as Porter's five forces), and its internal situation, resources and current strategies (for example, see the toolsets in Chapter 5, such as VRIO or the business model canvas). Use the information gained to describe the problem(s) or opportunity(ies) for the firm, such as whether current resources satisfy the demands of the external environment, whether it has a clearly defined strategy and competitive advantage, and whether it could take more advantage of external opportunities or needs to re-position itself to avoid serious weaknesses and to address external threats.

While often case challenges do not specifically ask for an analysis of the firm's performance or the performance consequences of certain solutions, analyzing performance aspects is an implicit key aspect in any management situation. Hence, you are advised (if possible) to analyze the firm's performance situation; that is, calculate relevant financial ratios (for example, profitability, cost structure, capital structure) and understand the financial implications of the problems or opportunities identified.

STEP 2: FORMULATE POSSIBLE SOLUTIONS, AND EVALUATE THEIR PROS, CONS AND POTENTIAL OUTCOMES

After having identified the problem or opportunities, the next step is to propose one or more potential solutions. This involves information about what the top management team should do, and why this is the right course of action. Hence, each part of your solution should be justifiable based on the findings of your analyses.

While some solutions are clearly better than others, there is in almost all cases no single, correct solution to the challenge. Therefore, it is essential to maintain an open mind and carefully evaluate the pros and cons of different potential solutions. We recommend that you not just take the first idea, but think about other solutions that may generate the same (or even better) results. Some of the most successful firms engage in scenario planning. That is, they develop several possible scenarios; these can relate to different outcomes or environmental developments that may matter for the success of the solutions developed. In this case, it makes sense to think about the likelihood of these scenarios and to identify the solution that works best under the most probable scenarios. Otherwise, it may also be useful to think of scenario planning with regard to developing a best, a worst and a trend case to visualize the range of potential outcomes of your proposed solution.

For real cases, you may sometimes find out what the management did. Be aware that this is not necessarily the best course of action. We recommend that you not stop your creative process here just because you found out what happened. Firms quite often make decisions on less thorough analyses, and yes, even big multinationals make mistakes. You may arrive at a different and even better solution. Thus, stand by your findings, as long as you can support them with solid analyses and reasoning.

STEP 3: DEVELOP AN IMPLEMENTATION PLAN

The final step is to develop a plan to implement the solution. To demonstrate the feasibility of your solution, you will need to explain how the solution can be put into action. This involves answering questions, such as: What activities need to be performed and how does this fit the firm's current activities, and what resources (for example, human resources, financial resources) are needed to implement the solution proposed? In addition, the implementation plan needs to specify the timeline and priority of actions (for example, what steps are taken first, and which are sequential in nature).

Finally, to demonstrate the feasibility of your solution, you can – if the case allows – demonstrate how you are going to finance the implementation of your solution (which may, depending on the case challenge, involve an evaluation of the payback period and break-even considerations). Ideally, you can demonstrate the outcomes (in the form of key performance indicators) that your solution will generate, in the best, worst or trend forecast. Often, this implementation plan may be supplemented by a risk analysis; that is, you identify risks that could affect the success of implementing your solution. Ideally, you also elaborate on ideas to mitigate these risks throughout the implementation phase.

STEP 4: DISCUSSING AND REPORTING CASE FINDINGS

Case discussion classes are most useful if everybody is prepared and willing to share thoughts and ideas. It is relevant that you focus on constructive feedback and demonstrate mutual respect – this does not imply that you need to agree with others' solutions. In most situations, perspectives, priorities and ideas will be considerably different. Thus, be prepared to be challenged, and feel free to challenge others. Constructive content-related conflict can be beneficial to the solutions developed and the learnings generated (in cross-cultural settings, you are invited to double-check this assumption using findings presented in Chapter 8).

In discussions as well as in reporting your analyses and solution, you must be able to convince your peers of their value by backing them up with sound logic and arguments. Lecturers generally provide their own guidelines regarding the content and format of a report, and you are advised to request specific guidelines. We recommend structuring the report using the questions involved in an elevator talk, in which you would explain what you have done, why you have done it and how you have done it. Hence, you first specify what it is that you propose; that is, you outline the key problem and the essence of your solution to the problem (for instance, start with an executive summary). Second, you demonstrate why you propose it; that is, you more thoroughly demonstrate your analysis of the situation, evaluate your solutions against other solutions and justify why you believe that your solution is best. Finally, you explain how it works and elaborate on the implementation plan.

NOTE

1. This guideline was inspired by Rothaermel's ideas on how to conduct a case analysis (see F. T. Rothaermel, 2015, *Strategic Management*, New York: McGraw Hill).

1
Analyzing international markets

Multinational enterprises (MNEs) operate in the international environment consisting of more than 214 discrete economies – 188 country markets and 26 economies with populations of more than 30,000 inhabitants (from numbers provided by the World Bank in 2020[1]). In describing this environment, authors often refer to rising "VUCA characteristics"; that is, volatility, uncertainty, complexity and ambiguity that challenge the managers of MNEs in developing successful strategies.

International business (IB) strategy aims at exploiting international opportunities while responding to threats in the international environment. Hence, for managers to develop IB strategy, they need to understand the volatile, uncertain, complex and ambiguous international context in which they operate. One step in confronting the VUCA environment is to collect relevant information, as this can narrow down the margin for errors in decision-making. In addition, as we are in a world of information overload, the decision-maker needs to identify what information is of relevance and how she or he can structure the information to differentiate interconnected from complementary aspects. We will in the following discuss indicators and conceptual frameworks that assist this understanding.

We differentiate the formal context from the informal context and introduce indicators and toolsets to analyze both. The formal context refers to the economic, political and regulatory environment of the firm. To generate an understanding of opportunities that may arise from the economic situation and development in a country, or an understanding of the threats that may stem from its political instability or poor legal system and procedures, several indicators and toolsets can be useful. In addition to the formal environment, the informal context also matters in IB. It refers to the values, norms and codes of conduct – sometimes simply summarized as "culture" – in international environments. Cultural dissimilarities can aggravate the cooperation between IB partners and pose a risk. Yet, cultural dissimilarities can also offer opportunities, namely profiting from more approaches to problem-solving and information processing. To exploit the opportunities and mitigate threats, you will need to understand what culture is and how you can identify relevant differences.

Hence, we will in the following discuss indicators and conceptual frameworks that characterize the economic environment, operationalize the political and regulatory context and measure and structure cultural values, and therewith assist with several decision challenges of relevance to the IB decision-maker introduced throughout this book.

1.1 ANALYZING THE FORMAL CONTEXT

1.1.1 The economic context

To understand the global economic order, international inter-dependencies and their development, we recommend the interpretation of several key indicators. First, to identify a country's position among the world's top economies, we recommend looking at the gross domestic product (GDP) and its development (typically measured as annual growth in percent) and components. Following the definition of the International Monetary Fund (IMF), the annual GDP measures the value of goods and services bought by the final consumers and manufactured in a country in a year. It is common to calculate the GDP per capita and the size of the country's middle class to understand the mean standard of living or wealth.

To analyze the structure of a country's GDP, it can be broken down along the contributions of different industries. Traditional statistics look at the agricultural sector versus the industry sector (for example, the relative value-added stemming from the agriculture, forestry and fishing sector versus the industry sector). Yet, new technologies and the new industrial revolution are changing the dynamism of IB and the structure of international relationships in many industries. Technologies, such as advanced robotics and artificial intelligence, create further automation in production; likewise, the digitalization of the supply chain (involving data clouds, the internet of things or blockchain technology) is forecasted to have a huge impact on internationalization patterns of firms. For instance, (capital-intensive) automation may reduce the need for firms to exploit lower labor costs abroad and may enforce insourcing and near-shoring of value-adding activities. In contrast, technologies such as 3D printing may facilitate the outsourcing and offshoring of activities to distributed manufacturing sites (see, for example, UNCTAD, 2020). Hence, for managers in many industries, there is a need to understand the development of the digital economy. In this context, the World Bank offers a digital adoption index (which is still subject to improvement and development). It is measured on a 0 to 1 scale and focuses on the supply side of digital adoption. It is the average of three sub-indices that more specifically relate to the business, citizen and government levels. The business level, for instance, comprises four components, namely business websites, secure servers, download speed and 3G coverage (for further information, see World Bank, 2016). Moreover, the global consumption database (also from the World Bank) offers data on the share of information and communications technology (ICT) consumption (purchases of telephone equipment and information-processing equipment among others). Organizations such as the Organisation for Economic Co-operation and Development (OECD) are likewise still in the process of developing full frameworks to measure the digital economy, yet provide lists of key indicators based on their current conceptualization (in 2020, 14 key indicators were presented; OECD, 2020). Key indicators involve broadband subscriptions per 100 inhabitants, enterprises' broadband connectivity by firm size, employment of ICT specialists across the economy, value added of the ICT sector and the evolution of ICT investments. Finally, organizations such as the International Federation of Robotics provide numbers on the operational stock of industrial robots (links to the relevant databases are provided on the book's website).

Second, to identify the extent to which countries are intertwined, "trade flows" – that is, exports and imports of goods and services – and inflows and outflows of foreign direct investment (FDI) are key in addition to potential trade or market agreements. FDI are investments in manufacturing or service facilities in a foreign country that involve management control and a long-term interest in being active in a country. The evaluation of trade and FDI in values (for example, in USD) provides information on worldwide developments. In addition, several ratios enable further interpretation: We can calculate the export or import dependency ratio for specific countries by dividing the total exports or imports (of a country) by its GDP. In addition, we look at the relationship between inflows and outflows. As regards trade, the difference between the value of a nation's exports and imports is the balance of trade, also referred to as "net exports." If a country exports more than it imports, it has a trade surplus or positive trade balance. A country that is a successful exporter makes goods and services that other nations buy, which is an indication for its competitiveness in the world market. Yet, a high share of exports in relation to GDP also reveals a high dependency on international trade. As regards FDI, the ratio of a country's share of global FDI inflows to its share of global GDP is called the "inward FDI performance index." Data providers such as the World Bank provide all relevant base indicators for its calculation; moreover, the World Bank provides the inward FDI-to-GDP ratio that is a proxy for the FDI performance index. A high FDI performance index indicates that a country is considered an attractive location to make long-term investments; as the index controls for GDP, it captures the influence of factors other than market size for attracting FDI. If a country's share of inward FDI matches its share in GDP, the FDI performance index is 1; a value greater than 1 indicates a larger share of FDI relative to GDP.

The flows of exports, imports and inward and outward FDI also depend to a large extent on political and regulatory agreements that may define: a free trade area (without intragroup tariffs), a customs union (that in addition involves common external tariffs), a common market (additionally including the free movement of goods, services, people and capital, such as the European Union, or EU), an economic union (additionally including common economic policies, that are in parts implemented in the EU) and a political union (that integrates major aspects of political and economic affairs, such as the United States).

Further relevant indicators to assess the "economic quality" or development of a country are annual inflation rates in percent (that is, the percentage increase in the prices of consumer goods and services), liabilities and external debts as a value or as a percentage share of GDP (that is, the country's total or foreign financial commitments or debts), unemployment rates (that is, the percentage of a country's total labor force that is without a job), labor costs, private consumption (on different categories, such as basic necessities, durables and luxury items), urbanization and the existence of regional economic powerhouses.

Table 1.1 provides an overview of the GDP of countries that either currently account for the greatest shares of worldwide GDP or are forecasted to account for the greatest shares of GDP by 2050. Looking at the GDP in billions of USD for 2019, we see that the United States currently accounts for 24 percent of the global GDP, while the current shares of China and India are at 16 percent and 3 percent, respectively. The consultancy PwC recently forecasted major changes to these shares in the upcoming decades, and estimates that in 2050 the United

Table 1.1 Economic indicators for selected countries, 2019, current USD

Selected countries[a] (alphabetical)	GDP (USD, billions)	GDP/capita (USD)	Exports (USD, billions)	Export dependence (%)	Trade balance (USD, billions)	FDI inflows (USD, billions)	FDI performance index
World	87,735	11,433	24,930	28	646	1,631	1.00
Brazil	1,840	8,717	260	14	5	69	2.02
China	14,280	10,216	2,631	18	132	156	0.59
Germany	3,861	46,467	1,813	47	219	72	1.00
India	2,869	2,099	546	19	-73	51	0.95
Indonesia	1,119	4,135	200	18	-4	25	1.20
Japan	5,082	40,246	905	18	-9	36	0.38
Mexico	1,269	9,946	493	39	-3	29	1.24
Russian Federation	1,700	11,585	482	28	129	32	1.01
United Kingdom	2,829	42,328	880	31	-35	2	0.04
United States	21,433	65,297	2,528	12	-577	352	0.88

[a] The world's top economies in 2050 according to a forecast by the consultancy PwC.
Source: World Bank data

States will account for 12 percent of world GDP, whereas China will account for 20 percent and India for 15 percent of world GDP (see PwC, 2017). Moreover, Table 1.1 provides an overview of trade and FDI flows. We observe that it is still a set of developed countries (that is, countries with mature economies and high GDPs) that rank top in terms of world trade and FDI; yet, emerging countries have become key players in the IB environment. Foremost, China has been implementing a going global policy and has been developing to a top exporter. Also, when looking at the FDI performance index, we see that countries like Brazil, Mexico and Indonesia perform well.

Emerging countries are of specific interest in IB as these offer future opportunities for firms; as formulated by the Boston Consulting Group, the future leaders in many global industries will be those firms that can best serve emerging markets. The most common definition of what constitutes an emerging market (for an overview, see Nielsen, Hannibal, and Larsen, 2018) is from Hoskisson et al. (2000): An emerging market satisfies two criteria, namely a rapid pace of economic development, and government policies that favor economic liberalization and the adoption of a free-market system. Building on this thinking, different organizations have created lists of emerging markets that relate to slightly different sets of indicators and thresholds. Popular classifications are: the BRIC countries, comprising Brazil, Russia, India and China, complemented by countries such as South Africa (BRICS), Eastern Europe and Turkey (BRICET), Mexico (BRICM); the MINT countries, covering Mexico, Indonesia, Nigeria and Turkey; the Next Eleven – Bangladesh, Egypt, Indonesia, Iran, Mexico, Nigeria, Pakistan, the Philippines, South Korea, Turkey, and Vietnam; and the CIVETS, comprising Columbia,

Indonesia, Vietnam, Egypt, Turkey and South Africa. The IMF likewise offers comprehensive lists of emerging markets that are structured along regions.

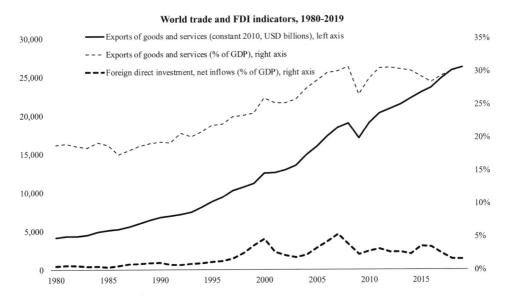

Source: World Bank data

Figure 1.1 World trade and FDI indicators, 1980–2019

Figure 1.1 presents the worldwide value of exports of goods and services in billions of USD from 1980 to 2019, which shows a continuous growth overall. The growth rate, however, fluctuates strongly from year to year with almost no growth or even negative growth rates in certain years of economic crisis; for instance, in 2001 after 9/11, and in 2009 as a result of the financial or subprime mortgage crisis (where bad subprime mortgages were packed into risky securities traded on the global financial marketplace). Hence, worldwide events, such as the Covid-19 pandemic, have an influence on world trade. Figure 1.1 moreover shows the development of worldwide exports as a percentage of the world GDP, which likewise demonstrates a steady growth and therewith a worldwide (growing) dependency on international trade. In 2019, the ratio was at 31 percent. In contrast, the development of FDI net inflows has been rather stable to declining in the last years – after a former period of growth. Yet, as indicated above, there are countries that increasingly attract FDI.

Organizations such as the World Bank provide a variety of indicators on trade, FDI, economic development and world consumption including relevant graphs and country-specific information. The databases offer user interfaces that enable the download of Excel files that can be customized to your information needs. The book's website provides the links to all relevant indicators introduced above as well as to further organizations providing data.

1.1.2 The political and regulatory context

In addition to the economic context, managers are advised to evaluate the political and regulatory or legal context in foreign countries. Theory posits and research has demonstrated that these aspects are key for location decisions of firms and matter for the performance outcomes of international activities (see Box 1.1). The CEO of Tesla, Elon Musk, who is in the process of setting up a huge manufacturing site in the German market, has for instance recently complained about the massive regulation on this process put forward by German authorities, which is slowing down his business procedures (Ohnsman and Persio, 2021). Yet, regulatory frameworks are of use, for instance, when it comes to the protection of property rights.

> **Box 1.1   Further insights: Theoretical background on institutions, location choice and performance**
>
> A key theoretical framework that is used to structure the analysis of the international context is institutional theory (North, 1991), and authors in IB usually refer to this framework by differentiating between different "formal" versus "informal" institutions.
>
> Formal institutions define the order in which firms operate and therewith create opportunities in and barriers to IB activities. Researchers differentiated formal institutions further into economic, political and regulatory formal institutions. A country's economic institutions influence the investment decisions of its individuals and organizations via influencing their access to capital and the value of capital in a country. Political institutions define a country's political processes, including the distribution of power within the government and participation of individuals in government procedures. They range from autocratic institutions with concentrated power in the hands of a few individuals to democratic institutions that distribute power among multiple individuals and encourage active participation of a country's citizens. Regulatory institutions set the rules that standardize business practices and create mechanisms to enforce the conformance to these rules (Holmes et al., 2013).
>
> Informal institutions comprise the beliefs, norms, values and business practices of a country and are reflected in a country's culture.
>
> Research has demonstrated that these institutions matter when it comes to location (or FDI) and trade decisions by firms (that is, the higher the quality of these institutional factors, the higher the FDI that is attracted; see, for example, Bailey, 2018). Moreover, they matter to the performance outcomes of IB activities worldwide (that is, the higher the distance between the institutions of the firm's home country and the foreign country, the lower is the performance; see Kostova et al., 2020).

In addition to several more comprehensive lists of indicators to assess the political and regulatory context (see, for example, Holmes et al., 2013), recent studies shortlisted key indicators (see Bailey, 2018) that correspond to sets of index values as provided by, for instance, the World Bank. The World Governance Indicators comprise six composite indices to measure the political and regulatory environment of a country, namely: voice and accountability, political stability and absence of violence, government effectiveness, regulatory quality, rule of law and control of corruption. These indices are based on more than 100 indicators that stem from

Table 1.2 World Governance Indicators of selected countries, 2019

Indicator	Definition	China value (rank)	Germany value (rank)	India value (rank)	Indonesia value (rank)	US value (rank)
Voice and accountability	Extent to which citizens can participate in selecting their government; freedom of expression, association and free media	-1.61 (6.40)	1.34 (95.07)	0.29 (57.64)	0.16 (52.71)	0.97 (78.82)
Political stability, absence of violence/terrorism	Likelihood that the government will be destabilized or overthrown by unconstitutional or violent means	-0.24 (38.10)	0.58 (66.67)	-0.70 (21.43)	-0.48 (28.10)	0.30 (57.62)
Government effectiveness	Quality of public/civil services; independence from political pressures; quality of policy formulation, implementation and credibility of government in these policies	0.52 (71.63)	1.59 (93.27)	0.17 (59.62)	0.18 (60.10)	1.49 (91.35)
Regulatory quality	Ability of the government to formulate/implement sound policies and regulations that permit/promote private sector development	-0.24 (42.79)	1.72 (96.15)	-0.16 (48.56)	-0.09 (51.44)	1.35 (88.94)
Rule of law	Extent to which agents have confidence in and abide by the rules of society; especially the quality of contract enforcement, property rights, the police and courts	-0.27 (45.19)	1.62 (92.31)	-0.03 (52.40)	-0.34 (42.31)	1.46 (89.90)
Control of corruption	Extent to which public power is exercised for private gain, including corruption, and "capture" of the state by elites and private interests	-0.32 (43.27)	1.90 (95.19)	-0.23 (47.60)	-0.42 (37.98)	1.22 (84.62)

Source: World Bank

30-plus data sources. The original or underlying indicators are perception-based – that is, they stem from surveys of firms and households – and are developed from assessments of information provided by commercial business providers, non-governmental organizations (NGOs), and so on. The indices are reported in two ways: the first is a range from around –2.5 to 2.5 (where higher values represent better governance; the range results from the statistical procedure used to aggregate individual scores); second, percentile ranks ranging from 0 (lowest) to 100 (highest) among all countries worldwide are provided (see Table 1.2 for numbers and Kaufman, Kraay, and Mastruzzi, 2010, for details on the methodology).

Several organizations provide alternative (in parts overlapping) compilations of indices that likewise target the assessment of the formal regulatory and political institutional context. For instance, the Heritage Foundation provides its Economic Freedom Index. It measures economic freedom with reference to 12 factors that are grouped into four categories of economic freedom: rule of law (that is, property rights, government integrity and judicial effectiveness), government size (that is, government spending, tax burden and fiscal health), regulatory efficiency (that is, business, labor and monetary freedom), and open markets (that is, trade, investment and financial freedom). The index is scaled from 0 to 100 and results from an average of indicators (with higher values indicating higher economic freedom). Currently, we observe rising protectionist tendencies – that is, more interventionism (for example, competition policies), more protectionism in trade and investment flows (for example, tariffs and non-tariff measures) – paired with more regional and bilateral economic cooperation, with a rather stable Economic Freedom Index for the world on average. The top three countries in 2021 along the Economic Freedom Index are Singapore (with a score of 89.7), New Zealand (83.9) and Australia (82.4). The bottom three countries are Cuba (with a score of 28.1), Venezuela (24.7) and finally North Korea (5.2). The United States is, for instance, in the group classified as "mostly free countries" (with a score of 74.8 and a drop by 1.8 points as compared to the previous year).

Another index that aims to assess the level of regulatory performance is the (ease of) doing business index by the World Bank. It measures the easiness of doing business in 10 categories: starting a business, dealing with construction permits, getting electricity, registering property, getting credit, protecting minority investors, paying taxes, trading across borders, enforcing contracts and resolving insolvency. A country's ease of doing business score is measured on a scale from 0 (lowest) to 100 (best performance). For instance, a score of 75 means that a country was 25 percentage points away from the best regulatory performance across all countries and time periods. Following on from the current ranking of countries, there would have been 21 countries in which the management tasks of Elon Musk could have been easier (considering only the category of dealing with construction permits, it would have been easier for him in 29 countries, as Germany is ranked 30).

We currently see a rising demand for sustainable and socially responsibly produced goods and services (for example, related to labor standards, social impact, gender equality) that is forecasted to make firms rethink their international operations, and – depending on the country under consideration – reflected in national regulations. Currently, the environmental aspects in particular seem to induce broader changes in the set-up of international production. These developments are reflected in policies and initiatives at the global level, such as the United Nations' (UN's) Sustainable Development Goals (the 2030 development agenda) in 2015, and the Paris Agreement of 2016 (ratified by 189 parties in 2020). In October 2019, the World Bank introduced a new data portal offering environmental, social and governance data that incorporates 67 indicators that relate to the 17 Sustainable Development Goals of the UN. The environment pillar comprises 27 indicators on emissions and pollution, natural capital endowment and management, energy use and security, environment/climate risk and resilience, and food security. The social pillar comprises 22 indicators on education and skills, employment (for example, children in employment), demography, poverty and inequality, health and nutrition, and access to services (for example, drinking water). The governance pillar comprises 18 indicators that show considerable overlap to the more generic regulatory and political, yet also economic indicators presented above. These are categorized as human rights, government effectiveness, stability and rule of law, economic environment, gender and innovation.

Finally, we observe a considerable increase in the flow of international migration in recent years, with more than 250 million international migrants worldwide (United Nations, 2017). The two countries with the highest absolute number of permanent migrant inflows and highest stocks of foreign-born population by far are the United States and Germany (OECD[2]). Migrants make up a considerable share of the labor force in many Western countries; for instance, currently around 15 percent in the United States and 12 percent in Germany (OECD). The OECD has a specific focus on migration and publishes a set of key indicators on international migration. Moreover, institutions specializing in migration (for example, the International Migration Institute, International Organization of Migration) have developed sets of migration governance indicators (again, see the book's website for relevant links).

1.1.3 A standard framework to assess the formal context

If it is about generating a more generic overview of different country markets, we recommend considering the yearly report by the World Economic Forum (WEF). It provides a very comprehensive set of indicators (including regulatory, political and economic indicators) that are supposed to measure a country's competitiveness. The Global Competitiveness Index is a composite index that builds on more than 100 indicators that are organized into 12 main drivers of productivity (called pillars): The first four pillars are institutions, infrastructure, ICT adoption, and macroeconomic stability (and are subsumed under the heading enabling environment). The next two pillars relate to human capital and are health and skills. Four further pillars relate to markets and comprise the product market, labor market, financial system and market size. The final two pillars relate to the innovative ecosystem and comprise business dynamism and innovation capability. The indicators are taken from secondary sources – for instance, from the World Bank – and complemented by survey data from the WEF's executive opinion survey, which is a global study involving about 15,000 business executives every year. Table 1.3 provides an overview of the pillars and subcategories that are involved in the Global Competitiveness Index.

The computation of the indicator aggregates the scores of underlying indicators by averaging from level (that is, the most disaggregated) to level, to the overall score. Hence, the overall score of a country is the average of the scores of the 12 pillars. In the report, scores are provided on a 0 to 100 scale, where 100 represents the optimal situation. While being very informative, the usage of data is a little less handy due to the publication format. Table 1.4 provides the scores of the 12 pillars for five selected countries in 2019. Comparing China, for instance, with India as another emerging market, we see that China has the relatively highest advantages as regards the adoption of ICT, and regarding the healthy life expectancy of its population. Also, it scores better regarding infrastructure, skills and innovation capability. The pillars and related indicators can be used to compare two or more countries that have been pre-selected as potential markets to be entered, ideally using indicators of specific relevance to the firm's business model (more information on this is found in Chapter 2).

Table 1.3 The pillars of the Global Competitiveness Index

Pillars	Lower-level indicators included
1. Institutions	
Security	Organized crime, homicide rate, terrorism incidence, reliability of police services
Social capital	Social capital
Checks and balances	Budget transparency, judicial independence, efficiency of legal framework in challenging regulations, freedom of the press
Public sector performance	Burden of government regulation, efficiency of legal framework in settling disputes, e-participation
Transparency	Incidence of corruption
Property rights	Property rights, intellectual property protection, quality of land administration
Corporate governance	Strength of auditing/accounting standards, conflict of interest regulation, shareholder governance
Future orientation of government	Government ensuring policy stability, government's responsiveness to change, legal framework's adaptability to digital business models, government's long-term vision, energy efficiency regulation, renewable energy regulation, environment-related treaties in force
2. Infrastructure	
Transport infrastructure	Road connectivity, quality of road infrastructure, railroad density, efficiency of train services, airport connectivity, efficiency of air transport services, liner shipping connectivity, efficiency of seaport services
Utility infrastructure	Electricity access, electricity supply quality, exposure to unsafe drinking water, reliability of water supply
3. ICT adoption	
ICT adoption	Mobile-cellular telephone subscriptions, mobile-broadband subscriptions, fixed-broadband internet subscriptions, fiber internet subscriptions, internet users
4. Macroeconomic stability	
Macroeconomic stability	Inflation, debt dynamics
5. Health	
Health	Healthy life expectancy
6. Skills	
Current workforce	Mean years of schooling
Skills of current workforce	Extent of staff training, quality of vocational training, skillset of graduates, digital skills among active populations, ease of finding skilled employees
Future workforce	School life expectancy
Skills of future workforce	Critical thinking in teaching, pupil-to-teacher ratio in primary education

Pillars	Lower-level indicators included
7. Product market	
Domestic competition	Distortive effect of taxes and subsidies of competition, extent of market dominance, competition in services
Trade openness	Prevalence of non-tariff barriers, trade tariffs, complexity of tariffs, border clearance efficiency
8. Labor market	
Flexibility	Redundancy costs, hiring and firing practices, cooperation in labor–employer relations, flexibility of wage determination, active labor market policies, workers' rights, ease of hiring foreign labor, internal labor mobility
Meritocracy and incentivization	Reliance on professional management, pay and productivity, ratio of wage and salaried female workers to male workers, labor tax rate
9. Financial system	
Depth	Domestic credit to private sector, financing of small and medium-sized enterprises (SMEs), venture capital availability, market capitalization, insurance premium
Stability	Soundness of banks, non-performing loans, credit gap, banks' regulatory capital ratio
10. Market size	
Market size	GDP, imports of goods and services
11. Business dynamism	
Administrative requirements	Costs of starting a business, time to start a business, insolvency recovery rate, insolvency regulatory framework
Entrepreneurial culture	Attitudes towards entrepreneurial risk, willingness to delegate authority, growth of innovative companies, companies embracing disruptive ideas
12. Innovation capability	
Interaction and diversity	Diversity of workforce, state of cluster development, international co-inventions, multi-stakeholder collaboration
Research and development (R&D)	Scientific publications, patent applications, R&D expenditures, research institutions' prominence
Commercialization	Buyer sophistication, trademark applications

Source: WEF Competitiveness Report

1.2 ANALYZING THE INFORMAL CONTEXT

1.2.1 Country cultures

Culture is the collective programming of the minds of a group of people that comprises shared core values, norms and modes of action. Understanding cultural similarities and dissimilarities between different groups of individuals – for instance, between different nations – is of relevance as it shapes the ways that these groups approach work and business.

There are several influential authors who have developed cultural classification schemes that aid this understanding. The most influential approach stems from the work of Hofstede.

Table 1.4 The Global Competitiveness Index of selected countries, 2019

Pillars	China	Germany	India	Indonesia	United States
1. Institutions	56.8	72.4	56.8	58.1	71.2
Security	79.2	80.9	56.4	77.2	76.7
Social capital	43.3	61.6	46.8	63.2	65.1
Checks and balances	36.0	71.2	51.9	57.2	72.0
Public sector performance	66.2	71.0	66.4	54.6	75.8
Transparency	39.0	80.0	41.0	38.0	71.0
Property rights	65.6	72.0	47.8	56.4	71.0
Corporate governance	59.7	63.3	74.2	62.3	69.6
Future orientation of government	65.3	79.0	69.7	55.9	68.2
2. Infrastructure	77.9	90.2	68.1	67.7	87.9
Transport infrastructure	68.9	84.3	66.4	56.1	79.6
Utility infrastructure	86.9	96.2	69.8	79.4	96.2
3. ICT adoption	78.5	70.0	32.1	55.4	74.3
4. Macroeconomic stability	98.8	100	90.0	90.0	99.8
5. Health	87.8	92.3	60.5	70.8	83.0
6. Skills	64.1	84.2	50.5	64.0	82.5
Current workforce	55.7	80.9	46.5	56.3	80.5
Skills of current workforce	59.4	67.6	52.9	59.4	71.7
Future workforce	72.5	87.4	54.5	71.7	84.4
Skills of future workforce	69.8	79.9	40.3	69.3	78.4
7. Product market	57.6	68.2	50.4	58.2	68.6
Domestic competition	57.5	69.7	56.9	57.0	70.2
Trade openness	57.6	66.7	43.9	59.5	67.0
8. Labor market	59.2	72.8	53.9	57.7	78.0
Flexibility	58.4	68.0	56.8	51.4	73.7
Meritocracy and incentivization	60.1	77.5	51.0	63.9	82.3
9. Financial system	75.0	79.1	69.5	64.0	91.0
Depth	67.3	69.9	58.6	43.3	89.1
Stability	84.6	90.6	83.0	89.9	93.4
10. Market size	100	86.0	93.7	82.4	99.5
11. Business dynamism	66.4	79.5	60.0	69.6	84.2
Administrative requirements	75.8	92.4	64.6	78.4	94.0
Entrepreneurial culture	57.0	66.7	55.5	60.8	74.4
12. Innovation capability	64.8	86.8	50.9	37.7	84.1
Interaction and diversity	48.2	77.6	43.4	46.2	76.0
Research and development	79.5	99.5	57.1	23.2	95.7
Commercialization	68.7	79.9	53.7	49.7	77.3

Source: WEF

In his 1980 study, he introduced a classification of cultural dimensions which originally covered four key factors determining the functioning of societies worldwide. These are the relation to authorities (that is, power distance), the relationship between the individual and the society (that is, individualism versus collectivism), the individual's concept of masculinity and femininity (that is, masculinity), and the way of dealing with conflicts, ambiguity and uncertainty (that is, uncertainty avoidance). In his first studies he surveyed more than 100,000 employees of technology corporation IBM in over 60 countries using items referring to these four aspects; he later validated and complemented these analyses by adding further respondent groups from other industries and countries and added two further dimensions, namely long-term orientation and indulgence versus restraint (see Hofstede, 2001; Hofstede, Hofstede and Minkov, 2010). A similar concept of classifying cultures is found in the GLOBE project, which builds on the thinking of Hofstede. The GLOBE research program involves investigators worldwide who study country cultures using interviews with middle managers in different firms and from different industries (see, for instance, the overview in House and Javidan, 2004). The project started in the early 1990s and covers several waves of data collection; the GLOBE 2020 study (which was ongoing at the time this book was written) aims to cover more than 160 countries. The GLOBE researchers refer to nine dimensions of culture; seven of these dimensions show similarity to what was defined in Hofstede (see Table 1.5).[3]

Both concepts refer to the idea of "power distance" as the extent to which the less powerful individuals expect and accept that power is distributed unequally. Likewise, both concepts refer to the idea of "individualism versus collectivism": in Hofstede, individualistic cultures are societies in which the ties between individuals are loose, whereas collectivism applies to societies in which people are integrated into strong, cohesive groups. In the GLOBE project, this dimension is re-conceptualized into, first, institutional collectivism, which refers to the encouragement of group loyalty even if individual goals suffer. Second, it includes in-group collectivism, which reflects the degree to which individuals are integrated into and loyal within their organizations or families. Hofstede's third dimension is labeled "masculinity versus femininity", because of considerable differences in surveying males and females: The masculine pole is characterized by goals such as high earnings, advancement opportunities and challenges, while femininity refers to good working relationships and cooperation. A society with distinct gender roles implying that men are supposed to be tough and focused on material success, whereas women are supposed to be more tender and concerned with the quality of life, is called masculine. In a feminine society, these gender roles overlap. This same concept is found in GLOBE, in which assertiveness and gender egalitarianism are differentiated.

Hofstede's fourth dimension is "uncertainty avoidance", which is similarly found in GLOBE: this implies feeling uncomfortable with uncertainty and ambiguity, and the need for rules, as well as the objective of having long-term work relationships. Hofstede furthermore added the idea of "long-term orientation" that corresponds to future orientation in GLOBE. In long-term or future-oriented cultures, individuals prepare for the future; for instance, by means of investing in education. Hofstede's final (and latest) dimension is "indulgence"; that is, an orientation towards enjoying life and having fun versus being restrained by strict social norms or controlling desires based on the way individuals were raised. The GLOBE frame-

Table 1.5 Cultural dimensions in Hofstede and GLOBE

Hofstede		GLOBE	
Dimension	Definition		Dimension
Power distance	Expectance and acceptance that power is distributed unequally		Power distance
Individualism vs collectivism	Loose ties; that is, individuals take care of themselves and their immediate families versus strong cohesive groups of individuals	Encouragement of collective distribution of resources and collective action	Institutional collectivism
		Loyalty and cohesiveness of individuals in their organizations or families	In-group collectivism
Masculinity vs femininity	Distinct gender roles: achievement, material success as male, and relationships, quality of life as female versus overlapping gender roles	Minimization of gender role differences	Gender egalitarianism
		Assertive, confrontational and aggressive individuals in social relationship	Assertiveness
Uncertainty avoidance	A strive to avoid uncertainty by relying on social norms, rituals and bureaucratic practices		Uncertainty avoidance
Long-term orientation	Engagement in future-oriented activities such as planning and investing into the future		Future orientation
Indulgence vs restraint	Desire to enjoy life and emphasis on play/leisure versus control of these desires due to social norms		
		Encouragement of performance and excellence	Performance orientation
		Encouragement of fairness, altruism, generosity and kindness	Humane orientation

work defines two additional dimensions, namely "performance" and "humane orientation." In cultures scoring high on performance orientation, training, development, excellence and performance are emphasized, whereas family and background count for less. Finally, humane orientation is a society's preference for altruistic, generous, fair and caring behaviors.

There are several resources that are provided by Geert Hofstede (and his son, Jan Gert), among them videos in which Geert Hofstede explains his framework of cultural dimensions and provides insights on individual dimensions. Furthermore, an organization called Hofstede Insights offers retrieval and comparison of country scores on all six dimensions. Similarly, GLOBE provides information about the study set-up and visualization of key findings on a website. The GLOBE project publishes the country scores identified in book tables that are in parts offered online. For instance, the 2004 data can be downloaded as an Excel file from its website (see the book's website for all relevant links).

While the two concepts are theoretically close, their measurement and therewith the resulting country scores provided differ to a larger extent (see, for example, Hauff and Richter, 2015). Let us for instance look at the development of the power distance index (see Table 1.6 for scores). In the Hofstede model, the power distance index has been computed on the basis of three questions, which capture the following aspects: nonmanagerial employees' perception that employees are afraid to disagree with their manager, subordinates' perception that their

Table 1.6 Cultural scores for selected countries

Selected culture scores	China	Germany	India	Indonesia	United States
Power distance (Hofstede)	80	35	77	78	40
Power distance, 1980s (Taras, Steel and Kirkman, 2012)	0.82	-0.46	1.17	1.17	-0.14
Power distance, 2000s (Taras et al., 2012)	0.18	-0.77	-0.28	n/a	-0.39
Power distance should be (GLOBE, 2004)	3.10	2.62	2.64	2.69	2.85
Power distance as is (GLOBE, 2004)	5.04	5.39	5.47	5.18	4.88
Institutional collectivism as is (GLOBE, 2004)	4.77	3.68	4.38	4.54	4.20
In-group collectivism as is (GLOBE, 2004)	5.80	4.27	5.92	5.68	4.25
Gender egalitarianism as is (GLOBE, 2004)	3.05	3.08	2.90	3.26	3.34
Assertiveness as is (GLOBE, 2004)	3.76	4.64	3.73	3.86	4.55
Uncertainty avoidance as is (GLOBE, 2004)	4.94	5.19	4.15	4.17	4.15
Future orientation as is (GLOBE, 2004)	3.75	4.11	4.19	3.86	4.15
Performance orientation as is (GLOBE, 2004)	4.45	4.17	4.25	4.41	4.49
Humane orientation as is (GLOBE, 2004)	4.36	3.29	4.57	4.69	4.17

boss tends to make decisions in an autocratic or persuasive/paternalistic way, and subordinates' preference for anything but a consultative style of decision-making by their boss. The index ranges from 0 for a small power distance to 100 for a large power distance.

The GLOBE project in contrast provides two different scores for each cultural dimension, namely a "should be" value and an "as is" practice. To measure power distance values, respondents are asked to indicate whether they believe that followers should obey their leader without question or question their leader when in disagreement, and that power should be concentrated at the top or shared throughout society. Based on these questions, a grand mean is calculated, which represents a country's power distance level. The same items are used for power distance practices, but in an "as is" format. As response categories ranged from 1 to 7, the power distance level ranges between 1 and 7 (where higher scores indicate a higher power distance level). As shown in Table 1.6, we see that there often is a gap between the as-is practice in a country and the value perceptions.

Finally, Taras and colleagues provided an updated set of national cultural scores along Hofstede's original dimensions in 2012 (see Taras et al., 2012). Their scores are based on a meta-analysis of 451 empirical studies which are consistent with the construct definitions by Hofstede (or with the items given in his measurement instrument). To calculate the cultural scores, cultural data from different studies were converted into common measures ranging from −2 to +2 (where low numbers indicate a low preference and high numbers a strong preference for a cultural facet). The authors provide different sets of national cultural scores for different decades, from the 1980s to the 2000s; hence, their scores indicate the direction and extent of cultural change in different nations. Taras et al. (2012) report that their meta-analytically derived scores match those of Hofstede from the 1980s quite closely with high correlations; however, correlations seem to drop over the decades analyzed. While the meta-analytic scores for power distance from the 1980s correlate to 0.91 with Hofstede's power distance values, this correlation drops to 0.70 in the 2000s. In contrast to Hofstede, who said that the differences between cultures reflected in his scores are rather stable, the authors therewith observe that cultural change is not uniform across countries and that these changes lead to substantial changes in the relative rankings of countries using these culture scores.

There are advocates for each of the three concepts presented, so there is no universal recommendation for one of the approaches. Using one or the other concept makes a difference, especially when using the values in quantitative models (see, for example, Hauff and Richter, 2015). As a new round of data collection is just about to be finalized in the GLOBE 2020 project, we would recommend referring to these scores as the ones most up to date (see the book's website for relevant links).

1.2.2 Clustering national cultures

The above cultural values can be used to bundle countries to cultural clusters. The cultural clustering by Ronen and Shenkar is the most famous in the IB literature. They provided a first clustering in 1985 and performed an update in 2013 (Ronen and Shenkar, 1985, 2013). Their 2013 clustering builds on a consolidation of 10 clustering studies that had been published after their initial study and utilized work-related values such as the ones proposed by Hofstede or GLOBE. Building on this information, they performed a cluster analysis. The procedure makes use of Euclidean distances (you will find further information on this in Chapter 2) and groups nations that show a low distance to each other. A basic description of their procedure to develop country clusters is as follows: The procedure starts with finding the most similar pair of countries building on dissimilarity calculations; it merges the two most similar countries into a single, new cluster; then it updates the dissimilarity calculations and again merges the most similar countries or sub-clusters; this process is continued till all countries are in one big cluster. As it is not the ultimate goal to put all countries into one group, but to develop clusters of congruent nations, we need to decide on a similarity cut-off point. For instance, we could opt for allowing a low country congruence within the clusters (relatively high dissimilarity) and therewith few clusters, or for enforcing high country congruence within the clusters (relatively low dissimilarity) and therewith a low number of clusters. Depending on this congruence cut-off, Ronen and Shenkar (2013) visualize the clustering of nations into global clusters (with relatively high dissimilarity) and sub-clusters (that show higher similarity among each other); see Figure 1.2.

Oftentimes, this or other clusterings are intuitively contrasted to one's own perception of culture and questions on the predictors of these clusters come up. While the clustering was developed based on cultural value surveys, Ronen and Shenkar (2013) also discuss further predictors of their clustering, namely geography (for example, Latin America, East Europe), language (for example, Anglo), religion (for example, the Confucian cluster), and historical ties (for example, the Germanic cluster between the African and Nordic which they suppose may reflect the German influence in East Africa in the 19th century).

ANALYZING INTERNATIONAL MARKETS

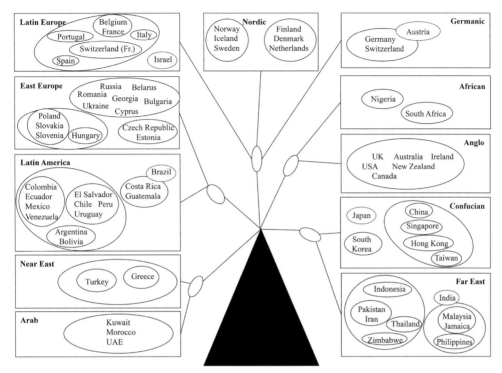

Source: Simplified from Ronen and Shenkar (2013)

Figure 1.2   Cultural clusters

1.2.3   Cultural archetypes and individual cultural value patterns

Several studies indicate that there is considerable heterogeneity in cultural value perceptions within countries. Thus, although culture is commonly assumed to be a shared property of a nation, individuals within countries can vary in their cultural values and there may be specific configurations of multiple cultural values, so-called cultural archetypes, that do not stop at national borders.

Past studies have identified different archetypes that are distributed among different countries (Venaik and Midgley, 2015; Richter et al., 2016). For instance, Richter et al. (2016) identify six archetypes in an illustrative study (see Figure 1.3): Archetype 1 is characterized as very individualistic and masculine; its members are therefore termed masculine individualists. In contrast, Archetype 2 resembles a constellation with a strong collectivistic and masculine orientation (masculine collectivists). Although some archetypes are disproportionally more represented in certain countries than in others, no single cultural archetype dominates a specific country. The highest percentage of concentrations of any archetype within a country is around 40 to 45 percent. For instance, there is a high share of masculine individualists (Archetype 1) in Russia (45 percent) and China (42 percent).

18 INTERNATIONAL BUSINESS STRATEGY AND CROSS-CULTURAL MANAGEMENT

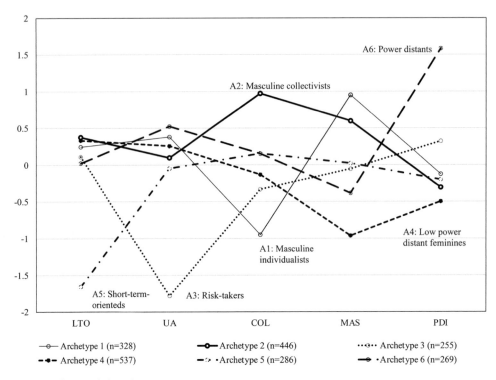

Source: Richter et al. (2016)

Figure 1.3 Cultural archetypes

Hence, cultural values may be more appropriately measured at the individual level. This is especially true when it comes to more specific contexts to be analyzed, such as the impact of culture on the work procedures in an organization, within a department or team. To measure cultural values on an individual level, there are various validated instruments that are ready to be used. Among these scales, the CVscale is most popular and has demonstrated good reliability (though there are criticisms of the scale; for instance, that it only measures collectivism, not individualism). Table 1.7 provides the questionnaire items of the CVscale that can be used to collect cultural values among individuals (see Yoo, Donthu and Lenartowicz, 2011). The cultural orientations are evaluated using a five-point scale from 1 = very unimportant to 5 = very important for the long-term orientation dimension, and 1 = strongly disagree to 5 = strongly agree for the remaining dimensions. Simple averages per dimension provide a good indication of the cultural context (readers with stronger method skills are invited to make use of factor scores for each dimension). Another scale that was thoroughly developed and offers a comprehensive set of items is the one presented by Sharma (2010). It moves a bit away from the work context and aims at providing a more general cultural framework that is applicable to diverse fields; for instance, including cross-cultural consumer research.

Table 1.7 Measuring cultural values at the individual level

Power distance

1. People in higher positions should make most decisions without consulting people in lower positions.
2. People in higher positions should not ask the opinions of people in lower positions too frequently.
3. People in higher positions should avoid social interaction with people in lower positions.
4. People in lower positions should not disagree with decisions by people in higher positions.
5. People in higher positions should not delegate important tasks to people in lower positions.

Uncertainty avoidance

1. It is important to have instructions spelled out in detail so that I always know what I am expected to do.
2. It is important to closely follow instructions and procedures.
3. Rules and regulations are important because they inform me of what is expected of me.
4. Standardized work procedures are helpful.
5. Instructions for operations are important.

Collectivism

1. Individuals should sacrifice self-interest for the group.
2. Individuals should stick with the group even through difficulties.
3. Group welfare is more important than individual rewards.
4. Group success is more important than individual success.
5. Individuals should only pursue their goals after considering the welfare of the group.
6. Group loyalty should be encouraged even if individual goals suffer.

Masculinity

1. It is more important for men to have a professional career than it is for women.
2. Men usually solve problems with logical analysis; women usually solve problems with intuition.
3. Solving difficult problems usually requires an active, forcible approach, which is typical of men.
4. There are some jobs that a man can always do better than a woman.

Long-term orientation

1. Careful management of money (Thrift)
2. Going on resolutely in spite of opposition (Persistence)
3. Personal steadiness and stability
4. Long-term planning
5. Giving up today's fund for success in the future
6. Working hard for success in the future.

Source: Yoo et al. (2011)

Depending on the decision-making challenge that you are facing, either of the concepts can be of use: If it is about analyzing cultural distance between nations, cultural values measured on the national level can be useful; if it is about clustering activities, understanding cultural clusters can be helpful; and if it is about more customized strategies towards your own organization, we recommend collecting values among your employees.

CHAPTER REVIEW QUESTIONS

1. Get an overview of the economic, political and regulatory context of your home country. What indicators would you have a look at, and why?
2. Imagine that you have just started your job at a clothing company that uses international suppliers in China, Bangladesh and Turkey to produce its fashion products. Soon, you will travel to these suppliers, and are asked to evaluate the situation in these countries. What kind of general indicators would you have a look at to get a basic understanding of the situation in these countries, and why?
3. What is meant by the term "emerging market" and which classifications of emerging markets are you aware of?
4. What are the key dimensions of culture that can be useful to understand the informal environment in international markets?
5. What are your thoughts on measuring culture: Is it useful? Possible? And, if so, to what extent?

NOTES

1. The World Bank DataBank, available at: https://databank.worldbank.org/.
2. Data available at: https://data.oecd.org/.
3. In addition to Hofstede and GLOBE, other popular concepts of culture are: the World Values Survey (see www.worldvaluessurvey.org), the "7 Dimensions of Culture" by Fons Trompenaars (Trompenaars and Hampden-Turner, 2020), and the framework of cultural value orientations by Shalom H. Schwartz (Schwartz, 2011).

REFERENCES

Bailey, N. (2018). Exploring the relationship between institutional factors and FDI attractiveness: A meta-analytic review. *International Business Review, 27*, 139–148.

Hauff, S., and Richter, N. F. (2015). Power distance and its moderating role in the relationship between situational job characteristics and job satisfaction: An empirical analysis using different cultural measures. *Cross Cultural Management: An International Journal, 22*, 68–89.

Hofstede, G., Hofstede, G. J., and Minkov, M. (2010). *Culture and Organizations: Software of the Mind – Intercultural Cooperation and its Importance for Survival*, Vol. 3. New York, NY: McGraw-Hill.

Hofstede, G. H. (2001). *Culture's Consequences: Comparing Values, Behaviors, Institutions, and Organizations across Nations*. Thousand Oaks, CA: SAGE.

Holmes, R. M., Miller, T. J., Hitt, M. A., and Salmador, M. P. (2013). The interrelationships among informal institutions, formal institutions, and inward foreign direct investment. *Journal of Management, 39*, 531–566.

Hoskisson, R. E., Eden, L., Lau, C. M., and Wright, M. (2000). Strategy in emerging economies. *Academy of Management Journal, 43*, 249–267.

House, R. J., and Javidan, M. (2004). Overview of GLOBE. In R. J. House, P. J. Hanges, M. Javidan, P. W. Dorfman and V. Gupta (Eds), *Culture, Leadership, and Organizations: The GLOBE Study of 62 Societies* (pp. 9–28). Thousand Oaks, CA: SAGE.

Kaufman, D., Kraay, A., and Mastruzzi, M. (2010). *The Worldwide Governance Indicators: Methodology and Analytical Issues*. Policy research working paper, World Bank.

Kostova, T., Beugelsdijk, S., Scott, W. R., Kunst, V. E., Chua, C. H., and van Essen, M. (2020). The construct of institutional distance through the lens of different institutional perspectives: Review, analysis, and recommendations. *Journal of International Business Studies, 51*, 467–497.

Nielsen, U. B., Hannibal, M., and Larsen, N. N. (2018). Reviewing emerging markets: Context, concepts and future research. *International Journal of Emerging Markets, 13*, 1679–1698.

North, D. C. (1991). Institutions. *Journal of Economic Perspectives, 5*, 97–112.

OECD (2020). *A Roadmap Toward a Common Framework for Measuring the Digital Economy*. Saudi Arabia: OECD.

Ohnsman, A., and Persio, S. L. (2021, May 18). Elon Musk's new Tesla plant runs into Germany's "bureaucratic hell", *Forbes*. www.forbes.com/sites/alanohnsman/2021/05/18/the-rules-even-tesla-berlin-gigafactory-elon-musk-cant-break/.

PwC (2017). *The Long View: How Will the Global Economic Order Change by 2050?* London: PwC.

Richter, N. F., Hauff, S., Schlägel, C., Gudergan, S. P., Ringle, C. M., and Gunkel, M. (2016). Using cultural archetypes in cross-cultural management studies. *Journal of International Management, 22*, 63–83.

Ronen, S., and Shenkar, O. (1985). Clustering countries on attitudinal dimensions: A review and synthesis. *Academy of Management Review, 10*, 435–454.

Ronen, S., and Shenkar, O. (2013). Mapping world cultures: Cluster formation, sources and implications. *Journal of International Business Studies, 44*, 867–897.

Schwartz, S. H., 2011. Studying values: Personal adventure, future directions. *Journal of Cross-Cultural Psychology, 42*, 307–319.

Sharma, P. (2010). Measuring personal cultural orientations: Scale development and validation. *Journal of the Academy of Marketing Science, 38*, 787–806.

Taras, V., Steel, P., and Kirkman, B. L. (2012). Improving national cultural indices using a longitudinal meta-analysis of Hofstede's dimensions. *Journal of World Business, 47*, 329–341.

Trompenaars, F., and Hampden-Turner, C. (2020). *Riding the Waves of Culture* (4th ed.). New York, NY: McGraw-Hill.

UNCTAD (United Nations Conference on Trade and Development) (2020). *World Investment Report 2020: International Production Beyond the Pandemic*. New York, NY: United Nations.

United Nations (2017). *International Migration Report*. New York, NY: United Nations.

Venaik, S., and Midgley, D. F. (2015). Mindscapes across landscapes: Archetypes of transnational and subnational culture. *Journal of International Business Studies, 46*, 1051–1079.

World Bank (2016). *Digital Adoption Index (DAI): Measuring the Global Spread of Digital Technologies*. Washington, DC: World Bank.

Yoo, B., Donthu, N., and Lenartowicz, T. (2011). Measuring Hofstede's five dimensions of cultural values at the individual level: Development and validation of CVSCALE. *Journal of International Consumer Marketing, 23*, 193–210.

1   CASE STUDY
MAGIC JUICE: A DISRUPTOR IN THE BUSINESS OF JUICE BARS

Dirk de Jong, the founder of Magic Juice, was very enthusiastic after the final negotiations with the large Dutch private equity fund DCC Capital. The result was that his successful juice bar, Magic Juice, received EUR 10 million in equity per January 1, 2017. The plans were big. Magic Juice should have air under its wings: Internationalization and expansion of the juice bar chain's brand required large capital and management competences, which Dirk and his partner Sofie Janssen did not feel they had at their disposal. The market potential for vegetable and low-sugar juice products seemed large and uncovered, and Magic Juice had shown the way. Its success had been unparalleled. In just seven years, Magic Juice has been established as the largest and most successful juice bar chain in the Netherlands with a turnover of EUR 5.79 million. Its team corresponded to a full-time equivalent of 64 employees, and it operated 12 juice bars. Moreover, Magic Juice also sold its vegetable juice products online.

FIRM HISTORY AND BACKGROUND

Magic Juice was founded in 2010 in Amsterdam, the Netherlands. The twenty-four-year-old Dirk de Jong established his first juice store on the corner of De Clercqstraat in Amsterdam. As a former elite runner on the Dutch national athletics team, Dirk was highly acquainted with strict diets and a strong focus on health and nutrition. The market for nutritious food was bland, and that fueled his ambition to change the narrative of health in fast food. Inspired by Howard Schultz and the journey of Starbucks, Dirk formed his goal to make high-quality healthy foods and drinks.

He started experimenting with the making of different types of juices. In order to find the healthiest juice types, he devoured one scientific article after another. While juice is enjoyed around the world, it is a controversial beverage. He learned that juice contains many important nutrients, such as antioxidants. However, there are some downsides attached to drinking juice: Often, juices are low in fiber and are high in sugar (particularly fruit juices). He threw himself into the production of tasty vegetable juices such as beets, carrots, broccoli, cucumbers, and so on, which – along with low-sugar fruit juices – were sold in his store. Dirk was working alone at his first location for almost one year. He struggled, working long hours, until one weekend when he had to take time off to visit some family members in Germany. Sofie Janssen, a regular customer who had previously expressed her interest in working behind the counter, offered her help to keep the store running in Dirk's absence. Later Dirk and Sofie became business partners.

At the beginning, Dirk was very conscious of creating a business model that was difficult for competitors to copy. Instead of a traditional coffee house or coffee bar environment, he created a special health store concept that quickly became known for the hip and relaxing atmosphere that customers encounter when they enter Magic Juice stores. In addition to healthy and fresh juices, he also offered nutritious and healthy dishes. Dirk visited some of the world's best vegetarian and vegan restaurants for inspiration. He composed menus consisting of various juices – often with "energetic names" such as Magic Energizer, Magic Kick, Magic King of Green, Magic Triathlon, Magic Base Jump, Magic-Juice-to-go – sandwiches (Magic's Sport Club, Magic Organic Raw, Magic Avocado, and so on), salad bowls, snacks, and shots and other beverages.

Dirk has a strong focus on employee development and training and has managed to create an extremely motivated team of employees that feel highly attached to the firm and convey the right health messages and offer top service to customers. Young, smart employees stand at the counter and lubricate a vegan avocado sandwich or squeeze juices to the tunes of French DJ lounge music. As the main idea for the stores' interior design, Dirk chose live vegetation (flowerpots) given the fact that plants, vegetables, and so on reflect the concept of the store's menu. The locations usually offer a spacious communal area outfitted with slick and colorful, contemporary furniture that reflects the color of the juice offerings.

To raise awareness about his juice bars, Dirk invited some of the most famous Dutch athletes, "health gurus," and other role models to tell their stories of healthy living and physical and mental training – events that all were very well attended. He also tried to make close collaborations with leading fitness clubs, sport colleges, sport clubs, and so on – however, with not much success. Dirk had plans for developing a Magic Healthy Food Trunk concept – a mobile healthy store – which could move to major events in athletics and other sports, as a counterpart to all the fast-food offerings that the public could buy. Within a few years, Magic Juice became a hyped juice bar chain with several stores in the largest Dutch cities, which attracted many young health-conscious people as well as sport athletes in particular.

Magic Juice also started selling its vegetable juice products online under the brand Magic. It felt quite natural, as the juice chain had gained a great deal of customer awareness. This predominantly involved sales via platforms offering lunch and dinner delivery (such as Thuisbezorg.nl), as well as online sales via its own website. Among many young people in the Netherlands, Magic Juice had achieved a kind of cult status in health drinking. It was primarily Sofie Janssen who built up that part of the business.

The company's vegetable juice products consist of high-quality natural ingredients, and they were marketed as healthy lifestyle soft drinks. The product assortment includes 11 different vegetable juices that are available in 250 ml (8.5 ounces), and 750 ml (25.4 ounces). For recognizability, the juices are sold under the same names as in the stores. The price for a 250 ml juice is EUR 2.50, and the price for 750 ml is EUR 4. A close friend of Dirk who studied design and arts developed Magic Juice's colorful logo and recommended a clean yet colorful design. Exhibit 1.1 shows the packs used for the online sales (please note that it is a black-and-white illustration). The firm's major communication channels were social media platforms; public relations, in the form of events with athletes, for example; its own website; and the Magic Juice stores.

WHERE TO GO NEXT?

In 2017, DCC Capital acquired 60 percent of the share capital in Magic Juice; Dirk de Jong got 35 percent, while Sofie Janssen took 5 percent. They both continued as board members of the firm: Dirk de Jong continued as CEO and Sofie Janssen became responsible for the online juice business. In order to internationalize Magic Juice, Dirk and Sofie hired Joe Garcia to take over the newly created position of Chief Operating Officer (COO). A 34-year-old American, Joe had a background in several leading American food retail chains, where he had developed new store concepts, including franchising models. After graduating from the University of North Carolina at Greensboro with an MBA degree, Joe started as a product manager at the large fruit company Chiquita Brands International.

After Joe familiarized himself with the situation at Magic Juice in 2017 (see also Exhibit 1.2), his first task as COO was to prepare an international expansion plan to exploit growth opportunities. The plan was to be presented at the first subsequent board meeting. Joe was a bit puzzled as to what include to in the plan. He wondered whether it should include considerations on the internationalization of Magic Juice as a bar chain and/or as a manufacturer of vegetable juice products. From the talks he had with the management team, Joe realized that there was some disagreement between Dirk and Sofie about how the internationalization process should be approached. Dirk believed that Magic Juice should aggressively go after spreading its shop concept by establishing juice stores in a number of foreign markets. Sofie was of the opinion that internationalization should firstly start by gradually building up the brand awareness of Magic Juice's vegetable juice products by expanding the online business to foreign markets. From her perspective, this could later be the basis for internationalization of the shop concept.

CASE EXHIBITS

Exhibit 1.1 Magic Juice: a selection of products

Exhibit 1.2   Magic Juice: Overview of selected performance indicators per 2017

Performance indicator	2017
Revenues	EUR 5.79 million
Gross profit/loss	EUR 4.89 million
Earnings before interest and tax (EBIT)	EUR 0.40 million
Employee full-time equivalents	64
Number of outlets	12

CASE QUESTIONS

In order to assist Joe in the preparation of an internationalization plan for Magic Juice, please discuss and answer the following questions and aspects: Which approach to internationalization do you think will be the right one – Dirk's or Sofie's? Make suggestions for main headings/themes that the internationalization plan should contain. Discuss the general opportunities, barriers and risks that the internationalization process may entail for Magic Juice. And discuss whether it is the right timing for Magic Juice to kick off the internationalization.

2
Selecting international markets

In Chapter 1, we introduced indicators and frameworks that assist in learning about international environments. This understanding usually follows a purpose, and one of the key purposes for which firms engage in the analysis of international environments is the identification of future markets to do business in – a process called international market selection (IMS). We define IMS as the process of establishing criteria for selecting country markets, classifying them according to the chosen criteria and selecting the markets that should be addressed in internationalization (see also Andersen and Strandskov, 1998; Kumar, Stam and Joachimsthaler, 1994).

While many decision-makers may still rely on a less structured IMS, we will in the following offer a normative perspective on the selection of markets using a rational decision-making process. There are two broad approaches to structure the IMS. The first is a top-down process, in which different country markets are selected based on their attractiveness and related risks. In particular, the attractiveness of markets strongly depends on the objectives (such as resource- or market-seeking objectives) that the firm pursues in its international activities. The second is a bottom-up market grouping in which we concentrate on markets which require the least adaptation (minimized costs) of our business procedures and products. Hence, in the first approach the decision-maker starts with a rather broad set of countries and performs a scoring process which identifies the most attractive ones. In contrast, in the second approach the decision-maker starts with a few international markets and orients the further expansion towards similar markets. Both approaches have different advantages that are more or less relevant depending on the firm's set-up and challenges.

We will first discuss the two approaches below. In addition, we will provide insights on a best-practice example at a retailer, which combines ideas of both approaches. Hence, the practical illustration highlights the need to customize the process to the firm's specifics. Finally, we will provide recommendations on the practicalities of the IMS, which involves several more technical or quantitative steps.

2.1   A TOP-DOWN OR RESTRICTED INTERNATIONAL MARKET SELECTION

2.1.1   Internationalization motives

Firms that follow a top-down or restricted selection process start with many international markets and then reduce the number of markets by identifying the most attractive ones.

The evaluation of the market's attractiveness depends (among other things) on the kind of opportunities firms seek in their international expansion. These can be classified into one or more of the following categories: resource-seeking, market-seeking, efficiency-seeking and strategic-asset-seeking.

Resource-seeking motives involve the access to specific resources, such as raw materials, components, local infrastructure, specifically skilled human resources and technological capabilities that are relevant for the firm's business model and strategy. Firms may benefit from operating in areas where, for instance, technologies are highly developed. Resource-seeking firms ask themselves where to find the relevant resources (and later how to best secure access to them), and on this basis identify the criteria of relevance for their market-selection process.

Market-seeking motives relate to seeking, sustaining and exploiting overseas markets. Typical considerations revolve around the present and future market size, including the presence of key customers. Firms can profit from transferring products (for example, in the maturity phase of the product lifecycle) and services to attractive foreign markets. Thereby, they increase their sales volumes (and often also efficiency, as they are able to amortize R&D costs and central overheads over a larger pool of customers). Depending on the product, network externalities may also occur if benefits from using a product increase with the number of consumers using compatible products (for example, in the software industry). Hence, the key question that guides the design of the market-selection process is where to find potential future customers.

Efficiency-seeking firms aim to benefit from a rationalization of their geographically dispersed value chains. That is, their key objective is to reduce their overall costs. Typically, this involves exploiting different costs of factor endowments (for example, firms that shift labor-intensive activities to countries with labor cost advantages). Moreover, a firm can benefit from the shared governance of geographically dispersed activities; for instance, it has economizing options in the procurement of raw materials that go beyond the possibilities of a single plant. These benefits are essentially economies of scale and scope. Economies of scale are cost savings that arise from large-scale production and from sharing fixed firm costs across a number of product units. Economies of scope are generated from using existing resources for diversified products or processes, leading to greater efficiency. A network of production units may also enable plant-level economies of scale owing to specialization. Specialization enables the firm to profit from the best matches between the resources available in their internal network and the specific advantages of various locations (for example, each plant specializes in some items rather than each plant producing the whole array). Hence, managers need to formulate market-selection criteria that are able to single out the most efficient location for each activity in their value chain.

Strategic-asset-seeking comprises the engagement in foreign markets to support strategic objectives, especially the protection and improvement of the firm's international competitive position. This involves the creation of a network of activities and capabilities in diverse environments to reduce location-specific risks, as the firm spreads investments over different countries (for example, smoothing out fluctuations in revenue streams), and to increase strategic and operational flexibility, as the firm has a portfolio of alternative sites to perform value-adding or support activities. Furthermore, and probably most relevant in today's business models, this involves learning goals and the development and improvement of capabilities. The key question to be answered by a firm is: "Where are the latest technologies and ideas that we can profit from in the long term?" Finally, moves to weaken the position of key competitors (for example, having a presence in an overseas market that is served by a specific competitor) also fall into this category. Lately, some outward foreign direct investment (FDI) from emerging economies involved the takeover of firms in economies that are more advanced in terms of technology, skills and management competences than the investing countries (for example, China, India). The Indian Tata Group is an example of an emerging-economy multinational enterprise that has made a series of acquisitions of technologically advanced but financially struggling businesses in the UK (namely Jaguar, Land-Rover and Tetley). The acquisitions were primarily motivated by Tata Group's ambitions to build managerial competences, for example, in the management of luxury brands. The acquired assets are strategic in the sense that they strengthen the capabilities of Tata Group not only in the local UK market but also in its global operations. Advanced technologies and international brand names contribute to strengthening Tata Group's global competitive position vis-à-vis its competitors back home, which in turn enhances the group's competitiveness globally (see Meyer, 2015).

2.1.2 Portfolio analyses

While firms may pursue several of the above objectives in their internationalization, it is important to develop a clear idea of the key objectives to be followed, as this – among other things – enables a prioritization of selection criteria and therewith a more accurate analytical market-selection process. To assess and compare the opportunities in different international markets in an analytical process, country portfolio analyses are used. Although the kind of opportunities to be looked at ultimately differ, there are some standard instruments, especially from the strategic management literature, that provide an idea of how to do it. Basically, the portfolio analyses assess the country markets along two key dimensions that offer room for customization regarding the specific firm objectives pursued. Three approaches are differentiated: First, we can focus the analysis on opportunities in the macro environment. Second, we can map a macro-environmental factor with an industry- or firm-specific factor. Third, we can compare opportunities and risks in international markets.

In their IMS model, Gaston-Breton and Martín (2011), for instance, concentrate on two (more generic, macro-environmental) dimensions of market attractiveness; that is, market potential and market development. To measure these two dimensions, they refer to the World Bank's development indicators. More specifically, they use gross domestic product (GDP), population, imports, and energy consumption to measure market potential; and GDP per capita, total employment rate, gross domestic expenditure on research and development, level of internet access and the Corruption Perceptions Index as indicators to measure market development. The usage of different indicators to measure the same dimension or bundling indicators and not looking at them separately follows two ideas: It should provide a reliable measurement of the dimension and avoids using multiple indicators that ultimately show a high content-related overlap and therewith redundancy. This procedure also avoids pitfalls that may result from an unbalanced number of indicators per dimension. To create a country score for each of the dimensions, the authors use a factor analysis; even if we are unfamiliar with this statistical technique, we can make use of a more basic two-step evaluation. That is, we use correlation coefficients (that can be calculated in Excel) to double-check a potential overlap between indicators (for example, between GDP and population), and in a second step create an index manually.

We demonstrate this in Box 2.1. In the example, we find a high correlation between the GDP and the total population (of 0.749); that is, countries with a high GDP also show a big total population, and vice versa. Therefore both GDP and total population are somewhat redundant and both measure the size of the market. Hence, we are in a next step advised to bundle these to a theoretical dimension, here market size. For the indicators that show high overlap (for example, indicated by a correlation coefficient of 0.7 or higher), we can manually create an index which bundles the overlapping indicators and measures the theoretical dimension (for example, market size). We will later introduce the technicalities of bundling indicators to a category (see Box 2.4).

Some authors propose to put an additional focus on the long-term market potential when it comes to the evaluation of opportunities in emerging markets. That is, they propose to use indicators that assess not only the current but also the long-term market growth opportunities in countries. A formula that has been used for this purpose is the following (based on Arnold and Quelch, 1998):

$$Q = (P + NP) * (DevGDP - AdjGDP)$$

In this formula, Q is the long-term market potential, P the national population, NP the population growth in the planning period, $DevGDP$ the average GDP per capita in developed markets, and $AdjGDP$ the GDP per capita in the country market adjusted to the purchasing power parity (PPP) level. Sakarya, Eckman and Hyllegard (2007), for instance, used the above formula to estimate the long-term market potential for several emerging markets for a US retailer in the textile industry. For $(P + NP)$, they used forecasts on population development. Population growth forecasts can be retrieved from the World Bank. For instance, the populations in Turkey and Argentina are forecasted to amount to 89.158 million and 49.191 million by 2030. For $DevGDP$ they used the group of seven countries' (the G7: Canada, France, Germany, Italy, Japan, the United Kingdom and the United States) average GDP per capita (in PPP numbers). Currently this yields an average GDP per capita of 55,116 (PPP, current international USD). The current GDP per capita levels (PPP, current international USD) in Turkey and Argentina are 27,875 and 22,947. Bringing it all together, this leads to a long-term market potential (2030) of 2,428,753.1 = 89.158 * (55,116–27,875) for Turkey, and of 1,582,425.3 = 49.191 * (55,116–22,947) for Argentina. These numbers cannot be interpreted as an absolute measure of future market size, yet they are proxies that can be interpreted as relative indicators to compare different markets – here indicating a higher market potential for Turkey.

> **Box 2.1 Further insights and example: Correlation coefficient between indicators**
>
> A basic procedure to understand overlap between indicators is to look at correlation coefficients that can be calculated in Excel (the book's website provides Excel templates). The correlation coefficient measures how strongly two indicators relate to each other. It ranges from −1 to 1, with −1 indicating a perfect negative relation and +1 a perfect positive relation. A correlation coefficient of zero indicates that there is no correlation or no relationship between the indicators. There are different rules of thumb on what constitutes a strong correlation: some authors propose that coefficients of 0.5 indicate a strong overlap; from experience in market-selection projects, we recommend using a threshold of 0.7 to identify high overlap (yet with some degrees of freedom for the researcher to use lower correlations if theoretically compelling).
>
> | 2019 | GDP (in USD, billions) | GDP per capita (in USD) | Population (in 1,000s) | Ease of doing business (rank) |
> |---|---|---|---|---|
> | Belarus | 63 | 6,698 | 9,418 | 49 |
> | Bosnia–Herzegovina | 20 | 6,109 | 3,301 | 90 |
> | Bulgaria | 69 | 9,828 | 6,976 | 61 |
> | Croatia | 61 | 14,944 | 4,065 | 51 |
> | Estonia | 31 | 23,718 | 1,327 | 18 |
> | Latvia | 34 | 17,819 | 1,914 | 19 |
> | Lithuania | 55 | 19,551 | 2,794 | 11 |
> | North Macedonia | 13 | 6,022 | 2,083 | 17 |
> | Poland | 596 | 15,695 | 37,965 | 40 |
> | Romania | 250 | 12,913 | 19,366 | 55 |
> | Serbia | 51 | 7,412 | 6,945 | 44 |
> | Slovak Republic | 105 | 19,266 | 5,454 | 45 |
> | Slovenia | 54 | 25,941 | 2,088 | 37 |
> | Ukraine | 154 | 3,659 | 44,386 | 64 |
>
> | | GDP (in USD, billions) | GDP per capita (in USD) | Population (in 1,000s) | Ease of doing business (rank) |
> |---|---|---|---|---|
> | GDP (in USD, billions) | 1 | | | |
> | GDP per capita (in USD) | 0.036 | 1 | | |
> | Population (in 1,000s) | 0.749 | −0.344 | 1 | |
> | Ease of doing business (rank) | 0.089 | −0.541 | 0.310 | 1 |
>
> Let us simulate the interpretation with an example: The above indicators were compiled (from the World Bank) for a list of 14 countries. Calculating the correlation coefficient between the four indicators (GDP, GDP per capita, population and ease of doing business), we find one strong correlation (of 0.749) between GDP and population, which points to a strong overlap and therewith to theoretically bundling these two indicators. The correlation coefficient between ease of doing business and GDP per capita is in absolute numbers also rather high (0.541), indicating statistical overlap. It is negative; that is, the higher the GDP per capita, the lower the ease-of-doing-business value – as ease of doing business is a ranking, the lower the value the better. Hence, countries with a higher GDP per capita show lower – and therefore better – ease-of-doing-business ranks. Here, it is up to the researcher to decide whether it makes sense (from a theoretical perspective) to summarize the two indicators to a category. We would argue that these are two different aspects, one measuring the wealth of a country (namely the GDP per capita), while the other measures the ease of starting a business and operating in a country. Hence, we would keep these as separate indicators in spite of a somewhat higher correlation coefficient.

The index scores for the two dimensions; that is, market development and market potential (either current or long term) can in the following be used to calculate an overall score using a specific weighting of the two dimensions which results in a country ranking. Alternatively, we can visualize the scores on each dimension and map the markets under consideration in a two-dimensional chart (see the left graph in Figure 2.1). Country markets that score high on both dimensions (for example, Country 1) would naturally be the ones that are considered most attractive. Markets that score high on one dimension but medium on the others are also attractive for investing. Country markets that score high on one dimension but low on another or medium on both (for example, Country 2, Country 3 and Country 4) are subject to a management decision or a selective strategy. That is, the decision will reflect the priorities to be set for the firm. The market development may, for instance, be more relevant for a producer of more expensive products that require a specific level of wealth. The country markets on the bottom left corner of the quadrant (for example, Country 5) are not attractive or least attractive.

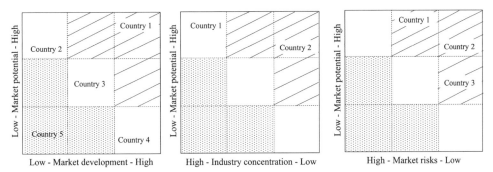

Figure 2.1 Macro-segmentation of countries

In addition to a pure macro-environmental approach, we can complement the analyses by using industry and/or firm-specific information, which is typical for standardized approaches in strategic management, such as the Boston Consulting Group's growth/share matrix.[1] The matrix plots a variable "internal to the firm" – that is, relative market share (the sales of a firm in comparison to the biggest competitor in the market) – against a variable "external to the firm" (that is, market growth).

Similarly, approaches to portfolio analysis in international markets refer to an assessment of market attractiveness (for example, a market potential indicator) and competitiveness in the industry. While market attractiveness may remain on the macro-environmental level, it can – if the data is available – be filtered for specific industries. Organizations (such as Marketline, Standard & Poor's, Gartner) provide reports for international markets that are specific to industry groups. Hence, they provide us with information on the size of specific segments in country markets. For instance, a producer of fruit juices may have an interest in the amount of money spent on fruit juices and how this spending developed over the last few years in different country markets, instead of (or in addition to) looking at the more generic GDP numbers. Furthermore, industry-specific information can relate to specific qualitative factors, such as whether the competition is based on price or quality features (which may be advantageous or disadvantageous for the firm). An idea to approach this analysis is to think of the three to four key success factors in an industry and more qualitatively assess the competitive situation in the local market using these factors. To identify these factors, consider the determinants of success that stem from the final product offering, from primary activities (for example, production, marketing and sales, and service) and support activities (for example, materials management, human resources and firm infrastructure, such as management systems). This already requires some level of analytical depth; firms that prefer to follow a keep-it-simple approach in the initial market screening therefore often use a quantitative standard approach to assess the competitiveness in the industry. That is, looking at market shares of competitors and calculating the concentration in the industry using indicators such as the Herfindahl–Hirschman Index (HHI; see, for example, Loetzner, 1994). The HHI varies between 100 and 10,000 and can be applied to the market shares (s) of firms in a market. In this context, it is the sum of the squared market shares of the competitors in a market:

$$HHI = \sum_{i=1}^{n} s_i^2$$

The higher the index, the more concentrated the market is on a few key competitors. Rules of thumb to interpret the market concentration are: values below 1,000 indicate a low market concentration, between 1,000 and 1,800 indicate a medium market concentration, and above 1,800 a high market concentration. Table 2.1 provides an example indicating a high concentration in Country 1 and a low concentration in Country 2. In markets which are highly concentrated, it may be difficult to get a foothold considering the market power of the dominant players. The mapping of the two dimensions (see the graph in the middle of Figure 2.1) can be interpreted following the same logic as applied above (note that the poles of the scale "low" and "high" for industry concentration are flipped). Naturally, this analysis may come to a different conclusion as compared to a market selection building on macro-environmental dimensions, only. For instance, looking at Country 1 and Country 2, the result of this analysis would favor Country 2 over Country 1. In addition to mapping markets, we can also combine the industry and market potential information to an overall score.

Table 2.1 Herfindahl–Hirschman Index to calculate market concentration

	Country 1		Country 2	
Firm	Market share (in %)	Market share (in millions of USD)	Market share (in %)	Market share (in millions of USD)
Firm A	74	557	13	100
Firm B	14	103	11	80
Firm C	8	60	6	47
Firm D	1	10	5	36
Firm E	1	9	4	28
Others*	2	13	61	461
Total	100	752	100	752
HHI (Market 1) = $74^2 + 14^2 + 8^2 + 1^2 + 1^2 + (4*0.5^2)$ = 5739			HHI (Market 2) = $13^2 + 11^2 + 6^2 + 5^2 + 4^2 + (30*2^2)$ = 487	

* Often industry numbers report an "Others" category that comprises a number of smaller players, the details of which are often not given. To calculate the HHI, we often need to make an assumption on the others. There is no standard way to do so: We propose to assume that each player in the Others category has a lower market share than the lowest share presented for a competitor.

The third approach is to compare opportunities and risks in international markets. That is, the analysis is complemented by an evaluation of country risks – the probability of future events in countries that could have negative effects on the functioning of firms. There are several frameworks available that offer a risk analysis of countries and rely on indicators provided by various organizations, such as the World Bank. Examples are the frameworks by the Political Risk Group, the French COFACE assessments, the Organisation for Economic Co-operation and Development's (OECD's) country risk classification, and the Robinson Country Risk assessment (see the relevant links on the book's website).

We discuss the latter as an illustrative example. Brown, Cavusgil and Lord (2015) introduced the Robinson Country Risk assessment, which is now promoted as the Robinson Country Intelligence Index. It comprises more than 450 variables for 199 countries. It does not provide new data, but combines data that is provided by institutions, such as the UN Conference on Trade and Development (UNCTAD), World Bank or World Trade Organization (WTO) using four broad dimensions: governance, economics, operations and society. These dimensions and their subdimensions (see Figure 2.2) receive a default weighting (of 25 percent each) to estimate an index value. The scores are scaled between 1 and 1,000 (1,000 is assigned to countries with the lowest risk and thus is the desirable pole of the scale). To report scores on this scale, there are several steps involved: The raw data is logarithmized to correct for highly skewed distributions, and standardized (using z-scores; that is, subtracting the mean from the logarithmized raw data point and dividing it by the standard deviation) and variables are aggregated using a weighted average.

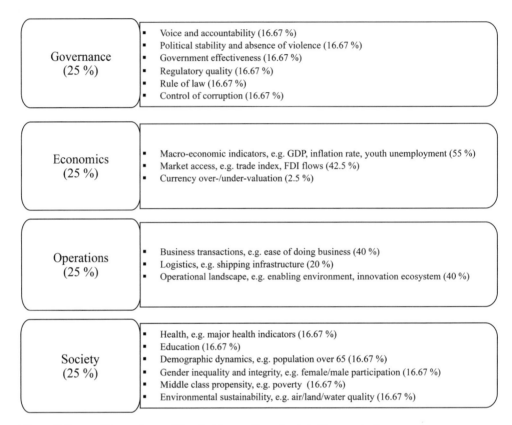

Figure 2.2 Dimensions of the Robinson Country Intelligence Index

One strength of the approach is that it can be customized. Dashboard access enables a customization of the index to one's own priorities by adjusting weights of dimensions, subdimensions or variables. Moreover, you can add or remove variables, alter the structure of dimensions and subdimensions and import your own data. While the customization service does not come for free (currently, the non-academic 12-month subscription comes at a price of USD 100), the overall scores as well as the aggregate scores for the four broad dimensions can be accessed for free. Again, the market attractiveness and country risks can finally be mapped against each other (see the right-hand graph in Figure 2.1). From this perspective, countries that show low risk and high potential (for example, Country 2) are most interesting. Further priorities depend on the risk profile of the investing firm. A firm with a risk-taking management may, for example, prefer Country 1 over Country 3.

The different implications that stem from the three approaches to the country scoring indicate that it may be worthwhile to combine all three perspectives. Before providing ideas on how this can be done, we discuss the bottom-up approach of IMS.

2.2 A BOTTOM-UP OR EXPANSIVE INTERNATIONAL MARKET SELECTION

2.2.1 Liabilities of foreignness

There are researchers that refer to international management as "management of distance" (Zaheer, Schomaker and Nachum, 2012). An approach that fits this logic is a bottom-up or expansive market selection. That is, we start with a few international markets and then select (further) international markets according to their similarity to our home market or to markets in which we are already active. This results in internationalization patterns that involve a low distance to foreign markets, the idea being that higher distance entails higher barriers to profiting from foreign activities or to exploiting opportunities in foreign markets. In the international business (IB) literature, the costs or barriers are often subsumed under the term "liabilities of foreignness" (LoF) (Zaheer, 1995 – some researchers use the term "liabilities of outsidership" to indicate that it is about not being part of the business network in a market; Johanson and Vahlne, 2009). These LoF have three primary sources: uncertainty, discrimination and complexity.

Uncertainty comes from the fact that we are unfamiliar or less familiar with new host environments and business networks. Costs related to uncertainty comprise costs of learning and adaptation to the new market. For instance, we will be confronted with additional information-search costs if we purchase or install facilities or develop external business networks in a market that we are unfamiliar with. This argument of uncertainty and insufficient knowledge about host country markets is key for internationalization-process scholars who developed an incremental internationalization-process model (from close to more distant markets) in the 1970s that has been updated several times in the meantime (see Box 2.2). Furthermore, firms can face costs arising from misbehavior through disrespect of regulations that they were unaware of. These so-called unfamiliarity hazards may come in the form of flawed product launches and the failure to comply with legal norms and cultural values. Research has demonstrated, for instance, that foreign subsidiaries face more labor lawsuit judgments than their local counterparts (Mezias, 2002).

Discriminatory costs result from discriminatory treatment of foreign firms vis-à-vis local firms by local stakeholders such as the government, suppliers or consumers. Discrimination can lead to lower sales volumes and to higher costs, for instance, if foreign firms are excluded from subsidies or if foreign products face specific tariffs. It can even lead to total losses in cases of expropriation of investments. Internationalization costs (in the form of lower sales volumes) can also increase dramatically owing to consumers' ethnocentric behavior; that is, a preference for buying home-country products.

> **Box 2.2   Further insights: Uppsala internationalization process model**
>
> In the mid-1970s, a team of researchers at Sweden's Uppsala University found that firms often develop their international operations in small steps, typically starting their international involvement by exports; thereafter they establish a sales subsidiary, and finally set up facilities to manufacture goods in the host country. Moreover, they observed a successive expansion from close to more distant markets from the home country (psychic distance). This internationalization pattern was supposed to be the outcome of a process of incremental adjustments described in a dynamic model: Decisions to commit further resources to overseas markets and the performance of a firm's current business activities are affected by former market commitments and market knowledge.
>
>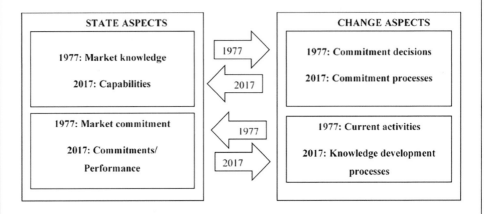
>
> **Figure 2.3** Uppsala internationalization process model
>
> In 2017, the authors proposed an updated or extended Uppsala model (Vahlne and Johanson, 2017). The 2017 model accounts for a stronger orientation towards processes (rather than structures), networks (rather than stand-alone units) and a more pro-active management in today's firms. In this model, internationalization is the outcome of a firm's actions to strengthen its position in the market, and the market is a network of interdependent and potentially international actors. This process is likewise represented in a dynamic model: There is continuous knowledge development in firms (for example, learning, creating and trust building). This knowledge may affect the evaluation of expected benefits and costs involved in the resource-commitment process (that is, the reconfiguration of resources). These commitments affect the capabilities of the firm (that is, a bundle of advantages that provide the firm with the potential to overcome LoF or liabilities of outsidership, such as superior technology and relationships). Hence, the mode of market entry is no longer the key measure of commitment, and the process model relates to an evaluation of the trade-off of advantages and disadvantages rather than to psychic distance.

As internationalization increases, it becomes more complex and difficult to manage. It requires dealing with additional transportation, communication, coordination and information-processing or simply governance or control costs. These additional processes or costs can be enhanced by geographic and especially cultural dispersion; the number of transactions and the differences encountered across regions are one of the main drivers of costs or LoF. These coordination costs occur, for instance, on the parent–subsidiary relationship level. Venturing abroad also causes costs for reading the international environment (for example, controlling of activities). These may include costs of monitoring trade policies and deliberations of multilateral economic institutions. Studies demonstrated that these costs matter to the performance of multinational firms (see Richter, 2010).

2.2.2 Managing distance

From this perspective, a first step in the management process is understanding the distance that is involved in working in specific international markets. For this purpose, we introduce two concepts: a management framework, namely the CAGE framework, and a calculation scheme.

A management concept that has gained popularity in the last years is the CAGE concept introduced by Ghemawat (2001) (see the video link on the book's website). Building on the observation that firms routinely overestimate the attractiveness of foreign markets, he perceived the need to develop a new toolset that places a specific focus on the potential barriers of internationalization and acknowledges that most of the costs and risks associated with internationalization result from distance. The framework differentiates between four dimensions of distance: cultural (C), administrative or political (A), geographic (G) and economic (E) distance. The forms of distance influence IB outcomes in different industries and firms in various ways, as indicated in Table 2.2.

Culture determines how individuals interact with one another and with firms and institutions; therefore, differences in cultural values, social norms, language and religious beliefs have the potential to create distance that can impact on business. For instance, certain products may trigger cultural associations or may carry a cultural identity (for example, food products). Therefore, culture may strongly influence preferences for products or product attributes. Likewise, preferences for product attributes may be triggered by cultural values. For example, Ghemawat (2001) refers to the Japanese preferring small household appliances as a reflection of a social value attached to space.

Second, distance can take the form of administrative or political distance. Most commonly administrative distance is reflected in barriers to foreign competition via tariffs, trade quotas or restrictions on FDI, or, in contrast, in subsidies and favorable treatment of home competitors in national regulations (for example, the EU's common market). Some industries are more prone to be protected and therefore receive higher national regulation, such as industries that are vital to national security; for more examples, see Table 2.2. The WTO provides a database with an overview of trade agreements in force and likewise offers a portal to access information on tariffs that are imposed on specific product categories, which may be helpful to generate a better understanding of the relevance of tariffs for the industry you are in.

Table 2.2 CAGE framework

Cultural distance (C)	Administrative distance (A)	Geographic distance (G)	Economic distance (E)
Attributes creating distance			
Different languages Different ethnicities Different religions Different social norms	Absence of colonial ties Absence of shared monetary or political association Political hostility Government policies Institutional weakness	Physical remoteness Lack of a common border Lack of sea or river access Weak transportation or communication links Differences in climates	Differences in consumer incomes Differences in costs and quality of: • natural/financial/human resources • infrastructure • intermediate inputs • information and knowledge
Industries or products affected by distance			
Products with high linguistic content (for example, TV) Products that affect cultural or national identity of consumers (for example, food) Product features vary in terms of: • size (for example, cars) • standards (for example, electronics) • packaging Products carry country-specific quality associations (for example, wine)	High government involvement in industries that are: • producers of staple goods (for example, electricity) • producers of other "entitlements" (for example, drugs) • large employers and large suppliers to government (for example, mass transportation) • national champions (for example, aerospace) • vital to national security (for example, telecommunications) • exploiters of national resources (for example, oil, mining) • subject to high sunk costs (for example, infrastructure)	Products that have a low value-to-weight or value-to-bulk ratio (for example, cement) Products that are fragile or perishable (for example, glass, fruit) Communications and connectivity are important (for example, financial services) Local supervision and operational requirements are high (for example, many services)	Nature of demand varies with income level (for example, cars) Economies of scale are important (for example, mobile phones) Labor and other factor cost differences are salient (for example, garments) Distribution or business systems are different (for example, insurance) Companies need to be responsive and agile (for example, home appliances)

Source: Ghemawat (2001: 140)

Third, geographic distance is of relevance. This relates to the distance in miles or kilometers, but also to aspects such as the true distance within countries (including infrastructure for transport and communication), the within-country distance to borders and the access to seaports. Geographic distance influences the transportation costs and is therefore more relevant to firms that have to transport products that have a low value-to-weight ratio or are fragile or perishable.

Finally, as regards economic distance, the most important attribute is the difference in wealth or income of consumers. In industries where firms offer a standardized product in different markets, managers aim to reduce economic distance and search for similar economic profiles. In other industries, however, managers are keen on exploiting arbitrage opportunities, such as lower labor costs (for example, the garment and footwear industries).

The idea of these distance considerations is that they are applied to evaluate countries or to complement country portfolio analyses by an evaluation of distance; this evaluation can be customized by taking industry characteristics as well as firm characteristics (for example, experience with internationalization) into account.

While the CAGE framework offers a frame to structure the analysis of distance, we also need to understand the amount of distance that is involved when comparing different country markets using indicators that measure culture, administration, geography and economics. Hence, we are in need of calculation schemes. While distance can be measured between various units (for example, individuals, teams and organizations), the measurement or calculation of distance between nations is most often used in IB. The easiest way to measure the distance between two nations is to use a Euclidean distance (ED) metric. The ED between two countries, 1 and 2, on an n-dimensional construct I is calculated as below, where I is represented by a country's score on a specific indicator; for instance, a score of a cultural dimension or of an institutional context indicator:

$$ED_{12} = \sqrt{\sum_{i=1}^{n}(I_{i1} - I_{i2})^2}$$

In their analysis of emerging markets for a US apparel retailer, Sakarya et al. (2007) refer to an ED metric. They assess the cultural distance between the United States and 12 emerging markets of interest to the retailer using the four original dimensions of Hofstede (see Table 2.3, into which we also integrated some calculation steps to better understand the above formula). Managers from developed economic systems often perceive a high level of uncertainty and psychic distance when it comes to emerging markets. This psychic distance is, however, subjective, with a high probability of stereotyping and generalizing without consideration of true individual country circumstances. Hence, the distance scores offer assistance as they quantify and validate the more subjective perception of uncertainty among managers. In the case of the US apparel retailer, the analysis assisted in quantifying the distances of Turkey vs Hong Kong to the United States, which were (to the managers surprisingly) similar.

Table 2.3 ED cultural distance scores between the United States and selected markets based on Hofstede values

Market	Power distance	Uncertainty avoidance	Individualism	Masculinity	Cultural distance [Σ(US score minus country's market score, squared)]
Argentina	49 [-9; 81]	86 [-40; 1,600]	46 [45; 2,025]	56 [6; 36]	61 [3,742]
Brazil	69 [-29; 841]	76 [-30; 900]	38 [53; 2,809]	49 [13; 169]	69 [4,719]
China	80 [-40; 1,600]	30 [16; 256]	20 [71; 5,041]	66 [-4; 16]	83 [6,913]
Hong Kong	68 [-28; 784]	29 [17; 289]	25 [66; 4,356]	57 [5; 25]	74 [5,454]
India	77 [-37; 1,369]	40 [6; 36]	48 [43; 1,849]	56 [6; 36]	57 [3,290]
Indonesia	78 [-38; 1,444]	48 [-2; 4]	14 [77; 5,929]	46 [16; 256]	87 [7,633]
Mexico	81 [-41; 1,681]	82 [-36; 1,296]	30 [61; 3,721]	69 [-7; 49]	82 [6,747]
Poland	68 [-28; 784]	93 [-47; 2,209]	60 [31; 961]	64 [-2; 4]	63 [3,958]
South Africa	49 [-9; 81]	49 [-3; 9]	65 [26; 676]	63 [-1; 1]	28 [767]
South Korea	60 [-20; 400]	85 [-39; 1,521]	18 [73; 5,329]	39 [23; 529]	88 [7,779]
Taiwan	58 [-18; 324]	69 [-23; 529]	17 [74; 5,476]	45 [17; 289]	81 [6,618]
Turkey	66 [-26; 676]	85 [-39; 1,521]	37 [54; 2,916]	45 [17; 289]	73 [5,402]
USA	40	46	91	62	

Note: The numbers in square parentheses indicate the score for the United States minus the score of the relevant country's market, followed by the same figure squared

An index that belongs to the family of ED metrics is the one by Kogut and Singh (1988; abbreviated as K&S in the following). They have introduced the index in the context of measuring national cultural differences (with reference to the Hofstede concept). The index is widely adopted and has become a standard instrument to measure distance in IB.[2] It is calculated as below. In its original form, I referred to a country's mean score on Hofstede's i^{th} dimension and N is the number of dimensions – at that time the four original dimensions of the Hofstede model (that is, power distance, individualism vs collectivism, masculinity and uncertainty avoidance). V_i is the variance of the ith dimension.

$$K \& S\ index_{12} = \sum_{i=1}^{N} \left\{ \left(I_{i1} - I_{i2} \right)^2 / V_i \right\} / N$$

The K&S index is an ED with variance correction that in addition divides the overall distance by the number of dimensions (N) (the ED formula in contrast takes the square root of the overall difference). One of the challenges with this index is that it is not always clear which variance to choose; for instance, the variance of all available country data or the variance within a subsample of countries. Theoretically, it would be recommendable to make use of the variance among the countries that are of relevance to the firm; for instance, the countries that a firm has invested into or the countries that it considers in the location choice (see Beugelsdijk, Ambos and Nell, 2018).

The distance metrics can be used on multidimensional constructs or on individual dimensions; whether you opt for one approach or another depends on what you are interested in measuring. In Box 2.3, we simulate the calculation of distance using the World Governance Indicators. The calculations assist managers when it comes to selecting markets using distance considerations. The book's website moreover provides an Excel spreadsheet that includes the example in Box 2.3 and the relevant formulas to calculate the distance between country pairs.

Box 2.3 Further insights and example: Distance calculations using the World Governance Indicators

We simulate the calculation of distances based on the World Governance Indicators for the countries given in Table 1.2 in Chapter 1 (China, Germany, India, Indonesia and the United States).

The ED between, for instance, China and Germany using the World Governance Indicators is 4.78. This results from:

$$ED_{12} = \sqrt{\begin{array}{l}(-1.61-1.34)^2 + (-0.24-0.58)^2 + (0.52-1.59)^2 + (-0.24-1.72)^2 + \\ (-0.27-1.62)^2 + (-0.32-1.9)^2\end{array}}$$

In contrast, the ED between China and India is 2.00, between China and Indonesia 1.82 and between China and the United States 3.97. That is, China and Germany are most distant when it comes to governance.

To calculate the K&S distance between China and Germany, we first need to determine the variance of each of the indicators among the countries of interest. For this purpose, we can use Excel, which has a standard formula to calculate the variances. Using Excel, we calculate the following variances for our five countries using the six indicators: voice and accountability = 1.29; political stability = 0.29; government effectiveness = 0.49; regulatory quality = 0.89; rule of law = 0.94; control of corruption = 1.13. Using these values, the K&S distance between China and Germany based on the World Governance Indicators is 23.93. This results from:

$$K\&S\ index_{12} = \left(\frac{(-1.61-1.34)^2}{1.29} + \frac{(-0.24-0.58)^2}{0.29} + \frac{(0.52-1.59)^2}{0.49} + \frac{(-0.24-1.72)^2}{0.89} + \frac{(-0.27-1.62)^2}{0.94} + \frac{(-0.32-1.9)^2}{1.13} \right) / 6$$

Calculating the distance to the other countries, we achieve an assessment of the relative distances. The K&S distance between China and India is 3.86, between China and Indonesia 2.90 and between China and the United States 16.23. That is, China and Germany are most distant when it comes to governance using the K&S index as well.

2.3 THE INTERNATIONAL MARKET SELECTION AT METRO GROUP

Metro Group is a Germany-based retailer with presence in more than 25 countries and more than 50 percent of foreign sales, and therefore one of the most internationalized firms in the industry. After a long period of international expansion that followed individual managerial projects, it has introduced a more structured (top-down) IMS process. It provided insights into its IMS process a few years after its implementation in the form of in-depth interviews and background materials. These relate to its cash-and-carry concept; that is, self-service shopping of food and non-food products by business customers (hotels, restaurants, caterers, and so on) in Metro's premises. In the following we discuss key selected steps in its IMS process to illustrate best business practices (the insights into Metro Group's IMS are based on Swoboda, Schwarz and Hälsig, 2007).

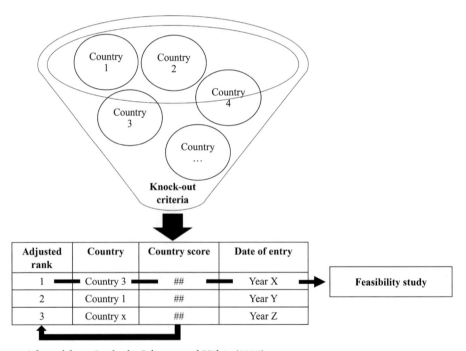

Source: Adapted from Swoboda, Schwarz and Hälsig (2007)

Figure 2.4   Metro Group's IMS process

Metro Group's IMS process (see Figure 2.4) starts with all countries, except for the countries in which they are already active. These receive an evaluation using "knock-out criteria": Countries that do not show enough potential and strong competitive intensity are excluded from any further evaluation. Moreover, Metro collects information on regulatory and economic knock-out indicators. Examples include legal uncertainty, a wholesale industry that is reserved exclusively for nationals, unfavorable tax regimes and financial dealbreakers such as inconvertible currencies.

This is followed by a scoring model that is applied to the remaining countries which survived the knock-out phase. The scoring concentrates on macro-economic data and leads to a country score based on the following criteria: GDP per capita (weighted 30 percent), private consumer spending (30 percent), population (10 percent), number of agglomerations/cities with a population of over 500,000 (10 percent), urban population (10 percent), the development of GDP per capita (4 percent), the development of private consumer spending (4 percent) and the development of inflation (2 percent). Hence the scoring focuses on market-seeking motives. The country score is used to create a preliminary country ranking that is then subject to an adjustment process. The adjustment is done using four aspects: First, Metro performs an adjustment by identifying potential gaps in the existing (country) portfolio that it aims to close. That is, if a country can be developed and operated from a business unit in a neighboring country, it will be moved to a higher rank. The second aspect that is considered in the adjustment process is potential benefits from synergies. If Metro is able to serve a market from neighboring countries with its existing operations, it will move this country up in the ranking due to the potential synergies in purchasing, logistics and administration (in the firm's history this led to a market entry into Moldavia, which was originally served from Romania). Third, potential trade-offs are analyzed: In light of limited investment capital available for expansion abroad, upgrading countries also means downgrading others that can thus only be entered at a later stage. Here, the management has to evaluate, for instance, whether postponing a market entry may result in not being able to enter the market anymore due to a rising competitive intensity in the meantime. In this context, managers need to evaluate whether there are relevant advantages or disadvantages of being a first-mover (see Table 2.4; Dykes and Kolev, 2018; Lieberman and Montgomery, 1988, 1998). Hence, the adjustment takes into account specific efficiency- and strategic-asset-seeking motives.

Table 2.4 Timing of market entry

First-mover advantages	First-mover disadvantages
Technological leadership, such as patents that protect new products on the market (for example, in the pharmaceutical industry) Pre-emption of (scarce) resources, such as: • attractive locations or slots (for example, cruise ferries in Scandinavia) • attractive stakeholders (for example, exclusive contracts with key suppliers, distributors, authorities) Creating the industry standard (for example, in the electronics industry) Buyers' perceived switching costs (for example, due to experiences built up with the first-mover products) Higher probability of creating brand loyalty (for example, due to established buying habits) Learning, experience and scale effects that create entry barriers for later entrants	Enabling free-rider effects; that is, the first mover does all the ground-work and the late-mover later profits from it Taking a potentially high market risk, such as market immaturity, including, for instance, the lack of infrastructure and business networks Facing higher uncertainty (for example, regarding the general fit of products to the market)

Fourth, provisional risks are analyzed: These include more short-term and current factors, such as political instability or economic problems.

Finally, these four adjustment process steps are complemented by a more qualitative analysis of the competitive situation in each country. This includes, for instance, the concentration ratio, the existence of a modern grocery market and saturation of the market related to the cash-and-carry concept, hypermarkets and warehouse clubs. If the top three to five retailers in the market account for more than 40 percent of the food retail volume, it is not very probable that the Metro Group will enter the market. The adjusted preliminary ranking results in the "country ranking pipeline." This involves future planning on when to enter which country or when to prepare a market entry to a country. This planning (including all pre-procedures) is updated annually.

Based on the country-ranking pipeline, the group's top executives decide whether to proceed with a more complex (and cost-intensive) evaluation of specific countries that takes the form of a three-stage feasibility process. Organization-wise, the feasibility process is conducted by an internal corporate development team, with the involvement of specific (external) experts if deemed necessary, and results in a recommendation to the executive board. The time period between kicking-off the feasibility process and opening an outlet in a country is typically two years.

The first step in this feasibility process is based on "desk research"; that is, information is gathered from specialized industry-related agencies, embassies, chambers of trade and industry, and statistics agencies to develop a more specific profile of the market. The economic, political, regulatory and competitive aspects are evaluated in more detail than in the initial scoring. For example, a feasibility analysis that Metro performed for the United Arab Emirates (UAE) revealed that this market and other countries in the same region did not provide enough market potential individually, and that a market entry would only be worthwhile if the entire Gulf region could be bundled (for example, to create relevant synergies between the country markets). As a result of this analysis, the market entry to the UAE was postponed.

In a second step, the Metro Group initiates initial visits to the country. These visits are performed by a team of two to four experts that are composed of, for instance, people from the corporate development team and can involve employees or partners from a neighboring country. Typically, they spend about a week in the country. They gather information, mainly from suppliers; develop deeper insights to validate the country-related desk research (for example, reviewing income-level statistics on the spot); and fill up information gaps (for example, on taxation aspects, willingness of officials and politicians to cooperate). Furthermore, surveys among the existing retail environment enable a fit analysis between the cash-and-carry format and the foreign customer preferences and habits (that is, the attractiveness of the business concept is analyzed). The data collection and analyses cover the number of potential customers by category (that is, the sales potential), average margins for food and non-food, and costs. Moreover, they cover the intensity of competition in the cash-and-carry or hypermarket sector and a validation or identification of potential new knock-out criteria.

If the above analyses are positive, a team of 10 to 15 experts covering all business functions (including sales, purchasing, finance, taxation, human resources and so forth) performs an in-depth analysis of the market that is accompanied by further trips to the country in a third step. This process is assisted by a feasibility manual, checklists and questionnaires that are used to estimate customer potential and spending, and the potential number of outlets in the long term. The process includes gathering information from institutions, such as the state and local government; from consultants; from customers (for example, via focus groups); and from suppliers. In addition to the above evaluations, a business plan is developed. This plan specifies how many stores are opened where and in what sequence, the estimated economic value added, the competitive position, the personnel requirements, and instruction and task structures, and involves a risk analysis. It results in a business case with an initial three-year strategy map. This business case indicates exactly the size of the investment, the time period and the potential return on investment to be expected. If the results of the feasibility study are not positive, the process is either stopped (for example, if the market entry is not advisable at all due to previously unknown restrictions or barriers) or postponed to a later date. If the results are positive, the top executives finally decide upon preparing a market entry.

2.4 AN INTERNATIONAL MARKET SELECTION TOOLSET

There is no true generalizable model to perform a market selection for all firms in all situations in a global context. The IMS needs to be adapted to the needs of the decision-maker. Hence, while we cannot offer a generalizable IMS process model, we can offer recommendations to approach the challenge and develop an individual toolset.

The first step in the IMS process is to develop a list of relevant countries that may be used to start the analysis. Depending on the size of the firm and the resources to perform a market screening, specific experiences, attitudes and potential regional strategies, this list may be shorter than the total number of countries available. We recommend only limiting the number of countries before starting the IMS process, if there are good, convincing reasons (for example, the product carries a cultural meaning and is therefore only of use in certain regional areas). Using today's databases, the additional costs of pre-screening additional markets using macro-environmental indicators are marginal. Organizations offer bulk downloads of indicators for all countries available in their database; hence making use of this "big data" seems warranted and may open up new perspectives. The number of countries can then be reduced by defining knock-out criteria.

The definition of knock-out criteria goes hand-in-hand with the definition of selection criteria. In this context, we recommend integrating all perspectives; that is, opportunities, risks, barriers or distance and industry characteristics. The indicators for each of these categories should receive a careful selection. To identify indicators, it may be helpful to start with an analysis of the key determinants of success related to the product or service and primary and secondary activities in the value chain. As discussed by Andersen and Strandskov (1998), it may be helpful to start the process with an open brainstorm, discussing such questions as "What do you think has to be considered for your company to select international markets successfully?" and "Why is that important?" This process can be supported by an interviewer who may further assist in uncovering the more fundamental ideas that go beyond surface reasons. This process may be supported by discussing and comparing a few markets. For instance, you may ask for the preferences for a market, and more importantly why this market is preferred (for example, ask whether somebody would prefer Turkey or the United States, and why); this way you can uncover key criteria that underly the choice and discuss whether they are actually most relevant to the firm. The indicators identified in this more open process can then be structured into either opportunities or risks, barriers and distance on both the macro-environmental and industry-specific level. We finally recommend contrasting this individually developed list of criteria to, and if needed complementing it with, the standard indicators discussed in the context of assessing the international environment. Potential standard indicators are summarized in Table 2.5.

Table 2.5 Recommendations on standard indicators to perform the IMS process

Opportunities	Risks, barriers, distance
Market potential:	Administrative/political/regulatory risks:
• GDP, population or urban population, and imports • *in the case of emerging markets:* long-term market potential • *if available:* market potential at the industry level; for example, spending on specific product categories	• World Governance Indicators (from the World Bank) • *if of relevance to the business model:* future orientation of government (for example, from the GCI) Economic risks: • inflation rate, unemployment rate, exchange rate volatility • market access (trade index, FDI flows) • domestic competition (for example, from the GCI)
Market development:	• *if available:* industry risks such as market shares of competitors (for example, HHI)
• GDP per capita, total employment rate	• *if of specific relevance to the business model:* financial system (for example, from the GCI)
If of relevance to the business model: Market innovation capability:	Socio-cultural risks:
• research and development indicators, interaction and diversity indicators and commercialization indicators (for example, from the Global Competitiveness Index, or GCI)	• health life expectancy, mean years of schooling (current or future; for example, from the GCI), size of the middle class • *or if more specifically following sustainability objectives:* social pillar; environment pillar (from the World Bank's database on environmental, social and governance data)
Information and communications technology (ICT) adoption:	*If of specific relevance to the business model:* Operational risks:
• level of internet access or ICT adoption indicators (for example, from the GCI)	• ease of doing business indicators (from the World Bank) • infrastructure (for example, transport and utility infrastructure from the GCI)
Labor market indicators:	
• wage levels (for example, from the International Labour Organization) • flexibility of the labor market (for example, from the GCI)	Cultural distance: • language, GLOBE/Hofstede indicators Geographic distance: • in the form of travel/transportation times/time zone differences

We may be tempted to include a large number of (equally weighted) indicators. However, this often does not contribute to the strength of the analysis but introduces significant redundancy into the analysis. Hence, there is a need to evaluate whether the indicators selected measure the same aspect or show high overlap. To assist the understanding of overlap, you can make use of the correlation analysis (see Box 2.1). If this analysis points to a high statistical overlap, evaluate whether this correlation reflects a content overlap or is just a mathematical fact. That is, ask whether the indicators can be subsumed under a certain headline or not. If yes, think of bundling the highly correlated indicators to an index that represents a dimension of interest; if not, you may also decide to keep highly correlated indicators in separate categories. In data collections from organizations, these dimensions are often already predefined; for example, the different pillars of the World Bank.

After understanding overlap and defining relevant dimensions, prioritize the criteria or dimensions. That is, evaluate which of the indicators or bundles of indicators are the most relevant ones. Studies indicate that IMS process models are more successful if the opportunities receive a higher weight than the risks, barriers or distance scores. In this context, you can also formulate further knock-out criteria or minimum levels that are necessary for a market to remain in the screening process. Hence, country markets not meeting the knock-out levels are excluded from the further market assessment.

As soon as this is done, rate the remaining countries using your indicators or indicator bundles. As the indicators are often measured in different units, such as scales from 1 to 5, US dollars or percentage values, you need to standardize them before you can create aggregate scores for countries and dimensions. We recommend standardizing the numbers to a scale going from 1 = low opportunities, high risks, high distance to 10 = high opportunities, low risks, low distance. To assign the original values to this scale, create an interval between the minimum and maximum values for each criterion (among the countries of interest). For instance, if using an indicator that measures a market opportunity, country markets are assigned a 1 in the case that their score on the indicator lies between the minimum and the minimum plus the interval.

$$Interval = \frac{Maximum - Minimum}{10}$$

As soon as all countries are rated, you can start the scoring; that is, creating a total score (either per dimension and/or overall) by summing up the weighted country scores on the 10-point scale. In Box 2.4, we illustrate the technicalities of this process using a simple example. We recommend using such a scoring process on the indicators that are relevant to your firm's setting to create a shortlist of the top five to six most interesting markets. You can then dive deeper into the shortlisted countries and engage in better understanding these markets and their peculiarities and synergies. For instance, you may incorporate data which you were unable to add to the overall scoring (for example, due to a lack of values, or challenges in their quantification) and may consider further evaluations on site before deciding upon a market entry.

Box 2.4 Further insights and example: Standardizing indicator data, country rating and scoring

Box 2.1 provided example data for four indicators – GDP, GDP per capita, population and ease of doing business – for 14 countries. We found a high statistical overlap between GDP and population. That is, we define three dimensions of relevance in our scoring: market size (GDP and population), market development (GDP per capita) and ease of doing business. We attribute the following weights to each of the three dimensions reflecting managerial priorities: 40 percent market size, 40 percent market development and 20 percent ease of doing business.

We standardize the indicators to create comparable scores using a 10-point scale. For this purpose, we calculate the minimum, maximum and interval on each indicator. Using this information, we assign a value of 1 to all countries having a GDP ≤ 71 (13+58); of 2 for countries having a GDP that is > 71 but ≤ 129 (71+58); and so forth (see the tables below). We flipped the scale for ease of doing business, as this is a ranking in which low values are better than high values.

	GDP (in USD, billions)	GDP per capita (in USD)	Population (in 1,000s)	Ease of doing business (rank)
Min.	13	3,659	1,327	11
Max.	596	25,941	44,386	90
Scale	10	10	10	10
Interval	58	2,228	4,306	8

Score	GDP (in USD, billions)	GDP per capita (in USD)	Population (in 1,000s)	Ease of doing business (rank)
1	≤ 71	≤ 5,887	≤ 5,633	> 82
2	> 71 but ≤ 129	> 5,887 but ≤ 8,115	> 5,633 but ≤ 9,939	> 74 but ≤ 82
3	> 129 but ≤ 188	> 8,115 but ≤ 10,344	> 9,939 but ≤ 14,245	> 66 but ≤ 74
4	> 188 but ≤ 246	> 10,344 but ≤ 12,572	> 14,245 but ≤ 18,551	> 58 but ≤ 66
5	> 246 but ≤ 304	> 12,572 but ≤ 14,800	> 18,551 but ≤ 22,857	> 51 but ≤ 58
6	> 304 but ≤ 363	> 14,800 but ≤ 17,028	> 22,857 but ≤ 27,162	> 43 but ≤ 51
7	> 363 but ≤ 421	> 17,028 but ≤ 19,256	> 27,162 but ≤ 31,468	> 35 but ≤ 43
8	> 421 but ≤ 479	> 19,256 but ≤ 21,484	> 31,468 but ≤ 35,774	> 27 but ≤ 35
9	> 479 but ≤ 538	> 21,484 but ≤ 23,713	> 35,774 but ≤ 40,080	> 19 but ≤ 27
10	> 538	> 23,713	> 40,080	≤ 19

Using the above standardization on the original country data (Box 2.1) yields the following scores on each indicator, which can now be used to create a market size index as – for instance – a simple average of the GDP and the population scores. Finally, using the above weights on each dimension, we calculate a total score for each country, indicating that the top three most attractive markets along this model are Poland, Estonia and Slovenia.

2019	GDP (in USD, billions)	Population (in 1,000s)	Market size	Market potential (GDP per capita)	Ease of doing business (rank)	Total score
Belarus	1	2	1.5	2	6	2.6
Bosnia–Herzegovina	1	1	1	2	1	1.4
Bulgaria	1	2	1.5	3	4	2.6
Croatia	1	1	1	6	5	3.8
Estonia	1	1	1	10	10	6.4
Latvia	1	1	1	7	9	5
Lithuania	1	1	1	8	10	5.6
North Macedonia	1	1	1	2	10	3.2
Poland	10	9	9.5	6	7	7.6
Romania	5	5	5	5	5	5
Serbia	1	2	1.5	2	6	2.6
Slovak Republic	2	1	1.5	8	6	5
Slovenia	1	1	1	10	7	5.8
Ukraine	3	10	6.5	1	4	3.8

CHAPTER REVIEW QUESTIONS

1. What is the difference between a top-down and a bottom-up IMS process? Which is the one to be preferred?
2. What are typical opportunities that firms seek in their internationalization, and how can these be classified into different motives?
3. What are relevant dimensions to be used in portfolio analyses of international markets?
4. How would you measure or assess country risk?
5. What are liabilities of foreignness (LoF), and how would you evaluate the relevance of these LoF in international business?
6. What are the CAGE dimensions? Discuss their relevance for different product categories or business models.
7. Why is it useful to avoid an overlap of indicators when performing a quantitative IMS?
8. What would be the most important indicators to look at if you are in the management board of a producer of fruit juices? How do these differ from the situation at a provider of software and a service to perform online interviews in various markets for business clients?

NOTES

1. Available at: www.bcg.com/about/overview/our-history/growth-share-matrix.
2. A third method that has received popularity in the last few years is the Mahalanobis index, which corrects for the co-variance between the dimensions. Research indicates that it provides similar findings to an ED metric in the case of totally uncorrelated or highly correlated indictators; hence it becomes relevant if looking at indicators that show both high and low correlations. Its calculation is a bit more complex – details are found here: Beugelsdijk, Ambos and Nell (2018); Berry, Guillén and Zhou (2010). The book's website moreover provides a link to a website with an Excel example.

REFERENCES

Andersen, P. H., and Strandskov, J. (1998). International market selection: A cognitive mapping perspective. *Journal of Global Marketing, 11*, 65–84.

Arnold, D. J., and Quelch, J. A. (1998). New strategies in emerging markets. *Sloan Management Review, 40*, 7–20.

Berry, H., Guillén, M. F., and Zhou, N. (2010). An institutional approach to cross-national distance. *Journal of International Business Studies, 41*, 1460–1480.

Beugelsdijk, S., Ambos, B., and Nell, P. C. (2018). Conceptualizing and measuring distance in international business research: Recurring questions and best practice guidelines. *Journal of International Business Studies, 49*, 1113–1137.

Brown, C. L., Cavusgil, S. T., and Lord, A. W. (2015). Country-risk measurement and analysis: A new conceptualization and managerial tool. *International Business Review, 24*, 246–265.

Dykes, B. J., and Kolev, K. D. (2018). Entry timing in foreign markets: A meta-analytic review and critique. *Journal of International Management, 24*, 404–416.

Gaston-Breton, C., and Martín, O. M. (2011). International market selection and segmentation: A two-stage model. *International Marketing Review, 28*, 267–290.

Ghemawat, P. (2001). Distance still matters: The hard reality of global expansion. *Harvard Business Review, 79*, 137–147.

Johanson, J., and Vahlne, J. E. (2009). The Uppsala internationalization process model revisited: From liability of foreignness to liability of outsidership. *Journal of International Business Studies, 40*, 1411–1431.

Kogut, B., and Singh, H. (1988). The effect of national culture on the choice of entry mode. *Journal of International Business Studies, 19*, 411–432.

Kumar, V., Stam, A., and Joachimsthaler, E. A. (1994). An interactive multicriteria approach to identifying potential foreign markets. *Journal of International Marketing, 2*, 29–52.

Lieberman, M. B., and Montgomery, D. B. (1988). First-mover advantages. *Strategic Management Journal, 9*, 41–58.

Lieberman, M. B., and Montgomery, D. B. (1998). First-mover (dis)advantages: Retrospective and link with the resource-based view. *Strategic Management Journal, 19*, 1111–1125.

Loetzner, T. (1994). *Einige Überlegungen zum Herfindahl-Index und seinen Erweiterungen.* (Dissertation), Universität Hohenheim, Düsseldorf.

Meyer, K. (2015). What is "strategic asset-seeking" FDI? *Multinational Business Review, 23*, 57–66.

Mezias, J. M. (2002). Identifying liabilities of foreignness and strategies to minimize their effects: The case of labor lawsuit judgments in the United States. *Strategic Management Journal, 23*, 229–244.

Raphael, Rina (2017, November 1). Coffee, sandwich, and a side of edgy: How Joe & The Juice aims to take over the U.S. *Fast Company.* www.fastcompany.com/3066489/coffee-sandwich-and-a-side-of-edgy-how-joe-the-juice-aims-to-take-over-the.

Richter, N. F. (2010). *Internationalisation and firm performance: An empirical analysis of German manufacturing firms.* Kovac: Hamburg.

Sakarya, S., Eckman, M., and Hyllegard, K. H. (2007). Market selection for international expansion. *Assessing Opportunities in Emerging Markets, 24*, 208–238.

Swoboda, B., Schwarz, S., and Hälsig, F. (2007). Towards a conceptual model of country market selection: Selection processes of retailers and C&C wholesalers. *International Review of Retail, Distribution and Consumer Research, 17*, 253–282.

Vahlne, J. E., and Johanson, J. (2017). From internationalization to evolution: The Uppsala model at 40 years. *Journal of International Business Studies, 48*, 1087–1102.

Zaheer, S. (1995). Overcoming the liability of foreignness. *Academy of Management Journal, 38*, 341–363.

Zaheer, S., Schomaker, M. S., and Nachum, L. (2012). Distance without direction: Restoring credibility to a much-loved construct. *Journal of International Business Studies, 43*, 18–27.

2 CASE STUDY
MARKET SELECTION AT MAGIC JUICE

COO Joe Garcia's strategic plan on internationalization includes a section on country markets that Magic Juice could target. Although the firm sees the whole world as its market for fruit and vegetable juices, Joe believes that the first step is to focus on European countries. On the basis of a preliminary screening, he selected 18 European countries for a further analysis. He asked an assistant to provide him with a description of the global and European markets in general, and a preliminary dataset consisting of several indicators that may be relevant to further screen and evaluate specific markets (see Exhibit 2.1).

THE FRUIT AND VEGETABLE JUICE MARKET

The global fruit and vegetable juice market accounts for a major share of the global beverage industry. The total market size of the fruit and vegetable market was estimated to be around USD 61 billion at the time of Magic Juice's internationalization plans. The fruit and vegetable juice market is a demanding segment in the beverage industry due to consumers' high and even increasing awareness of and preference for healthy products. Yet, the rising health consciousness among consumers is also driving the demand for specific products in the market, such as smoothies. For instance, Dirk de Jong was told that experts indicated that the global market for smoothies was projected to grow at a compound annual growth rate (CAGR) of 8.3 percent in the next five years.

The fruit and vegetable juice markets are segmented by the type of the major fruit/vegetable ingredient used, concentration of the juices (that is, the share of direct fruits in the juice), the clients served and geography. The market potential is influenced by health aspects, the geographical spread of locations and the availability of fruit and vegetable supplies. The juice market is driven by the consumer demand for healthy products; yet demand is also driven by the prevalent consumer trends and preferences for juice. Thus, the product development and the different blends that are to be introduced in markets have to follow specific consumer preferences that differ for various countries. The major threat or restraints in the market are diverse juice and flavor preferences among the consumers. That is, understanding the consumer requirements and opportunities in the markets and the key challenges or threats in country markets is a major part of developing a successful internationalization strategy.

The major markets for fruit and vegetable juice are North America, Asia and Europe. Industry reports on the global fruit and vegetable juice market (for example reports on the fruit and vegetable juice market provided by Research and Markets) indicate that it is dominated by major players like the Coca-Cola Company (with its brand Innocent Drinks), PepsiCo, Del Monte, CSC Brands LP and Eckes-Granini Group, among others. As the consumers value brand image and have specific regional flavor preferences, many regional brands and local players have a major share in their regional markets.

In the global vegetable juices segment, the United States, Canada, Japan, China and Europe were estimated to have a combined market size of USD 21 billion in 2018 (based on press releases from the industry; for example, at GlobeNewswire[1]). In recent years, the demand for juices produced from vegetables has been steadily gaining popularity, driven by their high nutritional content and relatively lower calorie content. Consumption of green vegetables in raw or juice form provides many health benefits, and thus is emerging as a must-have in a balanced diet. Consuming greens in juice form increases the overall intake of natural foods among adults and is an excellent way to get the required portion of greens in daily diets.

In many markets, the food and beverages industry is more strongly regulated. For instance, the European market for fruit and vegetable juice is highly regulated. According to the European Fruit Juice Association (AIJN), the market is subject to various national and EU laws and directives that regulate the safe manufacturing and correct labeling of these products.

THE EUROPEAN FOOD SERVICE MARKET: JUICE BARS

The juice bar market in Europe is relatively modest in size and structurally very fragmented. The number of stores is fluctuating somewhat over the years (in selected European countries; see Exhibit 2.2); the same is true for the total sales volumes generated, with a slight upwards tendency (see Exhibit 2.3). The juice bar market accounts for only a modest part of the food service market, including all bars and coffee shops. In Germany, for example, there were around 52,000 coffee shops/bars in 2017, of which the number of juice or smoothie outlets was only 959 (that is, a share below 2 percent). A similar situation was found in the United Kingdom. According to the market analysis carried out by the assistant of Joe Garcia, there is a high diversity in the markets as regards the number of independent juice/smoothie bars in contrast to the number of chained juice bars. In countries such as Austria, Greece, Hungary, Poland and Switzerland, there are only independent juice bars reported, and there is yet no chain formation to be observed (see Exhibit 2.2). The sales in juice/smoothie bars were highest in Germany (see Exhibit 2.3).

According to various industry and marketing experts, a key to success for juice bars is that customers can easily access the bars. Highly populated areas have the greatest number of customers, as well as the greatest number of outlets, owing to new trends in healthy lifestyles such as eating and drinking organic and vegan foods. For chained juice bars in particular, another success factor is the brand awareness and the unique selling proposition (USPs) that the juice bar chain conveys to the customer, while this has less significance for the independent, local juice bars.

Likewise, good inventory management is important as it is a key factor for maximizing margins. The costs of running a juice bar vary considerably depending on the number of bars or stores, ownership and locations. The numbers of customers that the business locations attract are heavily affecting the costs per unit. At the beginning of his start-up endeavor, Dirk was told that, as a rule of thumb, it requires a one-time investment of between EUR 80,000 and 110,000 (interior design, purchase of furniture, juicers, and so on) to open a bar or shop. A somewhat typical cost structure involves, among others, 15 to 18 percent expenses for raw materials and consumables, 35 to 40 percent expenses for staff and 25 to 30 percent expenses for premises, sales and distribution and offices. A typical return on sales in the industry, based on the earnings before interest and taxes, is around 6 percent.

COMPETITORS

While there are a number of national juice bar chains (for example, Jump Juice from Ireland, Tank Juice from New Zealand, and several in the United States – Nekter Juice Bar and Clean Juice, among others), there are only a few international juice bar chains. Some of the most prominent examples are Boost Juice, Jamba Juice, Smoothie King, Joe & The Juice and Zest Juices.

Boost Juice is an Australian retailer that sells fruit juices and smoothies. It was formed in 2000 by Janine Allis, an entrepreneur who opened her first store in Adelaide (Australia). Boost Juice expanded internationally with stores in Asia, Europe, South America and the United Kingdom, using franchising as an entry mode. In 2017, Boost Juice reported 270 stores in Australia and 197 further stores worldwide (that is, in total 467 stores). In 2007, the firm tried to acquire the Canadian juice bar Booster Juice, yet it did not succeed in this endeavor. Right from the start Janine devoted attention to the packaging: In 2000, she made use of Styrofoam cups with sustainable manufacturing to reduce costs and present Boost as an environmentally friendly brand. Later the cups were changed to paper cups. In addition, Boost Juice introduced the so-called Enviro-Cup, which can constantly be reused in the stores, with users of the cup receiving a discount of AUS 1 dollar per use.

Jamba Juice is a US-based firm that produces blended fruit and vegetable juices, smoothies and similar products. It is co-owned (with several other brands, such as Moe's Southwest Grill, Schlotzsky's, Carvel, Cinnabon, McAlister's Deli and Auntie Anne's) by Focus Brands. Focus Brands is an affiliate of the private equity firm Roark Capital Group (based in Georgia). It operates more than 6,000 stores. Jamba Juice was founded in 1990, with the first store located in San Luis Obispo (California). The founder, Kirk Perron, had a passion for active living, having fun and entrepreneurship. For 2018, Jamba Juice was forecasted to have more than 850 locations, and operations in 36 states in the United States, and in Japan, the Philippines, Taiwan, South Korea, Thailand and Indonesia. Most of the international stores or bars are franchises.

Another juice bar chain based in the United States is Smoothie King. It was founded in 1973 by Steve Kuhnau and has been using franchising since 1989. The number of locations has continued growing rapidly, from approximately 560 in 2008 to about 1,200 now. Thereof 970 stores are domestic locations and about 220 stores are outside the United States. In addition, Smoothie King has recently expanded to developing countries in the Asian region through franchising.

Of Danish origin, Joe & The Juice is a juice bar and coffee shop chain that is doing business around the globe. Currently, it lists over 300 locations in North America, Europe, Asia and Australia. The bars and shops serve coffee, tea, sandwiches, fresh juices, smoothies and veggie shots that are made with organic ingredients and prepared on the premises. It was founded in 2002 by Kaspar Basse, who is a former professional karate champion from Denmark. The firm established itself as the place to go to if you are a health-conscious person in love with freshly pressed juice (Raphael, 2017). The locations usually offer a spacious communal area outfitted with slick midcentury furniture, bright art, book-lined shelves and a free photo booth. In 2013, Valedo Partners bought Joe & The Juice for USD 48 million, though Basse retained a 10 percent stake. In 2016, General Atlantic invested in the firm to help fund the expansion of the juice bar chain into the United States.

Zest Fresh Juice Bar is a relatively new chain based in Belgium. The juice bar chain has 11 stores, most of which are located in Belgium, but juice bars have also been established in cities in neighboring countries (that is, in Amsterdam, in Luxembourg, and in Metz, France).

CASE EXHIBITS

Exhibit 2.1 Selected market indicators for selected countries (latest available period, if available 2019 forecasts)

Country	GDP (current USD, billions)[a]	GDP per capita (current, USD)[a]	Disposable income per capita (PPP, USD)[b]	Consumption of fruit and vegetable juice per capita (EUR)	Consumption of fruit and vegetables, five portions per day (% of population)[c]	Total population, (millions)[a]	Urban population, (millions)[a]	Share of population classified as obese in BMI[c]	Bloomberg's global health index (1–100)[d]	Ease of doing business (rank)[a]	Ease of doing business score (0–100)[a]
Austria	445	50,122	40,907	n.a.	7.2	8.88	5.20	14.3	86.3	27	78.8
Belgium	533	46,345	39,127	158	12.6	11.49	11.26	13.7	86.5	46	75.0
Czech Republic	251	23,490	29,142	74	9.1	10.67	7.89	18.7	77.6	41	76.3
Denmark	350	60,213	37,428	156	25.9	5.81	5.12	14.4	82.7	4	85.3
Finland	269	48,771	37,699	163	12.9	5.25	4.72	17.8	85.9	20	80.2
France	2,716	40,496	38,408	145	14.9	67.25	54.28	14.7	86.9	32	76.8
Germany	3,861	46,468	43,904	150	9.9	83.09	64.29	16.4	83.1	22	79.7
Greece	210	19,581	23,345	79	7.8	10.72	8.51	16.9	82.3	79	68.4
Hungary	163	16,730	23,020	88	10.1	9.77	7.00	20.6	65.7	52	73.4
Italy	2,004	33,226	33,580	109	11.8	59.73	42.25	10.5	91.6	58	72.9
Norway	403	75,420	42,793	320	6.5	5.35	4.42	12.6	89.1	9	82.6
Poland	596	15,695	23,549	55	10.1	37.97	22.79	16.7	70.3	40	76.4
Portugal	239	23,214	28,507	52	18.2	10.29	6.76	16.1	83.6	39	76.5
Slovak Republic	105	19,266	23,299	64	10.8	5.45	2.93	15.9	67.9	45	75.6
Spain	1,393	29,565	29,790	98	12.4	47.13	37.97	16.2	92.8	30	78.0
Sweden	531	51,648	36,626	170	9	10.28	9.02	13.4	90.2	10	82.0
The Netherlands	907	52,295	38,639	108	25	17.34	15.94	12.9	85.9	42	76.1
United Kingdom	2,829	42,329	36,553	149	33.1	66.84	55.91	19.8	84.3	8	83.6

Notes: (a) World Bank, (b) OECD, (c) Eurostat, (d) Bloomberg

Exhibit 2.2 Number of juice/smoothie bar stores in selected countries, 2015 to 2018 (data prepared by the marketing department of Magic Juice)

		2015	2016	2017	2018 (forecast)
Austria	Total number of stores	55	62	60	64
	Thereof: chained	0%	0%	0%	0%
Belgium	Total number of stores	77	80	78	85
	Thereof: chained	38%	37%	40%	44%
Denmark	Total number of stores	93	107	100	105
	Thereof: chained	55%	59%	57%	58%
Finland	Total number of stores	11	20	25	49
	Thereof: chained	100%	100%	100%	100%
France	Total number of stores	130	139	138	131
	Thereof: chained	25%	26%	27%	20%
Germany	Total number of stores	1267	1064	959	923
	Thereof: chained	6%	5%	3%	3%
Greece	Total number of stores	10	26	39	65
	Thereof: chained	0%	0%	0%	0%
Hungary	Total number of stores	92	101	103	111
	Thereof: chained	0%	0%	0%	0%
Italy	Total number of stores	19	33	33	46
	Thereof: chained	100%	100%	100%	100%
Norway	Total number of stores	30	45	42	48
	Thereof: chained	100%	100%	100%	100%
Poland	Total number of stores	173	184	188	199
	Thereof: chained	0%	0%	0%	0%
Portugal	Total number of stores	6	16	14	21
	Thereof: chained	0%	0%	0%	0%
Slovak Republic	Total number of stores	72	96	103	108
	Thereof: chained	14%	16%	18%	18%
Spain	Total number of stores	39	44	39	47
	Thereof: chained	50%	50%	49%	50%
Sweden	Total number of stores	169	194	200	210
	Thereof: chained	36%	42%	43%	45%
Switzerland	Total number of stores	33	40	39	46
	Thereof: chained	0%	0%	0%	0%
United Kingdom	Total number of stores	111	131	149	163
	Thereof: chained	58%	62%	66%	67%

Exhibit 2.3 Sales in juice/smoothie bars in selected countries (EUR, million), 2015 to 2018 (data prepared by the marketing department of Magic Juice)

		2015	2016	2017	2018 (forecast)
Austria	Total sales	15.1	17.3	17.0	18.8
	Thereof: chained	0%	0%	0%	0%
Belgium	Total sales	18.1	18.8	18.5	21.0
	Thereof: chained	63%	62%	64%	67%
Denmark	Total sales	48.2	52.4	53.1	56.2
	Thereof: chained	82%	82%	82%	82%
Finland	Total sales	2.4	7.4	9.1	17.3
	Thereof: chained	100%	100%	100%	100%
France	Total sales	18.1	20.1	19.2	16.9
	Thereof: chained	40%	44%	44%	35%
Germany	Total sales	197.3	166.2	132.5	130.7
	Thereof: chained	24%	21%	11%	11%
Greece	Total sales	1.4	3.7	5.7	9.5
	Thereof: chained	0%	0%	0%	0%
Hungary	Total sales	3.1	3.7	4.1	4.9
	Thereof: chained	0%	0%	0%	0%
Italy	Total sales	4.0	8.1	8.5	12.1
	Thereof: chained	100%	100%	100%	100%
Norway	Total sales	13.2	17.8	20.4	22.8
	Thereof: chained	100%	100%	100%	100%
Poland	Total sales	16.6	18.0	18.9	20.2
	Thereof: chained	0%	0%	0%	0%
Portugal	Total sales	0.5	1.4	1.2	1.7
	Thereof: chained	0%	0%	0%	0%
Slovak Republic	Total sales	2.7	3.5	4.4	4.9
	Thereof: chained	29%	29%	39%	40%
Spain	Total sales	7.9	9.3	14.1	15.4
	Thereof: chained	64%	63%	61%	61%
Sweden	Total sales	29.6	39.3	39.5	41.3
	Thereof: chained	60%	67%	67%	67%
Switzerland	Total sales	8.4	10.2	9.7	11.2
	Thereof: chained	0%	0%	0%	0%
United Kingdom	Total sales	32.2	39.0	48.2	56.2
	Thereof: chained	85%	87%	89%	90%

CASE QUESTIONS

Among other things, Joe Garcia ponders whether the market analysis should focus on national markets, urban areas (big cities), consumer segments and/or other relevant dimensions. He also asks himself: Should Magic Juice use a bottom-up or an expansive method in choosing foreign markets? Which potential screening criteria should be used for selecting markets; that is, should he include more or other indicators than have been proposed by the assistant? How should the market potential for Magic Juice's offerings be measured? Should Magic Juice enter one market first or several markets simultaneously? These are all questions that Joe wants to get clarified. In addition, to assist Joe in this endeavor, please provide him with a recommendation on the three to five most attractive countries to which the firm should expand next.

NOTE

1. See the latest report announcement here: www.globenewswire.com/news-release/2021/07/27/2269457/0/en/Global-Fruit-and-Vegetable-Juices-Market-to-Reach-199-4-Billion-by-2027.html.

3
Analyzing and selecting modes to enter, operate in and exit international markets

The choice of international entry mode has for decades been a highly persistent topic in international business (IB) and strategic marketing research. This is because it is widely recognized that international market success or failure is to a great extent determined by the entry mode that is chosen and enacted. An entry mode is an arrangement that enables the firm to launch its products in a foreign market, or transfer its technologies, capabilities or other resources to the foreign market. More formally, we define it as "a structural agreement that allows a firm to implement its product market strategy in a host country either by carrying out only the marketing operations (i.e., via export modes) or both production and marketing operations there by itself or in partnership with others (contractual modes, joint ventures, wholly owned operations)" (Sharma and Erramilli, 2004: 2).

Choosing an appropriate entry mode is one of the most important managerial decisions to be made when expanding business activities beyond borders. It is important because it establishes a "bridgehead" to a foreign market and changes the boundaries of the firm, and thus has long-term performance consequences. The entry mode decision also affects the firm's risk exposure (that is, the operational, commercial and political risks) as well as the size of earning opportunities in a foreign market. Moreover, the entry mode decision has significant influences on the control that the firm is able to exercise on other relevant areas in the foreign market, such as purchasing, manufacturing (costs and quality), and marketing and sales decisions (that is, product, price, placement and promotion).

In this chapter, we will present the commonly used entry mode alternatives in IB, and their advantages and disadvantages, and provide examples of where the respective entry modes are particularly relevant and widespread. We explain exporting modes, contracting modes and equity modes. Accordingly, the reader will gain insights into the factors that determine the choice of entry mode, including the underlying theories. To find the right entry mode, we offer a three-step entry mode screening process that the decision-maker can make use of in practice. In addition, we account for entry mode changes over time, including foreign market exit. The chapter will conclude with an example from the international fashion industry, where the determining factors are identified and discussed.

3.1　COMPLEXITY OF THE ENTRY MODE DECISION

In practice, the entry mode decision is highly complex. There are external, environmental factors (both home- and host-country factors) and internal, firm factors that affect the entry mode decision-making. The decision-making process involves three aspects: (i) why to enter (that is, the motives), (ii) when to enter (that is, the timing) and (iii) how to enter (that is, the modes of operations).

Different motives may influence the entry mode decision (see also Chapter 2). Market-seeking motives relate to a firm's goal of increasing its sales and/or market share of existing or new products. Resource-seeking motives are based on a desire to gain access to the critical resources in the host country (land, property, raw materials, infrastructure, and so on). Efficiency-seeking motives relate to the possibilities of exploiting different costs of factor endowments in the host country (for example, to achieve lower relative labor costs). Strategic-asset-seeking motives relate to creating or gaining access to resources and capabilities that complement existing core competencies to advance the global competitiveness of the firm (distinct from local host-country competitiveness). The different motives, individually or in combination, will generate various entry mode alternatives – some of which can be omitted in advance because they do not meet the aim of the entry. For example, market-seeking motives can be accommodated by the application of almost all modes of entry, and resource- and efficiency-seeking motives will typically be met through the use of foreign direct investment (FDI) and/or cooperative (joint venture, or JV) entry modes, while the fulfillment of strategic-asset-seeking motives often takes place through mergers and acquisitions (M&As).

The timing of entry is important because it over time determines the long-term business opportunities and competitiveness in the market. A too-slow and incremental market-entry process can lead to a loss of business opportunities, income and earnings. A too-rapid and investment-heavy entry process can result in large financial losses, and can ultimately lead to a withdrawal from the market. Expansion into a new market is risky because it involves liabilities of foreignness (LoF; see also Chapter 2): firms operating beyond their national borders have a fundamental disadvantage as compared to local firms or foreign firms already active in the market. In the case that we offer an existing product to a new geographic market, we can best manage the LoF by a gradual entry process, which maximizes the benefits of learning from prior experience, and thereby minimizes the hazard of failure. It allows us to learn more about foreign markets, before we increase commitments incrementally (for example, via subsequent investments into more functions and lines of business). However, if local or foreign competitors are already well established and highly competitive (for example, due to strong brands and/or distribution), we have to invest more massively from scratch to overcome the competitors' advantages, and this involves opting for higher-commitment entry modes. In the case that we plan to introduce a new product internationally and face a competitive landscape that is not well established, we can choose to opt for either a first-mover or a follower position depending on whether the "window of opportunity" is shorter or longer.

How to enter is a question of which entry mode alternatives are available and advantageous. Several scholars have offered typologies of entry modes. Some classify modes of entry into a continuum ranging from market to contracts to hierarchical modes, while others classify the modes into three categories: equity, non-equity and contract modes. Again, others differentiate between the level of ownership (that is, JVs versus wholly owned subsidiaries, or WOSs) and the establishment mode (that is, greenfield versus acquisition). In the following, we classify entry modes into two broad categories: non-equity modes and equity modes (see Figure 3.1; also see Pan and Tse, 2000). Non-equity modes are further split into export modes and contracting modes, while equity modes are split into equity JVs and WOSs that can be established by either greenfield investments or acquisitions. Strategic alliances may or may not include equity-, contracts- and market-based relationships and can thus be placed in both main categories depending on the specific arrangement.

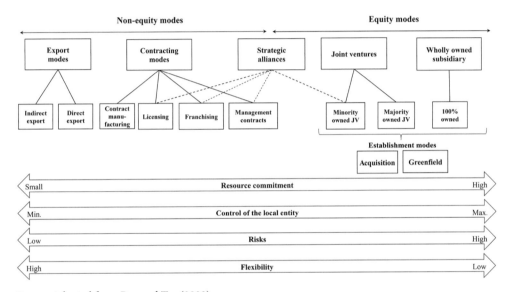

Source: Adapted from Pan and Tse (2000)

Figure 3.1 Entry modes

The entry modes can be evaluated using four main characteristics: (i) resource commitments, (ii) degree of control, (iii) degree of risk and (iv) degree of flexibility (for example, Schellenberg, Harker and Jafari, 2018).

Resource commitments are the dedicated assets and investments that in general cannot be employed for other uses without incurring costs. Resources may be tangible, such as financial resources and physical resources (plants and machines) or intangible, such as managerial skills, technological competences and intellectual property. The required resources vary with the entry mode, ranging from almost none with indirect exporting, to minimal training costs in franchising and licensing agreements, to extensive investments in plant facilities, machines and human resources in wholly owned production subsidiaries.

Control is an antecedent for determining the potential risks and rewards (for example, return on assets) for firms entering foreign markets. A high degree of control means that the decision-maker can influence the outcome of key decisions, while a low degree of control means that partner firms often influence key decisions. In franchising, for example, the control over operations is typically granted to the franchisee in exchange for some payment and for the promise to abide by the terms of the contract, while the licensor has little direct control. In a JV, control is shared formally according to ownership (for example, equity ownership above 50 percent can provide a partner with a higher number of directors on the board, which will increase control). WOSs are most attractive in terms of control, since this entry mode enables multinational enterprises (MNEs) to exert full control over the foreign business.

Risk has an individual and organizational dimension. Differences in risk perceptions exist at the individual level due to differences in cognitive biases, personal feelings and experiences (for example, international experiences) which affect entry mode decisions. At the organizational level, past successes and failures further influence risk behavior and thereby the entry mode decisions. Some decision-makers are risk-averse, while others have a higher willingness to accept risk. Risk-averse decision-makers will typically prefer low-resource-commitment entry modes (for example, indirect and direct export modes). In licensing agreements, the risk that the licensee reproduces and uses the licensor's technology in the future is fairly high.

Finally, the degree of flexibility relates to the possibilities of changing entry modes quickly and with minimal costs. If there are high switching costs due to high fixed investments (and sunk costs), firms will experience less flexibility in switching the entry mode. A high foreign market commitment leads to a higher degree of decision irreversibility and thereby to less flexibility in term of changing the entry mode.

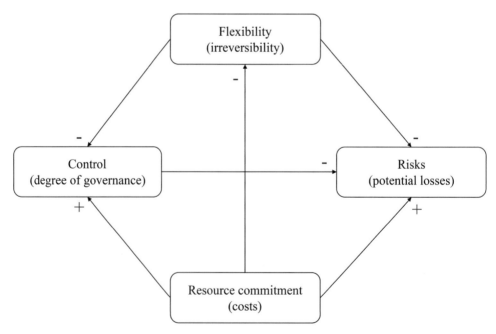

Figure 3.2   Entry mode decision trade-offs

Hence, equity modes differ significantly from non-equity modes in resource commitment, control, risk and flexibility, and resource commitment, risk, control and flexibility are highly interrelated (see Figure 3.2). For example, choosing a high-commitment entry mode such as a WOS increases the degree of control; however, it also leads to a higher perceived risk (and a potential high loss in the case of failure in the market). If, on the other hand, a low-commitment entry mode is chosen – for example, indirect export – the degree of control will be much more limited, yet also the risk will be correspondingly low. Contractual arrangements such as licensing and franchising are low-commitment entry modes but are also characterized by a low to medium degree of control and risk. The book's website provides a link to a good video introduction of a colleague on the different entry modes and their advantages and disadvantages, which we will dive deeper into in the following.

3.2 NON-EQUITY MODES

3.2.1 Export modes

Exporting is typically used in the case of an initial foreign market entry. In this situation firms have only little or no international experience and thus perceive a greater risk in entering the market. The exporting firm relies on manufacturing its products in its home market (or in a third country) and sells the products either directly or indirectly to a host country. For small and medium-sized firms (SMEs), exporting represents a viable entry mode in international markets because they are typically lacking resources (for example, financial and human resources), market power and knowledge to make stronger commitments.

Due to high search and negotiation costs in international markets, export intermediaries often play an important "middleman" role in international trade. They link buyers and sellers in different markets and assist in identifying customers and providers of the relevant financing options and distribution infrastructures. Furthermore, export intermediaries play a role in reducing knowledge gaps, uncertainties and other risks associated with operating in foreign markets because they possess host-country-specific knowledge. They can help to negotiate with foreign customers and to reduce commercial risks that are associated with a buyer's ability to pay. Hence, firms often prefer to use export intermediaries because they perform certain functions related to exporting better or at a lower cost than the firm could do. However, intermediaries also add to the cost of exporting, in particular in the form of transaction costs and rent extraction. There is also a loss of control when a firm uses export intermediaries.

With the rise of the internet, SMEs' transaction costs of doing business abroad (for example, costs associated with delivering goods or services to international customers) can be significantly reduced. The internet has led to entirely new ways for exporters to access markets and has improved their efficiency in terms of identifying customers, receiving orders and handling inquiries globally. In addition, through the acquisition of more reliable information about overseas markets, better communication with foreign buyers and closer monitoring of international operations using digital tools, exporting firms are nowadays in a better position to reduce the level of uncertainty in their IB transactions and to improve performance results. It has been argued that the internet and digitalization has made early internationalization a more viable and cost-effective option for SMEs (Katsikeas, Leonidou and Zeriti, 2019). The export mode covers several alternative forms and can be organized in a variety of ways (see Figure 3.3).

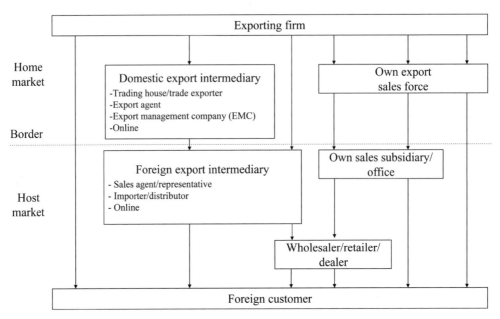

Figure 3.3   Alternative forms of exporting

Indirect exporting occurs when the firm does not take care of the exporting activities, but leaves these to a domestic intermediary – for instance, a domestic trading house, an export agent, an export management company (EMC) or an online intermediary – or uses a piggyback arrangement. As a result, the exporting firm loses significant control over the marketing of the product (that is, pricing, communication), but at the same time has a lower risk and needs to make fewer investments. Direct exporting means that a firm directly conveys or sells its products and services to an independent intermediary, such as an importer, a sales agent, a distributor or a retailer outside its home country. Foreign-based intermediaries are often involved in the exporting of the firm's products and services to other actors along the distribution channel (wholesaling) or are directly connected to the end-user or final consumer. Typically, the exporting firms are involved in handling documentation, physical delivery and pricing policies, while the foreign intermediary takes care of market contact and communication, product presentations (for example, show rooms) and eventually after-sales service.

Exporting through the firm's own sales force located in its domestic market is often preferred in business-to-business markets with few key customers that order in large sizes but require close contact. In this case, a traveling salesperson manages relationships with a small number of important customers which justify international travel costs. Different from a transaction-based view, relationship-marketing scholars emphasize that exporting can

Table 3.1 Pros and cons of foreign intermediaries versus a firm's own sales subsidiary

	Foreign intermediary (sales agent)	Sales subsidiary
Advantages	The sales agent can offer an existing organization The agent knows the foreign market and the corresponding business culture The agent can offer complementarities in sales (representing products by other principals) Small/limited investment	The sales may be concentrated on the exporting firm's products and services More and in-depth market knowledge Full control and independence of a third trading partner Prestige/showing commitment in relation to the host country
Disadvantages	The agent's priority of sales efforts (between principals) can give the exporting firm problems The agent's product and technical knowledge may often be inadequate The economic/commercial risks rely on the exporting firm and not the foreign intermediate	High preliminary investment costs Establishing of fixed capacity costs No sales complementarities (only selling the firm's own products) High risk and commitment
Issues/questions	Does the foreign intermediary have the right profile (segment, organization, employees)? Is the foreign intermediary offering suitable and proper forms of incentives and remuneration?	Market size versus fixed costs? Patience in relation to earnings? Requirements for product range (width and depth)?

best be understood by studying factors that shape the organizational interaction between the parties involved. The relationship-marketing literature has long recognized the importance of interpersonal relationships in business-to-business exchanges where both commitment and trust have central roles. According to the commitment-trust theory, commitment contributes to cooperation, reduced conflict and relationship longevity, and promotes long-term performance in cross-border relationships (Gu, Wang and Wang, 2019). Since many firms are confronted with the issue of whether to export through an intermediary or by using their own sales organization, Table 3.1 presents the pros and cons for the two alternatives.

3.2.2 Contracting modes

Contracting entry modes include a variety of arrangements, such as contract manufacturing, licensing, franchising and management contracts (Brouthers and McNicol, 2009). Contract manufacturing enables the firm to have a foreign source of inputs or intermediate products without the need to own its subcontractors and/or make large upstream investments. Payment is generally on a per-unit basis, and product-quality and product-specification requirements are important. Contract production is often preferred by firms that have a desire to (i) be close to their customers due to large transport distances and costs (for example, bulky products); (ii) produce where it is cheap (low labor costs), and where the product quality at the same time is satisfactory; and (iii) avoid tariffs, quotas and other trade barriers. Contract production is particularly widespread in industries such as textiles, footwear and furniture manufacturing and in business-to-business industries where various components and intermediaries are included in the production of finished products. Contract manufacturing offers a high degree of flexibility. If the contractor is dissatisfied with the product quality and/or the reliability of deliveries, a contract with another manufacturer can be placed.

Licensing is an entry mode in which the firm can establish local manufacturing of products and/or services in a foreign market without making heavy investments. A licensing agreement is an arrangement wherein the licensor (the seller) gives the licensee (the buyer) the right to use intangible property. These intangible properties include various categories, such as patents, production methods (formulas, processes, and designs), copyrights, trademarks and trade and brand names. Normally, the licensor is obliged to furnish sufficient information and assistance to the licensee. The licensee in return is obliged to use the rights in the agreed fashion and to pay compensation to the licensor. Hence, the licensee pays the licensor royalties or fees, which often are a combination of (i) a lump sum at the beginning of the agreement, (ii) a minimum royalty that guarantees a certain level of annual income for the use of the rights and (iii) a permanent (running) royalty typically expressed as a percentage of the final (customer) price or as a fixed sum of money per sold unit of the product.

Licensing is preferred by technology-intensive and service-oriented firms that (i) are too small to have the financial, organizational or marketing expertise for investment in wholly owned production subsidiaries, (ii) manufacture technological products with short product life cycles (that is, a short pay-back period) necessitating rapid international expansion, (iii) manufacture high-volume or bulky products and (iv) experience import constraints or barriers such as high tariffs or non-tariff barriers. Licensing agreements occur among others in high-tech and R&D-intensive industries (for example, the pharmaceutical industry, the electronic industry), in manufacturing industries with voluminous or bulky products (for example, beer, soft drinks, insulation materials) and in services and information industries characterized by copyrights for musical, literary or artistic compositions.

The world's top provider of streaming movies and television, Netflix, with approximately 200 million paid subscribers in more than 190 countries,[1] finances its content by constantly negotiating licensing deals with TV shows, networks and film producers. Licensing content involves obtaining the rights from the owners of a TV show or movie to stream the content through a service such as Netflix. Each licensing agreement varies based upon the needs of both parties. For example, the owner of a TV show could agree to allow Netflix to stream all seasons of its show for one, three or five years. The licensing agreement may limit Netflix to, or exclude it from, specific regions or markets. As competition continues to saturate the market, streaming service providers recognize the importance of exclusive content. Under an exclusive licensing agreement, the streaming distribution channel is reserved for a single platform. Exclusive licensing agreements are far more expensive than nonexclusive agreements, though they have the potential to drive greater numbers of subscribers over time.

Licensing is an economic way to enter a foreign market. It is a low-commitment entry mode that involves medium risk and medium to low control. However, licensing also has a number of disadvantages; among other things, the risk of technological appropriation by the licensee, who may become a future competitor, and the risk that the licensee does not live up to the licensor's quality requirements and expectations, especially if the license also includes the licensor's brand name, which could be undermined. Against this background, firms typically use licensing in smaller or low-priority international markets.

Franchising is a marketing-oriented method of selling in which the franchisor (the seller) grants the franchisee (the buyer) the right to use the product and its name and in return receives financial compensation (a management fee) as in a licensing agreement (Robson et al., 2018). We differentiate two types of franchising. First, in product and trade name franchising the franchisee can use the trade name, trademark and product line. Second, in business package franchising the franchisee gets access to a whole business model, including the franchisor's product line and trade name. The business package contains all elements necessary for a local franchisee to establish a business and to run it profitably. It may include the rights to use the product (trademarks and trade names), copyrights and designs, marketing and sales methods, and trade secrets, as well as managerial assistance from the franchisor in setting up and running local operations, including the transfer of business practices, instructions, training of employees, advertising, and so forth. The franchisor must deliver a well-developed, proven business model and operations manual of which standardization is a cornerstone, just as the brand has shown its strength in the marketplace.

Franchising represents an economical and risk-reducing way to enter a foreign market instead of investing from scratch in building one's own stores or outlets. Franchising combines the two kinds of advantages: the scale economics that can be generated on the side of the franchisor, and the local knowledge, goodwill and entrepreneurial talents on the side of the franchisee. It is therefore well-suited for testing and building a new and promising local market. Since the franchisee typically is a small independent investor who has working capital and local market knowledge but no or little business experience in selling the specific products, costs, risks and benefits are shared between the franchisor and the franchisee. The franchisor can also deal with a master franchisee that has the rights to open outlets on its own or to develop sub-franchisees in the country or region.

> **Box 3.1 Further insights: Conflicts in franchisor–franchisee relationships – the case of Georg Jensen A/S in China**
>
> With a history that spans more than 100 years, the Georg Jensen brand represents quality craftsmanship and timeless aesthetic design, producing lifestyle products ranging from hollowware to watches, jewelry and home products. Georg Jensen stands for timeless Scandinavian design and is sold almost all over the world.
>
> At the beginning of the millennium, Georg Jensen A/S (GJ) considered how to enter the large and booming Chinese market for its luxury design products. At that time, GJ had production facilities in Denmark and Thailand as well as about 100 stores in 12 countries, including flagship stores in some of the world's most important capitals. The first entry into mainland China took place in 2005 with the establishment of a flagship store at an attractive address in Beijing. With high expectations for the Chinese market, GJ decided to focus on a major expansion of its store network – not through GJ's own stores but though a franchise agreement with a partner.
>
> In 2009, GJ signed a master franchise agreement with a Danish-Chinese partner, Trayton Group (TG). In addition to designing, producing and marketing a wide range of products, including furniture, upholstery and lifestyle products, TG also distributed products from other Danish manufacturers in China. TG (with about 2,000 employees at that time) had operated in China since 1995 and had over the years gained

comprehensive knowledge about the Chinese market. Under the franchise contract, TG acquired exclusive rights to open GJ stores in two-thirds of the Chinese market (the richest, most attractive regions in the south and east) over the following period of 10 years. The plan was to open 15 stores by the end of 2012.

In 2011, TG had only opened four of GJ's five stores in China. With the aim of intensifying the expansion, TG insisted on getting the permission from GJ to sign agreements with independent sub-franchisees to open 20 to 30 more stores. GJ refused to give permission, but instead initiated a dialogue with other potential master franchisees in the part of China where TG already had exclusive rights. GJ believed that TG had not fulfilled the objectives of the franchising contract as agreed. By May 2012, GJ terminated the franchising agreement and suspended deliveries to TG. Against this background, TG was forced to close its four stores. Subsequently, TG sued GJ for breach of contract and demanded DKK 50 million (about EUR 6.8 million) to repurchase TG's distribution rights (that is, to compensate TG for investments in connection with store establishments, brand building, and so on). For the next two years, the two partners tried to reach a settlement, but failed. Instead, it came to arbitration, a case GJ lost in May 2014. GJ had to pay TG DKK 36 million (about EUR 4.9 million) plus legal costs, and so on.

For GJ, the conflict with its franchisee TG meant that the original plan to conquer the Chinese market for its luxury design products had to be completely abandoned. Consequently, GJ had to withdraw from the Chinese market and start over. GJ did not return until 2016 with the establishment of its own stores in a few Chinese cities.

Sources: Compiled from Danish newspapers; among others, *Berlingske Tidende*

Franchising fits the requirements of service and people-intensive industries, especially if these require a huge number of geographically dispersed outlets to serve the local markets. Retail businesses, fast food restaurants (such as McDonald's, Burger King, KFC and Pizza Hut), hotel chains (Hilton, Marriott and Sheraton), car repairs (Tuffy, Midas and AutoSmart), real estate services (Keller William, Century 21) are examples of businesses where franchising is particularly widespread. Franchising involves potential conflicts, which can complicate the cooperation between the franchisor and the franchisee and can ultimately lead to the termination of the legal contract. The biggest difficulties are the failure of either of the partners to live up to the terms of the legal agreement, and disagreements about objectives and the means of achieving profits. Box 3.1 provides an example of conflicts in a franchisor–franchisee relationship at Georg Jensen A/S in China. To achieve a well-functioning franchising collaboration, the parties should create a strong culture with common values and frequent and intensive communication, as well as ongoing monitoring of the results of the collaboration.

A management contract is an agreement between owners or investors of a project and a management company hired to deliver management expertise and know-how that is coordinating and overseeing the contract. A management contract is particularly relevant for an owner or investor who needs to gain management expertise from a contractor who possesses industry-specific competences and/or well-established experience in the field. Under a management contract, operational functions are handed over to the management company, which receives a fee for this assistance. Typical functions or operations include: (i) technical operations such as production; (ii) management of human resources, including training of personnel; (iii) financial management of the organization such as accounting; and (iv) marketing services, including promotions. The terms of a management contract differ depending on the kind of operation taking place and the parties involved. Typically, a management agreement will provide the management contractor with operational control of a specific organizational unit or the entire business. The management contractor will then take full responsibility of all operational decisions necessary to run the business.

Management contracts are most often used in service industries with large-scale functions, such as hotel management, property management and food service. For example, a hotel owner might have no interest in running the hotel, so instead she or he entrusts the operational management of the hotel to a management company. It is common for hotel management contracts to provide the managing firm with the control to service guests, maintain the premises, train employees and conduct marketing and other promotional services. Hotel management contracts tend to be long-term agreements due to the nature of the industry.

In IB, management contracts can be highly relevant in situations where host governments want foreigners to provide expertise in carrying out a specific project but do not want foreign ownership. Food service management contracts are often used in the public sector. Under these agreements, schools, sports facilities, nursing homes and public office buildings have their food facilities and services provided and managed by a management company.

3.3 EQUITY MODES

According to the World Bank, an FDI is an investment to acquire a lasting management interest (10 percent or more of voting stock) in a firm that operates in an economy other than that of the investor. It is the sum of equity capital, reinvestment of earnings, other long-term capital and short-term capital. The difference between FDI modes and contracting entry modes is related to equity. The fundamental characteristic of equity is that the owners or investors are paid *ex post*, namely from the profits that are generated through the investment. This contrasts with contracts that specify the payments to be made *ex ante* (for example, a royalty payment in a licensing agreement has to be agreed in advance, such as 5 percent per sold unit). Paying the investors and therewith the contributors of input *ex post* is efficient if it is difficult to define their contribution *ex ante* and if measuring it *ex post* is difficult (Brouthers and Hennart, 2007). Figure 3.4 shows entry mode alternatives in terms of the number of partners, equity and control-related aspects (see also Zahra and Elhagrasey, 1994).

FDI entry modes involve two main decisions: (i) the level of ownership – that is, the choice between WOS and JV; and (ii) the establishment mode – that is, the choice between greenfield investments and acquisitions. In addition, management needs to decide on the operational modes; that is, the choice of which parts of the value chain the firm should invest in (upstream versus downstream FDIs), which is discussed in further detail in Chapter 6.

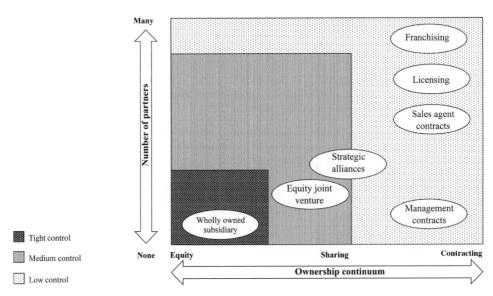

Figure 3.4   Entry modes: Number of partners, equity and control

3.3.1   Ownership modes: Wholly owned subsidiaries versus joint ventures/strategic alliances

A WOS is a firm whose common stock is 100 percent owned by another firm, the parent firm. Because there are no minority shareholders, the parent firm maintains full strategic and operational control of the foreign subsidiary. Foreign subsidiaries operate with the permission of the parent, which may or may not have direct input into the subsidiary's operations and management. WOSs are considered by firms that are willing to make a high commitment to the foreign market and have the financial strength to make the related high investments. In comparison with other entry modes, WOSs have high fixed initial costs (that is, high up-front investments) as well as ongoing re-investments in the venture, while JVs and contractual modes, for example, typically have lower fixed costs but higher variable costs (see, for example, Dikova and Brouthers, 2016).

WOSs can offer a wide range of benefits to the foreign investor. In addition to having full control, WOSs have in principle the most significant market impact and subsequent payouts. This, however, depends on the implementation capabilities of the foreign investor. In the long run, the return on investment (ROI) on WOSs is generally high, but in the short and medium term more moderate because it takes time to build up a production platform and a market presence (that is, investments into production facilities, channels of distributions and the creation of a customer base). In the case of a 100 percent acquisition of an existing foreign firm, the original investment also requires an up-front premium, which can make the pay-back time even longer. The speedy execution of strategic priorities is another advantage of WOSs. In the case of a new product launch, the parent company can ask the WOS to dedicate all its resources and capabilities to the project, while it will take longer if JVs or contractual entry modes are used. Faster execution means faster market penetration. Synergies in R&D, marketing and information technologies mean cost efficiencies and strong long-term strategic positioning. A further advantage of WOSs is that the parent and the subsidiary can use their combined size to negotiate better terms with suppliers and customers (for a further discussion, see Surdu and Mellahi, 2016).

The disadvantages of WOSs include a concentration of risk on the foreign investor and a potential loss of operational flexibility. By using a WOS as an entry mode, the foreign investor is strongly exposed to different types of risks: commercial, operational and political. Another disadvantage is that they require larger up-front investments that are considered more irreversible, or less flexible, than other entry modes. The irreversibility and sunk-cost risk of an investment increases with host-country uncertainty. This relates to the difficulties in anticipating future developments and to potential instability in the host market which may induce greater potential losses. In other words, a potentially wrong decision (for example, increase investments when situations become unfavorable or decrease investments when situations become favorable) would be exceedingly costly because established investments in foreign countries most often cannot be used for another purpose. Therefore, compared to other entry modes WOSs are less likely to change to another mode or to eventually lead to exiting the market due to less operational flexibility and high sunk costs (see also Song, 2014).

An equity JV is a partnership between two or more parties that involves the creation of a new business unit or firm. The two or more parties – for instance, a foreign investor and a local one – then share ownership and control in the new entity. JVs are motivated by several factors. First, a partner in a host country can help to speed up the market entry, and second, it can contribute to getting embedded in the new market; for instance, by negotiating with the host-country authorities. JVs help firms to gain an in-depth local understanding of distribution and marketing in a country. When Pepsi and Coca-Cola entered India, they used JVs to gain a better understanding of the distribution and logistics network in India. In the case where two or more partners have complementary resources (for example, within R&D, marketing), a JV arrangement can lead to new opportunities. Another major benefit of JVs is that they spread the risk of international expansion among the partners, and the partners likewise share the costs and investments (for example, in expensive R&D partnerships). Finally, firms also join forces to broaden the merchandise they have available, thereby gaining marketing efficiency and a better public image. In an online context, a JV can help companies to expand their subscriber base, enhance website traffic, gain international credibility and acquire complementary resources such as e-commerce capabilities.

However, JVs can also be enforced by the host country by restricting foreign ownership (for example, countries which do not allow WOSs); this is often the case if governments aim to gain access to important foreign technologies and know-how. In many emerging economies, foreign ownership is heavily regulated, if permitted at all. For example, JV laws exist in Russia, Eastern Europe, China and other formerly protected or centrally controlled economies. Several countries require some degree of local participation for operations in their country, necessitating the formation of JVs for firms seeking to expand into these markets beyond a simple exporting or contracting model.

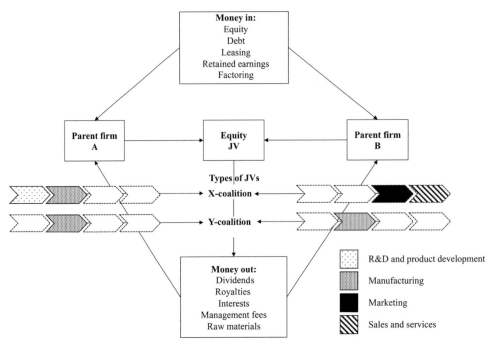

Figure 3.5   Equity joint ventures and types of coalitions

There are two types of JVs: X and Y coalitions (see Figure 3.5). X coalitions are formed when partners divide the value chain activities between themselves and offer complementary resources at each end of the chain. For example, partner A concentrates on R&D/product development and manufacturing, while partner B performs marketing, sales and service of the product. In this case A has core competencies in upstream functions, while B has core competencies in downstream activities. In Y coalitions, A and B both share one or more value chain activities with the purpose of sharing costs and risks. In the case of upstream Y coalitions, the two partners, for example, establish a joint production of components to achieve economies of scale, whereby the unit production costs can be reduced to benefit both partners (widely used in the automotive industry, for example). Downstream Y coalitions are formed if the two partners collaborate with regard to the marketing, distribution, and sales of and/or services related to the product.

The financing of a cross-border JV includes equity, debt, retained earnings, leasing and debt-factoring arrangements. The ownership split of the JV depends on how much each partner contributes in terms of equity (majority, minority, or 50–50), which ultimately determines who is in control and can influence key decisions. In managing JVs, potential for conflict can arise from: divergent goals of the two partners, different attitudes with respect to the sharing and repatriation of profits, different cultures and a lack of trust (among other things). Since cross-border JVs involve different countries with different legal/regulatory systems, legal controversies often emerge between the partners. This is particularly the case when mixing firms that are embedded in civil law systems (the legal system prevalent in most of Europe, other than the United Kingdom and Ireland) versus common law systems (for example, the United States and United Kingdom).

Often JVs are considered as second-best solutions that are chosen if WOSs are legally prohibited. In the case of no or few restrictions on foreign ownership, MNEs often choose WOSs either because JVs entail a high risk that crucial proprietary knowledge might leak to the JV partner, or because JVs are too complicated to manage. While JVs were the dominant type of ownership chosen by foreign investors into China until 2000, firms preferred to establish WOSs in most sectors given the continuing liberalization implemented by the Chinese government after the turn of the millennium. Firms that have changed from JVs to WOSs include, for example, large MNEs such as Mitsubishi, Siemens and Nestlé, as well as many SMEs (Puck, Holtbrügge and Mohr, 2009).

Strategic alliances represent a variety of purposive inter-organizational relationships between two or more partners that share compatible goals, strive for mutual benefits, contribute with differential resources and acknowledge a high level of mutual dependence (Child, Faulkner and Tallman, 2005). Strategic alliances differ from other types of collaborative arrangements because they occur in the context of a firm's long-term plans and seek to improve its competitive standing in global markets. Strategic alliances are not just limited to one-way transfers of resources, such as licensing, franchising and marketing agreements, but represent a spectrum of inter-organizational cooperative arrangements with a variety of governance mechanisms. In strategic alliances two or more partners may or may not have legal contracts and may or may not have provided equity funding in a separate entity (for example, non-equity ventures and JVs). What is common to all of these relationships is the commitment of the partnering organizations to jointly develop technology and/or to market products, share costs, access resources and integrate networks, thus strengthening their ability to keep pace with emerging requirements in the competitive marketplace.

Strategic alliances can be offensive or defensive. Offensive alliances focus on creating markets, defining industry standards and anticipating or responding to political developments or competitiveness with other firms. Defensive alliances aim to defend or strengthen an existing market position. Box 3.2 presents an example of a defensive type of strategic alliance commonly used within the airline industry. Here, cooperative marketing agreements, such as "codesharing," are used as a defensive weapon against other competitors.

> **Box 3.2   Further insights: Strategic alliances in the airline industry**
>
> Since the 1990s the airline industry has taken advantage of the formation of strategic alliances. For example, American Airlines, Cathay Pacific, British Airways and Qantas are among the partners in the Oneworld alliance, which integrates schedules and mileage programs. Another strategic alliance is Star Alliance, which is the largest in the world, consisting of 26 partners, and was founded by Lufthansa, Scandinavian Airlines, Thai Airlines, United Airlines and Air Canada in 1997.
>
> Strategic alliances in the airline industry include, among other things, cooperative marketing agreements called "codesharing." Codesharing is a practice between carriers in an alliance which allows each carrier to sell seats on specified flights that are operated by partners. For example, consider the codesharing between Air France and Delta on Air France's flight from Washington DC to Paris. This enables a passenger in Cincinnati to take a Delta plane to DC and connect to the Air France flight to Paris, all on a single itinerary purchased from Delta. This set-up effectively expands the route network for both airlines and allows them to coordinate flight schedules and share certain airport facilities. Moreover, it provides additional benefits to consumers who do not need to make separate reservations at multiple airlines to get to their destination.
>
> The phenomenon of codesharing can be explained by both efficiency and competitive motives. From the efficiency standpoint, codesharing effectively combines the networks of the allied airlines to provide expanded availability and streamlining of services. These efficiencies are exemplified in the "traditional" codeshared itinerary, in which a passenger flies on one partner's "flight segment" to connect to the codeshared flight segment that is operated by the other partner. A flight segment is defined as a nonstop flight between two airports, and the carrier that provides the aircraft and crew for this flight is referred to as the "operator." Under a codesharing arrangement, the operator's flight will have multiple airlines selling its seats, and the carrier who sells a given passenger the ticket is called the "marketer." Another efficiency gain from codesharing stems from the cooperation between airlines removing the elevated markups, or double margins, that are present when each airline sells its own flight segments separately.
>
> The competitive motives for codesharing are to gain or preserve market power. Like price and quality, codesharing is a tool that the airline uses to gain or protect market share from its competitors. As a codeshared flight segment has two codes, it is listed twice on the electronic flight listings known as global distribution systems, which facilitate most online marketing and reservation services (for example, Expedia, Booking.com). That is, a codeshared flight listing occupies more space on computer screens and can potentially crowd out competitors' listings. If both of the codesharing allies actually operate on the segment, this also leads customers to observe increased flight frequency, which may further boost the marketing benefit. Thus, codesharing gives allied airlines a marketing advantage over competitors by increasing the number of flight listings in computer databases, expanding the incumbents' passenger base, as well as sharing the marketing cost of attracting additional passengers. Furthermore, codesharing on a particular flight segment could also be used by alliance partners to compete against rivals in a variety of one-stop markets. In this case, it represents a joint attempt on behalf of the alliance carriers to divert market share away from a third-party competitor's indirect service to one of the endpoint airports of the codeshared segment. Due to its increasing presence in the airline industry, codesharing has drawn the attention of anti-trust authorities who are concerned about possible anti-competitive motives.
>
> *Source:* Adapted from Goertz and Shapiro (2012)

3.3.2 Establishment modes: Greenfield investments versus acquisitions

Entering a foreign market by FDI implies that the firm has to decide on the establishment mode. That is, the firm can either invest into building up resources from scratch, which is called "greenfield investment" or "*de novo*" investment," or it can acquire existing assets or shares of a firm that is already active in the market, which is called "acquisition." A greenfield investment implies an accumulation of capital and involves the creation of a new affiliate with supporting facilities: a new plant, an assembly factory, a warehouse, an R&D unit, a sales or marketing office, and so on. An acquisition involves the purchase of a firm located abroad; that is, a transfer of ownership. While the concepts of entry modes and establishment mode are closely related, the former considers the choice between market and hierarchy, while the latter focuses on the alternatives available within the hierarchical (or wholly owned) option.

While both greenfield investments and acquisitions are high-control, high-commitment and high-risk strategies for entering new markets, they differ in terms of timing, investment profile, implementation, and so forth (Alon, Elia and Li, 2020). Greenfield investments are associated with establishing a start-up, hiring and training new employees, sending employees from the parent organization (who are commonly called "expatriates") and gradually building the business with the knowledge of local institutions. It is a strategy to exploit firm-specific advantages that are difficult to separate from the parent MNE organization. Greenfield investments use the investor's technology, capital, know-how, and so on, which are transferred from the home- or third-country environment. That is, greenfield entry is easier when investors control key resources (firm-specific assets such as technology and know-how) that can be internally transferred and used as a source of competitive advantage in the host market.

In contrast to greenfield investments, acquisitions enable a rapid foreign entry. In acquisitions, resources, including technology, market power, knowledge, managerial capabilities and/or capital, are held by a local firm which has established production facilities, market knowledge, (access to) distribution channels, a brand name and/or a well-known customer base over a number of years. The advantage of acquisitions is the immediate availability of resources, which saves time for the foreign investor. In some cases, the MNE keeps the existing management structures. The former managers can facilitate the market entry and may enable a gradual learning process in dealing with the local environment in the new market. Acquisitions are most suitable if there are significant host-country competitive barriers to entry; for example, in the case of mature industries characterized by low to medium growth and eventually surplus capacities.

> **Box 3.3** **Further insights: The acquisition of Scottish & Newcastle**
>
> In autumn 2007, there were rumors that the UK-based brewing group Scottish & Newcastle (S&N) was for sale. S&N employed approximately 3,300 employees in its domestic market with breweries in Manchester, Reading, Dunston and Tadcaster, and about 15,000 employees in four breweries in other European markets. In addition, it had significant activities in Russia and East Asia and strong market positions for its three main brands: Baltika (owned with Carlsberg through the JV Baltic Brewery Holding, or BBH – a Russian brewing group), Foster's (a former Australian brand) and Kronenbourg 1664. Several global competitors, among them Heineken and Carlsberg, had an interest in acquiring S&N. That Carlsberg should be among the interested parties surprised S&N, as both firms had been (50–50) strategic partners in BBH for five years. S&N's chairman of the board announced that S&N was not for sale; it wanted to continue as an independent firm. In a press release in October 2007, Heineken and Carlsberg announced that they had formed a strategic alliance with the intention of bidding for all the shares in S&N. The alliance was spectacular: Two global competitors fighting for the same beer market could not have common interests – or could they?
>
> Carlsberg's ambitions were to take full control of BBH and its best-selling brand Baltika, one of the strongest and best positioned consumer brands in Russia. Between 2005 and 2007, the Russian beer market experienced an annual growth between 10 and 15 percent, and annual beer consumption had more than tripled from approximately 20 liters in the late 1990s to 67 liters in 2007. Due to Carlsberg's strong market position in France, it was interested in buying S&N's strong French brewery Kronenbourg. Several inquiries to S&N's management had revealed that S&N was not interested in selling its 50 percent share of the Russian brewing group to Carlsberg. In 2006, BBH had a market share of almost 35 percent of the Russian market, with up-to-date brewing factories. The agreement between Carlsberg and S&N also included a provision saying that if one of the partners wished to bid for the other party's 50 percent shareholding, the other could make a counteroffer. Should Carlsberg take over BBH 100 percent, there was no other option than to take full control of S&N. The problem, however, was that Carlsberg did not have the necessary capital to bid on S&N shares in 2007.
>
> For Heineken, S&N was an attractive firm because of its strong position in selected European countries. Heineken was more internationalized than Carlsberg, and especially known for its flagship brand and the sale of more than 200 different types of beers and brands. Heineken was particularly strong in Europe and the United States and was interested in acquiring S&N's operations in the United Kingdom, Ireland, Belgium, Portugal and Finland to further strengthen its European market position. S&N's strong competitive position in the United Kingdom with brands such as Newcastle Brown Ale, John Smith's beer and Foster's, as well as the Strongbow cider brand, was particularly attractive for Heineken.
>
> The acquisition plan of the Heineken–Carlsberg alliance was to split up S&N so that each of the two partners took over the parts of S&N that best fit into their respective business strategies. By splitting up S&N, there was also an expectation that the acquisition would not be overruled by European Union (EU) competition authorities; a significant risk if only one of the partners completed the acquisition of S&N. The takeover attempt of S&N took about three months. From the perspective of S&N, it was a hostile takeover. Throughout the end of 2007, three share offers from the Heineken–Carlsberg alliance were rejected outright, but after a renewed bidding round in January 2008, the shareholders of S&N could not reject an offer of 800 pence per share, corresponding to a total acquisition price of about USD 15.4 billion. The price per share was approximately 25 percent higher than the closing price on the date that the acquisition attempt was initiated. The final takeover bid was approximately 14 times S&N's earnings for 2006.
>
> *Sources:* Compiled from various sources, such as the *Financial Times* and *Borsen*

Box 3.3 gives an example of an acquisition in the European brewing industry, in which Heineken and Carlsberg formed a strategic alliance to acquire a British competitor. The Dutch–Danish partnership succeeded in carrying out a hostile acquisition, which after a split-up helped to strengthen both partners' market positions in Europe.

The choice of foreign establishment mode affects both current and future results of the FDI. Therefore, it is extremely important to analyze in depth the potential benefits and risks that are associated with choosing one or another entry mode and establishment mode. When deciding on the foreign establishment mode, investors should be aware that the consequences of wrong decisions can be very severe and highly irreversible.

3.4 AN ANALYTICAL FRAMEWORK TO GUIDE THE ENTRY MODE DECISION

Over the years, several theories and analytical frameworks have contributed explanatory factors that influence the entry mode choice. Five main schools of thought have been put forward to explain the choice of entry mode (see Box 3.4), which form the base to develop an analytical framework to guide the entry mode decision of managers facing this practical challenge.

More specifically, the different theoretical frameworks provide important explanatory variables in relation to entry mode choice. Some attribute particular importance to internal firm factors (that is, the resource-based view, or RBV, and the Uppsala model; see below); others emphasize the importance of host-country factors (the OLI – see below – and institutional theory), while still others focus on the importance of transactions (TCA; see below) in the choice between equity modes and non-equity modes.

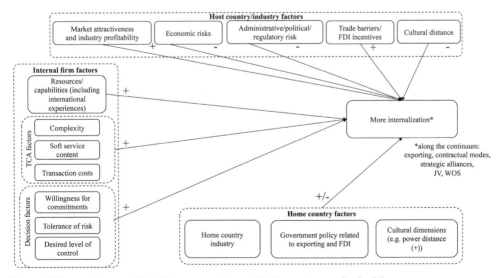

Figure 3.6 An analytical framework to guide the entry mode decision

We will in the following more systematically outline the factors that influence the entry mode decision (see Figure 3.6). In Figure 3.6, the direction of the various factors' influence on the entry mode choice is indicated via symbols: a (+) indicates a positive relation – a given factor will influence the mode choice towards an internalization solution (that is, equity modes). A (-) indicates a negative relation; that is, a factor pulls towards an externalization solution (that is, non-equity modes). We advise managers to look at factors that are classified into three main groups: internal firm factors, home-country factors and host-country factors. We will go through the relevant lines of arguments on each of these groups in the next sub-sections.

> **Box 3.4   Further insights: Theories that explain the entry mode choice**
>
> The Uppsala model of internationalization (see, for example, Johanson and Vahlne, 1977, 2009) is based on a set of behavioral assumptions concerning the importance of risk perception, uncertainties and experimental knowledge in doing IB. According to the Uppsala model, the choice of entry mode is a gradual process: When the firm first enters an overseas market, a low-resource-commitment mode such as exporting is desirable. As the firm acquires more knowledge and experience in that overseas market, it will assume a higher level of resource commitment with higher levels of risk and control, and potentially higher returns of its foreign operations with WOSs being the end of the continuum.
>
> According to transaction cost theory (TCA) or internalization theory (see, for example, Buckley and Casson, 1976; Williamson, 1987), the entry mode choice requires a comparison of the coordination costs associated with internalizing activities with the transaction costs arising from collaborating with a market partner. According to TCA, firms choose entry modes that minimize transaction costs associated with entering and operating in a foreign market, including the costs associated with finding, negotiating with, monitoring and enforcing contracts with a potential external partner. It is concerned with the costs of integrating an operation within the firm (internalization) as compared to the costs of using an external party (externalization). More specifically, firms prefer entry modes with a higher level of control (equity modes such as WOS or JV) when transaction costs are high. High transaction costs mainly stem from (internal and external) uncertainty (for example, information asymmetry in market-based relations; economic, political, and institutional risks), and asset specificity. In buyer–seller relationships, asset specificity occurs when the buyer must make investments that are specific to the seller. It consists of site, physical asset and human asset specificity and increases with the extent of losses that would be realized if the assets were used outside the specific context for which they were intended.
>
> The RBV (see, for example, Barney, 1991; Wernerfelt, 1995) suggests that firms either possess unique resources that they can exploit in foreign markets or use foreign markets to acquire or develop new resource-based advantages. To internationalize, firms have to possess firm-specific advantages (FSAs) – based on valuable, rare and inimitable resources – that allow them to outweigh the disadvantages they face in competing with already established host-country firms (that is, the LoF argument). The FSAs of firms rest on intangible (for example, proprietary knowledge, licenses, brands) and tangible resources (for example, financial and human capital, raw materials), that can be transferred to and exploited in foreign markets. The resources can either be developed by

the firm itself or acquired in connection with the choice of entry mode (for example, via strategic alliances or JVs).

The OLI framework suggests that FSAs (O-advantages), location advantages (L-advantages) and internalization advantages (I-advantages) together will influence the choice of entry mode (see, for example, Dunning, 2000). It combines insights from the RBV and the TCA with location theory by adding country-level factors. It is therefore also known as the "eclectic framework." First, the firms should possess O-advantages (for example, patents, copyrights, technical know-how and management skills) which enable them to compete in the host-country market. Second, the host country should provide L-advantages (for example, lower production and transportation cost, favorable taxation, lower risks, access to protected markets) which encourage outside firms to serve the market directly rather than going for exporting. And finally, the firms should have sufficient incentives to serve foreign markets through their internal organization; that is, I-advantages (such as lower transaction costs, minimum technology imitation, effective management and good quality control). If all three types of advantages exist, firms should make an FDI. The original OLI version explained three types of entry modes: exporting, licensing and FDI. In a later modified framework, O-advantages were broadened to include the skills and capabilities of partners, L-advantages were widened to include the spatial integration between locations and I-advantages were broadened to include the cooperative structures. With these changes, the framework can also explain cooperative modes.

The institutional theory (see, for example, North, 1991; Scott, 1995) suggests that the institutional environments in countries influence the entry mode choice, because they reflect the "rules of the game" that firms need to follow when they aim to participate in a host-country market. The central idea is that firms adopt structures and practices that are "isomorphic" to those of other firms in the foreign market because of their quest to attain legitimacy. Isomorphic pressures are a result of three institutional pillars: the regulative (that is, rules and laws that exist to ensure stability and order), normative (that is, social values, culture) and cognitive (that is, cognitive structure in a society) pillars; see also Chapter 1. Following this logic, firms choose an entry mode that will help them to gain legitimacy in and conform to the host-country environment. Therefore, firms are more likely to choose JVs over WOSs when regulative and normative institutional pressures in the host country are high. Moreover, firms also choose entry modes that were predominantly adopted by previous foreign firms.

3.4.1   Internal firm factors

In entering a foreign market, firms' decision-makers are well advised to first determine their primary goals and performance requirements. The entry-mode-related decision criteria are linked to managements' preference for speed, resource commitments, control, risk mitigation and flexibility. As has been shown, management must evaluate the various trade-offs involved: By using high-commitment or equity modes, managers will achieve a higher degree of control over their foreign operations, but at the same time also become more exposed to risk and experience a lower degree of flexibility. If firms use low-commitment modes, such as exporting or contracting modes, they will have an advantage of being less exposed to host-country risks and at the same time obtain a higher degree of flexibility, but will, as a significant disadvantage, achieve a lower degree of control.

In addition, the amount and quality of a firm's resources influence the entry mode decision. If firms possess extensive financial and human resources, they will be able to choose more investment-heavy entry modes, such as WOSs and JVs. Due to limited resources or fewer capabilities, SMEs are, for instance, more likely to enter foreign markets using exporting and contracting modes. As firms grow, they will increasingly use higher-commitment, higher-risk and higher-control operation modes. Moreover, if the firms' resources are highly unique and contribute to a sustainable competitive advantage, they will try to transfer resources to the foreign market using a high degree of control with the aim of protecting these strategically relevant resources (following the RBV). A specific resource or capability factor affecting entry mode choice is the international experience of the firm. It has an individual dimension related to the firm's managers as well as an organizational dimension (for example, operational routines). Experience plays a key role, because understanding how to operate effectively in a host market gives the firm the confidence necessary to increase its commitment to a market over time. In general, a firm's knowledge base increases with its international experiences and, as firms learn to operate across different modes over time, they are expected to make higher-commitment foreign entries to take control of their activities and reap higher rewards. Non-equity ventures become stepping stones on the way to engaging in FDI, such as a JV or WOS. The lower-commitment modes enable a firm to obtain knowledge about interacting with host institutional actors, such as governments, suppliers and customers. Building on this prior experience, firms tend to increase commitments and, in time, operate more independently and in the foreign market (as predicted in the Uppsala model).

Also, the nature of the product influences the entry mode choice. Product-related factors include: volume, weight, degree of specialization, service content (hardware/software), knowledge content, degree of technical complexity (for example, requirement for training the customer in the use of the product), repair and after-sales requirements. Closely related to the product per se is the nature of a transaction between the buyer and seller of inputs, intermediate products and final products. According to the TCA, transferring highly complex products with a significant component of tacit knowledge (for example, technologically complex and/or knowledge-intensive products) will make the choice of non-equity modes problematic as it involves high transaction costs (for example, drafting of a market-based contract). Box 3.5 presents the arguments from transaction-cost thinking in relation to whether a firm should enter a licensing agreement with a partner or should alternatively establish a WOS for production.

Box 3.5 Further insights: Transaction cost analysis: Licensing or WOS in a foreign market

A technology-intensive firm (the manufacturer) faces the question of whether it should choose to license its technological knowledge, production processes and trademarks to a partner, or make an FDI in a WOS for production.

The TCA argues that high transaction costs due to both high levels of information asymmetry and high asset specificity between a buyer and seller of technological know-how will favor the FDI in a WOS over a licensing agreement. In the exchange of technology, information asymmetry arises because the buyer of knowledge (the licensee) – vis-à-vis the seller – has limited knowledge of what she or he is buying and therefore has difficulties in evaluating the knowledge transfer. On the other hand, the seller of the technology (the licensor) has no guarantee that the buyer (the licensee) will not take advantage of the knowledge and/or commercialize the technology and later become a competitor. Therefore, patents are a potential solution of the information-asymmetry problem since they encourage the inventors to make their knowledge public for legal protection, but patents can hardly protect tacit knowledge.

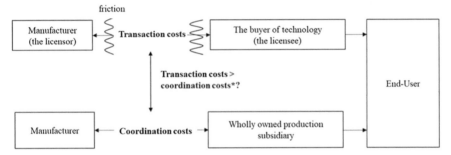

*transaction costs increase due to: - asymmetrical distribution of information that induces uncertainty; - asset-specific investments that increase the hold-up risk (e.g. missing remuneration/quality problems); - opportunistic behavior or a disagreement about goals/means and an increased risk of creating a competitor

Figure 3.7 Licensing vs WOS

Asset specificity occurs when the licensee, to absorb technology, must make investments that are specific to the seller of the technology. After they have made these investments, they bear the risk that the partner opportunistically alters the price or other aspects of the cooperation, a situation called "hold-up." To avoid such a hold-up situation, the partners draft a contract that specifies rights and obligations of both partners, the price for the life of transaction-specific investments and other conditions. While a licensing agreement or contract can mitigate opportunistic behavior by partners, its enforcement is far from perfect. For instance, how does the licensor ensure that the licensee manufactures the products at the agreed quality level? If this is not the case, the licensor's reputation may be damaged. Or how does the licensor ensure that the licensee does not expand to other markets or countries with the licensed product that has not been agreed upon?

According to the TCA, the manufacturer will choose a WOS if the transaction costs of using a third party (a licensee) are higher than the coordination costs to internalize into a WOS.

Equity modes are better to facilitate the transfer of tacit knowledge. In the case of services, the entry mode decision will mainly depend on whether it is a hard or soft service. Hard services are those where production and consumption are psychically separated or decoupled. For example, Microsoft's IT software services (such as office software, messaging software or payroll processing software) can be stored on a tangible medium and then transferred in a highly standardized way to end customers. Typically, the software service is licensed on a subscription basis and is centrally hosted. In soft services, on the other hand, production and consumption take place simultaneously (that is, the customer acts as a co-producer), which is why the manufacturer of soft services must be present in the foreign market. For example, operating in the hotel industry requires establishing a physical presence to provide the service in the foreign market (Pla-Barber, Villar and León-Darder, 2014). Hotel services are characterized by the intangibility and inseparability of production and consumption, which implies a high level of contact between producers and consumers. Often, soft services are tacit in nature and imperfectly transferrable across borders as they are embedded in the organization (for example, policies and systems), employees, culture and organizational routines. While tangible aspects are related to facilities, equally important is service quality, which determines customer satisfaction. Box 3.6 illustrates the importance of the product for the firm's choice of entry mode by comparing a carmaker's entry mode considerations with those of an IT software provider.

Box 3.6   Example: Entry mode considerations of a carmaker versus an IT software provider

Carmakers must identify who might be attracted to their cars, inform them of their features and persuade them to buy. Understanding buyer preferences and building consumer awareness in a foreign market takes time. Carmakers will typically ship cars and replacement parts to the foreign market by using either distributors or their own sales subsidiaries, who then deliver cars to an extensive network of dealers who sell the cars and do the repairs. Because buyers of cars still expect personal contacts in showrooms, and because they want repair facilities close by, the dealer network must be dense. Instead of subcontracting distribution to independent distributors, carmakers will rather prefer to invest in the costly and time-intensive task of building a network of wholesalers, who franchise and sometimes even own dealerships. Therefore, a carmaker's entry into a foreign market is a cumbersome and long-term process.

IT software providers face a different situation. Assume they have established a business model that is geared to reach individual programmers or small groups of programmers through the internet. All the necessary documentation to install their programs, as well as prices, is posted online, and prices can be paid by credit card. Since the customers are professionals, they need little handholding or assistance from IT software providers. Compared with carmakers, IT software providers do not spend too much time on persuading customers to buy. Selling to them requires no prior international experience; once the reputation of their software is spread out, professional customers seek them out. Since the business model is based on attracting customers worldwide using the internet, IT software providers do not need to invest in an extensive network of foreign sales subsidiaries.

For further insights, see Hennart (2013).

3.4.2 Home-country factors

Home-country factors can either force firms to expand internationally or encourage firms to choose certain entry mode strategies in foreign markets. An unfavorable industry environment at home (for example, relatively high labor costs or poor quality of factor inputs) can force firms to pursue international opportunities by making FDI instead of investing at home. The brewing company SABMiller, for example, chose to expand internationally in the first decade after the turn of the millennium to, among other reasons, escape a stifling environment in its home market of South Africa, and to form a new UK-based holding company, SAB plc.[2]

Home-country government policies and regulations can limit domestic firms' internationalization opportunities by imposing restrictions on their activities. For instance, in the 1970s the Indian government had imposed limitations and requirements for outward FDI, and Brazil also required approval of investment through exchange-control procedures. In contrast, the home-country environment can be supportive in establishing footholds in international markets for domestic firms. Governments' export-promotion programs, including financial and non-financial benefits, are primarily intended to reduce SMEs' problems in relation to LoF, but also to ensure employment in the domestic market.

In recent decades, governments from emerging market economies have announced policies to encourage FDI of their domestic firms. For example, the Chinese government emphasized a "go global" policy in the 2000s and encouraged the establishment of foreign affiliates and active participation in international M&A deals. Home-country government support may foster Chinese MNEs to springboard internationally without having accumulated much international experience. When a firm complies with or actively utilizes home-country government support, its risk-taking capabilities are heightened, thus reducing the necessity of prior international experience. Given the dominant role of state control in the Chinese economy, government support is likely to have profound effects on Chinese firms' internationalization (see, for example, Gaur, Ma and Ding, 2018).

Finally, cultural dimensions of the home-country environment are expected to influence the entry mode choice due to their associations with management style and decision-making. For example, it can be expected that the greater the power distance characterizing a firm's home-country culture (that is, centralized power and an autocratic management style), the more the firm will seek to get majority or full control of its entry mode. Also, firms originating from high-uncertainty-avoidance countries may prefer a clear structure and centralized decisions and thus full ownership and control, which can be achieved through a WOS. However, the empirical literature on the influence of home-country cultural dimensions on entry mode choice is rather ambiguous (Morschett, Schramm-Klein and Swoboda, 2010).

3.4.3 Host-country factors

The attractiveness of a foreign market is an important factor in market selection, and in the choice of entry mode too. The larger the foreign market and the higher the growth of the market in the last years, the more likely it is that a firm is willing to commit resources to this market. Generally, firms are assumed to enter attractive markets via a WOS because this is expected to provide the greatest potential for long-term profit and long-term market presence. Countries that are characterized by high market attractiveness are seen to have greater potential to absorb additional capacity, which provides an opportunity to improve firm efficiency by using high-commitment entry modes. A large host-country market implies that companies can expect returns that can compensate the higher risks associated with the commitment of resources. Higher returns are expected to come from the opportunity to gain economies of scale in manufacturing, distribution and sales in a host country with a high market attractiveness. In addition, market size is a proxy for transaction frequency, which also enhances the firm's propensity to choose equity entry modes from transaction-cost thinking.

The market attractiveness in a host country also depends on the industry competition, which can make the market attractive for foreign firms. Some industries are composed of many players and, thus, are intensely competitive, while others are dominated by a few large firms, resulting in a high degree of industry concentration. Similarly, industries vary in relation to the size of entry and exit barriers, which also have an influence on the choice of entry mode. In markets characterized by strong competition, profitability tends to be lower (see also the analytical framework to analyze industry profitability in Chapter 5) and therefore do not justify high resource commitments (for example, to set up a WOS). In addition, highly concentrated markets lead to small numbers bargaining. Compared to competitive markets, this increases the risk of opportunistic behavior of a potential partner. Thus, a highly concentrated market increases the transaction costs of cooperating, which makes internalization more attractive. Thus, transaction-cost thinking suggests that high industry concentration leads to equity entry modes.

Furthermore, economic risks need to be considered. A host-country market characterized by macroeconomic stability has minimized vulnerability to external shocks, which in turn increases its prospects for sustained economic growth. Macroeconomic stability acts as a buffer against currency and interest fluctuations in the global market. Exposure to currency fluctuations, large debt burdens and unmanaged inflation can cause economic crises and collapses in gross domestic product (GDP). Both the International Monetary Fund and the EU place an emphasis on macroeconomic stability. Indicators typically used to assess economic risk are the inflation rate, the unemployment rate, the exchange rate volatility and the health of government finances (see UNCTAD, 2016, and the overview in Chapter 2). The EU, for example, defined macroeconomic stability in the Maastricht Treaty using five indicators: (i) low and stable inflation (inflation rate below 3 percent), (ii) low long-term interest rates (restricted to 9 percent), (iii) low national debt relative to GDP (below 60 percent), (iv) low public deficits (not higher than 3 percent of GDP) and (v) currency stability (a fluctuation of at most 2.5 percent). When a host country's macroeconomic stability is high and predictable, economic risks are low and foreign investors will be inclined to enter the market with entry modes that necessitate a high commitment of resources. In contrast, instability and unpredictability will cause foreign firms to choose relatively low-commitment entry modes such as exports, or will make them completely stay out of the market.

Moreover, administrative, political and regulatory risks influence the entry mode decision. A key host-country factor is political and regulatory stability. Political stability can be defined in at least three ways: A first approach is to define it as the propensity for regime or govern-

Table 3.2 Example: Types of political risks

Risk types	Examples
Macro-political risks	
Expropriation/nationalization	Confiscation of a production unit/plant Forces sale of assets to government buyer at below-market prices Politically driven increase in state ownership of JV
War and terrorism	Border and closure of infrastructure (harbors, roads, and so on) due to interstate fights Politically motivated terrorist attacks against foreign investors
Capital controls	Limits on profit repatriation Administrative delays in approving capital transfers
Protests/strikes	Industrial actions and work stoppage at key suppliers Anti-firm protests
Regulatory change	Complex new environmental or labor standards Regulatory enforcement authority handed to state-owned company
Micro-political risks	
Bribery	Unforeseen border "taxes" on specific products
Taxation	Windfall taxes levied over "excessively high" profits Duplicate tax claims by/between central and local governments
License cancellation	Change to organization's license to operate
Forced divestiture	Assets or equity sell-offs due to protection of local firms

ment change. A second is to focus on the incidence of political upheaval or violence in a society (for example, terrorism). A third approach focuses on instability in policies rather than instability in regimes (that is, the degree to which fundamental policies – for instance, related to property rights – are subject to frequent changes). Accordingly, there are a number of indicators to measure political instability or risk in countries (see Chapters 1 and 2); for instance, the World Bank's political stability indicator. Political risks pose a threat to the profitability and sustainability of FDI. Examples are given in Table 3.2.

The most detrimental political risk is expropriation that occurs when a host government interferes with a foreign investor's fundamental ownership rights. This can take the form of a direct seizure of assets or it can be through a series of discriminatory actions, often called "creeping expropriation." Restrictions on profit repatriation occur when host governments arbitrarily limit the amount of profit that a foreign investor can remit from its local operations to the MNE headquarters' location.

Micro-political risks are those risk factors that are specific to an industry and may vary across different industries. They include contract defaults, regulatory changes, tax discriminations and forced divestiture. Forced divestiture, for example, is a country risk in which the MNE is forced to divest its business operation. An example of forced divestiture is the Indonesian subsidiary of the French retail giant Carrefour, which was ordered to sell the 75 percent stake it acquired in a smaller local rival in January 2008. In a study by Willis Towers Watson and Oxford Analytica (2019), a series of 20 structured interviews was conducted with panelists representing some of the world's leading MNEs. When asked about the most important types of risks faced today, participants mentioned regulatory risks most frequently. The study revealed that politically motivated regulatory change (with implications for tax rates, cross-border trade and exchange-transfer risks) has a significant impact on corporate risk exposure.

The size and nature of trade barriers (tariffs and non-tariffs) influence whether firms should export or make an FDI in production. High tariffs or quotas on the import of final products, intermediate goods and components speak for the establishment of local production either in the form of a licensed production or WOS. In the case of high tariffs on final products, firms can also choose assembly operations if the tariffs on imports of components and intermediate goods are significantly lower. Likewise, non-tariff barriers (such as trade and product regulations, import licenses, standards and preferences for local suppliers; for example, "buy national") influence entry mode choice, and encourage foreign firms to enter cooperation contracts or JVs with local partners. In several cases, host-country governments use incentives to attract FDI. There are three types of FDI incentives (UNCTAD, 2004): financial incentives (such as outright grants and loans at concessionary rates); fiscal incentives (such as tax holidays and reduced tax rates); and other incentives, including subsidized infrastructure or services, market preferences and regulatory concessions, such as exemptions from labor or environmental standards. Incentives can be used for attracting new FDI to a country (locational incentives) or for making foreign affiliates in a country undertake functions regarded as desirable, such as training, local sourcing, R&D or exporting (behavioral incentives). Most incentives do not discriminate between domestic and foreign investors, but they sometimes target one of the two. Incentives may also favor small firms over large, or vice versa. FDI incentives are offered by national, regional and local governments.

Finally, cultural distance (that is, the degree to which cultural values in the two countries concerned differ) influences the entry mode choice. Cultural distance implies differences in preferences, competition patterns and business rules between the host and home countries, but also indicates differences in managerial values, mindsets, norms and practices. High perceived cultural distance means that firms must deal with uncertainty in relation to planning, decision-making, communication, execution, and so on, which in turn increases the risk of operating in a host-country market and of the loss of firm resources. If there is a high cultural difference perceived by a firm's managers, they prefer entry modes which involve rather low resource commitments and secure high flexibility. Therefore, it is quite likely that a firm will avoid WOSs and will instead opt for JVs or even a lower-risk entry mode like exporting. An acquisition that grants access to another firm's capabilities is probably less efficient in the case of high cultural distance because integration costs are likely to be high. Cooperative entry modes such as JVs can therefore serve as a risk-reduction strategy in the case of high cultural distance between the firm's home- and host-country environments.

To decide upon the right entry mode, you need to analyze each of the individual factors presented above (internal firm factors, home-country factors and host-country factors) and then evaluate how the factors interact with each other. To facilitate this analysis, Figure 3.7 shows a three-step entry mode screening process. In the first screening, the entry mode alternatives are reduced to a realistic number; that is, those entry modes that do not meet the firm's goals and decision criteria or host-country restrictions are disregarded. The second step is based on a thorough internal analysis of firms' resources and product-related factors supplemented with an in-depth host-country analysis influencing the remaining entry mode alternatives.

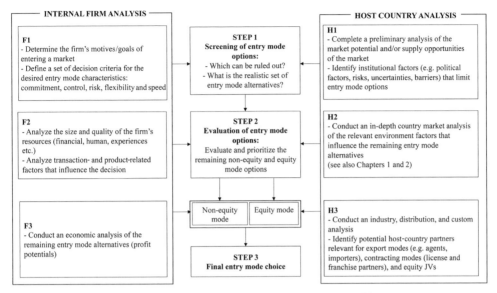

Figure 3.8 A three-step procedure to entry-mode decision-making

The third step that leads to the final entry mode choice is based partly on an analysis of the industry, channels of distribution and the customers, and partly on a financial analysis of the costs and revenues for each of the remaining and high-priority entry modes. Some of the analyses (especially in Step 2) were already part of the market-selection phase, yet with a different focus.

3.5 ENTRY MODE CHANGES OVER TIME AND FOREIGN MARKET EXIT

The literature on foreign entry modes has largely focused on the initial mode choice but less on how and why firms change operation modes over time. Operating in a turbulent environment means that firms by no means have a guarantee that an entry mode decision once made will remain the best way of serving a foreign market. Moreover, management's ambitions, goals and priorities change over time, just as the host-country conditions are constantly changing, which in turn will affect the evaluation of the entry mode decision. Changes of operation modes are important decisions as they concern firms' institutional arrangements that define the business framework of the activities in a country. Entry mode changes unfold in two ways: mode increases (that is, changes from an initial mode into a mode with higher commitment) or mode reductions (that is, changes from an initial mode into a mode with lower commitment). Various stimuli are important for mode increases as well as reductions. According to Swoboda, Olejnik and Morschett (2011), poor performance and negative host-country effects are more strongly linked to mode reductions, while firm internal factors and management's expectations and attitudes are strongly linked to mode increases.

In general, an increase to a higher commitment mode can be explained by internal and external factors, managerial expectations and performance-related factors. However, switching costs (that is, arising due to difficulties in changing the entry mode) are also important determinants. Switching costs fall into two categories. Take-down costs refer to the costs and revenue losses incurred by dismantling an existing foreign operation. Set-up costs are the costs and revenue losses of setting up a new foreign operation. They include the expenses related to recruiting and training new personnel in connection with the establishment of WOSs, as well as foreign-operation learning costs. Mode increases also depend on the actual mode shift in question. In cases of shifts within non-equity modes, several studies find that increasing transaction costs related to dissatisfaction with agency relations and increasing market expectations together with the accumulation of market knowledge are important factors in the decision to change from a sales agent to the firm's own sales subsidiary. But also switching costs matter: In exporter–agency relationships they typically consist of a severance payment that has to be made to a foreign sales agent with whom the cooperation is terminated, and of the potential losses of local sales due to customers residing with the distributor rather than the producer (Pedersen, Petersen and Benito, 2002). In the case of shifts within equity modes, research on international JVs shows that a power imbalance between partners and high levels of conflict increase the likelihood that a JV is transformed into a WOS (see Swoboda et al., 2011). According to the TCA, bringing special technological or management knowledge into JVs increases asset specificity and thus the extent of losses that would be realized if the assets were opportunistically used outside the specific context for which they were intended. To deal with the danger of opportunistic behavior of JV partners, the TCA suggests internalizing the use of these assets by establishing a WOS.

However, firms may also limit or reduce their operations in a host country and ultimately exit from foreign markets. Different terms have been used to call attention to the phenomenon of foreign market reduction and exit, such as de-internationalization, divestment, withdrawal, failure, closure, disengagement, liquidation, total sales and sell-off. De-internationalization refers to any voluntary or forced actions that reduce a firm's engagement in or exposure to current cross-border activities. The reduction of the foreign market commitment can take various forms, including the downsizing of foreign operations or withdrawal from that market; the switching from higher to lower commitment modes; the sell-off or closure of foreign sales, service or manufacturing subsidiaries; the reduction of the ownership stake in a foreign venture; and the seizure by local authorities of assets owned by foreign firms. The motives to reduce involvement in foreign markets fall into four groups: (i) lack of international experience (for example, insufficient market analysis preceding the entry mode decision; lack of information, inappropriate entry mode, too early or too late a start, maladjustment of the marketing mix in the foreign market requirement); (ii) changes in business strategy, such as further streamlining of a firm's activities, a change in foreign market priorities, or a shortage of necessary resources and consequently limited production capacity; (iii) changes in management; and (iv) poor financial results or increased incurred costs.

Some foreign market reductions and divestments are defensive, while others are voluntary. A defensive foreign divestment arises when the regional operations of an MNE incur losses over several years due to either internal problems or a hostile host-country environment (or both). A voluntary foreign market reduction, on the other hand, is based on MNE headquarters' desire for change in the overall business strategy, changes in the firm's foreign market portfolio and rationalization in the number of foreign units (for example, plants). Consequently, this means that even a well-run and profitable WOS for production can be replaced with a lower-commitment operation mode (for example, a sales subsidiary), as the headquarters wants to concentrate production on fewer foreign plants. Studies on foreign divestments have largely focused on defensive voluntary divestment, and they revealed that the divesting firms had little option but to divest. Often a very poor performance of a WOS was tolerated for many years; however, the onset of heavy losses at the parent firm provided the motivation for a divestment and triggered a review of operations that led to the closure of a loss-making wholly owned production plant (Richbell and Watts, 2000).

3.6 ENTRY MODES IN FASHION RETAILING, WITH A FOCUS ON BESTSELLER

We will illustrate a firm's entry mode considerations using an example from the international fashion industry (Bestseller A/S). To back-up the specific strategies at Bestseller, we will first provide a brief account of the factors related to the entry mode choice in the industry. International fashion retailers sell brands and/or operate stores in more than one country. They can select from a variety of entry modes, such as exporting their products, participating in franchising agreements, being involved in JVs and operational alliances, or the establishment of WOSs. In practice, retailers often use more than one entry mode for operating in different countries. For example, the US-based Tommy Hilfiger Inc. has a mixture of its own sales subsidiaries, its own stores and franchise stores in over 90 countries worldwide; the Italian retailer Diesel uses franchising in the North American market and has its own stores in Europe. Previous studies have identified several factors that are of specific relevance in the entry mode choice in fashion retailing that are grouped into internal firm factors and host-country factors (see Lu, Karpova and Fiore, 2009).

Brand equity is one of the most important internal factors in a fashion retailer's international expansion. Strong brand equity and brand values that relate to cosmopolitanism, exclusivity and design excellence have been identified as key competitive advantages in the industry. In accordance with the RBV, a brand equity advantage enhances a fashion retailer's capability to independently compete in the foreign market and encourages the retailer to select an ambitious approach with higher resource commitments. Moreover, a brand is vulnerable to potential opportunistic behaviors because of the self-interest of partners: There are potential goal conflicts between the retailer who aims at establishing a long-term brand value, and its local partners who may pursue short-term profits. Franchisees' insufficient concern for the brand image can, for instance, dilute brand equity (Lu et al., 2009).

Asset specificity is a second relevant internal factor. Asset specificity is related to the development of retail concepts and store environments, distribution management, inventory planning or product innovation. For example, a fashion retailer's competence in creating an original concept or a unique offering is an important source of specificity and competitive advantage (for instance, by catering to consumers who are inadequately served by local fashion brands). When a fashion retailer possesses highly specialized assets or unique capabilities, it is expected to exploit these assets using a higher-control entry mode.

Furthermore, financial capability is an important internal factor. Overseas fashion retailing involves a series of investments and associated costs, such as real estate investments, recruitment, volume-buying and marketing activities. It also often involves a large geographical spread, and management information systems to monitor and control the flow of stock and information, which further raise costs. Compared to a lower-control entry mode such as franchising that enables sharing costs with local partners, operating under a WOS puts severe financial constraints on a firm.

Finally, international experience is important in fashion retailing, since retailers need to cope with different cultural and regulatory contingencies. When a fashion retailer does not possess the international experience necessary for operating in a foreign market, forming a strategic alliance is a useful vehicle; likewise, franchising can help to overcome LoF by matching the local market knowledge of franchisees with their own brand advantages.

In addition, the fashion retailers are confronted with several relevant host country factors influencing their decision. For instance, a country like China is often perceived by Western companies as a market characterized by high country risk (commercial and political) and with a significant cultural distance. When macroeconomic risks and uncertainty are high, fashion retailers should limit their resource commitments and avoid higher-control entry modes due to high exit costs. The same is true when it comes to markets characterized by high cultural distance. Fashion retailers may feel intense pressure to serve customers who differ culturally from those with whom they have become accustomed. Examples of such differences include consumer product demands, key consumer reference groups, religious beliefs related to consumption and consumer aesthetic preferences (Lu et al., 2009). When countries or segments in country markets have high market potentials (size and growth) and limited market competition, international retailers should commit, in contrast, a high level of resources to exploit market opportunities and therefore select a higher-control entry mode.

This offers the relevant industry background to gain insights into Bestseller's entry into China (for which we compiled information from Hansen et al., 2010; business practice magazines; newspapers; and the firm's website). Bestseller A/S is an international fashion retailer with Danish roots that is family owned (by the Povlsen family). It offers fashion for women, men, teenagers and children and has a total turnover of about DKK 25 billion (about USD 4 billion). It sells more than 20 fashion brands, including: Jack & Jones, Vero Moda, ONLY and Vila. The brands are available online, in about 2,600 branded chain stores and 15,000 multi-brand and department stores across Europe, the Middle East, North America, Latin America and India. Bestseller does not have its own production facilities but cooperates with a high number of suppliers worldwide who are willing to meet Bestseller's code of conduct and chemical restrictions. Its main international competitors targeting the same consumers in the middle-price segment are GAP Inc. (from the United States), Zara (Spain) and H&M (Sweden). In terms of entry modes, Bestseller uses different modes in different countries. It has purchasing offices in Denmark, Italy, Turkey, India and China; its own sales subsidiaries in China, France, the Netherlands, Spain, the United Kingdom, Austria, Canada, Finland, Norway and Germany; its own showrooms for wholesalers in Austria, France, the United

Kingdom and Germany; logistic centers in Denmark, China and the Netherlands; and stores in more than 45 countries, of which a few are franchises.

Back in 1996, Bestseller was one of the first international fashion companies to enter the Chinese market, and has since established a strong and highly successful business there. In 1996 Dan Friis (who was then employed at the Danish East Asiatic Company) and Allen Warburg (who was then employed at McKinsey) approached owner and CEO Troels Holch Povlsen with the idea of entering the Chinese market. Jointly, they set up Bestseller Fashion Group China Ltd as an independent firm managed by Friis and Warburg. More specifically, Povlsen contributed 50 percent of the investment; the other half was provided by the two entrepreneurs. As they were unable to contribute the full amount on their own, the Danish Industrialization Fund for Developing Countries supported this endeavor, resulting in 30 percent cent of the capital provided by the fund, and 10 percent by each of the two entrepreneurs (in 2010 they bought the shares back from the fund). Bestseller Fashion Group China Ltd was a separate entity that outsourced clothes production in China. In terms of sales and distribution strategy, a multi-channel approach was used, consisting of a mixture of franchises and stores operated as WOSs. Within the first year, it opened 24 stores in nine different cities, and at the beginning of the millennium the firm introduced two main brands, Jack & Jones and Vero Moda. In 2000, Bestseller had 48 of its own stores and 24 franchises. In 2007 the total number of stores was increased to 1,800 (of which 960 were own stores and 840 were franchises, respectively). Hence, Bestseller decided on a mixture of an equity entry mode with franchising as a sub-mode, but why?

At the time of the entry Bestseller had several well-established international brands and the ability to leverage its European brand image in China. We know from the industry analysis that much of the brand building is done through shops; that is, there is some level of control needed over the point of sale. Developing retailing concepts in stores, moreover, involves some level of specificity (for example, store environments, distribution management, inventory planning). Bestseller already had firm-level experience in entering foreign markets and had some experience with doing business in Asia through its purchasing offices, operated at the time in Hong Kong and Beijing; in addition, the two entrepreneurs brought relevant international experience to the table.

The Chinese fashion retail market was highly fragmented at the time of the entry. Foreign luxury brands catered to the higher-price segment through outlets in upscale department stores or franchise shops, and a few international retailers dominated the market. However, this was not the case for the middle-price segment of the fashion market. In the period around the entry, the market demonstrated an impressive potential: From 1997 to 2003, consumer spending on clothes and footwear increased by 22 percent, and disposable income per capita in China's urban areas increased by more than 60 percent. There was a growing segment of young, fashion-conscious consumers. An estimate indicated that in Beijing alone there were 300,000 women with sufficient purchasing power to buy Bestseller products. That is, the market potential definitely justified high commitments. In China, before 2005 most foreign firms had to distribute their brands only through cooperation with local partners, which may have favored, among others, the franchising option. Based on the market potential, and the little competition faced, Bestseller China was able to establish an extensive sales network in a very short time.

In 2011, Bestseller announced that it intended to drop its franchising strategy and instead expand sales through the establishment of more of its own stores. At that time, the franchising business took up around 30 percent of the revenue in Bestseller. In a newspaper interview,[3] Dan Friis said: "When you own your own stores, it simply means fewer problems and more money in the long run." He continued: "This strategy strengthens our product range in the stores, our renovation of the stores will be faster, and we can get more training in sales and service. In addition, it is easier for us to negotiate locations for our four major brands when it is our own internal retail organization that conducts the negotiations together." Hence, we may assume that capital constraints, potentially a perceived lack of full host-country experience, and the regulatory forces had caused Bestseller to use franchising.

In 2021, Bestseller Fashion Group China Ltd is an independent firm, designs its own collections for more than 7,000 stores operating in more than 500 cities in China and sells an impressive list of different brands in China, among them ONLY, Jack & Jones and Vero Moda, which are all leading fashion brands in the market. Over 90 percent of the products sold in China are also produced in China. A key aspect of the Chinese strategy of Bestseller was the adaptation to local market conditions in terms of styles and models (more feminine and slender), and colors (more colorful), while still maintaining an overall European, Western design. Hence, the entry mode choice served the purpose of Bestseller, namely to sell price-competitive European clothing designs with a local touch to suit the tastes of millions of Chinese middle-class consumers – and thus was fundamental to its extraordinary success.

CHAPTER REVIEW QUESTIONS

1. What is the difference between indirect and direct exporting?
2. Discuss the relevant factors for motivating foreign distributors.
3. Why should a firm choose licensing as an entry mode strategy?
4. Why and under which host-country conditions do foreign firms prefer JV as an entry mode strategy?
5. Explain the difference between X and Y coalitions.
6. By which criteria would you evaluate whether a particular FDI activity was a success or failure?
7. Why are acquisitions often preferred vis-à-vis greenfield investments?
8. In Box 3.6, we discussed the entry mode challenges of car manufacturers. Explore the foreign market entry strategies of Tesla and compare it to the arguments presented in Box 3.6.
9. Assume that your relatively newly established firm that manufactures smaller industry robots used for packaging and labeling is considering entering the US market. Identify the key factors that influence the entry mode choice. Which entry mode alternatives do you think appear to be the most realistic?
10. Explain why Bestseller has dropped the franchise strategy and instead focuses on own stores. What does the theory say?

NOTES

1. Statista, available at: www.statista.com/statistics/250934/quarterly-number-of-netflix-streaming-subscribers-worldwide/.
2. Wikipedia, available at: https://en.wikipedia.org/wiki/South_African_Breweries.
3. Business.dk, January 10, 2011.

REFERENCES

Alon, I., Elia, S., and Li, S. (2020). Greenfield or M&A: An institutional and learning perspective on the establishment mode choice of Chinese outward investments. *Journal of International Management*, 26, 1–17.

Barney, J. B. (1991). Firm resources and sustained competitive advantage. *Journal of Management*, 17, 99–120.

Brouthers, K. D., and Hennart, J.-F. (2007). Boundaries of the firm: Insights from international entry mode research. *Journal of Management*, 33, 395–425.

Brouthers, L. E., and McNicol, J. P. (2009). International franchising and licensing. In M. Kotabe and K. Helsen (Eds), *The SAGE Handbook of International Marketing* (pp. 183–197). London: SAGE.

Buckley, P. J., and Casson, M. (1976). *The Future of the Multinational Enterprise*. London: Macmillan.

Child, J., Faulkner, D., and Tallman, S. (2005). *Cooperative Strategy: Managing Alliances, Networks, and Joint Ventures*. Oxford: Oxford University Press.

Dikova, D., and Brouthers, K. (2016). International establishment mode choice: Past, present and future. *Management International Review*, 56, 489–530.

Dunning, J. H. (2000). The eclectic paradigm as an envelope for economic and business theories of MNE activity. *International Business Review*, 9, 163–190.

Gaur, A. S., Ma, X., and Ding, Z. (2018). Home country supportiveness/unfavorableness and outward foreign direct investment from China. *Journal of International Business Studies*, 49, 324–345.

Goertz, C. F., and Shapiro, A. H. (2012). Strategic alliances as a response to the thread of entry: Evidence from airline codesharing. *International Journal of Industrial Organization*, 30, 735–747.

Gu, F. F., Wang, J. J., and Wang, D. T. (2019). The role of sales representatives in cross-cultural business-to-business relationships. *Industrial Marketing Management*, 78, 227–238.

Hansen, M. W., Larsen, M. M., Pedersen, T., and Petersen, B. (2010). *Strategies in Emerging Markets: A Case Book on Danish Multinational Corporations in China and India*. Copenhagen: Copenhagen Business School Press.

Hennart, J.-F. (2013). The accidental internationalists: A theory of born globals. *Entrepreneurship Theory and Practice*, 38, 117–135.

Johanson, J., and Vahlne, J.-E. (1977). The internationalization process of the firm: A model of knowledge development and increasing foreign market commitments. *Journal of International Business Studies*, 8, 23–32.

Johanson, J., and Vahlne, J.-E. (2009). The Uppsala internationalization process model revisited: From liability of foreignness to liability of outsidership. *Journal of International Business Studies*, 40, 1411–1431.

Katsikeas, C., Leonidou, L., and Zeriti, A. (2019). Revisiting international marketing strategy in a digital era: Opportunities, challenges, and research directions. *International Marketing Review*, 37, 405–425.

Lu, Y., Karpova, E. E., and Fiore, A. M. (2009). Factors influencing international fashion retailers' entry mode choice. *Journal of Fashion Marketing and Management*, 15, 58–75.

Morschett, D., Schramm-Klein, H., and Swoboda, B. (2010). Decades of entry modes: What do we really know about external antecedents of entry mode choice. *Journal of International Management*, 16, 60–77.

North, D. C. (1991). Institutions. *Journal of Economic Perspectives*, 5, 97–112.

Pan, Y., and Tse, D. K. (2000). The hierarchical model of market entry modes. *Journal of International Business Studies*, 31, 535–554.

Pedersen, T., Petersen, B., and Benito, G. R. G. (2002). Change of foreign operation method: Impetus and switching costs. *International Business Review, 11*, 325–345.

Pla-Barber, J., Villar, C., and León-Darder, F. (2014). Augmenting versus exploiting entry modes in soft services: Reconsidering the role of experiential knowledge. *International Marketing Review, 31*, 621–636.

Puck, J. F., Holtbrügge, D., and Mohr, A. T. (2009). Beyond entry mode choice: Explaining the conversion of joint ventures into wholly owned subsidiaries in the People's Republic of China. *Journal of International Business Studies, 40*, 388–404.

Richbell, S. M., and Watts, H. D. (2000). Plant closures in multiplant manufacturing firms: Adding an international perspective. *Management Decision, 38*, 80–88.

Robson, M. J., Kadile, V., Watson, K., and Clegg, L. J. (2018). International franchising relationships. In L. C. Leonidou, C. S. Katsikeas, S. Samiee and B. Aykol (Eds), *Advances in Global Marketing: A Research Anthology* (pp. 427–446). Cham: Springer.

Schellenberg, M., Harker, M. J., and Jafari, H. (2018). International market entry mode: A systematic literature review. *Journal of Strategic Marketing, 26*, 601–627.

Scott, W. R. (1995). *Institutions and Organizations*. Thousand Oaks, CA: SAGE.

Sharma, V. M., and Erramilli, M. K. (2004). Resource-based explanation of entry mode choice. *Journal of Marketing Theory & Practice, 12*, 1–18.

Song, S. (2014). Entry mode irreversibility, host market uncertainty, and foreign subsidiary exits. *Asian Pacific Journal of Management, 32*, 455–471.

Surdu, I., and Mellahi, K. (2016). Theoretical foundations of equity based foreign market entry decisions: A review of the literature and recommendations for future research. *International Business Review, 25*, 1169–1184.

Swoboda, B., Olejnik, E., and Morschett, D. (2011). Changes in foreign operation modes: Stimuli for increases versus reductions. *International Business Review, 20*, 578–590.

UNCTAD (United Nations Conference on Trade and Development) (2004). *Incentives*. New York, NY: UNCTAD.

UNCTAD (United Nations Conference on Trade and Development) (2016). *Development and Globalization: Facts and Figures*. Geneva: UNCTAD.

Wernerfelt, B. (1995). The resource-based view of the firm: Ten years after. *Strategic Management Journal, 16*, 171–174.

Williamson, O. E. (1987). *The Economic Institutions of Capitalism: Firms, Markets, Relational Contracting*. New York, NY: Free Press.

Willis Towers Watson/Oxford Analytica (2019). *How Are Leading Companies Managing Today's Political Risks?* London and Oxford: Willis Towers Watson/Oxford Analytica.

Zahra, S., and Elhagrasey, G. (1994). Strategic management of international joint ventures. *European Management Journal, 12*, 83–93.

3 CASE STUDY
MAGIC JUICE: WHICH ENTRY MODE(S) TO CHOOSE?

Joe Garcia recommended to the board that Magic Juice should enter several geographic markets at the same time from 2018. While he was still open for both the internationalization of the store concept and the alternative to go for distributing the juices only – for instance, using online channels – he felt that Dirk de Jong had already made up his mind that it should be stores that were launched first. The main question was which entry mode(s) Magic Juice should choose, and this depended on the strategies chosen and the peculiarities in the markets that were identified to be most promising.

Globally, franchising has been the major source of expansion for the leading juice and smoothie bar operators (for example, Smoothie King, Jamba Juice and Boost Juice). On the other hand, the successful Danish juice bar chain Joe & The Juice has established its own bars in many markets from 2012 to today, which means that the firm's expansion pattern has been fast and efficient, and not hampered by finding the right franchisees.

CASE QUESTIONS

Dirk feels that it would be good to approach the question of the entry mode with an open mindset, and would like to understand better how different entry mode options would work for Magic Juice; from his early days on, he has profited from screening the scientific literature and feels that there must be some theoretical guidelines on how to approach this question in a structured fashion.

Hence, Joe needs to prepare a report that visualizes the different entry modes for Dirk (for example, providing an overview of who is involved in the domestic and foreign markets and whether the entry mode option is viable for the challenge ahead). This should include an evaluation of the advantages and disadvantages for Magic Juice in using a non-equity mode versus an equity mode building on relevant theoretical frameworks and criteria. In addition, the report needs to provide an overview of considerations that relate to specific entry modes. For instance, if Magic Juice goes for franchising as an entry mode in some countries, what are further managerial challenges and issues involved? To conclude, Joe's report needs to demonstrate the most effective and long-term international mode of entry that Magic Juice should choose in the top three to five markets to be entered. Step into Joe's shoes and draft a report!

4
Entering markets with a partner

Firms that identify strategic alliances, joint ventures (JVs) or mergers and acquisitions (M&As) as a preferred mode to enter a foreign country need to solve additional challenges. As all of these entry modes involve the element of strategic partnership, managers need to identify the right partner and negotiate the conditions of the partnership – among them the right price – and in the case that an agreement is reached need to implement the right procedures to cooperate with or even integrate the partners to achieve the outlined objectives. The different forms of partnerships have several commonalities, yet also involve challenges that are different: In strategic alliances and JVs it is about organizing the cooperation, while a post-acquisition or merger situation requires the integration of two partners' organizations. As many toolsets are of relevance to several of these partnering modes, we decided to present them in one chapter and will comment on specifics in each of the sections.

Strategic partnerships have become a central approach for implementing international business strategies that are aimed at improving competitiveness, realizing synergies and strengthening innovativeness, yet they are not always successful. On the contrary, studies and consultancy reports indicate rather high (30 to 70 percent) rates of termination of strategic alliances and demonstrate that many M&As do not meet their objectives (see, for example, PwC, 2020; Rinaudo and Uhlaner, 2014). Hence, it is important to understand the determinants of success of these partnerships and identify managerial toolsets that assist good practice in tackling the partnering challenges. This has been done by academics who engaged in the study of partnering modes, yet also by consultants outlining best practices (for example, Gomes et al., 2013; Hoffmann and Schlosser, 2001; Wittmann, Hunt and Arnett, 2009).

In this chapter, we will discuss conceptual frameworks and toolsets that tackle the aspects in strategic partnerships that have been identified as detrimental to strategic success. In the pre-partnering phase, it is about selecting the right partner, negotiating the terms of the deal and paying the right price. Accordingly, the reader will be familiarized with relevant toolsets for partner selection, will receive advice on how to prepare a negotiation and will be introduced to the most common methods used to identify the right price and modes of payment in these deals. In the post-partnering phase, it is about making the arrangement work; that is, integrating the partners to the extent necessary, and managing and organizing the cooperation and its challenges. Accordingly, the reader will get insights into a set of conceptual frameworks to select the right strategy to integrate two (or more) partners in the new or the existing organizational set-up. In addition, accompanying aspects of change management, most importantly leadership, speed of integration and communication, are discussed. Finally, toolsets for the accompanying cultural integration are presented. Practical examples are provided in each of the sections. Table 4.1 provides an overview of the critical success factors that we will concentrate on in the following.

Table 4.1 Critical success factors in the pre- and post-partnering stage

Phase	Critical success factors
Pre-partnering phase	Strategic and organizational fit of the partner (selecting the right partner) Paying the right price Negotiations
Post-partnering phase	Integration approaches/strategies Cultural integration Best practices to manage the integration of partners

4.1 SELECTING THE RIGHT PARTNER

Finding the right partner is one of the keys to success in partnerships. To select the right partner, you first need to develop a clear understanding of the strategic objectives of the partnership in the market, and of the resources and capabilities that are necessary to fulfill these objectives. You can then use this understanding to screen relevant partners and to evaluate their fit (this analysis may even lead to a re-evaluation of the actual need for the partnership). A good partner offers capabilities or resources that you do not have yourself; that is, brings complementary resources to the partnership (Gudergan et al., 2012). To evaluate the value of these complementary resources, you need to understand which resources are required to meet your strategic objectives in the upcoming three to five years in the market. This assists in identifying the resource gap that needs to be filled by the partner and results in a desirable resource profile that can be used to screen and evaluate potential partners.

Table 4.2 provides an example of a matrix that can assist in the development of an ideal partner profile. In addition to visualizing a decision matrix, it also provides an overview of different motives for entering a partnership. We note that in business practice, it is sometimes not possible to enter a partnership with the ideal partner, and the second- or even third-best partner has to be chosen, as the ideal partner may not be for sale, may be unwilling to enter a partnership or simply requests too high a price.

In addition to the complementarity of resources, the partners need to demonstrate fit on further strategic dimensions. This involves ensuring that the strategic motives and orientations of the two partners entering the partnership do not conflict. This relates to different time horizons involved: It is important that the long-term objectives of the two partners are not in conflict and that the benefits that the partners are looking for can be sustained. A good strategic fit exists where the partnership serves each partner's long-term strategic ambitions. In addition, the strategic fit of two partners will be higher if the partnership is of high relevance to both partners, and if there is a strong need for the partnership on both sides of the collaboration. Hence, strategic fit considerations should involve an analysis of the partners' positioning, financial capacity and networks (for example, is the partner an industry leader or follower?) to understand each partner's need to enter the collaboration. Moreover, a good fit is likely to emerge if the partners are of equal size. Research findings suggest that partnerships in which

Table 4.2 Criteria for rating partnership opportunities

Partnering motives	Necessary capabilities/resources?	Available capabilities/resources?	Where are the gaps (that is, what does the partner need to bring)?
Market- or product-related • Market-seeking • Acquiring means of distribution • Complementarity of goods and services to market • Overcoming legal/regulatory barriers • Legitimation, bandwagon effect • Following industry trends			
Resource- or learning-related • Gaining access to new technology, and converging technology • Learning and internalization of tacit, collective and embedded capabilities • Developing products, technologies, resources • Developing technical standards • Co-specialization			
Efficiency-related • Obtaining economies of scale • Cost-sharing, pooling of resources • Restructuring, improving performance			
Strategic-asset- or risk-related • Achieving vertical integration • Recreating and extending supply links to adjust to environmental changes • Diversifying into new businesses • Risk reduction and risk diversification • Cooperation of potential rivals/to pre-empt competitors			

Source: Own table; partnering motives adapted from Todeva and Knoke (2005), Varadarajan and Cunningham (1995)

one partner is very small in relation to the other can result in suboptimal outcomes or low performance (Gomes et al., 2013). Explanations are that the small partner tends to be neglected in the future design of the collaboration. Hence, if you are entering a partnership with a considerably larger partner, you are well advised to evaluate the partner's history of collaborations. Ultimately, while understanding the partner's (true) motives to engage in the collaboration is of relevance to safeguard the success of the collaboration in the long term, it may not be straightforward. In addition to getting in touch with potential partners, you may engage in role play among your own team members to unfold hidden motives on the other side.

Finally, to ensure that the partnership works later, organizational and cultural dissimilarity needs to be identified. Differences in organizational cultures (yet also national cultures) have the potential to create misunderstanding and tensions when it comes to the organization of work. Consultancies regularly report that soft or relationship problems are among the key causes of failures in strategic alliances. Hence, for quite some time a recommendation was to avoid organizational cultural clash and more actively avoid partnering with dissimilar partners. In more recent academic research projects and consulting practice, the focus is more on the management of cultural differences and on a positive lens on cultural differences. In addition, the relevance of these differences depends on the form of the partnership: Differences are clearly more relevant in partnerships that necessitate the integration of organizational cultures; for instance, if an organizational unit is formed that combines elements of both cultures. Yet, no matter which perspective is followed, a key recommendation is to make cultural assessment part of the due diligence process to either avoid cultural challenges or be able to later manage the difference. To identify organizational (culture) fit, the following are key aspects: First, organizational structures are of relevance; that is, centralized versus decentralized structures with a concentrated or decentralized locus of power. Second, management and leadership styles are of relevance; that is, for instance, collaborative versus autocratic decision-making, performance orientation and the question of group versus individual orientation in performance measurement, and reinforcement or incentives provided in the form of rewards or recognition. Third, the level and kind of formalization is relevant. This involves formal procedures for decision-making, financial or accounting procedures and the degree of documentation of policies and rules. Fourth, the risk tolerance of the management board is key; that is, whether there is a risk-taking or risk-avoiding climate. Fifth, an evaluation of distance along formal and informal institutional contexts is advised that may point to critical areas to be managed in the later partnership. For this purpose, you are invited to make use of the frameworks discussed in Chapters 1 and 2. Sixth, whether individuals in top positions have a high potential to get along with each other is worth evaluation.

To gain further insights into the strategic and organizational fit between two partners, it is a good idea that the individual partners score their organizations on relevant dimensions (see an example in Table 4.3). In addition, the partners may score each other to reveal differences in perceived organizational cultures between the two sides. Aggregating the individual scores to the organizational level and then comparing the scores can signal fit or misfit. Moreover, as there will not be a perfect partner in most situations, the identification of areas of misfit may point to aspects that should be more actively managed throughout the partnership in a later phase of the partnering process.

Before being able to evaluate potential partners, these need to be identified. A typical starting point is to draw attention to existing distributors, suppliers and customers. Furthermore, business networks, industry associations, business directories, embassies and specialized consultancies may help in the identification of partners. A toolset that engages managers to think more broadly about potential partners is a "partner map." This map should involve both current and potential participants in industries and industry segments that may represent customers, suppliers, complementors and competitors that may create value in the partnership. Starting the evaluation using four fundamental ways of value creation that partners may offer – namely by reducing input costs, by reducing operating costs, by increasing customers' willingness to pay and by accessing new markets – has demonstrated usefulness among executives. Likewise, using an approach that differentiates partners by supply, demand, competitor and complementor relationships is recommended. These approaches trigger a broader thinking

Table 4.3 Assessment of strategic and organizational (cultural) fit

Fit category	1	2	3	4	5
Strategic orientation/objectives					
Strategic importance of the partnership: low to high	Low				High
Need for a partner (for example, financials, firm size): low to high	Low				High
Time horizon: short- to long-term	Short				Long
Organizational cultures					
Structure: centralized versus decentralized/locus of power	Centralized				Decentralized
Decision-making: autocratic versus collaborative	Autocratic				Collaborative
Performance orientation towards groups or individuals	Group				Individuals
Formalization: low to high	Low				High
Risk tolerance: risk-taking to risk-avoiding	Risk-taking				Risk-avoiding
Complementary categories: fit between national cultures and the potential fit between top managers – low to high	Low				High

about potential partners and avoid focusing too early on the micro or firm level; in the best case, they assist in finding potential future opportunities. For instance, a firm in the online travel industry may first identify: airlines, hotel chains and car rentals as potential supply-related partners; corporate travel departments, and channels that are accessed by individual travelers, as customer-related partners; traditional and online travel brokers as competitor-related partners; and internet search engines or travel magazines as complementor-related partners. Second, it may continue the search for specific partners along the above lines (Holmberg and Cummings, 2009).

To support the selection of the right partner, Cummings and Holmberg (2012) propose using a scoring model that compares different partners and generates an overall fit score. Table 4.4 provides an example of such a scoring model and includes factors that are related to the motives for the partnership, here called "task-specific factors of success" (for example, Europe-wide distribution channels), and "partnering-related factors of success" (for example, similarity of organizational cultures) that fit traditional research on the determinants of success. In addition, the example includes risk-related aspects, such as the spillover of proprietary knowledge or negative effects on reputation if the partnership fails. All of these aspects are rated on a scale from 1 to 10 with higher values indicating a more positive rating; that is, better distribution channels, higher similarity of cultures and a lower spillover of proprietary knowledge. Finally, an overall fit is calculated that reflects different weights attributed to the task-, partnering- and risk-related aspects, and indicates a better fit of Firm A as compared to Firm B for the partnership evaluated in Table 4.4.

Table 4.4 Partner scoring

Success factors	Relative importance	Partner A	Partner B
Task fit (related to the motives of the partnership)		8.4	6.8
Europe-wide distribution channels	40%	10	6
Strong local brand	40%	7	6
Strong host-government relations	20%	8	10
Partnering fit		6.5	8.6
Similarity in organizational cultures	10%	8	6
Compatible supply chain management (SCM) system	15%	5	9
Importance of alliance to partner	15%	9	10
Senior management compatibility	30%	5	8
Collaboration track records	30%	7	9
Risk fit		7.0	3.5
Negative reputation if alliance fails	50%	5	5
Spillover of proprietary knowledge	50%	9	2
Overall fit		7.9	6.6
Task fit	70%	*8.4*	*6.8*
Partnering fit	15%	*6.5*	*8.6*
Risk fit	15%	*7.0*	*3.5*

Source: Adapted from Cummings and Holmberg (2012)

4.2 PAYING THE RIGHT PRICE

As soon as a good partner is identified, the next question to be answered is the one on the right price for the partnership. Paying too much can be a cause of failure, as it raises the bar to achieve relevant paybacks, no matter which form of payment is chosen. In a non-equity contractual agreement, management considerations may focus on royalties, whereas managers in an equity-based M&A deal need to determine a price to pay upfront to enter the deal. In the following, we will discuss key examples and the most common valuation methods that assist in understanding the strategic considerations when it comes to valuation.

4.2.1 Valuation methods

The most common approach to determine the value of a (equity-based) partnership is to look at the net present value (NPV) of cash flows (CF) (see, for example, DePamphilis, 2010). The NPV concept discounts all relevant future CF related to the partnership project to the present value, following the idea that future cash is of less value to the firm than current cash. If the NPV is positive, a partnering project is financially viable. The interest rate that is used for the discounting is the weighted average cost of capital (WACC). The WACC is the weighted average of costs that accrue for borrowing capital from externals (that is, debt) and from owners (that is, equity). The calculation of future CF relies among other aspects on forecasts of future revenues that are again determined by forecasts on prices and sold units over a certain period; hence, there is a considerable amount of uncertainty involved in these calculations. Therefore, managers are well advised to simulate different scenarios, such as a best-, trend- and worst-case scenario of future CF, to understand the possible range of outcomes.

In a practical setting, managers need to identify the relevant CF, approximate the WACC and specify their time horizon. The time horizon ultimately is a matter of managerial objectives and decision-making: ideally it should equate with the typical time span used for strategic planning. Typical time frames used in the evaluation of partnerships range from five to 10 years, yet some firms use longer horizons. For instance, Johannes Dietsch, the former CFO at Bayer (a Germany-based pharmaceutical and drug company), explained its long-term practices in partnering evaluations in an interview in the context of a merger with the US-based firm Monsanto, and indicated that it used a 15-year time horizon (Döhle, 2017). To determine the WACC, and first the costs that accrue from borrowed capital, a typical approach is to use long-term average interest rates for bonds issued by firms with a good credit rating. Bayer, for instance, uses the long-term average interest rates for 10-year bonds, which in 2018 was about 4 percent; as interest for borrowed capital is tax deductible, this yielded about 3 percent for its calculations. The equity capital costs reflect what shareholders or investors expect when they invest into the firm. In the case of Bayer, Dietsch explained that it looks at the historical excess return of the stock market in comparison with government securities and then adds in a coefficient called beta, which reflects the fluctuation of the Bayer share price compared with the market as a whole. In 2018, this was 8.6 percent for equity capital. To establish the WACC, Bayer weighted the two interest rates: equity capital was weighted at 80 percent and borrowed capital at 20 percent using the proportion from the stock market rather than the balance sheet, the argument being that this is what an investor who buys a share wants to see interest on. This resulted in a WACC of 7.5 percent at Bayer at the time. Finally, to determine the NPV, managers need to compile an overview of CF. As a general rule, you should refer to the free CF; that is, the sum of after-tax earnings, plus non-cash expenses (mainly depreciation and amortization), minus the capital investment (CAPEX) and minus the change in working capital (that is, current assets minus current liabilities), as given in the formula below:

Free CF = EBIT (1-t) + Non-cash expenses – CAPEX – ΔNWC

where: *EBIT* = earnings before interest and taxes, *t* = tax rate, *CAPEX* = capital expenditures for fixed assets, and ΔNWC = change in net working capital (current assets – current liabilities).

Box 4.1 provides an example and exercise of an NPV calculation that a European car manufacturer performed to determine the attractiveness of a JV project with a competitor in Asia. In addition, the book's website provides an Excel sheet with formula advice that can be used to simulate different scenarios involving this example or further practical challenges.

ENTERING MARKETS WITH A PARTNER

Box 4.1 Exercise and example: NPV considerations in a JV of a European car manufacturer

The CEO of a Europe-based global manufacturer of cars provided insights into its valuation process in a JV with a competitor in Asia. The two partners envisaged the following: The European partner should provide a factory in the Asian market to the JV, which would then be managed by both partners. In addition, the European manufacturer should provide technological know-how on car and engine technology to the JV which was licensed to the JV and should create royalties at the European partner's side. The Asian partner should provide its sales and distribution network in the market to the JV. Finally, both partners should provide cash in the form of equity and loans to the JV. The European manufacturer performed evaluations under the directive to achieve a pay-back after 10 years and an NPV of at least EUR 40 million. The valuation process for the JV was based on considerations related to the location, the types of products and estimated price points. Due to the uncertainties involved, different scenarios were constructed. To develop a financial plan, these strategic considerations were backed up with financial numbers, such as target prices for specific components. Doing the financial planning, two kinds of plans were developed, one that was officially labeled "Joint venture business plan" and one internal plan that involved internal aspects and additional flows to the parent, such as the royalties for patents to be used in the JV. The internal plan was not made official to the partner at this stage. The business plan for the JV more specifically involved the following:

- Volumes were planned at 150,000 cars and 400,000 engines to be manufactured, with a slightly lower number to be assumed in the first two years of the JV.
- The average prices were estimated at EUR 6,500 for cars and EUR 1,000 for the engines.
- EBIT margins typically ranged from 11 to 15 percent for cars and 14 to 19 percent for engines.
- Using the considerations on volumes, the required investment into manufacturing capacity was estimated to total EUR 700 million that had to a major extent (64 percent) be spent upfront respectively in the first year.
- Non-cash expenses (especially depreciation) were estimated at about EUR 60,000 per year.
- Change in working capital was approximated at 1.5 percent of revenues in each year.
- The WACC was set at 7.5 percent, and a tax rate of 35 percent was applied.

These numbers were used to perform an NPV estimation (see below); in the example a trend scenario was developed using the average EBIT margins and the numbers given above.
If you were to advise the CEO of the European car manufacturer:

- How would you evaluate the resulting NPV results based on the trend scenario?
- Which further scenarios would you estimate?
- And what are your results on these scenarios (you may want to use the Excel sheet provided on the book's website)?
- How would you summarize your findings on the scenarios, and what are potential further strategic actions to be explored?

	Year 0	Year 1	Year 2	Year 3	Year 4	Year 5	Year 6	Year 7	Year 8	Year 9	Year 10
Cars											
Units		75,000	100,000	150,000	150,000	150,000	150,000	150,000	150,000	150,000	150,000
Price		6,500	6,500	6,500	6,500	6,500	6,500	6,500	6,500	6,500	6,500
Revenues (= units * price)		487,500,000	650,000,000	975,000,000	975,000,000	975,000,000	975,000,000	975,000,000	975,000,000	975,000,000	975,000,000
EBIT-margin in %		13%	13%	13%	13%	13%	13%	13%	13%	13%	13%
EBIT (= revenues * EBIT-margin)		63,375,000	84,500,000	126,750,000	126,750,000	126,750,000	126,750,000	126,750,000	126,750,000	126,750,000	126,750,000
Engines											
Units		200,000	300,000	400,000	400,000	400,000	400,000	400,000	400,000	400,000	400,000
Price		1,000	1,000	1,000	1,000	1,000	1,000	1,000	1,000	1,000	1,000
Revenues (= units * price)		200,000,000	300,000,000	400,000,000	400,000,000	400,000,000	400,000,000	400,000,000	400,000,000	400,000,000	400,000,000
EBIT-margin in %		16.5%	16.5%	16.5%	16.5%	16.5%	16.5%	16.5%	16.5%	16.5%	16.5%
EBIT (= revenues * EBIT-margin)		33,000,000	49,500,000	66,000,000	66,000,000	66,000,000	66,000,000	66,000,000	66,000,000	66,000,000	66,000,000
Total revenues (cars + engines)		687,500,000	950,000,000	1,375,000,000	1,375,000,000	1,375,000,000	1,375,000,000	1,375,000,000	1,375,000,000	1,375,000,000	1,375,000,000
Total EBIT (cars + engines)		96,375,000	134,000,000	192,750,000	192,750,000	192,750,000	192,750,000	192,750,000	192,750,000	192,750,000	192,750,000
Tax rate 35%											
EBIT (1-t)		62,643,750	87,100,000	125,287,500	125,287,500	125,287,500	125,287,500	125,287,500	125,287,500	125,287,500	125,287,500
Non-cash expenses (depreciation)		33,731,250	46,900,000	67,462,500	67,462,500	67,462,500	67,462,500	57,462,500	67,462,500	67,462,500	67,462,500
		60,000	60,000	60,000	60,000	60,000	60,000	60,000	60,000	60,000	60,000
Change in working capital (% of revenues) 1.5%		10,312,500.00	14,250,000.00	20,625,000.00	20,625,000.00	20,625,000.00	20,625,000.00	20,625,000.00	20,625,000.00	20,625,000.00	20,625,000.00
CAPEX	-700,000,000										
Free cash flow	-700,000,000	52,391,250	72,910,000	104,722,500	104,722,500	104,722,500	104,722,500	104,722,500	104,722,500	104,722,500	104,722,500
WACC (discount rate) 7.5%	1.0000	0.9302	0.8653	0.8050	0.7488	0.6966	0.6480	0.6028	0.5607	0.5216	0.4852
NPV free cash flow	-700,000,000	48,736,047	63,091,401	84,297,483	78,416,263	72,945,361	67,856,150	63,122,000	58,718,140	54,621,525	50,810,721
NPV cumulative free cash flow	-700,000,000	-651,263,953	-588,172,553	-503,875,069	-425,458,806	-352,513,445	-284,657,295	-221,535,294	-162,817,155	-108,195,630	-57,384,908

Figure 4.1 NPV estimations, trend scenario

Using the CF approach in the case of an M&A, two kinds of future CF have to be taken into consideration: The first is the future CF of the partner that you aim to acquire (that is, the stand-alone value). This is calculated building on the partner's forecasted business activities, and represents the value that the partner alone brings to the M&A. In a perfect world, if the partner is listed on the stock market, its market capitalization should represent the partner's stand-alone value. In addition to the stand-alone value, you need to consider the synergy value. M&As usually generate synergies by merging the two partners; for instance, in the form of cost savings and revenue enhancement. These should be reflected in the future CF stemming from synergies. However, you must also deduct the costs of conducting an M&A (for example, the implementation costs, employees' compensations, competitors' gains, and so on). These considerations provide an overview of the range of prices to be paid for the deal; see Figure 4.2. In a regular setting, a partner would not sell its business for a price that is below the stand-alone value. From the perspective of the buying partner, the price should not be above the stand-alone value plus the synergy value, as the buyer would not profit from a price higher than this. Hence, this provides a base to start preparing the (price) negotiation. Empirical evidence shows that the buying firm often over-evaluates the synergy potential and underestimates the implementation costs in M&As.

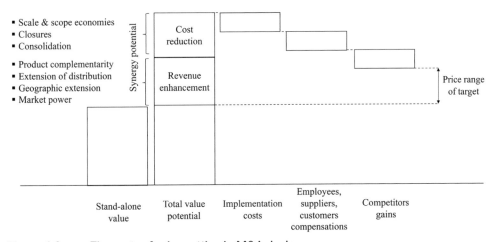

Figure 4.2 Elements of price setting in M&A deals

While the CF approach is most common, there are two further valuation methods of relevance in the case of M&A. These are asset-based valuation and comparable valuation. Asset-based valuation of a target firm is "the value today"; that is, the net realizable value of the assets and liabilities as a going concern (for example, revenues and costs over five years, including risks and growth prospects). Comparable valuation, which is often used in deals when the target firm is not listed on the stock market, is a kind of benchmark valuation based on the industry/country's recent deals or market valuation of comparable businesses. The valuation of the target firm is typically done by using earnings or sales; for instance, the average profit margin (EBITDA; earnings before interest, taxes, depreciation and amortization) within the last three years multiplied by the multiple. The multiple can, for instance, be the enterprise-value-to-EBITDA ratio. This ratio averaged at a value of around 13 over the last few years for the S&P500 list (as per 2020). You can then estimate the benchmark enterprise value by multiplying the EBITDA by the enterprise-value-to-EBITDA ratio that is available for your industry or a reference business. The book's website provides links to videos that provide further examples of all three valuation methods.

4.2.2   Form of payment

Decision-making on the right price does not stop at the valuation but has to involve considerations on the form of payment. In M&As there are basically two key options: a cash deal – a transfer of money for shares; and a stock deal – an exchange of shares. For instance, in a study of 447 M&A deals announced by European listed firms, 12 percent used a stock deal, 71 percent a cash deal and 18 percent a combination of stock and cash (Feito-Ruiz and Menéndez-Requejo, 2013). The two forms of payments have different implications related to the bearing of risks on the side of the two partners, which are illustrated in Box 4.2. Basically, in a cash deal the shareholders of the acquiring partner take on the entire risk that the forecasted synergy value will not materialize. In a stock deal, the later operational risk-sharing depends on the resulting ownership structure from the deal and in addition involves a risk stemming from the fluctuation of share prices on the market. Hence, in deciding upon cash versus (different forms of) stock deals, managers considering the acquisition of a partner are well advised to evaluate whether the partner's stock market value is fair, overvalued or undervalued, and the risk that is attached to the synergy value (see Box 4.2 for further insights).

As mentioned earlier, in September 2016 the Germany-based Bayer AG signed a merger agreement with Monsanto, a US agrichemicals firm. The agreement was to buy Monsanto at USD 128 per share in an all-cash transaction for USD 62 billion in total. The deal was then the largest overseas deal that a German company had ever signed. The partners expected synergies of approximately USD 1.5 billion after three years of the merger, and additional benefits from integrating the two firms in the longer term. In June 2018, Bayer successfully completed the takeover of Monsanto, with Bayer becoming the sole owner. The price of the deal included a substantial premium of 44 percent over Monsanto's share price of USD 89.03 in May 2016; that is, a premium of USD 43 billion. Hence, Bayer investors must have estimated a considerably higher synergy value emerging during the 15 years after the merger to justify the price. The transaction was financed through a combination of debt and equity on the side of Bayer and, as indicated in the explanation earlier, the Bayer side was the one that would bear the full risk if these expected synergies did not materialize.

> **Box 4.2   Further insights: Cash versus stock deals in M&A**
>
> To illustrate cash versus stock deals, let us assume that Buyer wants to acquire its competitor Seller.
> - Facts about Buyer: The market capitalization is USD 5 billion; 50 million shares priced at USD 100 per share.
> - Facts about Seller: The market capitalization is USD 2.8 billion; 40 million shares priced at USD 70 per share.
>
> The managers of Buyer estimate that by merging the two firms, a synergy value of USD 1.7 billion can be created.
>
> ### The cash-deal scenario
>
> Buyer offers to buy all shares of Seller at USD 100 per share; hence, the total value is USD 4 billion and therefore USD 1.2 billion above the stand-alone value of Seller (the USD 1.2 billion is also called the "premium above the market value"). Then the expected net gain to Buyer, which is called the "shareholder value added," is the difference between the estimated value of the synergies and the acquisition premium, here USD 1.7 minus USD 1.2 billion = USD 0.5 billion.
>
> If the synergy value does not materialize, Buyer would fully shoulder the loss of the premium of USD 1.2 billion paid.
>
> ### The stock-deal scenario
>
> - *Fixed-share deal:* Buyer offers one of its shares for each of Seller's shares; hence, the total value (at the time of the offer) is again USD 4 billion with a shareholder value added of USD 0.5 billion. Yet, the resulting ownership structure is different: The new firm has 90 million shares and Buyer's shareholders own 55.5 percent of these shares, so their share in the shareholder value added is at 55.5 percent of the USD 0.5 billion only (that is, USD 0.2775 billion); the rest goes to the shareholders of Seller who are now shareholders in an enlarged Buyer.
>
>   If the synergy value does not materialize, the loss of the premium would also be shared between the two partners.
>
>   The only way that Buyer's original shareholders can obtain the same shareholder value added from the stock deal as compared to the cash deal would be by offering Seller fewer shares – the acceptance of this offer is then depending on the perception of Seller's shareholders of the future value of the merged firm. In addition, as the value of shares may fluctuate between the announcement of the offer and the closing date, the shareholders at Seller are vulnerable to a fall in the price of Buyer's stocks.
> - *Fixed-value deal:* Buyer offers to enter a stock deal that fixes the total value of shares at USD 4 billion; that is, the number of shares issued is not fixed until the closing date and depends on the price prevailing at the time of the deal.
>
>   For instance, assume that Buyer's share price has fallen from USD 100 per share to USD 76 per share at the time of the deal. Now, Buyer has to issue 52.6 million shares to give the shareholders of Seller the promised USD 4 billion. This will result in a new share of ownership for Buyer's shareholders of only 48.7 percent. As a result, the proportional ownership of the merged entity is left in doubt until closing. Here, the shareholders at Buyer bear the price risk on its shares between announcement and closing.
>
>   From the above ownership structures, it becomes obvious that the risk considerations also depend on the relative size of the buyer and the seller.
>
> *Source:* Adapted from Rappaport and Sirower (1999)

In a strategic alliance or a JV involving equity, the approach is similar. The CF that need to be considered involve CF representing the synergy value of the two partners entering the alliance; for instance, increased sales due to joint marketing and cost savings stemming from synergies in R&D, manufacturing, marketing or other processes. In addition, in a JV in which an autonomous economic entity is created, there is a direct value stemming from this entity that is distributed to the partners of the JV.

Finally, partnerships also often involve contractual agreements and therewith agreements on specific forms of payments. A key form of payment is rents, often called "royalties." Royalties accrue, for instance, if a partner is granted the right to use a certain technology, knowledge and brand name (in a certain geographic area, field of use, and so on); see also Chapter 3. Here, managers need to decide upon the right price. Again, the considerations would start at determining the NPV of CF or profits that are attributable to the right or patent. As this may be hard to determine in reality, firms often rely on industry averages to determine the royalties. Usually these fall between 10 and 30 percent of the profit generated (with lower rates in situations of high risk to the buyer of the right). In some industries there are good statistics available that factorize this risk, such as in the pharmaceutical industry. The average royalty rates here depend on the particular stage of the patent development (for example, patent issued: 1 to 2 percent; with clinical trials: 3 to 4 percent; with government approval: 5 to 7 percent). If the negotiating parties do not have statistics at hand, an arbitrary – yet to some extent accepted – rule of thumb is 25 percent (see, for example, Courtois, McPhee and Rerolle, 2012). Profits are considered an efficient base for calculating the royalty, the idea being that the buying partner has a self-interest in maximizing this parameter which will then automatically maximize the rents for the seller. Still, managers are advised to evaluate potential incentives stemming from different base numbers of royalty; for instance, with regard to maintaining a certain product-quality level. In addition to a royalty that comes as a share of value measure (which is clearly the dominant approach), the contract can also involve a per-unit royalty (that is, a fixed amount of money paid for every unit of the product). The partners may agree on upfront one-time payments that are effective when the contract is signed, or agree on a minimum royalty payment, or payments that are bound to certain project milestones.

4.3 NEGOTIATIONS

In almost all partnerships, negotiations involve conflicting aims of the partners, as the interest in getting the best deal for their own organization is often strongest. While resulting power issues cannot fully be avoided, both partners should follow a cooperative mindset because a partnership that starts with an unhappy partner at the beginning will probably not be sustained. Hence, ultimately the negotiations need to create a mutual understanding of both sides' strategic interests and fit, and need to accomplish a plan for the later cooperation that settles key aspects of the future collaboration. In addition, negotiations can be an opportunity to build trust between the partners.

There are a few recommendations that have the potential to positively influence the negotiation outcome; that is, appointing the right team for the negotiation, good preparation for the negotiation, the negotiation process itself and the formalization of the final agreement.

As regards the appointment of the right team for the negotiation, we recommend involving both senior executives and middle-level or operational managers (for example, division heads, legal, financial, market and technical experts) in the negotiation process. This way, you combine the commitment and information on strategic parameters at the senior level with the potential to evaluate fit on the day-to-day issues. In partnerships involving strong cultural dissimilarities, it is of value to involve a language interpreter or a consultant who bridges the cultural differences.

Table 4.5 Aspects to clarify prior to the negotiation

	Our organization	The partner	The partnership
Objectives	Our objectives? Key requirements for the partnership to achieve our objectives? Fit of the partnership with our strategy? Our expectations from the partnership?	The partner's objectives? Key requirements for the partnership to meet our partner's objectives? Fit of the partnership with the partner's strategy? The partner's expectations from the partnership?	Objectives of the partnership (if an individual entity/project)? Strategy for the partnership (if an individual entity/project)?
Resources/strengths	What do we bring to the partnership? (Including managerial or human resources that we bring to the partnership and/or that we want to preserve)	What does the partner bring to the partnership?	Does the partnership have VRIO resources (if an individual entity/project)[a]?
Risks	What potential obstacles to success/and or risks are involved in the partnership from our perspective?	What potential obstacles to success or risks are involved in the partnership from the partner's perspective?	What are the risks that the partnership is confronted with?
Negotiation levers	What concessions are we willing to make? What are we not willing to provide or to compromise on (for example, management and staffing)?	What concessions will our partner request? What are the deal-breakers from the partner's perspective?	What is in the best interest of the partnership?

Note: [a] The partners must consider if the resources are valuable (V), rare (R) and costly to imitate (I), and if the partnership is organized to capture the value of the resource (O); see Chapter 5 for further details.

Second, you need to prepare well for the negotiation, which involves you developing a clear understanding of your expectations of the partnership and the commitments that you are willing to make. That is, you need to be aware of your strategic objectives for the partnership, how it contributes to these strategic objectives and what you expect from the partnership – information that you should have at hand from the previous analyses. Accordingly, it is useful for you to develop an understanding of the key requirements for the partnership to meet your strategic objectives and identify potential obstacles or risks that may hinder success. Putting yourself in the shoes of your partner is likewise essential. In this regard, it may be valuable to involve an individual from your own team who is not agreeing to the partnership and takes a more critical viewpoint which helps challenge the (maybe too positive) assumptions of the team that negotiates with the potential partner. Finally, it is a good idea to understand your own negotiation levers beforehand; that is, aspects that you are not willing to make concessions on in contrast to aspects that could be granted to the partner. Table 4.5 provides an overview of pre-negotiation questions that can assist in your preparation. Box 4.3 provides an overview of typical pitfalls to avoid in negotiations.

> **Box 4.3   Further insights: Typical pitfalls in negotiations**
>
> 1. Poor planning: Successful negotiators make detailed plans; they know their priorities and options. Hence, prepare a written goals and analysis sheet for yourself.
> 2. Thinking that the set-up of the issues under discussion is fixed: Usually it is not. Do not fall into the "I cannot expect to get everything I want" trap without exploring opportunities.
> 3. Failing to pay attention to your opponent: Try to get inside your partner's head by framing; you can better influence your partner's point of view if she or he understands/accepts your view of the situation.
> 4. Assuming that cross-cultural negotiations are just like "local" negotiations: They are not, due to all the differences in communication, styles and value systems that are influencing both sides.
> 5. Paying too much attention to anchors: This is relevant when it comes to, for instance, the price for a deal; if there are two offers on the table, often the partners feel that these are anchors fixing the range of possible outcomes. If the offer provided by the partner is far lower than what you are aiming for, it may be a bad idea to start compromising, building on this as a reference point.
> 6. Caving in too quickly: Never give anyone their first offer. Experience shows that if a partner accepts an offer without bargaining, this may even cause a feeling of having offered the service or goods for too little.
> 7. Do not gloat: As you may find yourself on the same bargaining table again one day, do not do a dance of joy in front of the partner if you feel that you have made a sweet deal (and would have made the deal for less).
>
> *Source:* Adapted from Buell (2007)

As soon as the negotiations are kicked off, the first meetings should be used to get to know each other better and clarify mutual interests and goals. Research recommends that it is better to not put emphasis too early on legal technicalities, and first focus more on operational aspects, clarity of goals, resource allocation and desired results. To avoid friction, it is relevant that the negotiating team knows exactly what to achieve until when, and what kind of information it is allowed to share at which stage of the negotiation process. Ultimately, the negotiation process needs to relate to several key aspects summarized in Table 4.6. Agreements achieved need to be formalized in a letter of intent, which usually is a non-binding document (yet, in some legal

Table 4.6 Typical items in a partnership agreement/letter of intent (see also Lasserre, 2018)

Strategic objectives	Mission, vision, and ideally strategy statement (see also Chapter 5)
Contributions of the partners	Identification of resources to be used or contributed by the partners, involving: technology, facilities, brand, distribution; in addition, financial resources, including equity-sharing
Management and staffing	Board configuration, positions (including recruitment, careers and management roles), decision-making procedures, control mechanisms and remuneration
Collaboration	Conflict-resolution mechanisms, renewal, extinction
Legal rights	Ownership of technologies developed in the partnership, rights to use and market resources (for example, technologies, brands), rights related to territories and new developments, identification of legal liabilities (for example, warranties, obligations)
Valuation	Assets, price, distribution of value, valuation formulas (see the last section), royalties, cost-sharing

contexts, it may actually have a binding character; hence, it is recommended that you involve legal experts at this stage). The letter of intent is a good piece of pre-work that will facilitate the design of the binding legal agreement, in which legal counselors should be involved.

If both partners have no experience with partnerships, but plan to create a strategic alliance or an M&A, it may be a good idea to engage in a smaller-scale joint project or a JV which allows the partners to see whether they are able to interact. This enables both partners to build trust and understand differences and similarities related to strategy and organization.

The book's website provides a fictional illustration of a negotiation situation between two European banks: a German partner with a dominant presence and numerous branches in the Hamburg region, and a Danish partner with strong expertise in online banking and digital services. The two partners are in the situation of negotiating basic aspects of the M&A deal, including leadership and organizational set-up, such as headquartering. The descriptions can be used to simulate a negotiation situation.

4.4 INTEGRATION APPROACHES

As soon as an agreement has been reached, some forms of partnerships, especially M&As, require an organizational integration of the partners. Hence, managers need to develop a strategy that determines the extent to which the two partners' systems and business functions will be combined and the degree to which employees from both sides collaborate. This also relates to the speed of integrating the two partners and accompanying change management or leadership.

The right approach to integrating the partners is a key determinant of success, yet it depends on the context and the characteristics of the partners. Hence, recommendations on how to approach this process have to reflect these contingencies. A well-known framework that can guide managerial decision-making was proposed by Haspelagh and Jemison (1991) for M&A partnerships. Building on an evaluation of (i) the strategic interdependence between the partners to achieve synergy and (ii) the organizational autonomy of the partners that is needed to respond to differences in the market environment, they derived three ideal integration approaches: a preservation approach, an absorption approach and a symbiotic approach (see Figure 4.3).

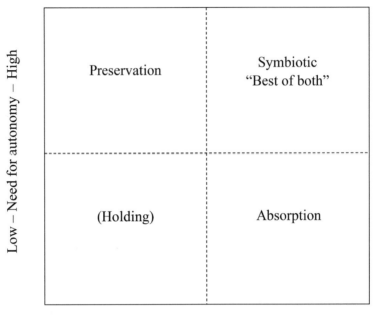

Source: Adapted from Haspelagh and Jemison (1991)

Figure 4.3   Integration approaches

In partnerships which require high levels of autonomy, and in which partners have limited strategic interdependence, a preservation mode is recommended. As there are no or few benefits from interdependencies and there is the need to have autonomy to respond to market requirements, the key objective is to preserve the identity and autonomy of the acquired partner to maintain the partner's sources of competitive advantage. This involves keeping the existing management to the extent possible and then progressively learning the rules of the game from the partner's side. Here, integration may come in the form of accounting management, and providing access to logistics, or IT or distribution facilities; the integration of human resources focuses on learning (rather than controlling the partner).

In partnerships which require low levels of autonomy of the partners and in which the partners demonstrate a high strategic interdependence, an absorption approach is proposed. In an absorption approach, the boundaries between the partners are dissolved, and the organizational structures and operational processes are fully consolidated into the acquiring partner. This involves a significant degree of change, especially at the acquired partner, and may involve several challenges when it comes to eliminating positions that perform redundant tasks. Hence, this approach needs good planning of the integration, the set-up of a transition structure and good project and change management. An example is the deal between Hewlett-Packard and Compaq (see Ellis and Lamont, 2004) that was motivated by the need to improve costs and market position. Both partners engaged in extensive integration-planning efforts prior to completing the deal that involved an appointed integration manager and a detailed schedule of integration milestones. To achieve the cost-based synergies, a consolidation of purchasing and manufacturing functions and an elimination of overlapping product offerings was realized, which led to a reduction of 7 percent in the combined workforce. Hence, the strategic integration needed to be accompanied by a management of workforce reduction that minimized potential disruptions during the change process. Acknowledging the critical role of timing, they aimed to realize two-thirds of the envisaged cost savings within the first six months of the partnership.

In partnerships which involve both high strategic interdependence and a high need for organizational autonomy, a symbiotic approach to integration is proposed. This is often the case in horizontal acquisitions that offer a high potential for synergies, but likewise involve differences in market context that require the partners to maintain autonomy. In this approach, the partners start from co-existing (as in a preservation mode) and become increasingly capable of identifying sources of synergies and profiting from interactions. Hence, the partners start with a preservation-like mode and they gradually integrate by using the best practices from both partners. Thereby, a symbiotic approach requires both partners to change, the idea being that the combined entity will profit from the core competencies and leading practices of both partners. It is therefore recommended to likewise implement a transition management structure that coordinates integration activities and helps to identify best practices. The pace is comparatively slower, as in an absorption approach. An example of a partnership that followed a symbiotic integration approach is the deal between Suiza Foods and Dean Foods (see Ellis and Lamont, 2004). The primary motives for the deal included increasing size, leveraging complementary product offerings, expanding geographic market coverage and achieving synergies. The partners initiated a strong integration related to the consolidation of manufacturing and distribution activities, and eliminated redundant sources of costs. In addition, the partners engaged in identifying the best of both to exploit new growth opportunities, and to leverage the resources and capabilities of the partners. Top management statements at the time of the deal stressed that the integration should provide the opportunity to learn from each other, and to improve the business by adopting the best practices of each partner.

A fourth type of post-acquisition style can be conceptualized (holding), where the non-integration is not indicated due to autonomy needs but results from a lack of concern for the integration. Hence, in a holding approach, there is simply no intention to integrate the two partners. Haspelagh and Jemison (1991) did not encounter any examples of this type of acquisition.

4.5 CULTURAL INTEGRATION

Cultural integration is a key determinant of success in partnerships. Cultural differences can be a source of competitive advantage if managed appropriately. This starts with an analysis of the key similarities and differences between the partners. In addition to the integration model by Haspelagh and Jemison (1991) that focuses on procedural or resource integration, there is a model of sociocultural integration proposed by Nahavandi and Malekzadeh (1988) that offers some guidance. Building on the acculturation literature, they refer to four modes of acculturation in partnerships (which in parts overlap with the model by Haspelagh and Jemison, 1991, in terms of the labels used).

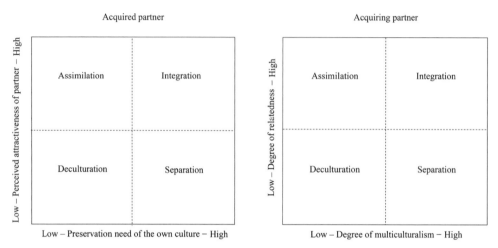

Source: Adapted from Nahavandi and Malekzadeh (1988)

Figure 4.4   Cultural integration

The preferred mode on each side of the partnership can be identified using two dimensions. From the acquired partner's perspective (see Figure 4.4, left), the two dimensions are (i) the degree to which members perceive their own culture and practices as valuable and worth retaining and (ii) the degree to which they are willing to adopt the acquirer's culture and practices or seek positive relations with the acquirer. From the acquiring partner's perspective, the two dimensions are (i) the degree to which the partner is multicultural (that is, the degree to which the organization values cultural diversity) and (ii) the degree of relatedness of the two partners (for example, whether the partners are working in a very related business). If the acquirer is not very diverse and rewards conformity, it is likely to encourage its new partner to adopt the acquirer's culture in order to avoid friction. If the two partners' businesses are very similar, the acquirer is likely to try to impose its culture and practices on the partner in order to achieve synergies.

Depending on the two dimensions, four modes of acculturation may be preferred from the perspective of the acquirer and acquired partner: integration, assimilation, separation and deculturation. In an integration approach, the acquired partner maintains its own beliefs, cultural values and behavioral practices, but is fine with being integrated into the acquiring partner's structure. This calls for the acquirer's willingness to allow that the partner maintains a certain level of independence. Overall, an integration mode entails changes on both sides; that is, some degree of change in culture and practices at both partners without one partner's dominance. In an assimilation approach, one partner adopts the culture and systems

Table 4.7 Cultural integration planning

Cultural lever	Key differences	Integration actions	Timing	Responsibility
Acculturation modes preferred				
Organizational cultures • Structure: centralized versus decentralized/locus of power • Decision-making: autocratic versus collaborative • Performance orientation towards groups or individuals • Formalization: low to high • Risk tolerance: risk-taking to risk-avoiding				
National cultures (for example, using the four key dimensions of Hofstede, Hofstede and Minkov, 2010) • Power distance • Individualism versus collectivism • Masculinity versus femininity • Uncertainty avoidance Alternatively, you can use the scores proposed by Meyer (2014) that we will introduce in Chapter 8.				

Source: Adapted from Galpin (2014)

of the other partner. This may occur if the acquired partner has been unsuccessful, or if the employees and managers perceive that their culture and practices are aggravating performance. Overall, the acquired partner is absorbed into the acquiring partner. In a separation approach, the cultures and practices are preserved on both sides. Separation implies that there will be minimal cultural exchange between the two partners. Each partner continues to do business following its own culture and practices. This can be the case if the acquired partner refuses to adopt the culture of the acquirer and is allowed to do so. Fourth, a deculturation approach (also called "marginality") occurs when members of the acquired partner do not value their own culture and organizational practices, but also are not willing to adopt the culture of the acquiring partner. This results in a loss of identity and cultural stress, and is a non-desirable option.

The authors propose that a congruence between the preferred approach to acculturation between the partners is a facilitator of success of the partnership, as it will result in less stress over acculturation and involves lower levels of organizational resistance, and we support this idea from our own consulting practice.

An analysis of acculturation approaches can be based on the analysis already initiated during the partner-selection process that can be enriched at this stage. That is, you first identify the key differences between the partners and formulate actions that could be used to mitigate differences, if of relevance with regard to the acculturation mode preferred and fitting the strategic agenda on both sides. For this purpose, we recommend developing a cultural integration plan; an example is given in Table 4.7. Our website provides links to interviews with business practitioners commenting on their best practices in this cultural change process.

4.6 BEST PRACTICES TO INTEGRATE THE PARTNERS

The realization of the integration between the partners has been in the focus of consulting practice, which indicates that several relevant activities need to be planned and performed (see Galpin, 2014). These involve the implementation of, first, executive leadership roles and responsibilities that ensure the right level of commitment from the top level. Second, an integration taskforce or infrastructure that specifies relevant teams to work on transitional and synergy-related tasks is invaluable. Third, an overall communication strategy needs to be developed that manages rumors, ensures two-way communication and helps to develop or keep a positive attitude towards the change. Fourth, structure, staffing and recruiting that ensures that the best individual will win the job in a fair process, and ensures that key talent will be retained, is advised. Fifth, cultural integration that takes an analytical approach to identify and mitigate culture clash is recommended. Sixth, human resource management that enables the right incentives for desired employee behavior is advised. Seventh, tracking and reporting performance using key performance indicators is useful. Finally, all of the above should be integrated into a project management approach that involves relevant milestones and connects strategies developed to an ongoing due diligence process building on and enriching the detailed analyses that have been part of the pre-partnering phase. Legal counseling is not only advised but required in most partnering deals, making this an integral part of the integration phase as well. Figure 4.5 offers a simplified timeline of activities.

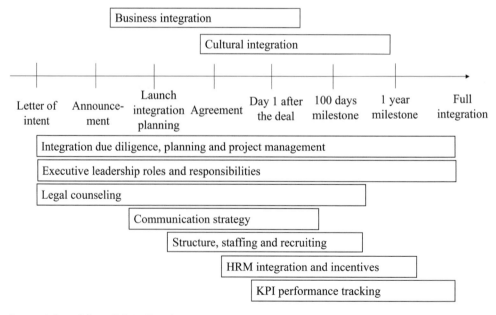

Source: Adapted from Galpin (2014)
Note: HRM = human resource management, KPI = key performance indicator(s)

Figure 4.5   Cultural integration

The timeline given in Figure 4.5 refers to two kinds of milestones, a 100-days and a one-year milestone. The speed of integrating partners has been identified as an antecedent to success, though this may feel uncomfortable. A too-slow process may cause uncertainty, and can lead to rumors and deteriorate employee morale. Yet, speed may also be a challenge; a slow integration helps to reduce conflicts and contributes to trust-building. While we do not have an exact optimal speed, business practice offers a few rules of thumb on appropriate milestones that relate to periods between 90 and 100 days.

Among the aspects given in Figure 4.5, a key determinant of success is implementing leadership; successful partnerships demonstrate clarity in leadership roles early on. That is, the top executives and, depending on the size, an integration manager need to be determined as early as possible. The latter may be of use to enable that the partners still have a chance to devote attention to the day-to-day business challenges during the transition process. The top management team may be appointed from outside of the partnership, this being advantageous to catalyze the combination process and to allow significant changes on both sides, or from the partners' current teams to allow insider knowledge. There is no straightforward recommendation on the best approach, but what is crucial is to ensure that the top managers bring the right capabilities needed to master the integration challenge. General capabilities of these individuals comprise: strategic management skills, credibility among all involved parties, relationship-building capabilities, diplomacy, creative problem-solving skills, strong negotiation skills, technical competence, tolerance for ambiguity and cross-cultural competencies. Both partners' approval of the individuals selected and of the positions' specifics (such as performance and compensation packages) additionally mitigate future management and leadership challenges.

Another key determinant of success is the communication strategy. An effective communication strategy ensures that there are no surprises for employees, including managers who are part of the new organization, as a result of press releases. That is, external press releases come after the dissemination of information to staff. Management needs to ensure that internal managers who have not directly been involved in the integration process are briefed and in turn brief their employees. In addition, research indicates that communication is not just words but is followed up with action. Hence, be careful with what you communicate and promise.

Another traditional management best practice to be followed is the measurement and reporting of performance. An approach that is useful for this performance tracking is that of a balanced scorecard (see Chapter 5). For tracking performance, measures should be developed that relate to financial outcomes, the customer, internal systems and employees or further stakeholders. The key performance indicators to be selected and tracked may also be adapted throughout the lifetime of the partnership. Experience shows that you should put more emphasis on softer measures (for example, partnership quality) at the early stages, and turn to more hard facts in the later stages of the partnership. This tracking can also be combined with the establishment of a learning process during the partnership, so that lessons learned will assist the success of future partnerships.

4.7 ADIDAS AND REEBOK: WHAT WENT WRONG?

In 2021 the sporting goods multinational enterprise (MNE) Adidas announced that it would sell Reebok, about 15 years after it acquired its competitor. Compiling insights from diverse press releases, information from the two firms and an earlier case analysis (see Schmid et al., 2018), we will present the acquisition journey.

Adidas is a German sporting goods firm headquartered in Herzogenaurach. It was founded by Adi Dassler in 1949 and over the decades developed into a global player in the sporting goods market. In the 2000s the MNE was led by Herbert Hainer. In 2005, Adidas was in the top two in the sporting goods market, with sales of USD 7.9 billion. At the time, the US-based Nike was the market leader, with sales of USD 13.7 billion, and third was Reebok, headquartered in the United States as well, with sales of USD 3.8 billion.

In 2005 Adidas decided to acquire Reebok in a "friendly takeover" agreed on by Herbert Hainer and Paul Fireman, who was the chairman at Reebok. The acquisition was officially done on January 31, 2006, as a share deal of USD 3.8 billion, in which Adidas offered USD 59 for each share of Reebok (a premium of around 34 percent). Adidas was paying about 10.7 times Reebok's EBITDA according to Bloomberg data. The idea of the deal was that uniting the two sporting goods firms would provide Adidas with several benefits, and Paul Fireman had a likewise positive attitude towards the deal, indicating that "Adidas is the perfect partner for Reebok. With Adidas, we are able to offer an enhanced portfolio of global brands that truly addresses the needs of today's and tomorrow's consumers."[1]

A key benefit of the partnership would be size: Adidas was able to increase its sales volume, catching up to the sales of market leader Nike, and world market leadership was a declared goal in Adidas's mission statement at the time. Size was expected to bring several further benefits: synergies and economies of scale in operations (as the joint firm would, for instance, manufacture 70 million more sport shoes every year), and more bargaining power towards

Table 4.8 Complementary resources of Adidas and Reebok in 2005

	Adidas	Reebok
Dominant regions	Europe Asia	United States United Kingdom
Dominant customer segments	Men, performance-oriented athletes in all age groups	Men and women, leisure-oriented individuals, younger age groups
Dominant types of sports	Soccer Athletics European sports	Fitness Tennis US sports
Price segments	Medium to high pricing	Medium pricing
Key distribution channels	Specialized retailers for sporting goods Retail store chains for sporting goods	Department stores Fashion boutiques
Sponsoring contracts	FIFA soccer World Cup UEFA soccer Champions League UEFA soccer Europa League Olympic Games	NBA (US basketball league) NFL (US football league) NHL (US ice hockey league) MLB (US baseball league)

Source: Adapted from Schmid et al. (2018: 37)

Asian suppliers and American retailers. The leaders expected synergies in sales, marketing and distribution (40 percent), shared services and IT (40 percent) and global operations (20 percent) – without significant reductions in the workforces after the acquisition. Second, complementarities were key. Table 4.8 provides an overview of the complementary resources of the two firms. Two key complementarities that Adidas aimed to profit from were Reebok's knowledge and foothold in the US sporting goods market and the female and leisure-oriented sports market. Therefore, Adidas went for the deal in 2005, although experts expressed critical comments, mostly revolving around two aspects: a lack of clear branding and missing innovations at Reebok, and the question of whether Adidas would be capable of successfully integrating the two firms.

While Adidas had strong branding and was considered a professional and authentic sports brand, Reebok's branding was somewhat fuzzy. Formerly good branding as an authentic and high-quality sporting goods firm became diluted by targeting products likewise to the fashion and lifestyle segment without a clear positioning of different sub-brands for these submarkets (Reebok offered more than 15 different versions of the Reebok logo that could not be differentiated by the customer). As Reebok's communication was mainly targeted to the US market, its branding was clearly weaker in all other parts of the world. In addition, its products were perceived as somewhat outdated and sold at high discounts in department stores. Reebok's sales suffered from unreliability in its product deliveries and long lead times (resulting in high inventories at retailers). The profitability at Reebok, measured as the return on sales, was

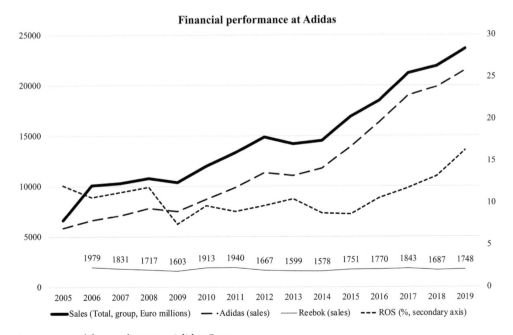

Source: Annual financial reports, Adidas Group

Figure 4.6 Development of the financial performance at the Adidas Group

around 7 percent in the year that the deal was decided and considerably lower than that of Adidas, which had a return on sales of around 12 percent (see Figure 4.6). Both leaders agreed that a new brand called Adidas–Reebok was not a feasible option, and wanted to maintain the positioning of the two brands. However, they also wanted to profit from coordinating, for instance, product launches, and aimed at carefully positioning the two brands for different target groups.

In terms of cultural fit, analysts acknowledged that two quite different national cultures were involved, yet the organizational or industry cultures demonstrated quite some similarity. The passion for sports was visible in the headquarters at both partners (for example, having various sporting facilities on site, a casual style, and so on) and they shared a common goal, namely to "beat Nike." Finally, Adidas already had a multicultural workforce and was open to diversity, with English as its firm language, which was deemed to be a facilitator.

As the management of Adidas had generated several learnings from a former rather difficult acquisition, it devoted attention to the integration process of the partner. It implemented integrative structures right from the start: The management appointed eight integration work groups that were supposed to develop proposals to integrate work procedures involving the unification of group-wide standards, reporting systems, and the like. They were supposed to identify synergies related to costs and sales, and developed blueprints for a new organization. Including sub-teams, more than 1,500 employees worked for about six months in this process. The teams were filled by employees from both the Adidas and Reebok sides (in parity). In addition, a project management and steering board was created that controlled the progress and achievement of objectives (for about two to three years after the acquisition).

The organizational integration followed the objective to work as one firm with a regional set-up by 2007. Yet this integration was supposed to focus on the supporting functions, and on functions that were not close to the customer, such as sourcing, logistics, IT, finance and human resources. The brands were supposed to be managed individually, with one person in charge to manage the marketing and sales of Adidas and one for the marketing and sales of Reebok. The two so-called brand presidents reported directly to CEO Herbert Hainer. In 2008 Adidas replaced the top management at the Reebok side and implemented a close friend of Hainer, who was later replaced again by Reebok's then marketing officer Matt O'Toole in cooperation with Adidas Global Brands executive Erich Stammiger. The back-office activities were supposed to be mainly integrated into the German headquarters whenever feasible, or integrated at other subsidiaries. As regards the filling of the key positions within the new group, an open process was created that enabled the employees on both sides to apply for a position, with the best one winning. Furthermore, some successful managers from Adidas were sent to the Reebok sites to support the implementation of Adidas's culture, and some key positions were quickly filled with Adidas managers following a precise analysis performed in the pre-partnering phase. Hence, there were different kinds of integration approaches used for different functions in the firm, a kind of preservation for the marketing and sales aspect and an absorption for the remaining functions with some elements of "best of both" as regards staffing at the middle and lower management levels. This process managed to not make Reebok employees feel absorbed by Adidas.

> **Box 4.4 Further insights: Decisions and events in the branding of Adidas and Reebok**
>
> After the acquisition, the idea was to reposition Reebok as a leading sporting goods brand with US attributes, aiming at wellness and lifestyle-oriented female and male athletes. Outside the United States, running and sports and lifestyle apparel for females in particular were promoted and sporting goods for team sports (basketball, football, soccer, cricket) were only regionally promoted extensions.
>
> Reebok repurchased some brand selling rights from foreign distributors with the aim of increasing profit margins and enabling an integrated brand management worldwide. In addition, Rebook transferred the sponsoring rights for the professional basketball league in the United States and a professional British soccer club (Liverpool FC) to Adidas.
>
> Several advertising campaigns were launched that did not really succeed in anchoring the new positioning aimed for in customers' minds. In addition, sales did suffer from retailers being reluctant to put both Adidas and Reebok on their shelves for products with overlap; that is, for products targeting the same segments.
>
> In 2012, Reebok initiated a focus on the CrossFit segment and implemented a new logo (the Reebok delta, which replaced the variety of logos). It developed a new distribution strategy with FitHubs selling Reebok at partnering gyms.
>
> In 2014, Adidas presented disappointing results. These were attributed to Adidas struggling in the US market, a golf brand not performing well and exchange rate issues in the Russian market impacting the financial results. However, the media was attacking the Reebok brand, which admittedly performed at the lowest level (sales: EUR 1,578 million) since the acquisition of the brand (sales: EUR 1,979 million).
>
> In 2016, the CrossFit initiative turned out to be a good idea, with growing sales at Reebok (see Figure 4.6). More than 13,000 CrossFit gyms with about 4 million members promoted Reebok worldwide. However, Adidas was still suffering in the US market due to a "too European" image and new competitors attacking the market (especially Under Armour). Adidas implemented a new president for the North American business, Mark King, and a new CEO, Kasper Rørsted (coming from Henkel with experience from Compaq and Hewlett-Packard).
>
> The new leadership aimed to add American flavor to the Adidas products. An increased marketing budget; several contracts with professionals in basketball, baseball and football; and new design studios in several sport hotspots in the United States (among other countries) paid off for Adidas. The idea was to make Adidas the best sports brand and Reebok the best fitness brand.
>
> In 2018, Reebok was profitable again and sales grew slightly at the end of 2019; yet the pandemic interrupted this development with declining sales.
>
> At this point Adidas was choosing to sell rather than to continue to invest in Reebok. In an interview Rørsted acknowledged that Adidas may have lost focus on Reebok, and Reebok may have suffered from the strengthening of the Adidas brand (Höpner and Hofer, 2021).
>
> *Sources:* Schmid et al. (2018), information from the press/media

The integration process was accompanied by a transparent communication strategy with the CEO visiting the Reebok headquarters and an intranet site on the specifics of the integration process among other things. In periodical intervals, employees were surveyed to understand how their feelings about the acquisition were developing. All of these efforts nurtured a strong sense of belonging for the Reebok employees. That is, Adidas seemed to have done its homework when it came to organizing the post-acquisition integration. Still, it did not turn out to be a complete success. *Ex post*, this is mainly attributed to an unsuccessful brand management of Reebok. Yet, we argue that rather it was an unsuccessful coordination of managing the two brands that made the Reebok brand suffer. Box 4.4 presents the decisions and events in the process after the acquisition.

CHAPTER REVIEW QUESTIONS

1. What are the key success factors in partnering entry modes?
2. Which indicators would you use to identify whether a potential partner is a good fit? How would you prioritize the different aspects?
3. What is the key valuation mode used to determine a price to pay for a partnership? How does it basically work (for example, which components do you need to look at, what are the assumptions that influence the valuation)?
4. How would you prepare for the negotiation process with a partner?
5. What are potential "don'ts" in negotiations that surprised you?
6. If you have agreed to collaborate with a partner, how would you approach the integration of the partner related to both the organizational structure and cultural practices?
7. Reflect on the best practice to integrate partners.
8. Reflecting on the Adidas and Reebok case, what would you have done differently as the leader of Adidas? Do you think it was a bad deal for Adidas after all?

NOTE

1. Adidas-Group press release, "Adidas-Salomon to combine with Reebok and create €9 billion footprint in global athletic footwear, apparel and hardware markets," August 3, 2005. www.adidas-group.com/en/media/news-archive/press-releases/2005/adidas-salomon-combine-reebok-and-create-9-billion-footprint-glo/.

REFERENCES

Buell, B. (2007, January 15). Negotiation strategy: Seven common pitfalls to avoid. Insights by Stanford Business. www.gsb.stanford.edu/insights/negotiation-strategy-seven-common-pitfalls-avoid.

Courtois, Y., McPhee, D., and Rerolle, J. F. (2012). Profitability and royalty rates across industries: Some preliminary evidence. KPMG. https://assets.kpmg/content/dam/kpmg/pdf/2015/09/gvi-profitability.pdf.

Cummings, J. L., and Holmberg, S. R. (2012). Best-fit alliance partners: The use of critical success factors in a comprehensive partner selection process. *Long Range Planning, 45,* 136–159.

DePamphilis, D. M. (2010). A primer on merger and acquisition cash-flow valuation. In D. M. DePamphilis (Ed.), *Mergers, Acquisitions, and Other Restructuring Activities* (5th ed., pp. 241–279). San Diego, CA: Academic Press.

Döhle, P. (2017). Johannes Dietsch im Interview: Wie rechnet Bayer? Brand eins. www.brandeins.de/magazine/brand-eins-wirtschaftsmagazin/2017/umsonst/wie-rechnet-bayer.

Ellis, K., and Lamont, B. T. (2004). "Ideal" acquisition integration approaches in related acquisitions of equals: A test of long-held beliefs. *Advances in Mergers and Acquisitions*, 3, 81–102.

Feito-Ruiz, I., and Menéndez-Requejo, S. (2013). *Mergers and Acquisitions Valuations: Cash vs Stock Payment* (SSRN ed.). https://ssrn.com/abstract=2290954.

Galpin, T. J. (2014). *The Complete Guide to Mergers and Acquisitions: Process Tools to Support M&A Integration at Every Level*. New York, NY: John Wiley & Sons.

Gomes, E., Angwin, D. N., Weber, Y., and Tarba, S. Y. (2013). Critical success factors through the mergers and acquisitions process: Revealing pre- and post-M&A connections for improved performance. *Thunderbird International Business Review*, 55, 13–35.

Gudergan, S. P., Devinney, T., Richter, N. F., and Ellis, R. S. (2012). Strategic implications for (non-equity) alliance performance. *Long Range Planning*, 45, 451–76.

Haspelagh, P., and Jemison, W. (1991). *Managing Acquisitions: Creating Value Through Corporate Renewal*. New York, NY: Free Press.

Hoffmann, W. H., and Schlosser, R. (2001). Success factors of strategic alliances in small and medium-sized enterprises: An empirical survey. *Long Range Planning*, 34, 357–381.

Hofstede, G., Hofstede, G. J., and Minkov, M. (2010). *Culture and Organizations: Software of the Mind – Intercultural Cooperation and its Importance for Survival*, Vol. 3. New York, NY: McGraw-Hill.

Holmberg, S. R., and Cummings, J. L. (2009). Building successful strategic alliances. *Long Range Planning*, 42, 164–193.

Höpner, A., and Hofer, J. (2021, May 11). Warum sich Adidas von seiner US-Marke Reebok trennen will. *Handelsblatt*. www.handelsblatt.com/unternehmen/handel-konsumgueter/bilanzcheck-warum-sich-adidas-von-seiner-us-marke-reebok-trennen-will/27157146.html?ticket=ST-583070-lpjiAqsBv4nerEm2Xzb1-cas01.example.org.

Lasserre, P. (2018). *Global Strategic Management* (4th ed.). London: Palgrave.

Meyer, E. (2014). *The Culture Map: Breaking through the Invisible Boundaries of Global Business*. New York, NY: PublicAffairs.

Nahavandi, A., and Malekzadeh, A. R. (1988). Acculturation in mergers and acquisitions. *Academy of Management Review*, 13, 79–90.

PwC (2020). Evolving with agility: PwC's 2020 M&A Integration Survey. www.pwc.com/us/en/services/deals/library/ma-integration-survey.html.

Rappaport, A., and Sirower, M. L. (1999). Stock or cash? The trade-offs for buyers and sellers in mergers and acquisitions. *Harvard Business Review*, November–December, 147–158.

Rinaudo, E. K., and Uhlaner, R. (2014). Joint ventures on the rise. *McKinsey Insights*, November 1.

Schmid, S., Dauth, T., Kotulla, T., and Leding, P. (2018). Adidas and Reebok: Is acquiring easier than integrating? In S. Schmid (Ed.), *Internationalization of Business: Cases on Strategy Formulation and Implementation* (pp. 27–61). Cham: Springer.

Todeva, E., and Knoke, D. (2005). Strategic alliances and models of collaboration. *Management Decision*, 43, 123–148.

Varadarajan, P. R., and Cunningham, M. H. (1995). Strategic alliances: A synthesis of conceptual foundations. *Journal of the Academy of Marketing Science*, 23, 282–296.

Wittmann, C. M., Hunt, S. D., and Arnett, D. B. (2009). Explaining alliance success: Competences, resources, relational factors and resource-advantage theory. *Industrial Marketing Management*, 38, 743–756.

4 CASE STUDY
MAGIC JUICE: ENTERING A PARTNERSHIP?

MAGIC JUICE'S INTERNATIONALIZATION IN THE MEANTIME

By the end of 2020/beginning of 2021, Magic Juice is looking back at three adventurous years of internationalization after it started thinking about its expansion in 2017. It entered four foreign markets. In 2018 it expanded its business to Germany and Austria, and in 2019 it expanded to France and the United Kingdom, using different entry modes in the different markets (see Exhibit 4.1 for the details). In Austria, the United Kingdom and France some outlets were operated under a franchise model, for which Magic Juice requested a franchise fee of 5 percent of annual sales of its business partners in addition to an upfront payment of EUR 25,000 per outlet.

When Dirk de Jong looked at the consolidated figures for Magic Juice (see Exhibit 4.2), he was very satisfied with the developments made. Revenues were growing and the profitability of Magic Juice measured via the return on sales developed from 7 percent in 2017, to 10 percent in 2018, to 14 percent in 2019. In 2020 Magic Juice was, like the whole world, suffering from the consequences of the Covid-19 pandemic. Though it was able to buffer some of the declines in sales with its take-away, online delivery and Trunk concept options, it was the first year with declining sales overall. Thanks to some government-run programs, it was able to keep the great majority of employees; and thanks to the negotiation skills of Sofie Janssen, who managed to reduce costs by, for instance, renegotiating some of the rents during the crisis, its profitability only dropped to 4 percent, which was comparably good in the industry. Hence, Dirk and the rest of the team had a very positive outlook on the situation. At a recent event, Dirk said: "We are confident that we are on the right way to success; results in the past years demonstrated that our ideas work in various markets. Also, the reopening of markets showed that our customers were looking forward to returning to our juice bars. This is a good feeling and nurtures our belief in the future!"

AN INTERESTING OPPORTUNITY UPCOMING?

In the wake of the Covid-19 crisis, one of the partners of the Dutch private capital fund DCC Capital, Anton de Vries, who is also the chairman of the board of Magic Juice, received an inquiry from an investment banker. On behalf of a client, the banker wishes to initiate discussions about a possible collaboration with Magic Juice. Initially, the information is sparse and not very concrete. The inquiry comes from a vertically integrated juice producer that – according to the briefing – is considering establishing juice bars in Spain and Portugal with a partner. This is the message De Vries received at the beginning of the negotiations, but later it turned out that the interest goes even further, namely towards a potential M&A!

The inquiry comes from the Catalonia-based firm Zumo Saludable. Zumo Saludable manufactures a wide range of fruit and vegetable juice products that are sold nationally and internationally to both the grocery and retail sectors. It produces more than 45 million liters of juice annually, including juice from peaches, nectarines, apples, pears, mandarin oranges, lemons, grapefruits, strawberries, cherries, apricots, kiwis, plums, tomatoes, carrots, broccoli, cucumber and more. Due to its excellent raw materials, Zumo Saludable has for some years been one of the main suppliers of fresh fruits, vegetables and juice concentrates for Magic Juice.

Zumo Saludable was founded in 1990 through a merger of various fruit cooperatives. Its sales amounted to EUR 49 million in 2019, and the firm was exporting around 40 percent of its production of juices, nectars, purees and concentrates, primarily to Central and Eastern Europe, followed by Japan, Australia and the Middle East. Zumo Saludable has its own sales offices in Germany, France, Poland and Japan. In addition, it has production sites in two Catalonian locations that still have production capacity left.

Zumo Saludable has continuously invested in its plants and in new technologies, filling systems and packaging lines. Since 2015, strong investments have been made in projects devoted to modernizing and optimizing the plants. While investments in packaging have focused for the most part on the construction of new PET (polyethylene terephthalate – a type of plastic) bottle filling lines during the past few years, there has also been increasing attention on the construction of a new glass line, as reusable glass bottles have returned. The firm has had solid financial results in the past few years (see Exhibit 4.3; Exhibit 4.4 provides additional information on its balance sheet). According to one representative of Zumo Saludable, its key success factor has been: "Our geographic location in an area known for its excellent and outstanding quality of fruits and vegetables; our close relationships with the owner-cooperatives; our versatility and flexibility and our high investment capacity."

Previously, Zumo Saludable tried to establish a juice bar chain in Spain, but without much success. According to the investment banker, the management of Zumo Saludable has made significant preparations for the endeavor, including the identification of the best locations in the major Spanish and Portuguese cities: Madrid, Barcelona, Sevilla, Lisbon and Porto. Contacts have been made with a number of real estate firms to conclude lease agreements for some of the best main- and side-street locations. However, Zumo Saludable lacked the necessary marketing know-how and knowledge about running a juice bar. In addition, it did not have the necessary management power and expertise to carry out such a project. In fact, Zumo Saludable was in a sort of transitional situation with a need for generational change. Its management was patriarchal, without much dynamism – it was mostly concerned with running the firm efficiently, which it did well. The organization was classically divided into functions. Standardization of procedures and formalized processes were among the organizational mechanisms used. Among the firm's owners, there was also interest in selling the business.

Under great secrecy, Anton de Vries and Dirk de Jong began talks with the board representatives of Zumo Saludable. The talks first started with discussions on the possibilities of establishing an equity JV (50–50), which would aim to run a juice bar chain in Spain and Portugal under the brand name of Magic Juice. In addition to providing the JV with capital, Magic Juice would also contribute with its management know-how and its brand name, and Zumo Saludable would be responsible for product development and juice manufacturing, including logistics. The ambitions were great: In the upcoming three years, a minimum of 25 juice bars were to be established in Spain and 15 in Portugal, respectively.

A letter of intent was signed to ensure the process of further negotiations.

In the ensuing months of negotiations, Anton de Vries realized that the owners of Zumo Saludable were actually interested in selling the entire firm; preferably to a business partner from the industry who aimed to realize the firm's ambitions to integrate its business further toward the consumers. Anton sees a great potential in a partnership with Zumo Saludable. By collaborating, the Magic Juice bar chain could position itself more strongly in the hard-hit European food service industry. Many bars, coffee shops and restaurants have been closed due to the Covid-19 crisis. The structural change in the European food service industry is expected to continue, and he thinks that only the most capital-rich firms will survive this development. Anton believes that it is especially in times of recession, or after a major crisis, that one should invest. He also believes that Magic Juice will gain better control of its entire supply chain by partnering with a producer of fruit and vegetable juices.

CASE EXHIBITS

Exhibit 4.1　International expansion at Magic Juice, 2017–2020

Markets and key information	2017	2018	2019	2020
Netherlands (home market)				
Number of outlets	12	15	19	19
Thereof wholly owned	12	15	19	19
Thereof franchising	0	0	0	0
Germany				
Number of outlets	0	6	18	18
Thereof wholly owned	0	6	18	18
Thereof franchising	0	0	0	0
Austria				
Number of outlets	0	4	4	4
Thereof wholly owned	0	0	0	0
Thereof franchising	0	4	4	4
United Kingdom				
Number of outlets	0	0	12	12
Thereof wholly owned	0	0	8	8
Thereof franchising	0	0	4	4
France				
Number of outlets	0	0	7	7
Thereof wholly owned	0	0	2	2
Thereof franchising	0	0	5	5

Exhibit 4.2 Magic Juice's financial situation, 2017–2020 (all numbers in EUR, millions)

	2017	2018	2019	2020
Revenues	5.79	10.33	23.32	17.44
Other operating income (mostly franchise)		0.17	0.45	0.17
Expenses for raw materials and consumables	0.90	1.61	3.65	2.73
Gross profit/loss	4.89	8.89	20.12	14.87
Other external expenses (mostly premises, sales and distribution, office)	1.59	2.74	6.10	5.06
Staff expenses	2.20	3.92	8.24	6.53
Depreciation and amortization	0.69	1.19	2.63	2.63
EBIT	0.40	1.03	3.16	0.66
Financial result	0.12	0.15	0.20	0.04
Profit/loss before tax	0.52	1.18	3.36	0.70

Exhibit 4.3 Profit and loss statement of Zumo Saludable SA, 2017–2019 (all numbers in EUR, millions)

	2017	2018	2019
Revenues	48.21	50.26	48.97
Material costs	34.58	35.03	34.23
Other operating income/expenses	-6.09	-6.53	-5.93
Personnel costs	3.74	4.03	4.14
Depreciation and amortization	1.50	1.60	1.61
EBIT	2.30	3.07	3.06
Financial result	0.14	-0.03	0.12
Profit/loss before tax	2.44	3.04	3.18

Exhibit 4.4 Balance sheet of Zumo Saludable SA in 2019 (all numbers in EUR, millions)

	December 31, 2019
Total assets	28.28
Property, plant and equipment	10.30
Intangible assets	4.05
Non-current financial assets	3.78
Inventories	3.83
Trade and other receivables	3.91
Cash and cash equivalents	2.41
Total equity and liabilities	28.28
Equity	13.76
Liabilities	14.52

CASE QUESTIONS

Throughout this period of negotiation, Dirk is having a hard time understanding the potential opportunity faced. He wonders about the strategic rationales of Magic Juice, but likewise about the strategic objectives of DCC Capital to enter a partnership with Zumo Saludable. In addition, he wonders whether Zumo Saludable is the ideal partner, or if there are better options. If yes, what form of partnership should Magic Juice or DCC Capital choose: an equity JV with the aim of establishing a juice bar chain in Spain and Portugal under the brand name of Magic Juice? Or would it be better to acquire Zumo Saludable and integrate the company into Magic Juice? In addition, although he has maneuvered the financial part of the business well so far, he is puzzled about the financial consequences of each option and which elements he would need to think of to find the right price if acquisition is the way forward. What are your recommendations?

5 Developing strategy and strategic positioning in international markets

To a certain extent, international strategies reflect extreme versions of market segmentation and positioning, which are part of all strategy-development processes. That is, managers in multinational enterprises (MNEs) can, to a certain extent, profit from applying the classical strategy frameworks. These classical frameworks comprise various schools of thought that guide our understanding of strategy and strategy development (see Table 5.1). In the following, we will take a prescriptive view on strategy that involves tools for developing strategy and assists managers in analyzing markets and the firm. Hence, we define a strategy as a plan and a set of goal-directed actions to build and sustain a competitive advantage in selected (national and international) markets. Following the classical thinking, an MNE has a competitive advantage when its profitability is greater than the average profitability of all firms in the industry; if the MNE is able to maintain this above-average profitability over a number of years, it has a sustained competitive advantage. At the core, a competitive advantage is driven by a firm's strategic positioning in the market.

In addition to the application of the classical strategy toolset, challenges in international business (IB) also constitute an individual domain. Differences in cultural, political, legal, and technological environments are much greater in international markets as compared to domestic markets that warrant strategy frameworks specific to IB. These are primarily related to achieving local adaptation (or "responsiveness" of business) and building regional or global integration (or "regionalization" or "globalization" of business). That is, MNEs may be forced to adapt their positioning to local requirements and to respond to specific market needs to achieve a competitive advantage, or can offer a standardized product and service portfolio and therewith profit from economies of scale.

In this chapter, we will first introduce a key element in strategy, namely strategy statements. Building on that, we will demonstrate how different strategic analyses assist managers in understanding complex issues in the business environment. Thereafter we will introduce toolsets and concepts to develop a strategic positioning that results in a sustained competitive advantage and ultimately leads to superior profitability in (national and) international markets. We illustrate several of these aspects on a business practice example of a furniture retailer. Finally, we introduce indicators and concepts that assist in measuring and monitoring the success of strategies adopted.

Table 5.1 Schools of thought in strategy

School of thought	Main message	Key ideas/orientation	Strategy formation
Planning (Ansoff)	Strategy relates the firm to its environment.	Analytical, rational planning process, prescriptive (what should)	Systematic analysis of external and internal factors to evaluate strategic alternatives
Positioning (Porter)	Strategy creates a unique position based on activities differentiating from rivals.	Analytical, rational planning process, prescriptive (what should)	Analysis of external (industry) forces and internal factors to find defendable position/competitive advantage
Resource-based view (Barney)	Sustainable competitive advantage arises from (valuable, rare, inimitable, non-substitutable) resources.	Formal analytical process, prescriptive (what should)	Develop and implement strategies based on control of unique resources
Learning, configuration (Mintzberg)	Strategy emerges and is planned, but it is hard to steer changes.	Too complex and uncertain a world for rigid plans to work, descriptive (what is)	Strategy is a partly emergent and partly planned process in which a certain course of action stabilizes, the focus is on the organization
Strategy-as-practice (Whittington)	Strategy is formed by the daily practices performed by strategists.	Day-to-day activities in local contexts, descriptive (what is)	The day-to-day practices of strategists underpin organizational strategy-formation processes, the focus is on the individual strategist

Source: Adapted from Baraldi et al. (2007)

5.1 CRAFTING A STRATEGY

5.1.1 Strategy statements

An MNE's strategy can be summarized in statements (see the overview in Figure 5.1). A mission statement describes what the firm does; typically this involves answers to questions such as what customer groups your firm satisfies, which customer needs are satisfied and how they are satisfied. Hence, it spells out the underlying motivation for being in business. For instance, an insurance company may specify the mission to provide financial security to consumers. A firm's values guide managers and employees in their behavior, as they spell out how they should behave. The vision specifies the desired future state of the firm and articulates what the firm would like to achieve in the future. Although all three statements are useful to define your business, the mission and vision statements in particular are often not unique; several insurance companies, for instance, may have the same mission statement. Moreover, they are less useful in developing goal-directed actions in business. A statement that is more concrete, ideally unique and able to guide practical action is the strategy statement.

The first element of a strategy statement is the definition of a strategic objective. Ideally, this is a single precise objective that will drive the business over the next five to 10 years. Hence, instead of specifying something like "we seek to grow profitably," you need to decide whether

DEVELOPING STRATEGY AND STRATEGIC POSITIONING

it is about growing the business or becoming more profitable to guide the actions of your sales force, for example. Moreover, the objective should be specific, measurable and time-bound to offer the necessary practical relevance. For instance, in the strategy statement given in Figure 5.2, the single objective is "To grow to 17,000 financial advisers by 2030."

Source: Adapted from Collis and Rukstad (2008)

Figure 5.1   A hierarchy of strategic statements

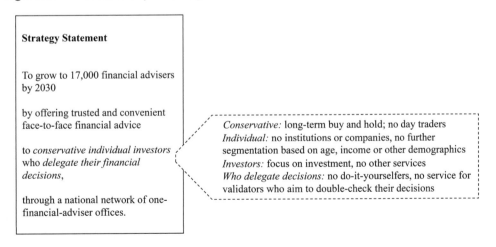

Source: Adapted from Collis and Rukstad (2008)

Figure 5.2   A strategy statement

In addition to the core objective, you may specify subordinate goals that follow from the strategic objective; ideally these are likewise specific, measurable and time-bound. Consulting practice has demonstrated the implications of changing the primary objective (see Collis and Rukstad, 2008): When Boeing, for example, changed its primary objective from being the largest to being the most profitable player in the aircraft industry, it restructured the whole organization. It shifted resources from sales (as it was no longer about competing with Airbus on every deal) to efficiency in manufacturing (that is, it considerably reduced manufacturing over-capacity that was built to flexibly serve customer demand in the earlier set-up – it was able to flexibly deliver more than half a peak year's demand).

The second element is a definition of the firm's scope. This involves three aspects that may vary in relevance for specific strategy statements: customer or offering, geographic location and vertical integration. Clearly defining the boundaries in those areas (that is, who do you target, where and through which channels) will assist managers and employees in setting the right priorities on activities. For instance, in Figure 5.2 the customer and offering are specified as "financial advice to *conservative individual investors* who *delegate their financial decisions.*" The statement provides additional information on these terms to leave no room for misinterpretation. The geographic location is in this example limited to a national level and the channel is defined as the firm's own offices.

Given that the development of a sustainable competitive advantage is the essence of strategy, the third element of the strategy statement is most important: the definition of the advantage. The definition of a firm's competitive advantage consists of the customer value proposition and a reason to believe or the (combination of) activities that allow the firm (alone) to deliver the value proposed. A strategy and the resulting strategy statement that does not explain why customers should buy the firm's products or services will most probably fail. For instance, in Figure 5.2 the advantage is specified as financial advice that can be "trusted" and is "convenient" and "face-to-face" and is delivered "through a national network of one-financial-adviser offices." To arrive at the final wording of such a strategy statement can be a lengthy process, yet it is relevant to define the essence of your strategy, to ensure that it can be easily communicated and to generate the relevant understanding among managers or employees.

Consulting practice demonstrates that many firms lack a clear strategy statement, though its value is undisputed. Furthermore, and even more problematic, many firms even lack a clear strategy, which is the basis for crafting a strategy statement. There are several toolsets that assist in the development of a strategy. Basically, all toolsets involve an analysis of the context and industry landscape; an analysis of customer needs and of competitors and their strategies; and an assessment of the firm's capabilities. Some authors refer to this as finding "the sweet spot that aligns the firm's capabilities with customer needs in a way that competitors cannot match given the changing external context" (Collis and Rukstad, 2008: 89), which is helpful to initiate the strategy-development process (see Figure 5.3).

While in practice competitive advantage often relates to profitability, conceptually it can be understood as the difference between the perceived value that customers attach to a firm's offering (that is, their willingness to pay for a product) (W), and the total costs for producing that offering (C). This is defined as the economic value added (EVA = W − C); the higher the EVA, the higher is the competitive advantage. Therefore, the first fundamental decision that

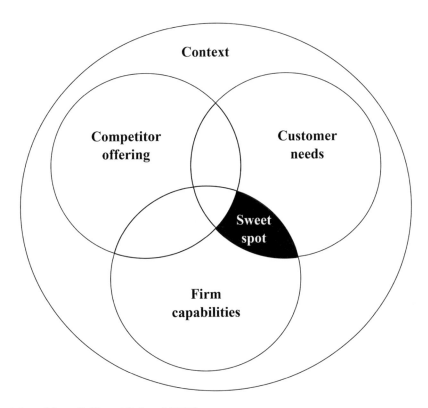

Source: Adapted from Collis and Rukstad (2008)

Figure 5.3 The sweet spot

managers need to make is whether to focus on a cost or value positioning to ultimately increase their firm's EVA. Hence, there are two fundamental, generic business strategies: cost leadership and differentiation. A cost-leadership strategy aims to create similar value for customers by offering products at lower costs or lower prices to its customers. A differentiation strategy aims to create higher value for customers by offering products that present some unique features and therefore allow a price premium. In addition to these two fundamentally different strategies, the manager may further detail the strategy by defining its scope; that is, either targeting a narrow part of a market and very specific customer groups or a broader market that may comprise many different segments or even the mass market. If targeting a narrow market, authors refer to the terms "focused cost leadership" and "focused differentiation strategy." Montblanc, for example, follows a (focused) differentiation strategy by offering exquisite pens at more than USD 100 for a specific segment of customers; BIC in contrast offers pens for the mass market at a low price and follows a cost-leadership strategy.

5.1.2 Strategic analyses

A first toolset that may help to guide strategic decision-making is Porter's five forces (Porter, 2008). To understand industry competition and assess the profitability potential, Porter proposed an analysis of the industry's underlying structure using five forces (see Table 5.2). Understanding these forces is likewise useful to guide decisions about strategic positioning.

The first force is the threat of entry. New entrants into a market aim to gain market share, and put pressure on costs and prices as they bring new capacity to the industry; hence, their entrance into the market influences the industry's profit potential. The threat of entry depends on the entry barriers and on the reactions that can be expected from the firms who are already in the market (incumbents). To understand the latter, it can be useful to assess market entries of other entrants in the past, and to follow public statements of incumbents.

The second force is the power of suppliers. If they are powerful, they keep more of the value produced for themselves; for example, by charging higher prices, limiting quality or services, and by shifting costs to industry participants.

The third force is the power of buyers. Buyers who are powerful can put pressure on prices and on quality and service standards, and may thus put pressure on the industry's profitability. Buyers are powerful if they have the power to negotiate, and if they are price-sensitive. Table 5.2 provides an overview of sources for high negotiation power and price sensitivity. Most of these sources apply to both business-to-business and final consumers; consumers tend to be more price-sensitive if they purchase products that are undifferentiated and expensive in relation to their incomes, and if the product quality has limited consequences on their lives.

The fourth force is the threat of substitutes. A substitute product performs similar functions as the industry's product and may appear in a very different industry (for example, videoconferencing as a substitute to business travel). If the threat of substitutes is high, the profitability in the industry suffers.

Finally, the fifth force is the rivalry among the existing competitors, which limits the industry's profitability, especially if the intensity of competition is high and if the competition is based on price. Competition on other facets, such as a specific product, service or brand features is less likely to erode industry profitability, as it increases the customer value and enables higher prices (Porter, 2008).

To perform Porter's five-forces analysis, we recommend following several best practices that assist in avoiding key pitfalls in using the tool (see Porter, 2008). The first step in the analysis is to define the relevant industry; that is, to define the products that belong to the industry and the geographic scope to be analyzed. To identify the boundaries of the industry, we recommend looking at whether the industry structure is the same or similar (for example, the same or similar buyers, suppliers, barriers to entry) for different potential products or regions that are of relevance. If it is very similar or the same, the products or regions are to be understood as belonging to the same industry and should be analyzed together. As a rule of thumb, you should treat the industries or regions as distinct if there are large differences in at least one of the forces, or if the differences involve more than one force. Second, you need to identify the buyers, suppliers, competitors, substitutes and potential entrants. Third, you need to understand the industry structure and its underlying drivers (see Table 5.2) and identify which of the

Table 5.2 Porter's five forces

Threat of entry	Lower threat of entry if entry barriers are high and if incumbent reactions to market entry are strong. High entry barriers may stem from: • supply-side economies of scale (if firms that produce at larger volumes enjoy lower costs per unit) • network effects (if the willingness to buy the product increases with the number of other buyers) • customer switching costs; that is, costs (for example, modifying processes) faced when changing suppliers • capital requirements (for example, large financial investment into facilities, inventories, up-front advertising) • incumbent cost/quality advantages (for example, proprietary technology, access to most favorable locations) • unequal access to distribution channels (for example, wholesale or retail channels blocked by incumbents) • restrictive government policy (for example, licensing requirements and restrictions on foreign investments)
Power of suppliers	The power of suppliers is high if: • suppliers are more concentrated than the industry they sell to • suppliers do not depend heavily on the industry for their revenues (for example, if serving several industries) • industry participants face switching costs if changing suppliers • suppliers offer products that are differentiated and not generic or me-too (that is, similar to products offered by other firms in the market) • there is no substitute for what the suppliers provide • the supplier can (credibly threaten to) integrate forwards into the industry
Power of buyers	The power of buyers is high if they have negotiation leverage and are price-sensitive. Buyers have negotiation power if: • there are few buyers, or if the purchase volume of buyers is large relative to a single vendor's size • the industry's products are standardized or undifferentiated • buyers face few switching costs in changing vendors • buyers can (credibly threaten to) integrate backwards and produce the product themselves Buyers are price-sensitive if: • the product bought represents a significant fraction of the buyer's costs or procurement budget • the buyers earn low profits or are in need of cash or otherwise under pressure to trim costs • the quality of the buyer's products or services is little affected by the industry's product • the product has little effect on the buyer's other costs
Threat of substitutes	The threat of a substitute is high if: • the substitute offers an attractive price–performance trade-off to the industry's product • the buyer's costs of switching to the substitute are low
Intensity of rivalry	The intensity of rivalry is greatest if: • competitors are numerous or are roughly equal in size and power • industry growth is slow • exit barriers are high (that is, the flip side of entry barriers) • rivals are highly committed and have aspirations for leadership or goals that go beyond profitability • firms cannot read each other's signals well (for example, if they lack familiarity and have differing goals) Rivalry is destructive if the focus of competition is on price, which most likely occurs if: • products or services of rivals are nearly identical and there are few switching costs for buyers • fixed costs are high and marginal costs are low • capacity must be expanded to be efficient • the product is perishable

Source: Adapted from Porter (2008)

forces are strong and which are weak. For this purpose, we recommend looking at the forces in a more quantitative than qualitative fashion and engage in a rigorous analysis that goes above and beyond a qualitative list of aspects. For instance, rather than just making a qualitative statement on the price sensitivity of buyers, go into the details and add information on the underlying drivers, such as the percentage of costs that the product accounts for on the side of the buyer. In this context you will also need to define the appropriate time horizon. To not confuse cyclical changes with structural developments, we recommend taking a three- to five-year time horizon and looking at average numbers over this period. To better understand the strengths of the forces, you are advised to generate an understanding of how the forces influence your financials (for example, balance sheets and income statements). For instance, if a stronger rivalry in the industry is assumed to affect prices, you are advised to generate an understanding of how this will affect your margins. In this context you may also test the validity of the analysis and test whether it is consistent with the actual long-run profitability in the industry and whether it enables you to explain why certain players are specifically profitable. These more in-depth analyses will sharpen your understanding of strategic opportunities and enable you to focus your attention on the most important forces in the industry. Fourth, and finally, you are advised to assess likely positive and negative future changes in each of the five forces, including an analysis of whether there are forces that are impacted by your competitor developments, your own developments or entrants, or if shifts in one of the forces trigger reactions in other forces in the future.

A theoretical framework that shifts the focus from the industry to the firm, and therefore adds a relevant perspective to develop strategy, is the resource-based view (Barney, 1991). It assists you in identifying your firm's core competencies; that is, the resources and/or capabilities that have the potential to create a sustained competitive advantage. Resources are broadly defined in this model and encompass tangible and intangible resources. Tangible resources are physical entities, such as land, buildings, equipment, inventory and money. Intangible resources are nonphysical entities that are created by the firm's managers and employees, such as brand names, the firm's reputation, the knowledge that employees have gained through experience, and the firm's intellectual property, including patents, copyrights and trademarks. Capabilities are understood as firm-specific resources that improve the productivity of other resources that the firm possesses; that is, they often reside in an organization's rules, routines and procedures. A resource or capability can be a source of competitive advantage, and therefore form a core competency, if it exhibits VRIO attributes; that is, it must be valuable (V), rare (R) and costly to imitate (I), and the firm must be organized to capture the value of the resource (O). Hence, the VRIO framework can be used as a decision tree to identify firm resources that have the potential to provide the firm with a sustained competitive advantage (see Table 5.3). If you are able to answer all four questions with "yes" for a specific resource, it has the relevant attributes to deliver a sustained competitive advantage to your firm.

A resource is valuable if it increases the perceived value of a firm's products or services in the mind of its (potential) customers. This can be due to attractive features or a lower price. An example of a valuable resource at a car producer is its knowledge in designing and producing

Table 5.3 The VRIO framework

Valuable?	Rare?	Costly to imitate?	Exploited by organization?	Implications
No	-/-	-/-	No	Competitive disadvantage
Yes	No	-/-	Limited	Competitive parity
Yes	Yes	No	Partially	Temporary competitive advantage
Yes	Yes	Yes	Yes	Sustained competitive advantage

Source: Adapted from Barney and Hesterly (2015: 103)

efficient engines. A resource is rare if there is only one firm or a small number of firms that possess it. At the time Toyota built its initial position in car manufacturing, its lean manufacturing system was valuable and rare, as it enabled the firm to lower production costs and to simultaneously increase the quality of its products. A resource is costly to imitate if other firms are unable to develop or buy the resource at a reasonable price. If the resource is not costly to imitate, other firms will most probably acquire or develop the resource themselves and therewith restore competitive parity. If a resource in contrast qualifies as valuable, rare and costly to imitate, then it is a core competency that has the potential to provide the firm with a sustained competitive advantage. To finally provide the firm with a sustained competitive advantage, the firm needs to be able to capture the resource's value-creation potential; that is, it needs to have the right organizational structures and coordination systems to exploit its VRI resources.

Research has demonstrated that the VRIO framework is able to predict firm performance (for example, Bresser and Powalla, 2012; Crook et al., 2008) and therefore is of strong relevance to managerial practice. Yet, research has also demonstrated that managers and researchers do not tap the full potential of the toolset in practical settings. In addition to its more static nature, one aspect that is challenging in practical settings is the identification of relevant resources. To select resources for the VRIO analysis, we recommend choosing one of two conceptual frameworks; that is, either a distinction into tangible and intangible resources or using an analysis of the value chain with its primary and support activities (see Chapter 6 for further details on value chains). Hence, before analyzing different resources, ensure that you create a more comprehensive list of relevant resources for your firm. Mentally reviewing the value chain activities for relevant resources may assist in this process. An example that is using the value chain framework to structure the resources to be analyzed is provided in Table 5.4.

The VRIO analysis in Table 5.4 indicates that the example firm has several resources that have VRIO attributes and offer the firm a sustained competitive advantage: Among the primary activities, it is the firm's brand image in the industry, and its distribution and customer service network, that provide a sustained competitive advantage. Furthermore, its research and development (R&D) capabilities, which empowered the firm to constantly innovate in its market, are a source of sustained competitive advantage. Furthermore, its organizational culture and human resource management system contribute to its innovation capability and therefore to this source of competitive advantage.

Table 5.4 VRIO example along the value chain

Resources	Reasons	Valuable	Rare	Costly to imitate	Exploited by organization
Support activities					
Organizational culture	Open culture with strong diversity management triggering creativity and ideas for innovative products	Yes	Yes	Yes	Yes
HR management	Acquiring and developing motivated and excellent employees that enable exploitation and exploration advantages	Yes	Yes	Yes	Yes
Information systems	Well-functioning enterprise resource planning (ERP) system that creates operational excellence	Yes	No		
Materials management	Access to superior components through contracts with key suppliers	Yes	Yes	No	
Primary activities					
R&D	Spends 6.4 percent of total sales on R&D (more than the industry average), enabling a continuous flow of innovations	Yes	Yes	Yes	Yes
Production facility	One manufacturing plant with a production capacity of 435,000 units per year, enabling relevant economies of scale	Yes	No		
Operational excellence	Excellence and experience in production, enabling premium product quality	Yes	No		
Distribution network	Strong nationwide distribution network with 4,200 dealer touch points, enabling relevant responsiveness to customer needs	Yes	Yes	Yes	Yes
Brand	One of the most recognized brands in the industry (which can be leveraged in this and other markets)	Yes	Yes	Yes	Yes
Customer service	57 service centers with 24-hour service that enable high customer experience in case of complaints	Yes	Yes	Medium	Yes

Another toolset that helps to craft strategy is an analysis of the strengths, weaknesses, opportunities and threats (SWOT). It synthesizes the information from previous analyses conducted on the external environmental factors and internal resources. While the analysis starts with gathering information, the aim of a SWOT goes above and beyond a laundry list of data. In a first step, managers need to identify the most significant and strategically important internal and external factors that will affect their business. The list of opportunities summarizes favorable trends and developments in the external environment that have the potential to increase the firm's sales and profits or to offer new business opportunities. A correct application of a SWOT ensures that opportunities listed are not confused with business strategies; in this step it is about identifying external opportunities or developments observed in the world or relevant markets, and not strategies – mixing the two causes confusion. The list of threats summarizes unfavorable trends and developments that have the potential to deteriorate sales and profits. While this may seem to be of less interest to opportunity recognition, it is important to plan around events that could impede the future business performance. The VRIO analysis is a good base to identify strengths and weaknesses. Importantly, both strengths and weaknesses are relative strengths and weaknesses to the competition (that are rare). Moreover, it is about strengths and weaknesses that matter to the customer (that is, we recommend focusing on the strengths or weaknesses that are customer-relevant or valuable). A way to think about weaknesses is to understand the required competencies in the industry or what most customers require that the firm does not possess.

In a second step, the SWOT matrix (see Table 5.5) is used to develop strategic alternatives: Strategic alternatives can be SO – that is, strategies that make use of strengths to exploit external opportunities; WT – to eliminate or minimize weaknesses to mitigate an external threat; ST – to use a strength to minimize the effect of an external threat; and WO – to improve a weakness and take advantage of an opportunity. The example presented in Table 5.5 for a producer of air conditioning already demonstrates that developing strategic alternatives might be challenging (for example, think of potential W1T1 strategies). In a third step, management needs to evaluate the advantages and disadvantages of each strategic alternative to finally select one or more alternatives to pursue.

While the SWOT analysis is one of the most popular managerial tools, consultancy practice demonstrates that its usage in part lacks professionalism (see, for example, Hill and Westbrook, 1997). In many firms quite long lists of SWOT factors are produced involving 40 factors; that is, 10 factors in each category, or even more which are not further prioritized. Sometimes the same factor is listed under two different categories (for example, listed as an opportunity and threat) without further explanation. Finally, we often see that the distinction between internal and external factors is not kept and the lists mix, for instance, strengths with opportunities.

Table 5.5 SWOT with example items for a producer of air conditioning

	Opportunities O1. Growth of middle-class segment in high-temperature countries X and Y	Threats T1. Rising costs for electricity
Strengths		
S1. High R&D spending for product innovation S2. Strong brand in the industry	S2O1: Use the strong brand to achieve high share of the market in X and Y	S1T1: Foster innovation that saves energy
Weaknesses		
W1. Insufficient distribution network in country X W2. Insufficient distribution network in country Y (with low urbanization)	W1O1: Develop distribution network in key urban areas of country X W2O1: Develop distribution partnerships in country Y to ensure delivery in a situation of low urbanization	W1T1: …

To ensure analytical rigor, we therefore highlight several recommendations on using SWOT (Coman and Ronen, 2009): First, concentrating on four or five key items per list is useful for the steps that follow. These may be identified by evaluating which factors have the potential to substantially impact the firm's sales, profits and long-term positioning. This also includes the elimination of redundancy and irrelevant aspects and the identification of potential underlying cause–effect relationships, for instance, to identify core problems that underlie several weaknesses. Furthermore, consultancy practice calls for items that are actionable or at least allow the definition of actionable strategic alternatives. In this context, we recommend to be as precise as possible in defining or listing the factors and to avoid vagueness. Finally, it is important to highlight that it is a tool to develop strategy, hence it should not stop at listing SWO and T.

In Table 5.5, a strategic (SO) alternative is to use the firm's brand to achieve a high share of the market in a certain country market. If this is what is prioritized by managers, the next step to develop strategy is defining the value proposition and therewith the positioning in the new country market.

5.2 DEVELOPING A GLOBAL OR LOCAL POSITIONING

5.2.1 Identifying customer needs and viable segments

A firm that is entering a new market needs to develop a competitive positioning in this market. This process is supported by several toolsets from the strategic marketing literature: In a first step, you need to define the market. This definition can be derived or taken from the previous analyses of the industry using Porter's five forces which already specify whether national country markets are looked at separately or whether markets are analyzed jointly. In a second step, customer needs and, if possible, segments of customers with different needs

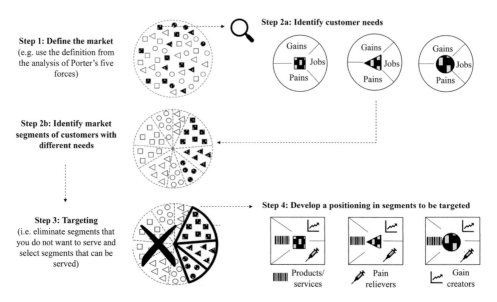

Figure 5.4   The process of developing a positioning and value proposition

are identified. The third step is called "targeting"; that is, selecting the market segments you want to serve. The fourth step is to position your firm and your products and services within the segments you aim to serve; that is, you define a value proposition and the relevant products. Figure 5.4 visualizes this process.

"Customer needs" are desires and wants that can be satisfied by means of the attributes or characteristics of a product. In many markets the customer needs go beyond basic functional needs that are relevant for the product category (for example, being able to make a phone call with a smartphone). Often emotional and social needs play a relevant role in the purchasing decision as well (for example, using a smartphone of a certain brand that is perceived as innovative and technologically superior). Firms that offer products which satisfy specific additional emotional or social needs often profit from a higher or premium price for their product. Charles Revson, the founder of cosmetics producer Revlon, once formulated it this way: "In the factory we make cosmetics, in the drugstore we sell hope."[1] Moreover, in most markets these customer needs are different for different customer groups. The process of gaining a deeper understanding of the customer needs of different customer groups is called "segmentation." In segmentation, the market is divided into groups of customers who are maximally similar within the group, but maximally different between groups.

"Segmenting" a market is relevant as it enables firms to better understand the diversity of customer needs and choose the segments that they can best satisfy and profit from under given resource constraints. It involves two important sub-steps: dividing the market into segments and profiling the segments along their customer needs. To segment a market, you can refer to different segmentation criteria: First, there are criteria that are independent of the relationship with the industry's product. These include less progressive criteria, such as demographics (for example, age, gender, income) and geography as well as more progressive psychographic criteria (for example, lifestyles, interests) and needs-based criteria. Second, there are criteria that involve information about the relationship between the customer and the product (for example, usage patterns, involvement with the product category, and the stage in the buying and decision-making process). In practice, often a combination of different methods of segmenting the market is used, as each method offers useful information. However, there usually is a primary criterion to segment the market – the more strongly this is related to the final customer needs (that is, the more progressive), the easier it is later to develop a relevant positioning.

One contemporary strategy concept that aims at identifying relevant customer needs is the idea of "jobs to be done" and the identification of the pains and gains that are attributed to these jobs (Christensen et al., 2016; Osterwalder et al., 2014). Jobs offer a more comprehensive understanding of facets that may be relevant for positioning. A customer job is a task that a customer is aiming to perform or complete, a problem she or he is trying to solve, and/or a need that she or he is aiming to satisfy. An example often referred to in this context is that a customer does not buy a power drill because she or he wants a quarter-inch drill, but because she or he wants a quarter-inch hole (hence, the quarter-inch hole in the wall is the job that the customer wants to get done). As in traditional marketing, jobs can be functional (that is, if customers try to perform a specific task; for example, eat healthily), social (if customers want to look good or gain status), and personal or emotional (if customers seek an emotional state such as feeling good). The idea of the concept is to understand the jobs that customers need

Table 5.6 Identify customer needs by understanding pains and gains

Trigger questions to identify pains	Trigger questions to identify gains
What makes customers feel bad, frustrated, annoyed? Which features are customers currently missing in products sold? Are there performance issues that annoy them or malfunctions they cite? What are the main difficulties and challenges customers encounter? Do they have difficulties getting certain things done? What negative social consequences do customers encounter/fear? Are they afraid of loss of face, power, trust or status? What (financial, social, technical) risks do customers fear? What is keeping customers awake at night? What are their big issues, concerns and worries? Are customers using a solution the "wrong" way? What barriers (for example, up-front investment costs) are keeping your customers from adopting a value proposition? How do your customers define (too) costly? Is it about too much time, too much money or too much effort to be made?	What quality levels do customers expect, and what do they wish to have more or less of? How do current products delight your customers? Which features do they enjoy? What would make your customers' lives easier? Would they enjoy more services or lower costs? What positive social consequences do customers desire? What makes them look good? What increases their power or their status? What are customers looking for most? Are they searching for good design, guarantees or specific or more features? What do customers dream about? What do they aspire to achieve, or what would be a big relief to them? How do your customers measure success and failure? How do they gauge performance or cost? What would increase the likelihood of customers adopting a value proposition (for example, lower costs, less investment, lower risk, better quality)? Which savings would make customers happy (time, money or effort)?

Source: Adapted from Osterwalder et al. (2014: 15, 17)

to get done, the context in which the jobs need to get done and potential pains (that is, aspects that annoy customers or are risky before, during and after trying to get a job done) and gains (the benefits that customers expect or desire or that surprise them). Pains include potential bad or undesired outcomes and side effects; gains include aspects such as functional utility, gaining social status, inducing positive emotions and saving costs. Table 5.6 gives an overview of questions that assist in identifying customer needs using pains and gains.

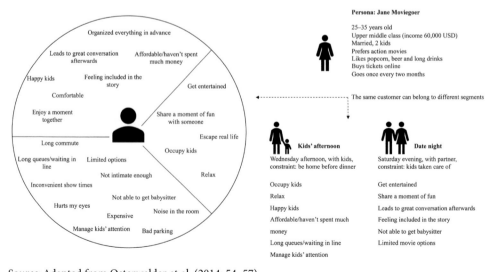

Source: Adapted from Osterwalder et al. (2014: 54–57)

Figure 5.5 Example of a customer profile

While you may decide to involve professionals in market research to identify customer needs and segments, putting yourself into your customers' shoes is an exercise that will assist you in developing a customer profile. For this process, you first select a customer segment (often using less progressive criteria and more intuitively) that you want to profile. Second, you identify the jobs that these customers want to get done. Third, you identify the customer pains, and fourth, the gains. Finally, you are invited to prioritize jobs, pains and gains to differentiate the essential from the nice-to-have or acceptable gains and pains. An example of a customer profile is provided in Figure 5.5. Moreover, we recommend getting in touch with your (potential) customers and learn about their needs directly.

For segments to be truly meaningful and useful for the later positioning process, the needs of customers (related to the product and or purchase process) in one segment must be distinct from those in other segments. Otherwise, the benefits of segmenting cannot be realized, and resources may be wasted as two value propositions and accompanying product offerings are developed, although one would be sufficient to satisfy the two segments. The customer profile developed in the context of the "jobs to be done" analysis maybe used to identify overlap. You may likewise more traditionally develop a description of the customers within the segments. Answering the following questions may guide this process: What benefits are customers seeking? How do they use the product? Who is in the segment (that is, what are their demographics)? Furthermore, the usage of "personas" may be a helpful toolset. Personas capture segment characteristics in the form of a fictionalized typical or average customer within a segment. An example of a persona is given in Figure 5.5 (Jane Moviegoer).

Independent from the concept used to develop a customer profile, we recommend enriching these profiles further with information on the size of the segment and its potential growth, the channels through which customers buy the product, how often or how much of the products

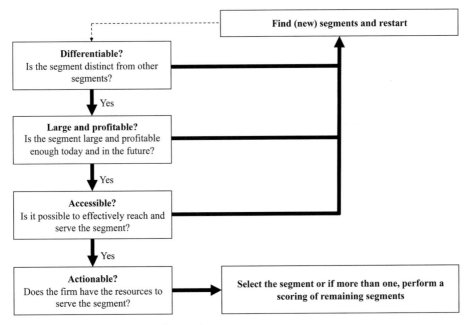

Figure 5.6 The process of targeting

customers buy, and the nature of competition in each of the segments, as this will be needed in the next step. The information on the customer segments is used to target relevant segments; that is, to choose which segments to serve and which not to serve. First, we recommend filtering the segments using the criteria provided in the decision tree in Figure 5.6 (see Freytag and Clarke, 2001 for a business-to-business decision tree). Second, we recommend evaluating the remaining segments using a scoring model. Popular criteria for this process are the segment size, growth rate, competitive intensity, synergy with other aspects of the organization, and fit with the firm's resources and overall strategy. Alternatively, and depending on the flexibility of your business and firm, you may first develop ideas on relevant potential positionings in the market and then do the scoring.

5.2.2 Developing value propositions

For the segments to target, the firm needs to develop its "value proposition" and therewith its positioning in the market. In this process step, it is about creating an offering that satisfies the needs of the sweet-spot customers. This can be one overarching positioning of the firm in a specific market segment, yet can also involve the development of different value propositions for different market segments targeted individually. Marketing practice and research has demonstrated that there are six relevant criteria to develop a strong positioning in a market – some of these are very similar to what we are familiar with from the VRIO framework: (i) relevance (that is, do customers care or see a value in the positioning), (ii) uniqueness (is the positioning different from what competitors offer or is it rare), (iii) attainability (are we able to deliver this value proposition or are we organized to capture its value), and (iv) sustainability (can we maintain the value proposition over a long-term period). Furthermore, two criteria are of relevance for a strong positioning: (v) clarity (that is, will customers and further stakeholders easily understand the essence or main message of our positioning) and (vi) credibility (will customers and stakeholders believe that we can deliver this value positioning). While we have discussed strategy statements earlier, firms are in this process step advised to develop a positioning statement that relates more specifically to the product offering. Best practices indicate that it should involve the target (as in the above strategy statement), the frame of reference (that basically defines the market), the point of difference (that is, the aspects that make the offering unique), the key benefit (that will satisfy the customer most) and the reason to believe. An example often referred to is the positioning statement of Snickers: *Among snackers, Snickers is the candy bar that satisfies your hunger because it is packed with peanuts* (Fossas, 2016). The *target group* are *snackers*, the *market* or *frame of reference* are the brands of *candy bars* (and not, for instance, the industry for convenience meals), the *point of difference* and *key benefit* are bundled in the statement that it *satisfies your hunger*, and the *reason to believe* is that it is *packed with peanuts*. The reason to believe can be a facet that is inherent in the product or in the company; here it is a facet that is inherent in the product.

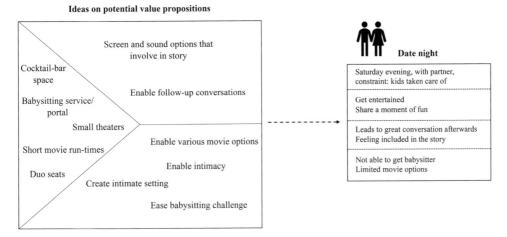

Figure 5.7 Example of ideas on a customer value map

To develop such a value positioning, you can make use of your "jobs to be done" analyses. For this purpose, list the products and services that you currently serve. This includes all kinds of offerings; in addition to tangible products, this also includes intangible offerings, such as copyrights and digital benefits (for example, online recommendations). Second, identify and outline pain-relievers. That is, understand how your products and services currently help your customers in avoiding pains by eliminating or diminishing undesired outcomes and risks. Third, identify and specify gain-creators by understanding how your products and services currently create desirable outcomes and benefits for your potential customers. Finally, you should prioritize these aspects based on the importance to customers. You will most probably not be able to address all pains and gains of customers, but need to and should focus on those that are most relevant and make a difference for customers. This exercise can be separated using different customer groups; that is, using your segmentation of the market. Hence, it is about deciding which kind of offering you tailor to which customer group. Finally, it becomes obvious that this exercise may likewise assist you in developing an understanding of how your current products and services may need to be adapted to create gains and to relieve pains of relevant customer groups. Figure 5.7 provides an example of ideas generated on a customer value map to target a specific segment of individuals who consume movies.

The translation of strategy into action takes place in the firm's business model. It details and summarizes the firm's tactics and initiatives to achieve the strategic objectives. It explains how the firm conducts its business with its buyers, suppliers and partners; and formulates a blueprint of actions and initiatives (including structures, processes, cultures and procedures). A toolset that supports the process of translating strategy into action points is the "business model canvas" (Osterwalder et al., 2014). It basically offers a tool to visualize the key elements of your business; that is, the customer segments and value proposition that we discussed in detail above. Moreover, it suggests listing the channels that are or should be used to deliver the value proposition. It comprises communication channels as well as distribution and sales channels. Furthermore, it suggests listing the customer relationships that are established or should be established with customers in different segments (for example, should it be a personal, personalized relationship or not?). Then it suggests listing the key resources (here understood as assets), activities and partnerships that are of key relevance to deliver the value proposition. A good way to think about these key resources (and activities and partnerships) is the VRIO framework using a broad definition of resources. Finally, the business model canvas highlights the relevance of visualizing revenue streams (that is, how does the organization capture value, what prices are customers willing to pay), costs structures (all costs incurred to operate the business model) and the resulting profits (by subtracting the total costs from the total revenue streams in the canvas). Figure 5.8 provides an example of a business model canvas. Alexander Osterwalder offers video explanations of the business model canvas that we recommend watching (relevant links are provided on the book's website).

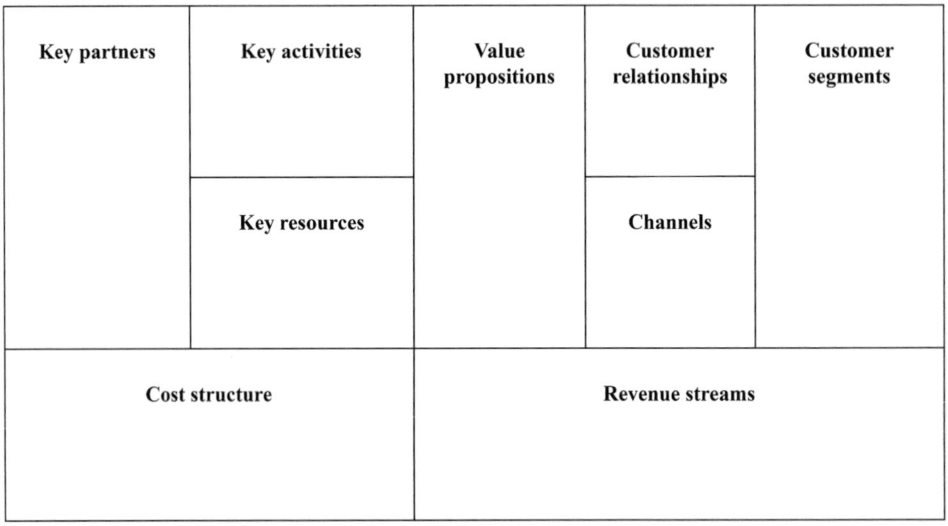

Key partners	Key activities	Value propositions	Customer relationships	Customer segments
	Key resources		Channels	
Cost structure |||| Revenue streams			

Source: Adapted from Osterwalder et al. (2014: XVII)

Figure 5.8 The business model canvas

5.2.3 Integrating value propositions or not

We may now ask ourselves: What is different about international as opposed to domestic strategy? Basically, it is the contexts that the MNE is confronted with, and the question of whether the firm should follow a uniform positioning worldwide or a localized positioning that is customized to the local or regional markets. MNEs have two options: First, they can target a universal segment across countries if such a universal segment exists. Second, they can pursue different segments in the different markets. When focusing on a uniform segment, management needs to decide whether to use the same positioning or tailor the positioning to the individual country markets.

Table 5.7 Forces for localization, regionalization and globalization

Forces for ...	Major drivers	Benefits	Industry examples
Globalization/global integration	Fewer international trade barriers High speed of innovation and short product lifecycles Global convergence of customer needs Digitalization	Global economies of scale (standardized products) Global coordination benefits Global learning benefits Global arbitrage benefits	Container shipping Civil aircraft Bulk chemicals Electronics (for example, microchips, computers)
Regionalization/regional integration	Regional trading blocks Regional distribution networks and logistics Supra-national institutions	Regional economies of scale Regional coordination benefits Regional learning benefits Regional customization benefits	Brewing Logistic services Automotive
Localization/responsiveness	National cultural consumption peculiarities National formal institutional requirements Transport barriers	Benefits of local customer orientation (for example, customer loyalty, price premium) Local market proximity and closeness benefits (for example, competitive edge and creation of market-entry barriers)	Food Car repair Business services Personal care

In general, if target customers have very similar needs worldwide, a uniform positioning may work and enables the generation of global scale benefits, among others. Yet, it is not only about customer needs in the international domain. There are several sets of forces that shape the competitive structure of industries and market segments. Table 5.7 provides an overview of localization forces, yet also regionalization and globalization forces that shape the international context of positioning (which are often discussed in IB; see Hollensen, 2020; Lasserre, 2018).

The geographic locus of international business opportunities can refer to a single country or a region (a set of countries), or it can be global (geographically unconstrained). Several cultural, commercial, technical and legal factors, and so on, may differ from country to country, and therefore create a great pressure for local responsiveness or localization. Responding to local customer preferences and tastes requires customizing the value proposition (that is, customizing products and processes). For example, consumers may prefer products that are sensitive to their specific lifestyles, to their habits, social codes and buying practices. This is often the case for products with high cultural content, such as foods or personal-care products, that are sensitive to levels of economic development and/or involve high levels of personal interaction. Responding to local differences in legal factors, technical standards and commercial factors implies adaptation in various dimensions of the firms' marketing mix (for example, product design, branding, distribution, pricing and after-sales service).

For many industries, there are groups of countries that are relatively similar to each other (and relatively dissimilar to countries in other regions), offering benefits of regionalization. While regions may be separated by oceans, large time zone differences and so forth, regional cultural, social or economic commonalities may exist and thereby reduce the influence of geographic distance on business. In addition, supra-national institutions, regional trade blocks or unions (for example, the EU; ASEAN, or Association of Southeast Asian Nations; NAFTA, or North American Free Trade Agreement; Mercosur) reduce economic distance. Common industrial policies, R&D policies, and elimination of intra-regional tariff and non-tariff barriers improve inter-regional linkages and improve economies of scale and scope opportunities for the MNE. Furthermore, regional integration results in a higher similarity in economic structures (for example, tax regimes, competition laws, procurement regulations, corporate governance practices) offering benefits on the regional level.

At the global level, similarities in customer preferences, trade and distributions practices, and technological diffusion and new communication channels prevail across national borders due to a worldwide convergence of markets and competition. The emergence of major globalization drivers has been due to a wide range of political, technological, social and competitive factors that have characterized the world since the beginning of the 1970s. Liberalization of the world trade and capital flows (reducing tariffs and other trade and investment barriers) has progressively opened markets, technological processes in logistics and telecommunication have lowered the transportation and communication costs, and international travel and the diffusion of lifestyles have increased brand awareness of consumers worldwide and created global brands. Box 5.1 provides examples of how the internet has influenced the drivers and barriers of globalization.

Box 5.1   Further insights: Internet/digitalization effects on globalization and global strategy

The internet increases global commonality in customer needs, enables global customers, facilitates global channels and supports global marketing. For instance, computer manufacturer Dell has shifted its marketing and ordering systems to the web, enabling worldwide access to its product portfolio. Online retailers such as Amazon open up a wide global reach even to small and medium-sized firms. The internet enhances access to global sourcing opportunities, can speed up global logistics and helps in exploiting differences in country costs. For instance, internet technologies are used to create networks between firms cooperating along the value chain (for example, to exchange information and components in the automotive industries), and platforms such as Alibaba generate worldwide access to manufacturers. The internet makes competitor comparisons easier, which can aid the firm in its strategy development, yet also aids the customer in comparing offerings. Finally, the internet can assist in side-stepping trade barriers. It is difficult for most governments to monitor or tax services exchanged via the internet. For products and services ordered online but delivered physically, governments should theoretically be able to catch these at the frontier customs; yet, in practice, most governments miss a high volume of relatively low-value items.

Therefore, the internet has provided firms with several opportunities when it comes to global strategy development. It offers global market participation, enables firms comparatively easy routes to global marketing, allows firms to be both global and local, reduces the need to have local physical presence and enables the pooling of expertise online.

Source: Adapted from Yip (2000)

Forces for regional or global integration include economies of scale and scope, which require standardization and coordination of the MNE's foreign operations to reap global or regional cost efficiencies. On the other hand, pressures for responsiveness are driven by national or regional differences in consumer preferences, culture, institutions, and so forth, which require tailoring or adapting the MNE's activities to each country or regional environment with the aim of increasing customer value. Hence, while the benefits of integration are primarily cost-based, the benefits of responsiveness are primarily revenue-based (allowing differentiation to reach customer niches).

A strategy development toolset that guides managers in deciding upon their strategic set-up is the integration-responsiveness (IR) framework either in its classic (see Bartlett and Ghoshal, 2000) or extended version (see Verbeke and Asmussen, 2016), which relates to industry pressures or forces for integration (regionally or globally) and pressures or forces for responsiveness (see Figure 5.9). That is, the IR framework helps managers to map their strategic options given prevailing pressures for adaptation to local needs and global standardization in their industries, maximizing economies of scale (EOS) and reducing duplication, thus achieving efficiency.

In some industries global forces dominate, and firms in those industries can sustain competitive advantages only if they are present in the key markets of the world, and/or if they integrate and coordinate their activities worldwide in a centralized fashion. In these industries/segments, customers demand highly standardized products and expect global delivery of products and services, uniform characteristics of global pricing, and so on. In global industries, the customers and competitors are typically also operating worldwide: Global customers operate with centralized and highly standardized procurement, and the competitors in global industries have strong competitive positions in all important geographical markets and segments. Examples of global industries are civil aircraft, microprocessors, container shipping and bulk chemicals. In these industries MNEs are encouraged to follow a global strategy that maximizes global EOS and provides customers with worldwide competitive and standardized products that meet universal needs.

Other industries are characterized by almost purely local forces on both the demand and supply sides. Local industries are industries in which firms can sustain competitive advantages within the boundaries of nations/countries. Firms operating in multi-local industries may either be domestic firms within each country or MNE subsidiaries operating independently of each other in the respective countries. Food, car repair, business services (for example, business lawyers) and personal care are examples of local/domestic industries. A strong pressure to respond locally, and to generate EOS on a national level, encourages MNEs to adopt a multinational strategy with locally adapted products and processes.

Furthermore, there are industries that are characterized by a mixture of global and local forces. In industries such as telecommunication equipment and pharmaceuticals, both global and local forces dominate simultaneously. Hence, competitiveness cannot be achieved without achieving the benefits of global coordination and scale economies and, at the same time, creating local market proximity (for example, distribution), closeness and local customization (for

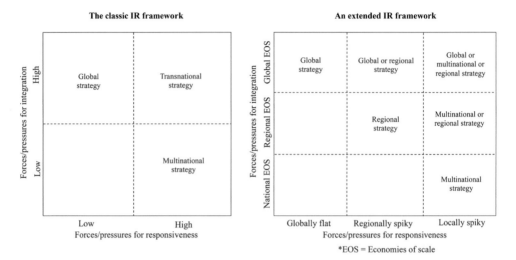

Source: Adapted from Verbeke and Asmussen (2016)

Figure 5.9 The IR framework

example, adapt to legal or health requirements, and local product standards; see for instance Castillo Apraiz et al., 2020)). If the MNE faces both high forces for integration and responsiveness, a transnational strategy may be appropriate (as outlined in the classic IR framework). The transnational strategy is a balanced strategy, where the MNE examines the "tensions" or "trade-offs" between global integration and local responsiveness and often "mixes" local and global strategy elements in a normative and practical way. For example, global product standardization (that is, the MNE produces one standardized product for the global market) is combined with different marketing/distribution strategies tailored to the nations in which the MNE operates, and local adaptation within part of the marketing mix (for example, pricing, packaging and labeling).

In the literature, it has often been debated what strategic orientation MNEs follow, and empirically it has been difficult to find evidence for a general spread of the global strategy and transnational strategy. A strong school of thought argues that most industries are not global but regional. Rugman (2005) argues that most businesses by MNEs take place in regional blocks. Box 5.2 presents empirical evidence on whether MNEs follow regional or global strategies.

> **Box 5.2   Further insights: Regional or global strategies of MNEs**
>
> A team of researchers around Professor Alan Rugman has brought to the forefront the assertion that "global" companies are, in fact, regional in nature. Studying the 2002 Fortune Global 500 firms, which account for over 90 percent of the world's stock of foreign direct investment, they identified four types of MNEs: home-region-oriented (that is, at least 50 percent of the MNE's sales are concentrated in the home region), bi-regional-oriented (less than 50 percent of the MNE's sales are in the home region, and at least 20 percent in another region of the Triad – North America, Europe and Asia), host-region-oriented (the MNE must have more than 50 percent of its sales in a host region of the Triad), and global-oriented (the MNE has at least 20 percent of its sales in each of the three Triad regions, but less than 50 percent of its sales in any of the three regions).
>
> As given in the table below, a majority of the MNEs were home-region-oriented (88 percent), while only a few had a global orientation (3 percent), suggesting that much work on corporate globalization is normative, rather than accurately describing reality (Rugman and Verbeke, 2004). Based on equivalent data for the 2017 Fortune Global 500 list, a study by Rosa, Gugler and Verbeke (2020) confirms that many MNEs are still home-region-oriented, but to a lesser extent than before, with 9 percent having a global orientation. Studies demonstrate that these orientations have relevant implications for the performance of MNEs (see for instance Richter, 2007)
>
> | | 2002 | | 2017 | |
> | --- | --- | --- | --- | --- |
> | Geographic orientation | Number of MNEs | % of MNEs | Number of MNEs | % of MNEs |
> | Global | 9 | 3 | 36 | 9 |
> | Home-regional | 320 | 88 | 286 | 74 |
> | Bi-regional | 25 | 7 | 39 | 10 |
> | Host-regional | 11 | 3 | 25 | 7 |
> | No data/insufficient data | 135 | - | 118 | - |
> | Total | 500 | 100 | 500 | 100 |
>
> Examples of global-oriented MNEs are: Royal Dutch Shell, Daimler, BMW Group, Trafigura Group (all Europe); Apple, IBM, Procter & Gamble, United Technologies, Coca-Cola (North America); Hyundai Motor (Yen), Kia Motors, Lenovo Group, Canon and Mizuho Financial (Asia).

Hence, there are industries in which regional forces dominate due to geographical and cultural proximity, combined with growing market attractiveness and fewer trade barriers (for example, the EU market). The proliferation of regional drivers implies that firms seek to develop regional products and services (that is, identify common denominators across local consumer preferences within the region) and market these via regional brands, regional key accounts and regional distribution centers. Examples of regional industries are the automotive and brewing industries. In industries where both forces for responsiveness and integration are regional, a purely regional strategy is optimal. In this case, no substantial scale or scope economies are gained by standardizing beyond the level of regions, and little is gained by adaptation below the regional level (that is, to different countries within each region). Hence, a single nation will be too small to allow cost-efficient production, but the region is large enough for achieving a minimum efficient scale. A regional strategy can be viewed either as a "halfway house" between a multinational and global strategy or as a transition post-globalization to regionalization. In the latter case, a new view of globalization can be interpreted to be a collection of regional strategies. This is most evident in the automotive industry, where the largest manufacturers have abandoned global strategies in favor of regional structures (including regional competition and consolidation across regions). Hence, regionalization can be viewed as an optimal strategy, whereby firms effectively balance responsiveness to local markets with the integration benefits of control. Likewise, a regional strategy may also be an optimal response to the extremes of both forces for global integration and local responsiveness: Even if there are local responsiveness pressures within each region, the regional approach can improve the firm-level response to these pressures, because it will at least accommodate inter-regional differences. Similarly, even if there are global EOS to be reaped, a regional strategy can improve integration by obtaining at least a significant part of the EOS.

In his textbook, Lasserre (2018) offers a list of questions that can assist in identifying the forces for either integration or responsiveness in an industry. In Table 5.8, we provide an adapted version of his questionnaire. The first eight questions represent the forces for integration, while the remaining questions represent the forces for localization. To identify the importance of the forces you can sum up the points in questions 1 to 8 and divide the total by 8, which provides the strength of integration forces (the higher the value the higher the forces); if you sum up the points in questions 9 to 14 and divide the total by 6, this provides the strength of localization forces. You can use these scores to map the business in a matrix, in which a score of 3 constitutes the average.

The book's website offers an Excel tool to perform the relevant calculations automatically. To exercise this, we encourage you to assess the strength of forces for integration and localization for a producer and retailer of furniture, such as IKEA. Following on from your analysis, which strategic set-up would you recommend to the management of IKEA?

Table 5.8 Positioning a business on the IR framework

N	Question	1 point	5 points	Points
	Forces for integration; to what extent …			Σ(Q1:Q8) / 8
1	Do customers have similar demands for functionality and design across countries?	Very different	Very similar	
2	Do products and services have a high proportion of standard components across countries?	Low proportion	High proportion	
3	Are customers/distributors themselves operating in different countries and buying centrally your products or services?	Buying locally	Buying centrally	
4	Are significant EOS in your industry important for the product cost (that is, are high volumes needed to obtain low costs)?	Not so important	Very important	
5	Is the speed of introducing new products worldwide important for competitiveness?	Not so important	Very important	
6	Are the sales of your product or service based on technical or cultural factors?	Highly cultural	Highly technical	
7	Can experience gained in other countries be successfully applied in other countries?	Cannot be applied	Can be applied to a huge extent	
8	Do competitors in your industry operate in a standardized way across countries, and are they successful in doing so?	Competitors are localizing	Competitors are standardizing	
	Forces for responsiveness; to what extent …			Σ(Q9:Q14) / 6
9	Can pricing be different from country to country without introducing dysfunctionalities?	It has to be consistent	It can be very different	
10	Does distribution channel management differ from country to country?	Not so different	Very different	
11	Do business regulations and contexts differ from country to country, requiring big differences in local practices?	Not too different	Highly different	
12	Do products or services require a high degree of customization to customers?	Low customization	High customization	
13	Are transportation costs high compared to the product costs?	Not so high	Very high	
14	Is the customer interface critical for success?	Not critical	Very critical	

Source: Adapted from Lasserre (2018)

5.3 MONITORING STRATEGIC SUCCESS

A good strategy and positioning should lead to superior firm performance, while a poor positioning leads to inferior performance. To monitor strategic success, we need to measure firm performance. This is usually done with reference to accounting-based financial performance indicators (see Hult et al., 2008). Most common are profitability ratios, such as the return on sales, return on assets and return on equity.

Table 5.9 Overview of selected performance indicators to understand, monitor and benchmark strategic success

Indicator	Formula	Meaning
Return on sales (ROS)	Net income / sales; alternatively: EBIT / sales	How well the firm is producing profits from sales
Return on assets (ROA)	Net income / assets; alternatively: EBIT / assets	How well the firm is producing profits from its assets
Return on equity (ROE)	Net income / equity; alternatively: EBIT / equity	How well the firm is producing profits from its equity
Sales per employee	Sales / number of employees	The productivity of the labor force
Administration intensity; alternatively: sales and administration intensity	Administration costs / sales; alternatively: SGA / sales	How much of sales the firm spends on administration (and sales)
R&D intensity	R&D costs / sales	How much of sales the firm spends on research and development
Inventory turnover	Sales / average inventory; alternatively: COGS / average inventory	The number of times the inventory is sold or used in a time period
Average days to sell inventory	365 days / inventory turnover	The average number of days to sell the inventory
Asset turnover	Sales / average total assets	How efficient the firm is at using its assets to generate sales
Receivable turnover	Sales / average accounts receivable	How efficient the firm is at collecting accounts receivable
Debt to equity	Total debts / total equity	The (risk, leverage in the) capital structure
Debt ratio	Total debts / total assets	The percentage of a firm's assets that are financed by debts
Market-to-book ratio or price-to-book ratio	(Stock price × number of shares) / total stockholders' equity	The market valuation of a firm relative to its book value
Price–earnings (PE) ratio	Stock price / EPS	The firm's share price relative to its earnings per share

Note: Average X = (beginning X + ending X) / 2; COGS = cost of goods sold; EBIT = earnings before interest and taxes; EPS = profit / outstanding shares; SGA = selling, general and administrative expenses.

Table 5.9 provides an overview of financial performance indicators. These ratios are usually used for benchmarking purposes; that is, comparing your own performance with the performance of competitors in specific markets or in specific business segments. For instance, the return on sales provides information on how much of the firm's sales is converted into profits. Further ratios assist in understanding the efficiency and drivers of profitability: The productivity of the labor force can be assessed by looking at the sales per employee. Furthermore, it may be of interest to understand the administration intensity and research and development intensity of your firm in relation to other players in the market (that is, how much of your sales do you spend on administrative overheads and how much do you invest into exploring new options). Furthermore, you may look at inventory turnover. Inventory turnover indicates the number of times the inventory is sold or used in a certain period and can be used to calculate the average number of days to sell the inventory. Then, the asset turnover and receivables turnover are interesting to look at: The asset turnover measures how well the firm leverages its assets, such as property, plant and equipment to generate sales, and the receivables turnover measures the efficiency in collecting accounts receivable. From a financial perspective, you may complement the analysis by indicators that look at the capital structure (for example, the debt-to-equity ratio and the debt ratio).

All of the ratios given in Table 5.9 are based on income statements and balance sheets facilitating their use for benchmarking; that is, an assessment of the relative profitability and competitive performance. Practitioners and academics have criticized them for being backwards-looking, as they refer to historical data and with their focus on accounting information neglect intangible values (for example, see Gallagher and Andrew, 2003; Richter et al., 2017). In addition to accounting-based indicators, there are several indicators that relate to shareholders. From this perspective, two further aspects often come into play: risk, and a more forwards-looking assessment of the firm's performance that also accounts for intangible resources and is reflected in the market price of the firm's stock.

As regards risks, the assumption is that riskier investments should yield higher returns. Hence, performance is understood as the risk-adjusted return and expressed as the excess return over a benchmark return yielded per unit of risk taken. This is referred to as the Sharpe Measure (see below). The total shareholder return (R_i) is defined as the increase of investor capital, in terms of stock prices and dividend payments in relation to the capital employed (that is, amount spent on shares at the beginning of the period). Potential benchmark returns (R_f) are the returns investors demand from investments which bear no risk, such as certain government bonds and returns reflected in stock-market indices. As regards risk, the Sharpe Measure refers to the standard deviation of the annual rate of return as a measure of risk (σ_i) in order to indicate the volatility of returns. The Sharpe Measure is often provided for firms traded via stock markets and is more commonly used for evaluating investment options than for pure benchmarking. Comparing the investments in two international firms according to their Sharpe Measures, investors are advised to invest in the firm with the higher ratio, because it yields more return for the same risk.

$$Sharpe\ Measure = \frac{R_i - R_f}{\sigma_i}$$

The market price of the firm's stock is supposed to reflect all available information about a firm's past, current and future performance. In evaluating competitive advantage, a comparison of a competitor's share price development and market capitalization is useful. The market capitalization captures the total market value of a firm's outstanding shares at a given point in time. For instance, if a firm has 10 million shares outstanding, and each share is traded at USD 120, the market capitalization is USD 1.2 billion. Firms can be benchmarked against a competitor from the industry (or to a broader market index, if the firm is more diversified). A disadvantage of stock-market indicators is that they are more volatile in the short term and involve effects that may be caused by irrational moods/actions of investors. Hence, the market price is often less objective than expected.

Box 5.3 presents an example of input data that can be used for benchmarking. Think of how you would evaluate these numbers if you were among the management team of Firm A. Box 5.4 at the end of this section provides a benchmarking scenario that was developed by a manager in Firm A and presents the actions taken by the top management team. Develop your own approach first, before you explore Box 5.4.

Box 5.3   Exercise: Input data that can be used for benchmarking

Firm A has collected the following financial indicators for four competitors. It entered the market later than all the competitors in the market and focused on achieving growth in the last few years.

	Firm A	Competitor 1	Competitor 2	Competitor 3	Competitor 4
Income statement	USD (1,000s)	USD (1,000s)	USD (1,000s)	USD (1,000s)	USD (1,000s)
Sales	$4,286.28	$1,837.86	$19,512.01	$26,745.05	$62,157.61
Cost of goods	$2,906.41	$1,267.30	$13,885.72	$5,627.38	$51,057.38
Gross margin (GM)	$1,379.86	$570.56	$5,626.29	$21,117.67	$11,100.23
SGA	$839.92	$261.27	$3,179.91	$12,840.97	$7,510.45
thereof: R&D	$270.38	$88.35	$714.85	$3,917.61	$3,270.03
EBIT	$539.94	$309.29	$2,446.38	$8,276.70	$3,589.78
Taxes, interest, and so on	$40.44	$84.81	$308.50	$2,568.17	$952.70
Net income	$499.50	$224.48	$2,137.89	$5,708.53	$2,637.08
Balance sheet	USD (1,000s)	USD (1,000s)	USD (1,000s)	USD (1,000s)	USD (1,000s)
Cash, and cash equivalents	$429.63	$58.26	$10,120.11	$7,767.76	$6,392.39
Accounts receivable	$749.25	$329.13	$1,253.25	$6,165.16	$5,660.66
Inventory	$347.45	$237.04	$270.27	$2,252.25	$8,113.11
Other current assets	$304.30	$60.36	$2,879.88	$767.77	$2,839.84
Property, plant and equipment	$759.20	$558.00	$1,581.00	$7,753.00	$7,975.00
Other non-current assets	$1,818.00	$888.80	$1,115.00	$5,243.00	$20,836.00
Total assets	$4,407.83	$2,131.58	$17,219.51	$29,948.94	$51,816.98
Accounts payable	$350.35	$160.76	$3,393.39	$3,485.48	$16,217.20
Other short-term liabilities	$1,289.39	$320.62	$3,084.08	$5,970.97	$13,513.50
Non-current liabilities	$864.10	$683.30	$750.00	$5,181.00	$17,354.00
Total liabilities	$2,503.84	$1,164.68	$7,227.47	$14,637.45	$47,084.70
Equity	$1,903.99	$966.90	$9,992.04	$15,311.49	$4,732.28
Total liabilities and equity	$4,407.83	$2,131.58	$17,219.51	$29,948.94	$51,816.98
Further information					
Number of employees	16,100	10,500	17,780	66,750	154,200
Market capitalization (in USD 1,000s)	$8,038.73	$4,677.37	$135,845.51	$76,831.76	$83,508.32
P/E ratio	16.8	25.8	68.5	17.6	38.0
Five-year sales growth, CAGR*	5.7	4.5	7.9	4.1	2.2
Five-year net income growth, CAGR*	10.2	6.5	21.1	7.3	-2.0

Think of:

1. What would be the 10 key ratios that you would look at as a manager of Firm A to benchmark your performance?
2. Would you benchmark Firm A to all competitors given above, or only to specific ones? What are further ideas to make the benchmarking more specific?
3. How do you interpret the numbers in your key ratios, and what recommendations can you derive from these numbers?

* To calculate a compound annual growth rate (CAGR), you can use the following formula:

$$CAGR = \left(\frac{EV}{BV}\right)^{\frac{1}{n}} - 1$$

where: EV is the value at the end of the period (for example, after five years), BV is the value at the beginning of the period (for example, at the beginning of the first year), and n is the number of years (for example, five).

There are further performance perspectives that can likewise assist a more forwards-looking assessment of the firm's performance. Commonly used are (i) operational performance measures that cover the determinants of success that might lead to financial performance, such as product-market outcomes (market share, new product introduction and product quality) and internal process outcomes (such as employee satisfaction and process quality); and (ii) overall effectiveness measures that represent a wider conceptualization of performance involving indicators such as reputation, survival and achievement of goals.

A concept that aims to broaden the focus to these wider perspectives is the "balanced scorecard." A balanced scorecard summarizes multiple internal and external performance metrics that go beyond financial metrics. Managers using the balanced scorecard develop metrics that can be used to measure and monitor the progress on the strategic objectives outlined. Hence, the balanced scorecard can be customized to measuring the key aspects of relevance to the firm and its management. In light of the social responsibility imperative in many markets, an updated version of the balanced scorecard was recently proposed that suggests broadening the focus from shareholders to stakeholders and takes into account the fact that social and environmental aspects gained relevance in the last years (Kaplan and McMillan, 2020). It recommends designing key performance indicators (KPIs) around four categories of metrics: The first category is called "outcomes." It comprises financial, environmental and societal performance indicators. The latter two may include indicators that measure usage of energy, usage of water, waste reduction, amount of recycled materials used, reduction in packaging and transportation costs, donations to local schools and higher quality of life for local residents (for example, higher household incomes, improved health, reduced inequality). The second category (formerly called "customers") is (now) called "stakeholders" (that is, how do stakeholders such as customers, employees and suppliers view the firm and its offering). The idea is that there may be firms whose value proposition not only focuses on its customers, but also on the interests of stakeholders (for example, it may involve aspects such as maximizing the use of public resources or optimizing the harvesting conditions of a product in a certain market; see the example in Kaplan and McMillan, 2020). The third category is called the "internal process perspective" and looks at the key competencies and activities that are needed to achieve the firm's objectives. The fourth and final category is called the "enablers' perspective" and concerns how we ensure long-term future competitiveness; for instance, via coordinating across stakeholders, building good leadership and organizational structures.

Managers who have formulated a strategy statement and have implemented their strategic objectives, segments and value propositions into a business model canvas have the relevant input information to start developing relevant KPIs. To be able to monitor progress or performance on these objectives, they will need to engage in specifying the relevant metrics that fit their individual situations. As the two toolsets were developed independently of each other, the categories do not 100 percent fit, yet an assignment of the canvas categories to a balanced scorecard is possible (see the example in Figure 5.10).

Firms are free to design their own scorecard dimensions. The dimensions in the business model canvas and in the balanced scorecard approach assist, however, in covering all relevant aspects. Consulting practice stresses the need to select KPIs that are able to measure facets and goals formulated in the strategy statement (see, for example, PricewaterhouseCoopers, 2007). Consultants observe that many managers still focus too much on financial performance indicators even though their strategies may enforce measures that more directly measure the fulfillment of strategic objectives. For instance, if the strategic focus is on maximizing customer experience, customer metrics may offer a more direct measurement of success. Also, KPIs depend on the industry; for instance, a retailer may be interested in sales per square foot and customer satisfaction as KPIs. The number of KPIs used depends on the firm, its strategy, its industry and the number of segments (that may need individual reporting), yet consulting experience demonstrates that between four and 10 measures offer a good picture. In designing a list of KPIs or a balanced scorecard, we recommend explaining why you believe that a certain indicator is of relevance (in addition to the relevant calculation details). The example in Figure 5.10 should assist in designing your own scorecard.

DEVELOPING STRATEGY AND STRATEGIC POSITIONING

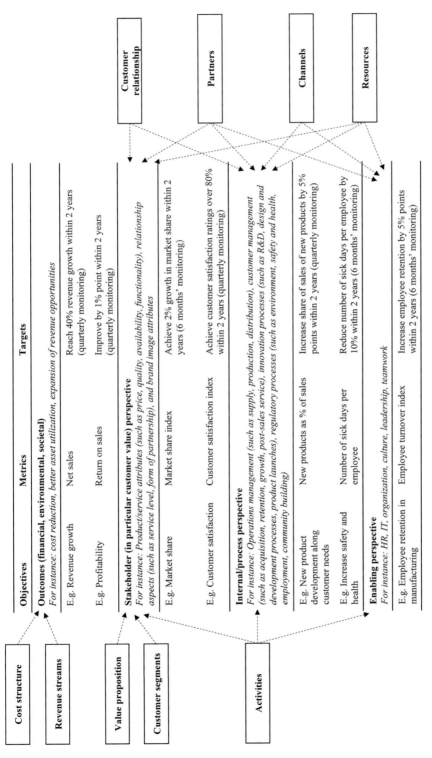

Figure 5.10 Example of a balanced scorecard

Box 5.4 Exercise: A benchmarking scenario developed by a manager of Firm A

The manager of Firm A selected and calculated 10 ratios given below in italics (the table provides further ratios that assist you in comparing it to your own approach). The manager compared the performance of Firm A against three benchmarks: first, the average ratios for all competitors (*Average comp.*); second, against Competitor 2, who is comparable in size (*Number of employees*); and third, against the top competitor on each indicator (*Top score/player per indicator*).

Benchmarking indicators (selected by the manager of Firm A)	Firm A	Competitor 1	Competitor 2	Competitor 3	Competitor 4	Average comp.	Top score/player per indicator	
Five-year sales growth, CAGR	5.7	4.5	7.9	4.1	2.2	4.7	7.9	2
GM / sales	32.2%	31.0%	28.8%	79.0%	17.9%	39.2%	79.0%	3
EBIT / sales	12.6%	16.8%	12.5%	30.9%	5.8%	16.5%	30.9%	3
ROS	11.7%	12.2%	11.0%	21.3%	4.2%	12.2%	21.3%	3
ROE	26.2%	23.2%	21.4%	37.3%	55.7%	34.4%	55.7%	4
ROA	11.3%	10.5%	12.4%	19.1%	5.1%	11.8%	19.1%	3
Speed (asset turnover, proxy)	1.0	0.9	1.1	0.9	1.2	1.0	1.2	4
Revenue / employees	$266	$175	$1,097	$401	$403	$519	$1,097	2
GM / employees	$86	$54	$316	$316	$72	$190	$316	2
EBIT / employees	$34	$29	$138	$124	$23	$79	$138	2
R&D / sales	6.3%	4.8%	3.7%	14.6%	5.3%	7.1%	14.6%	3
SGA / sales	19.6%	14.2%	16.3%	48.0%	12.1%	22.7%	12.1%	4
Receivable turnover (proxy)	5.7	5.6	15.6	4.3	11.0	9.1	15.6	2
Inventory turnover (proxy)	8.4	5.3	51.4	2.5	6.3	16.4	51.4	2
Inventory days	43.6	68.3	7.1	146.1	58.0	69.9	7.1	2
Market-to-book value	4.2	4.8	13.6	5.0	17.6	10.3	17.6	4

Firm A's growth strategy worked out well: its sales are growing comparatively stronger than the market; yet Competitor 2 showed an even stronger CAGR. It has a lower intensity of SGA expenses than its competitors, yet again has invested more than Competitor 2. This may point to a well-channeled marketing budget and a reasonable administrative structure. Profitability is an issue of concern: Firm A remains below average with regard to EBIT/sales, ROS and ROA and far below the profitability of Competitor 3 (who demonstrates outstanding results). This may be triggered by a more unfavorable cost structure or comparably low prices. Likewise, labor productivity is an issue. Firm A is far from achieving the productivity ratios of competitors, which may be triggered by its relative newness in the market, and/or by relatively lower price levels (induced by the focus on growth).

In addition, it presents a non-optimal number of days in inventory especially compared to Competitor 2. Also, the receivables turnover points to improvement potential: Firm A is less efficient in collecting accounts receivables than its competitors. Looking at the market ratios, it is a clear under-performer; the stock market does not acknowledge that it may have a good growth rate, and seems to not trust in its future performance in contrast to values presented for Competitor 2 and Competitor 4.

The following actions were taken by the managers: (i) They initiated an assessment of price levels with regard to potential price increases; (ii) they advised the marketing and corporate communication departments to evaluate recent communication activities with regard to increasing the perceived value of both the firm itself and the products and services offered; (iii) they initiated an evaluation of employee productivity – instead of thinking about workforce reduction, they put a focus on training needs, system support and process improvements, and in this context they advised identifying lessons to be learned from competitors on the organization of the supply chain; and (iv) they advised the accounting department to assess options to shorten customer credit and to put more pressure on customers to adhere to the payment terms agreed.

5.4 STRATEGIC POSITIONING AND STRATEGY AT IKEA

The strategic positioning and the adoption of successful international strategies is a challenging task and even big players with a good portfolio of experiences in international markets face difficulties to successfully implement procedures in various markets. If you have used the grid provided in Table 5.8, you may have encountered the difficulties in assessing international forces for integration and responsiveness. We will demonstrate the practical challenges in identifying the best positioning in international markets by looking at some of the moves and learnings at IKEA (the following is based on information published in business magazines, IKEA reports, information generated in interviews with IKEA managers, and analyses provided in Jonsson and Foss, 2011, and Johansson and Thelander, 2009).

IKEA was founded in 1943 by Ingvar Kamprad. Using the initials of his name, his parent's farm and his hometown, he opened the first IKEA store in Sweden in 1958. Today, IKEA is among the world's largest furniture retailers with 463 outlets and business activities in more than 50 markets (per 2021). It is a privately held company owned by the Stichting INGKA Foundation registered in the Netherlands that is effectively controlled by the Kamprad family.

The early internationalization of IKEA was characterized by an exploratory trial and error process with moves to Norway (1963) and Denmark (1969), followed by Switzerland (1973) and Germany (1974). During the late 1970s IKEA entered Japan. This was (as with several of the earlier internationalization moves) less a strategic selection of the market, but an unplanned move: An export department started to sell IKEA products to firms in Japan, which then sold IKEA products at high prices in small IKEA corners in big malls. This conflicted with the management's idea of IKEA's positioning. The top management was dissatisfied with the lack of control over these activities, which ultimately led to a full withdrawal from the Japanese market in the 1970s. As a result, IKEA created a special unit, Inter IKEA Systems, that was from then on responsible for controlling internationalization activities. In addition, it triggered management efforts to further conceptualize the IKEA business idea for IB and led to a homogenization of the IKEA product offering and store concepts across countries. The following internationalization moves were characterized by replication and the idea to realize cost efficiencies from exploiting EOS. The replication was based on IKEA values and beliefs codified in an internal statement called *Testament of a Furniture Dealer* that was later extended. Hence, the focus shifted to a fully standardized approach or global strategy with standardized store formats (in blue and yellow, the Swedish national colors), uniform promotion and product ranges, following the notion "we shall be one IKEA, one business idea and one culture" expressed by Ingvar Kamprad (Jonsson and Foss, 2011). Efforts became fully concentrated at the headquarters and the management saw no need to learn from subsidiaries.

The full replication of one positioning or value proposition to various international markets (that is, the global strategy model) induced several failures. In the US market, for instance, IKEA suffered from not adapting to the needs of the American customer for bigger beds and kitchen cabinets. Therefore, IKEA shifted towards what was called a "flexible replication" that mixed elements of global standardization and national responsiveness. This involved the realization that IKEA stores all over the world needed to carry a core product range (for example, the Billy bookcase), so that EOS could be realized and the IKEA brand could be recognized all over the world.

IKEA's global positioning involves being an affordable vendor that offers products that are functional and come for relatively low prices. In addition, more recently, sustainability has been added as a core value; that is, products, production and distribution should be as sustainable as possible. IKEA's store format and design follow a fixed format or traffic flow with a selection of furniture being displayed in roomlike settings, and a self-service warehouse section offering ready-to-assemble furniture. The operating procedures at IKEA are standardized and codified with several manuals detailing procedures, and expatriates being sent to local markets to ensure that these standards are kept. As an element of local adaptation, local managers were allowed to add products to the offering in their markets. Yet, further market responsiveness turned out to be essential.

In 1998 IKEA opened its first store in Shanghai and faced several challenges in its internationalization to China that were induced by its positioning in the market. IKEA's formulated vision was to "create a better everyday life for many people" and its value proposition was to "offer a wider range of well-designed, functional home-furnishing products at prices so low that as many people as possible will be able to afford them." The target customer was defined as earning a low to middle income. This worked well in many European countries and further markets that were entered previously. However, this value proposition clashed with the Chinese perception of IKEA's product offering, which caused confusion in the market. Prices seen as low in Europe and North America were considered high by Chinese consumers. Customer surveys demonstrated that IKEA was thought to target the middle to high income classes in China. In addition, IKEA's products were considered high-end. Following its global strategy, IKEA also followed sustainability values in China and implemented several environmentally friendly measures. However, Chinese consumers seemed to be annoyed when asked to pay extra for plastic bags, and they did not want to bring their own shopping bags. Also,

Table 5.10 Selected differences in the positioning of IKEA between Europe and China

	Europe	China
Value proposition	Stylish, functional Sustainable furniture	Good quality Western-styled furniture
Product and service offering	Self-pick-up and self-assembly (yet with recent moves to offer more assembly services)	Self-pick-up and self-assembly yet heavily supported by delivery and assembly services offered
Pricing	Low-cost	Affordable
Target group	Low and middle classes (everybody)	Well educated, middle class (white collar)
Store, logistics and operations	Suburban stores next to highways City center stores to reach younger, urban shoppers Sourcing from developing nations (for example, China, Malaysia) and shipping to Europe	Outskirt stores next to rail networks City center stores to reach younger, urban shoppers Local sourcing and factories to avoid import taxes

most suppliers in China did not have the technologies that were necessary to provide products that met IKEA's green standards. The store design that invited customers to feel comfortable in the roomlike settings induced several incidents involving beds being occupied with customers actually sleeping in them and families who felt so at home in the dining rooms that they started to eat in there. Finally, also the pick-up concept created challenges, as the majority of Chinese customers did not have a car, and self-assembly was not something that was appealing to customers in China.

In fact, for the first 10 years after entering China, IKEA remained unprofitable in this market and was unable to achieve a competitive advantage. To create a competitive advantage and resolve the profitability problems, IKEA needed to make several strategic adjustments in China. This included a strong repositioning and a quest for lower prices (see Table 5.10 for an overview of differences in the positioning of IKEA in Europe and China). IKEA changed its target group in China to young, middle-class professionals, who are well-educated singles or families with a double income. This new target segment was open to a Western lifestyle, which was advantageous for a Western brand. Thereby, IKEA needed to reposition its brand, especially promoting the Western style, which was a long-term process in China. Furthermore, IKEA needed to work on its pricing. Low prices had always been a key factor of success at IKEA, yet in the Chinese market its prices were higher than those of local competitors. Hence, IKEA took several moves (in particular, local sourcing) towards lowering its price levels, and reduced prices by about 60 percent between 2000 and 2018. These price cuts did not allow it to fully follow up on the sustainability positioning, as the market and suppliers did not offer the relevant technologies. Assisting them to adopt these technologies would have meant higher costs, which was not perceived to be an option in the market. In addition, IKEA offered further home delivery options and started to offer a fee-based assembly service. Store locations were planned close to railway stations. As for the product range, IKEA introduced several localized products to attract more Chinese consumers. For instance, it offered a stronger variety of balcony furniture, as many houses in China have balconies, or hallway furniture, as it is common for a Chinese house to have a hallway leading to the living room. As regards the level of comfort in the in-store room settings, IKEA does not seem to have found a standard: In 2015, a Beijing IKEA store used loudspeaker broadcasts to ask customers to not fall asleep on the beds or occupy sofas for too long, yet media reports show that IKEA's management often accepts that many Chinese customers visit the stores to take a nap.

The above adjustments turned out to be successful around 2017. Sales demonstrated good growth rates of about 14 percent, and IKEA turned profitable and has been growing its China business further. Now, it aims to use the experience gained in China when it comes to becoming successful in further emerging markets (such as India).

CHAPTER REVIEW QUESTIONS

1. What is referred to as the "sweet spot" in strategy development? And what are three key toolsets that can assist you in identifying a sweet spot in a market?
2. What is meant by the term "economic value added" (EVA)?
3. What are the two fundamental/generic business strategies? Can you provide examples of firms following the two strategic alternatives?
4. What are the relevant process steps in developing a good strategic positioning in a market? What are key toolsets that can assist you in this endeavor?
5. How can you identify a firm's core competencies?
6. Discuss relevant best practices in performing a SWOT analysis.
7. Discuss the idea of jobs to be done. Do you think that this is of value for managers? If so, where do you see the strengths and weaknesses of the concept?
8. How do you evaluate if a firm has developed a strong positioning in a market?
9. What is the IR framework and how can you make use of it in developing an international strategy?
10. Discuss how the digitalization trend may influence the development of international positionings?
11. What is a balanced scorecard?
12. If you were to develop a balanced scorecard for a furniture retailer (such as IKEA), which indicators would you include?

NOTE

1. Revlon company information, available at: www.revloninc.com/our-company/our-founders.php.

REFERENCES

Baraldi, E., Brennan, R., Harrison, D., Tunisini, A., and Zolkiewski, J. (2007). Strategic thinking and the IMP approach: A comparative analysis. *Industrial Marketing Management*, 36, 879–894.

Barney, J. (1991). Firm resources and sustained competitive advantage. *Journal of Management*, 17, 99–120.

Barney, J. B., and Hesterly, W. S. (2015). *Strategic Management and Competitive Advantage*. Boston, MA: Pearson.

Bartlett, C. A., and Ghoshal, S. (2000). *Transnational Management: Text, Cases and Reading in Cross-Border Management* (3rd ed.). Boston, MA: McGraw Hill.

Bresser, R. K. F., and Powalla, C. (2012). Practical implications of the resource-based view: Assessing the predictive power of the VRIO-framework. *Zeitschrift für Betriebswirtschaft*, 82, 335–359.

Castillo Apraiz, J., Richter, N. F., Matey de Antonio, J., and Gudergan, S. P. (2020). The role of competitive strategy in the performance impact of exploitation and exploration quality management practices. *European Business Review*, 33, 127–153.

Christensen, C. M., Hall, T., Dillon, K., and Duncan, D. S. (2016). Know your customers' "jobs to be done." *Harvard Business Review*, September 2016, 54–62.

Collis, D. J., and Rukstad, M. G. (2008). Can you say what your strategy is? *Harvard Business Review*, April 2008, 82–90.

Coman, A., and Ronen, B. (2009). Focused SWOT: Diagnosing critical strengths and weaknesses. *International Journal of Production Research*, 47, 5677–5689.

Crook, T. R., Ketchen, D. J., Combs, J. G., and Todd, S. Y. (2008). Strategic resources and performance: A meta-analysis. *Strategic Management Journal*, 29, 1141–1154.

European Fruit Juice Association (2018). *2018 Liquid Fruit Market Report*. Brussels: AIJN.

Fossas, D. (2016). Developing your market positioning. Linkedin. www.linkedin.com/pulse/marketing-mondays-developing-your-market-positioning-david-fossas.

Freytag, P. V., and Clarke, A. H. (2001). Business to business market segmentation. *Industrial Marketing Management*, 30, 473–486.

Gallagher, T. J., and Andrew, J. D. (2003). *Financial Management: Principles and Practice* (3rd ed.). Upper Saddle River, NJ: Prentice Hall.

Hill, T., and Westbrook, R. (1997). SWOT analysis: It's time for a product recall. *Long Range Planning*, 30, 46–52.

Hollensen, S. (2020). *Global Marketing* (8th ed.). Harlow: Pearson.

Hult, G. T. M., Ketchen Jr., D. J., Griffith, D. A., Chabowski, B. R., Hamman, M. K., Dykes, B. J., … Cavusgil, S. T. (2008). An assessment of the measurement of performance in international business research. *Journal of International Business Studies*, 39, 1064–1080.

Johansson, U., and Thelander, Å. (2009). A standardised approach to the world? IKEA in China. *International Journal of Quality and Service Sciences*, 1, 199–219.

Jonsson, A., and Foss, N. J. (2011). International expansion through flexible replication: Learning from the internationalization experience of IKEA. *Journal of International Business Studies*, 42, 1079–1102.

Kaplan, R. S., and McMillan, D. (2020). Updating the Balanced Scorecard for triple bottom line strategies. *Harvard Business School Working Paper* 21–028, 1–23.

Lasserre, P. (2018). *Global Strategic Management* (4th ed.). London: Palgrave.

Osterwalder, A., Pigneur, Y., Bernarda, G., and Smith, A. (2014). *Value Proposition Design: How to Create Products and Services Customers Want*. Hoboken, NJ: John Wiley & Sons.

Porter, M. (2008). The five competitive forces that shape strategy. *Harvard Business Review*, 86, 78–93.

Richter, N. F. (2007). Intra-regional sales and the internationalization and performance relationship. In A. M. Rugman (Ed.), *Research in Global Strategic Management* (Vol. 13, pp. 359–381). Amsterdam: Elsevier.

PricewaterhouseCoopers (2007). *Guide to Key Performance Indicators: Communicating the Measures that Matter*. London: PricewaterhouseCoopers.

Richter, N. F., Schmidt, R., Ladwig, T. J., and Wulhorst, F. (2017). A critical perspective on the measurement of performance in the empirical multinationality and performance literature. *Critical Perspectives on International Business*, *13*, 94–118.

Rosa, B., Gugler, P., and Verbeke, A. (2020). Regional and global strategies of MNEs: Revisiting Rugman and Verbeke (2004). *Journal of International Business Studies*, *51*, 1045–1053.

Rugman, A. M. (2005). *The Regional Multinationals: MNEs and "Global" Strategic Management*. Cambridge: Cambridge University Press.

Rugman, A. M., and Verbeke, A. (2004). Regional transnationals and triad strategy. *Transnational Corporations*, *13*, 1–20.

Verbeke, A., and Asmussen, C. (2016). Global, local, or regional? The locus of MNE strategies. *Journal of Management Studies*, *53*, 1051–1075.

Yip, G. S. (2000). Global strategy in the internet era. *Business Strategy Review*, *11*, 1–14.

5   CASE STUDY
MAGIC JUICE: STRATEGY AND POSITIONING

A CHALLENGING PERIOD FOR MAGIC JUICE

The year 2020 was a challenging one for Magic Juice. Covid-19 hit the food service industry, including juice bars, hard and several entrepreneurs had to close down their operations. Magic Juice tried to meet the big challenges by adapting the business to the unpleasant circumstances: Juice bars were forced to stand idle for several weeks and months in Magic Juice's markets; some employees left the firm. Yet the online sales, and especially the catering business, were expanded – the Magic Healthy Food Trunk concept also kept the business running.

Dirk de Jong, the founder and inventor of Magic Juice, was positive about the future past Covid and convinced that his ideas had a fruitful future. In retrospect, he had started his business as a kind of disruptor – by breaking market boundaries and by developing a juice bar concept that had not been seen elsewhere at the time. Within just 10 years he – with funding from DCC Capital – had expanded his juice bar business to four countries. There were now 60 juice bars under the brand name of Magic Juice: 19 in the Netherlands, 18 in Germany, four in Austria, 12 in the United Kingdom, and seven in France. The performance in the various markets entered was quite diversified, and it was hard for Dirk to identify whether this was part of the set-up challenge, due to the different entry modes or maybe a result of the business model not performing equally well in the different markets. In addition to the home market, the best results seemed to be created in Germany, followed by the United Kingdom. Somewhat poorer results came from Austria and France. The accounting team has compiled a few numbers for Dirk (see Exhibit 5.1). Yet, he felt that he was missing a true overview of KPIs that would guide him in steering the international business of Magic Juice.

Magic Juice's mission had always been to make healthy living a lifestyle and not an obligation. Magic Juice's customers were healthy, quality-conscious, life-oriented people who were willing to pay a premium price for a high-end product. However, some critical questions haunted Dirk: Was the business model of Magic Juice ready for a diversity of markets? Was Magic Juice's brand properly positioned in relation to customers and competitors? And what is the influence of megatrends in food services, which Magic Juice needs to take into consideration to ensure long-term success? All of these questions came in addition to still being concerned with the potential partnership. Dirk decided that it was time to consolidate knowledge and gather thoughts and ideas.

MAGIC JUICE'S GAME-CHANGER CAMP: TOWARDS 2025

In Spring 2021, Magic Juice's "Game-Changer Camp" was held. The idea was – over three weekends in April and May – to explore and shift the juice chain's overall strategic direction towards 2025. Basic strategic issues that had not been touched upon since the firm's birth, such as its customer segmentation, value proposition and business modeling, were addressed. No discussions were sacred. Participants were the top management, the board of directors, selected senior team members and two external strategy consultants.

Joe Garcia and his marketing assistant had prepared various materials for the camp (see Exhibits 5.2-5.4). The main conclusion of a recent market analysis was, among other things, that Magic Juice's juice – in the eyes of the customers – "delivers a more intimate, inspiring atmosphere and more nutritious, better tasting products compared to its main competitors." So far, so good, but the market analysis also pointed out some weaknesses. In some markets, Magic Juice's stores were weakly positioned, which might have been caused by not being locally responsive enough to these markets (for example, different strengths of the vegan trend in European markets, differences in flavor preferences and most likely also problems with pricing). The location was also of great importance to how a juice bar performed, so the question was whether the stores' locations were best situated to serve the key customer.

At the camp, Dirk and Sofie Janssen gave various presentations. Dirk acknowledged that it was still important for customers to experience Magic Juice as a chain that served high-quality, healthy and nutritious food and drinks. From his perspective, the focus should, however, be turned away from "what is served" to "how it is served." "And that is where the employees come in," he stated. Dirk believes that Magic Juice's customers need a stronger personal experience and/or service. In his view, the Danish Joe & Juice chain has shown the way: The staff, called "juicers," are encouraged to be themselves in how they dress and talk, and even play their own music. They are encouraged to joke around, discuss the news and share their favorite albums with customers; that is, bring their personalities to work. The idea is that employee freedom fosters a strong relationship between the "juicers" and the customers. Dirk believes that Magic Juice should work on "how to develop a unique culture and environment," since "it is the ambience and the emotional factors that will differentiate us in the longer run," as he stated at the camp.

A senior executive has created his own version of the value chain proposition canvas, a toolset he read about in a newspaper. Within the juice bar category, he thinks there are four main pillars of the product/brand offerings that a firm can play around with: (i) experience – that is, weaving the product/brand into an entire experience, especially online; (ii) values – matching consumers' values on ethics, sustainability and functionality; (iii) materials – use of a novel or underused ingredient, typically but not necessarily through inclusion of natural, "free from" ingredients; and (iv) the price.

In her presentation, Sofie especially highlighted the "personalization trend" in food eating and preparation as well as the channel reinvention that is currently under development in food services. She has observed that newly established food firms have disrupted the traditional "routes to market" by building business models based on blended formats, subscription, on-demand and consumer-to-consumer. She had lately heard about a Belgian start-up company, Alberts Robots, also known as Alberts Smoothie Stations. It lets consumers create their own juice blends from a selection of 10 different fruits, either via an app or on a machine as they shop in a supermarket or take a break at work. In addition, Alberts gives users the options of connecting their calendars to its system, so that the smoothie stations will know if a user just exercised and it can ping them a suggestion for a thirst-quenching blend. At the camp, Sofie argued that Magic Juice should focus more on spreading its strong brand name on several platforms and channels, where online business is combined with the physical juice bars.

Many views and questions were addressed at the camp. One of the team members asked whether Magic Juice's main customer group was precisely defined (for example, whether vegans, super athletes and health-conscious consumers were sub-segments or belonged to the same broad target group) and whether the customer group(s) vary across the countries in which the chain operated. Another wanted to know what constituted Magic Juice as a lifestyle food brand. A strategy consultant proposed using the value proposition canvas to better understand the consumers and how their preferences fitted with the core competencies of Magic Juice.

CASE EXHIBITS

Exhibit 5.1 Magic Juice performance figures for various markets for 2019 (financial figures in EUR, millions)

Markets and key information	2019
Netherlands	
Total revenues including franchise income	9.79
Thereof: income from franchise	0
Full-time equivalent number of employees	96
Germany	
Total revenues including franchise income	8.87
Thereof: income from franchise	0
Full-time equivalent number of employees	99
Austria	
Total revenues including franchise income	0.07
Thereof: income from franchise	0.07
Full-time equivalent number of employees	0
United Kingdom	
Total revenues including franchise income	4.12
Thereof: income from franchise	0.18
Full-time equivalent number of employees	46
France	
Total revenues including franchise income	0.93
Thereof: income from franchise	0.21
Full-time equivalent number of employees	10

Exhibit 5.2 Megatrends in food and food services

Based on several market analyses from leading international marketing agencies and consultants, Joe Garcia and his staff have summarized what they consider to be the most important megatrends that Magic Juice must relate to. They pay particular attention to what is called the megatrends hierarchy in foods (see also Exhibit 5.3).

Healthy living is one of the megatrends in the industry, with the focus shifting from diets and the control of weight to good nutrition and natural wellbeing. Related to this trend, the industry experienced a growth in raw foods; that is, uncooked (not heated above 48°C) or unprocessed food that therefore still has most of its natural vitamins and minerals.

One of the core drivers in food consumption is indulgence. Yet, what actually constitutes indulgence is changing and different for different national markets: Consumers feel indulged by different products, in different occasions and on different regional areas.

A third megatrend is ethical living: This relates to vegan food as being one of the most important lifestyle movements of the 21st century. This also relates to consumption ethics involving, for instance, shopping locally (indeed, 30 percent of consumers surveyed report that they prefer shopping locally).

Furthermore, consumers' motives in food consumption go beyond possession of products; they are about experiencing the product. This relates to a higher need to engage customers; for instance, through personalization of products and diets. Consumers (especially millennials) expect products that are customized to their needs, and a personalized interaction with brands. Brands and products have to meet the requirement of fitting into fragmented, busy lives of individuals, and have to be conveniently accessible around the clock – a trend that went hand in hand with rising urbanization. In addition, firms have to present the right brand personalities that enable the consumer to differentiate himself or herself through the products consumed.

Likewise, shopping behavior is reinvented in various markets. In 2021, the traditional channels for buying food, namely supermarkets and hypermarkets, account for less than 50 percent of the trade. Especially in Western markets, business models involving subscription services and mixtures of online and offline services are demonstrating a high growth rate.

Also, market frontiers are shifting with ongoing migration trends. A forecast indicates that in 2050, one out of three consumers will be Muslim, which will influence the relevance of halal food in Western markets. Migration flows into Western markets will induce an uptick in Syrian- and Middle Eastern-inspired flavors. Also, as the disposable incomes of the Muslim-populated markets are increasing at a comparably faster rate, we will see more premium foods carrying the halal label.

Projections indicate that the household type with the strongest growth globally is the single-person household; that is, those inevitably consuming single-portion foods and snacks rather than complex/large meals. Meanwhile, the inequality between low- and high-income groups is worsening, with the low-income segment growing at a much faster rate than a decade ago all over the world, which influences demand for certain product categories.

Finally, also in the food sector, technology is becoming more important. This relates not only to the distribution and delivery of food, but also to the way consumers interact with and evaluate the products they intend to buy (for example, consumers' reviews are becoming more important, technologies reconnect manufactures and consumers, social media enables niche firms to reach a broader market, and artificial intelligence and big data are relevant tools for the food retailer and producer).

Source: Adapted from Euromonitor International

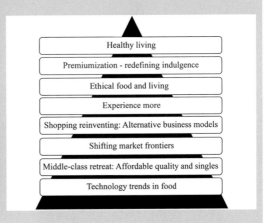

Source: Adapted from Euromonitor International

Exhibit 5.3 Megatrends hierarchy in foods

Exhibit 5.4 Fruit juice market profiles

Country	Key conclusions from strategy consultants	Dominant flavors	Dominant packaging	Take-home vs in-store consumption*
Netherlands	Confusion on the health benefit of juices; consumers seem unable to differentiate fruit sugars from added sugars. There is a need for educating consumers by effective communication on the wellness credentials of juice.	Mixed: 46% Orange: 29% Apple: 10% Grapefruit: 1% Nut/seeds: 1%	Carton: 72% Plastic: 21% Glass: 6%	Take-home: 90% In-store: 10%
Austria	Trend for locally produced organic fruits and vegetables, fair trade offerings; consumers request products with functional benefits (for example, additional antioxidants); uptrading by consumers (that is, consumers being willing to pay more for a higher-quality or better product or service) is forecasted.	Orange: 40% Apple: 26% Mixed: 19% Berries: 5% Mango 2%	Carton: 59% Plastic: 27% Glass: 10%	Take-home: 58% In-store: 19%
Germany	The juice segment is benefiting from a general trend toward natural products in the market (for example, organic variants, smoothies). Consumers are increasingly informed and able to distinguish high from low quality. Price promotions are frequent, and consumers are price-sensitive even in the premium segment.	Orange: 34% Apple: 22% Mixed: 22% Vegetable: 3% Grape: 3%	Carton: 37% Plastic: 52% Glass: 10%	Take-home: 79% In-store: 21%
United Kingdom	Sugar tax (not on juices) has induced various competitors to increasingly use vegetables in juices to reduce sugar content. The freshly pressed fruit juice segment is still emerging and suffers from consumers perceiving it to be too expensive. The juice segment faces competition from a growing trend towards coconut waters.	Orange: 56% Apple: 12% Mixed: 9% Berries: 5% Pineapple: 4%	Carton: 64% Plastic: 30% Glass: 5%	Take-home: 80% In-store: 12%
France	Premiumization of fruit juice segment observed (yet with a buy-less-but-higher-quality attitude); the health trend uplifts preferences for organic products and fruit/vegetable mixes. The market still suffers from debates on the sugar content of juice.	Orange: 48% Mixed: 23% Apple: 12% Pineapple: 3% Grape: 2%	Carton: 57% Plastic: 32% Glass: 7%	Take-home: 89% In-store: 11%

* In countries where the percentages do not add up to 100 per cent, an individual "On the go" category accounts for the remaining percentage points.

Source: Adapted from European Fruit Juice Association (2018)

CASE QUESTIONS

In spite of all the preparation for the camp, Dirk, Joe and Sofie understood the need to re-assess some of their basic strategic ideas, starting with the questions of how to segment the market and how they would actually define or profile their target customer. In addition, they really wanted to work on the positioning of Magic Juice. Hence, they saw a need to better define its core value proposition and pains and gains in various markets that are related to the use of the chain's offerings. As a start, the team wanted to understand the value proposition canvas with a deeper dive into the home market and the foreign markets entered. A question here was about how Magic Juice actually performed vis-à-vis its main competitors. To ease internal firm communication, they wanted to have a true value proposition outlined for Magic Juice. And ultimately, they wanted to see an evaluation of the strategic proposals that Dirk and Sofie presented at the camp. In addition to the question of strategic set-up, Dirk wondered about how he could prioritize his attention to different markets via a more structured overview of KPIs. Throw your expertise to the table and assist them in these challenges.

6
Designing global value chains

Since the early 2000s, the global value chain (GVC) concept has gained popularity within analyses of the international expansion and geographical fragmentation of supply chains. A GVC combines functions and operations worldwide through which goods and services are produced, distributed and consumed. While GVCs are often looked at primarily from a trade perspective, they are very much a function of the activities and business processes of multinational enterprises (MNEs). Approximately 80 percent of global trade is linked to the international production networks of MNEs (UNCTAD, 2020). MNEs are the lead firms that coordinate the complex structure of cross-border trade and collaboration taking place between MNE subsidiaries, contractual partners, specialized suppliers and customers (referred to as a "global value chain," "global commodity chain," "global production network" or "global factory"). Often, the production sites are located in low-cost developing countries. These are then closely linked with lead-firm buyers who are often located in major consumer markets in North America and Europe. Therewith, a new global divide in industrial organization has emerged: a development from hierarchically organized MNEs (that is, vertically integrated value chains) to MNEs that are international lead firms in a GVC. GVCs do not only refer to manufacturing firms. They likewise characterize service MNEs and firms using digital business models (for example, IT firms that generate revenues from dispersed foreign locations without investing in production in a conventional sense) (see Kano, Tsang, and Yeung, 2020).

In this chapter, we will explain the relevant concepts and frameworks related to the analysis of GVCs. We will introduce the elements that characterize a value chain, and familiarize the reader with the historical development and rise of GVCs. We will discuss the factors that influence the configuration of GVCs. The reader will be familiarized with alternative governance and control mechanisms that the firm can choose in connection with the GVC configuration. In addition, we will derive alternative GVC strategies for managers, based on key decision variables. We will supplement the GVC analysis with industry and firm examples and end the chapter with a more comprehensive discussion of practices at a Danish shoe manufacturer.

6.1 UNDERSTANDING GLOBAL VALUE CHAINS

6.1.1 Elements of the value chain and value added

Basically, a value chain is a systematic means of displaying and categorizing the firm's activities that relate to the design, production, marketing, delivery and support of its products or services. Porter (1985) introduced the value chain concept as a framework for developing strategy and achieving competitiveness by directing attention to the entire system of a firm's activities. In Porter's classical value chain analysis, activities are physically and technologically distinct but can be grouped into primary activities (inbound logistics, operations, outbound logistics, marketing and sales, and after-sales service) and support activities (procurement, technology development, HR development and infrastructure). They are the building blocks used by firms to create value for their buyers. Value is the amount that buyers are willing to pay for the products or services provided by the firm (also referred to as "perceived value"). In line with our understanding of strategy, the overall aim is to offer products or services with a perceived value that is higher than the cost of creating these products or services. The added value (that is, the difference between the perceived value and the cost) is the firm's profit, or "margin."

The value chain includes both value and cost drivers; that is, structural factors that explain why the firm generates costs and value via its activities. To achieve a competitive advantage (or a firm-specific advantage; FSA) a firm either provides a comparable customer value more efficiently than its competitors (that is, at lower cost), or performs activities at comparable cost in unique ways that create more value to the customers than the competitors and, hence, command a premium price (differentiation). Accordingly, the firm can identify value chain activities that are not worth the cost or do not fit the desired quality, and therefore are outsourced to third partners. Or the firm can keep the identified activities in-house, but alternatively decide to perform them outside its home market (offshoring).

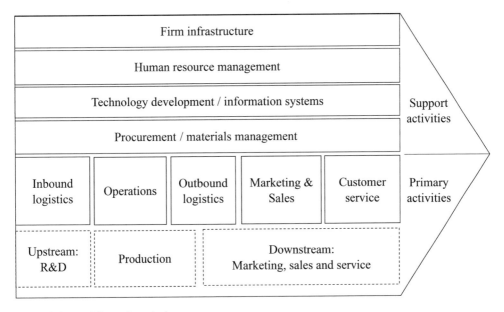

Figure 6.1   The value chain

Figure 6.1 shows Porter's classical value chain (as introduced above), and a simplified value chain that only includes basic primary activities. The simplified value chain differentiates three parts: upstream activities (that are related to inputs), downstream activities (that are output- or market-related activities) and the middle part of activities. Upstream activities comprise basic and applied research, design, engineering and activities related to product quality. Downstream activities comprise, among others, marketing, advertising, brand management, distribution, sales, delivery and customer services. Activities in the middle part of the value chain comprise purchasing, manufacturing, assembly, packaging and quality management.

The value chain is not a collection of independent activities. Rather, it is a system of *interdependent* activities within the firm. Decisions made in one value activity (for example, procurement) may affect another value activity (for example, operations). Since procurement is, for instance, responsible for the quality of inputs, it will probably affect the (cost of) production (and therefore operations) and eventually even the product quality. Likewise, a technologically well-developed product will probably affect the customer support services in a positive way. Clear communication and coordination between and across the value chain activities are therefore just as important as the activities themselves. Consequently, a firm also needs to optimize the links between activities to create value in an efficient way; sometimes, services are referred to as the glue that holds value chain activities together and ensures that they function in a fluid manner.

The identification of all the individual activities of the value chain that will make up the full value of the product is not trivial in practice. Especially as the firm's value chain is embedded in a large stream of network activities in the total supply chain of goods and services. Furthermore, value chains may be local, regional or global. Ali-Yrkkö et al. (2011) demonstrate this complexity in their analysis of the value added in the GVC of a smartphone; see Box 6.1 for further insights.

To understand the activities involved in the GVC, we differentiate four "levels of aggregation": tasks, occupations, stages and products (see Baldwin, 2013, and Figure 6.2). Tasks are all the activities and functions that must be performed to get the product into the consumers' hand. Occupations are a group of tasks that are performed by an individual worker or a skilled employee. Stages are a collection of occupations that are performed in proximity due to the need for face-to-face interaction between the tasks performed by workers or employees. Products are the outputs, which also include after-sales services. When it comes to the coordination in GVCs, it is critical to identify the aggregation of tasks to individual occupations and the stages of occupations based on the need for proximity.

This need for proximity (for example, for face-to-face interaction), or at least the solutions that can comfort this need and induce proximity over distance, has changed in recent years, as we will discuss next.

| Box 6.1 | Further insights: The value added in the GVC of Nokia's N95 smartphone |

A detailed breakdown of the value chain of producing and selling the Nokia N95 smartphone illustrates the difficulties in disentangling the individual GVC activities and their value added. At the time, Nokia launched its then newest smartphone under the slogan "It's what computers have become"; it had, among other things, a new operating system and a new slider design that offered different menus when sliding right or left on the screen.

The key value chain of the Nokia N95 was differentiated with five stages: (i) mines, refiners and raw material traders; (ii) component vendors and assemblers that create subcomponents and provide subassembly – actors that are involved in these first two stages account for 11 percent of the value added; (iii) technology and software licensors, who account for 3 percent of the value added; (iv) Nokia, which is responsible for final assembly and therefore captures 50 percent of the value added; and (v) distribution channel partners selling the product to the consumer/end-user. These downstream actors (distributors and retailers) account for 14 percent of the value added (see the table below). Subcontractors of vendors and unaccountable inputs capture the remaining 22 percent.

Actor	Share of value added
Suppliers of material inputs	11%
Software and other firms selling licenses	3%
Nokia	50%
Distributors	3%
Retailers	11%
Unaccountable inputs	3%
Vendors of vendors	19%

The 50 percent that is attributed to Nokia is allocated to direct and indirect labor costs that accrue in-house (such as manufacturing and assembly; innovation; marketing, including advertising design; financial; administrative; and management functions), asset depreciation, investments and operating profit. Breaking this down to the value per phone (that at the time had a retail price of EUR 546), Nokia's value added amounted to 269 EUR. According to Ali-Yrkkö et al. (2011), the ultimate final assembly accounted for only EUR 11. The remaining shares of Nokia's part of the value chain are mainly made up of its internal support activities and costs, namely EUR 169, and an operating profit of EUR 89.

In terms of the value-added breakdown of the N95 by major regions, it was estimated that over 50 percent of value added was captured in Finland and the other EU-27 countries, even though the final assembly was done in China and a large part of the final sales occurred in the United States. The reason was that the EU countries were dominant in the branding, development, design and management.

Source: Adapted from Ali-Yrkkö et al. (2011)

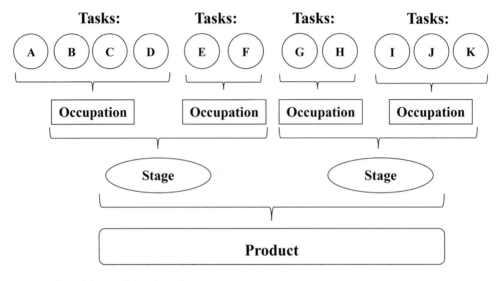

Source: Adapted from Baldwin (2013)

Figure 6.2 Tasks, occupations, stages and product

6.1.2 The rise of the global value chain and the "smiling curve"

Traditionally, classical supply chains were best coordinated by bundling all stages and activities in a single factory with the aim of reducing costs and risk. Starting in the mid-1960s, however, manufacturing firms sliced up their supply chains in the search for low-cost or capable suppliers in offshore locations; that is, they have been engaging in global outsourcing. In particular, in the 1980s and 1990s an "unbundling" of the value chain was observed, leading to fractionalization and dispersion. *Fractionalization* concerns the unbundling of the value chains into finer stages of manufacturing, logistics, marketing and sales. *Dispersion* relates to the geographical unbundling of stages. Large retailers and firms offering private brands (that is, in-house brands) have done the same as manufacturers earlier and started searching for offshore suppliers of consumer goods, which led to a shift from producer-driven to customer-driven value chains.

Producer-driven GVCs are nowadays typically found in high-tech sectors such as the semiconstructor or pharmaceuticals industries. Because these industries rely on technology and R&D, lead firms are placed upstream and control product designs as well as most of the assembly activities that are fragmented in different countries. In buyer-driven GVCs, retailers and marketers control all the downstream activities and often also the manufacturing part of the chain. GVCs with lower needs for capital, and those relying on fewer skilled workers, are generally organized this way.

In the 1990s and 2000s, GVCs with activities that encompass various nations around the globe grew exponentially, covering finished products as well as components and subassemblies, and affecting manufacturing industries as well as energy and food production, and all kinds of services from call centers to accounting, to medical procedures and core R&D. That is, we have witnessed a "trade in value added" and "trade in tasks" (see Gereffi and Lee, 2012). Today, world trade and production are increasingly structured around GVCs; that is, value chains are spread over several countries – a development that is characterized by two phases of unbundling. First, since transport and communication costs became much cheaper, it became possible to relocate the value chain: goods, information and people to a certain extent transferred across locations. Second, with new information and communication technologies (ICT) – that is, the internet, computerized tasks and robots – more stages emerged, and as the transmission of ideas, instructions and information was facilitated, value chains over longer distances were enabled. Authors refer to this as "globalization's second unbundling" (an unbundling of the stages of production due to ICT; see Baldwin, 2013, and Figure 6.3).

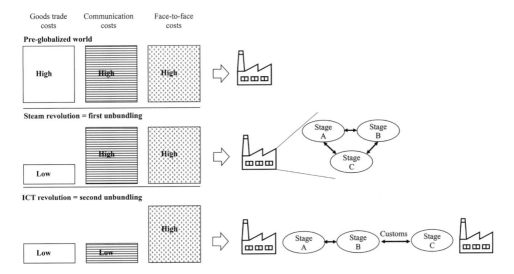

Source: Adapted from Baldwin (2013)

Figure 6.3 Stages of globalization and unbundling

Hence, the second unbundling induced a geographical fragmentation of production processes across the globe following the comparative advantages of locations. For MNEs, key factors pulled them in the direction of specializing and spreading the value chain over several locations (dispersion forces): considerable wage differences (high factor price differentials) encouraged the location of labor-intensive stages of the value chain in low-wage locations in Asia and the skilled intensive stages in high-wage locations in Europe or the United States (vertical specialization). However, low wages alone do not explain dispersion to several locations; also, firm-specific differentiation benefits and excellence in performing specific value chain stages played an important role in horizontal specialization. On the other hand, supply- and demand-side linkages, such as big markets, learning and spill-over effects, are local agglomeration forces that encouraged geographical clustering. For example, large customers in huge consumer markets attracted further suppliers in their own locations, and suppliers attracted more suppliers (which was, for instance, the case in China, sometimes referred to as "the world's production factory").

Countries specialized in specific tasks or business functions, such as assembly operations in the case of China and business services in the case of India, rather than in specific industries. New evidence suggests that there is a trend towards a regionalization of GVCs. This is due to various factors, including the growing importance of large emerging economies and regional trade agreements (see Gereffi and Fernandez-Stark, 2016; International Bank for Reconstruction and Development, 2017). The international fragmentation of production is a powerful source of increased efficiency and firms' competitiveness. Today, according to Organisation for Economic Co-operation and Development (OECD) figures,[1] more than half of the world's manufactured imports are intermediate goods (primary goods, parts and components, and semi-finished products), and more than 70 percent of the world's service imports are intermediate services.

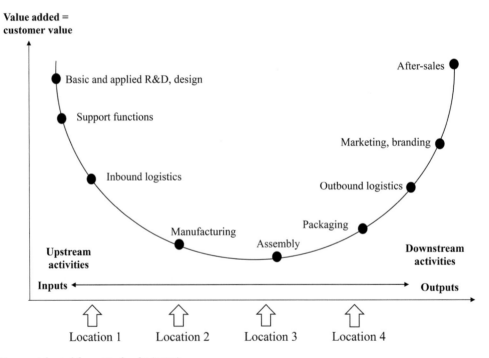

Source: Adapted from Mudambi (2008)

Figure 6.4   Value added in the value chain: The smiling curve

A result of this process is an observation known as the "smiling curve" or the "smile of value creation," which shows the value added at each stage of the value chain; see Figure 6.4. Activities at the ends of the value chain are largely located in advanced economies (high-income countries), while those in the middle of the chain are moving (or have been moved) to emerging economies. Examples of the "smiling curve" and the pattern of locational disaggregation are found in several industries. In the automotive sector, the GVC of General Motors' Pontiac Le Mans and Ford's Fiesta incorporate design and marketing in advanced economies and assembly in emerging economies. The fabrication (especially assembly) involves less value creation than it did before the second unbundling – the "smile" deepened, so to speak (Mudambi, 2008).

The "smile of value creation" is a dynamic process. At both ends of the value chain, innovations create new industries related to upstream activities (for example, from basic to applied R&D), and downstream activities (for example, new online business models emerging from innovations in distribution and marketing). MNEs in advanced economies that control the end of the value chain are faced with an increasingly competitive landscape, including entrants from emerging markets. Due to knowledge spill-over effects, emerging economies have a strong incentive to catch up and improve their competitiveness in activities that involve a higher added value. Research-intensive firms, such as bio-tech companies, and ICT-based firms, increasingly locate R&D in countries such as India and Brazil and therewith create a further knowledge spill-over into emerging markets. In the mobile handset industry, for example, high-value-added activities appear at the ends of the value chain. Firms from emerging markets, such as Huawei (China), that started as electronics manufacturing service firms that supplied private-label products to MNEs in advanced economies, have recently developed strong marketing competences to develop their own brands. Thus, they now put competitive pressures on smartphone manufacturers such as Apple (see also Mudambi, 2008).

> **Box 6.2   Further insights: Trends that will reshape tomorrow's GVC**
>
> A recent report (UNCTAD, 2020) forecasts the following developments of relevance to the GVC of the future. It is expected that:
>
> 1. The application of digital technologies on GVCs will result in more integrated production processes, a reduction in governance and transaction costs, and more effective coordination of complex value chains. Due to digital technologies such as the internet of things and big data applications, the importance of intangibles in the value chain is expected to be increased and will shift the value added to the ends of the "smile curve" – hence central parts of the curve will be flattened.
> 2. The application of automation and the availability of cheaper (and smaller) industrial robots is expected to reduce (potentially dramatically) the competitive advantages of low-cost manufacturing hubs in developing economies and may therefore trigger a wave of reshoring of key parts of the GVC.
> 3. The application of 3D printing technology (additive manufacturing) is potentially the most revolutionizing technology in the context of GVCs. It enables a shift from mass production and economies of scale (EOS) to mass customization. The implications are greatest for those industries profiting from mass customization (for example, the footwear industry) and niche segments organized in long, vertically disintegrated value chains. This 3D printing points to a value chain configuration characterized by small-scale, localized manufacturing for which it would imply simultaneous re-bundling and offshoring of many steps (indicating a deepening of the "smile").

Further dynamic changes to the GVC are upcoming and influenced by new technologies and the digitalization shift; in addition, global megatrends such as the sustainability imperative will shape the GVCs of tomorrow. A recent report has investigated how new technological developments (in particular) will reshape GVCs, and provides (at this stage speculative) conclusions (see Box 6.2 for further insights).

6.2 VALUE CHAIN STRATEGIES

6.2.1 Value chain configurations and their determinants

While Porter's value chain concept puts specific emphasis on the configuration of activities within the firm to improve competitiveness, the GVC analysis focuses on the generation and transfer of value within the whole business system and production network (that is, value activities within the same firm or among different firms). A GVC analysis goes beyond extending Porter's value chain approach to a global level. Its main objective is to understand the interplay between value-distribution mechanisms and the organization of the international production–consumption networks. Key questions that managers need to answer for their GVCs are: Who are the GVC actors? What kinds of rules exist? Is it a competitive or a cooperative GVC? What generates successful (effective) GVCs?

Table 6.1 Determinants of GVC length, geographical distribution and governance

Determinant	Impact	Relationship L	GD	GC
Arbitrage opportunities (labor costs, regulatory, tax)	Differences in labor costs are the origin of efficiency-seeking investment and international production networks	+	+	
Concentration of supply, demand and/or know-how and technology	Geographical dispersion of the upstream and downstream parts of the value chain is determined by locations of demand, critical supply sources and technology/talent		-	
Trade cost	Higher trade costs (for example, tariffs, administrative procedures) make up a higher share of products/components that cross borders multiple times	-	-	
Transportation costs	Transportation costs influence the sourcing and location decisions of firms; they will affect both the physical length of value chains and the geographical spread	-	-	
Transaction costs (between actors in the supply chains)	Transaction costs (for example, difficulties in transmitting information, product specifications, quality control) determine the degree to which lead firms use outsourcing, and the number of steps in value chains	-		+
Modularity of production	The degree to which production can be broken up in discrete tasks is a driver for the degree of fragmentation	+	+	
Gains from specialization	The gains from specialization in tasks along the value chain are a key driver of fragmentation, closely linked with EOS at task level	+		

Determinant	Impact	Relationship		
		L	GD	GC
Economies of scale	EOS at the value chain task level are equivalent to the gain of specialization and lead to more fragmentation; EOS in integrated production processes can have the opposite effect	+/-	-	
Innovation/intellectual property intensity	Higher intellectual property intensity tends to lead to more closely controlled internalized value chains, closer to home	-	-	+
Degree of product differentiation/ customization	The need for customization tends to lead to more decentralized value addition (and higher geographical spread)	-	+	+/-

Note: The columns on the right denote a positive/negative relationship to the length of the value chain (L), the geographic distribution of the value chain (GD), and the governance of the value chain (GC)
Source: UNCTAD (2020)

We describe the configuration of the GVC using several dimensions (following UNCTAD, 2020): the length of the value chain, the geographic distribution of value chain activities and the governance of the value chain; see Table 6.1. The length or degree of fragmentation of the value chain determines the extent to which a given value chain allows vertical integration and specialization, the spatial separation of individual activities and the exploitation of differences in factor cost across locations (countries). The length of value chains depends on a number of factors. These comprise, among others, the degree of modularity of production processes in the industry (that is, the extent to which production processes can be sliced up into distinct and discrete steps), economic gains of specialization in specific production tasks, and EOS through similar or complementary tasks. For example, a high degree of production modularity and a high degree of EOS and specialization lead to longer value chains.

The factors that influence the geographical spread of value added include the importance of trade and transportation costs, the degree of labor cost differentials across locations, the international opportunities for exploiting tax or regulatory arbitrage, and the degree of concentration of natural and/or intellectual resources required for production. For example, high trade and transportation costs as well as a high concentration of resources required for production result in economic disincentives for a wider dispersion of value chain activities. In contrast, high labor cost differentials and tax arbitrage potentials in an industry speak for spreading value chain activities to these locations to profit from the arbitrage opportunities.

The governance or coordination of value chain activities unfolds on a spectrum from low levels of control over external suppliers of inputs to full control through internalization (that is, the firm performs the activity by using its own organizational units). The governance dimension is closely related to the choice of entry mode (see Chapter 3). It is a choice between exporting, all kinds of intermediary levels of control exercised through various contracts (for example, through licensing and franchising) and foreign direct investment (FDI). The governance decision, or the decision on whether the firm prefers to fully control the value chain or not, depends on several industry- and transaction-specific factors. If the firm over time has developed strong FSAs (such as fundamental R&D or active ingredients in pharmaceutical products), a high degree of control provides the management with the best opportunity to protect and disseminate these FSAs. In addition to the governance of the value chain via the

INTERNATIONAL BUSINESS STRATEGY AND CROSS-CULTURAL MANAGEMENT

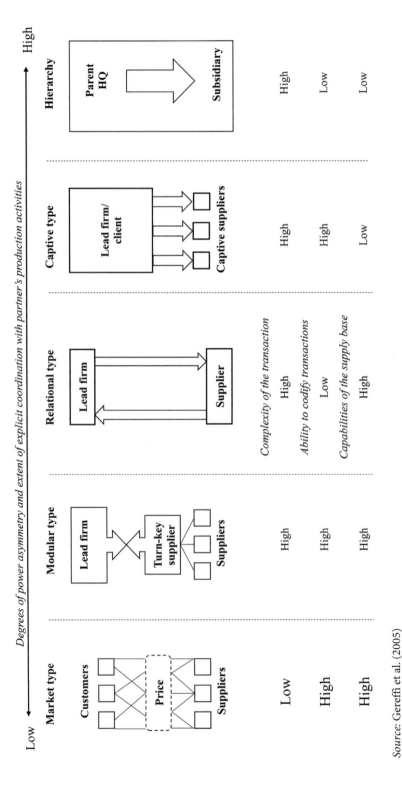

Source: Gereffi et al. (2005)

Figure 6.5 Typology of global value chains

market (market type) and the vertical integration (hierarchy), we differentiate between three further forms of GVCs: the modular, relational and captive GVC (see also Gereffi, Humphrey and Sturgeon, 2005, and Figure 6.5).

Market governance refers to simple transactions, in which suppliers make products involving little coordination with buyers, with the price as the central governance mechanism. *Modular governance* refers to suppliers manufacturing products based on a customer's (the lead MNE) specifications; products are more complex but information on the production is relatively easy to codify using standardized information exchange (for example, Original Equipment Manufacturer supplies). *Relational governance* emerges when buyers and suppliers need to exchange complex information; here, frequent interactions and knowledge-sharing based on mutual trust and social ties are critical to successfully coordinate value chain activities. *Captive governance* is characterized by a group of small suppliers that depend on one or a few buyers; here, the suppliers usually operate under conditions set by, and often specific to, demanding buyers or lead MNEs. Finally, *hierarchical governance* in value chains involves managerial control within the lead firms that develop and manufacture the goods in-house (see Gereffi and Lee, 2012).

Superior efficiency in these GVCs is created by designing governance systems that fit the attributes of transactions in a cost-economizing way, and competitive advantage arises from the capabilities of firms to select the most efficient mix of internal activities and external contracts. The form of governance (for example, modular, relational or captive) can change as an industry evolves and matures, and governance patterns within an industry can vary from one stage of the value chain to another (Kano et al., 2020). Box 6.3 provides several examples of GVCs in different industries.

Box 6.3   Further insights: GVCs in different industries

The GVC of motor vehicles is largely organized through a hierarchical structure, with the large automotive manufacturers positioned on top of the pyramid as lead firms responsible for the design, branding and final assembly. Both outsourcing and offshoring have pushed the international fragmentation of production quite far in this industry. One level down, first-tier suppliers produce complete subsystems by cooperating with a large network of lower-tier suppliers and subcontractors. Close relationships have developed, especially between car assemblers and first-tier suppliers, as these have taken up a larger role in the whole production process, including design. These suppliers have increasingly developed into global suppliers since lead firms demanded that they have a global presence and system-design capabilities.

The chemicals industry is characterized by the presence of a multitude of different GVCs. The value chain begins with raw materials (in particular, oil and gas) which are transformed into petrochemicals, base chemicals, polymers, specialties and active ingredients. The chemical industry provides inputs to many other industries since its products are used in multiple applications across industries. Products in the early stages of the chemical GVC include more commodity-type products; that is, products which are produced in high volumes and sold at low unit values to mass markets. Specialty products are typically produced in the later stages of the chemical GVC and incorporate larger degrees of complexity often linked to higher R&D and marketing investments.

The agri-food industry is a further example of an industry that is increasingly structured around GVCs led by food processors and retailers. Supermarket chains such as Walmart, Tesco and Carrefour work with food importers and exporters, and control how products are grown and harvested. As most consumers have changed their food consumption habits and now ask for food quality and safety, they need to ensure that the quality and food safety standards are met along the value chain, which requires vertical coordination. Therefore, it is important for the retail sector to be able to follow the product's journey through the entire value chain. At the same time, FDI and trade liberalization have given opportunities for firms to reorganize their value chains. A relatively small number of firms now organize the global supply of food, and link small producers in developed and developing countries to consumers all over the world. For instance, Nutella, the hazelnut and cocoa brand of Ferrero International SA, which is headquartered in Italy, is produced in five factories in Europe, one in Russia, one in North America, two in South America and one in Australia. These produce about 250,000 tons of Nutella per year. Some inputs, such as skimmed milk, are locally supplied, while others are globally supplied: hazelnuts come from Turkey, palm oil from Malaysia, cocoa from Nigeria, sugar from Brazil and vanilla flavor from France. Nutella is then sold in 75 countries through sales offices and agents.

An increasing number of business services previously supplied within firms have been outsourced and offshored and have become an integral part of the GVC. The share of business services in international trade has steadily increased over the last 20 years, in particular when it comes to computer services and legal, accounting, management consulting and public relations services. For instance, in the case of the financial services value chain, inputs are money and information, and the firms involved include commercial banks, investment banks, securities brokers, asset management firms, securities exchanges and trusts. Firms raise funds by taking deposits or by issuing securities, and make loans or trade securities. The value chain goes from lenders to borrowers, and the products are divided into credit intermediaries and financial intermediaries. There are also firms providing supporting services and advice to facilitate these transactions.

Sources: De Backer and Miroudot (2013), Gereffi and Fernandez-Stark (2016)

6.2.2   Strategic options to configure the value chain

When it comes to the strategic design of the GVC, we need to answer two fundamental questions regarding the control and location of the value chain activities: First, which activities should the firm own, and which activities should be left to external partners (that is, which to insource or outsource)? And second, where should the firm locate the value chain activities (that is, onshore or offshore)?

"Insourcing" is reincorporating an activity to the firm that was formerly outsourced to an external partner, while "outsourcing" is associated with the decision to obtain intermediate goods, components, final products or services from an external partner that were traditionally produced internally (see also Foerstl, Kirchoff, and Bals, 2016). Ultimately, this make-or-buy decision is related to the issue of control of the firm regarding the value chain activities. In a vertical integration strategy, we take advantage of an internalization of activities; that is, we control multiple value chain activities and enhance the efficiency and effectiveness of each activity. In contrast, a specialization strategy focuses on controlling the key value-creating activities and core competences within the chain, while outsourcing all other rather peripheral activities (that is, externalization). "Onshoring" is the relocation of a value chain activity, a business function or task to a more productive or lower-cost location in the firms' home-country environment. In contrast, "offshoring" refers to relocating the activity to a different country that either remains within or moves outside the firm. This home-or-abroad decision is related to the issue of where to locate the value chain activities. The firm can take advantage of the comparative advantages of locations, which leads to a wider geographic dispersion of its activities, or it can choose to concentrate its value chain activities in its domestic market.

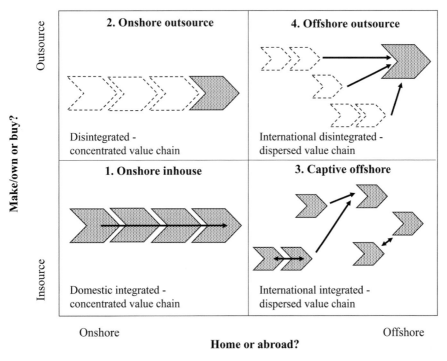

Figure 6.6   Value chain strategies

In principle, the firm has four basic strategies to follow that are represented in Figure 6.6: (1) onshore in-house, (2) onshore outsource, (3) captive offshore, or (4) offshore outsource (Mudambi, 2008). A firm following an onshore in-house strategy chooses to have a home-country-concentrated, dispersed value chain. It prefers to own and carry out all activities along the value chain, and locates some activities at different places in the domestic market. While the in-house production results in a high degree of management control of the value chain activities, it also leads to an increasing organizational commitment to a specific type of technology that may constrain flexibility in the long run. For example, in the footwear industry there are producers that follow an onshore in-house strategy, namely the US-based New Balance Inc., which owns shoemaker Dunham (lately New Balance Inc. has opened its first store in London), and big Chinese shoemakers such as Belle International Holdings Ltd, Red Dragonfly Footwear Co. Ltd. and Spider King, who offer their local brands to huge home markets.

Alternatively, a firm following an onshore outsource strategy leaves the less-value-creating activities to other firms in the home country – that is, to subcontractors – and concentrates on those functions and tasks where it has a competitive advantage. Through outsourcing, the flexibility in terms of switching partners is increased and the investments in plant and equipment can be reduced, which results in lower fixed costs.

A captive offshore strategy is primarily driven by expectations of lower production costs, but also other factors such as access to talent and qualified labor, learning opportunities and new markets. A firm following a captive offshore strategy usually does so to keep full control of the dispersed activities in host markets; this internalization results in reduced transaction costs as a result, but at the same time also increases internal coordination costs. The captive offshore strategy is, for instance, used by several international shoe manufacturers; among others, the Italian fashion company Geox S.p.A. (with its own factories in China, Vietnam, Indonesia, South Korea, Brazil and Serbia), and Timberland (owned by the fashion brand VF Corporation Inc., which also owns the North Face, Wrangler and Lee brands), which manufactures its boots, boat shoes and sneakers in a number of offshore locations.

Finally, the fourth option is an offshore outsource strategy that is highly flexible (and complex). It is designed to continuously identify potential new foreign value chain partners who can most cheaply and efficiently take over the least-value-creating part of the value chain while at the same time monitoring subcontractors' technological competencies, quality and performance. Most of the international top 10 sport shoe brands, such as Nike and Adidas, follow an offshore outsource strategy.

By 2020 Nike Inc. used more than 500 independent factories (contract manufacturers) and material suppliers located in 41 countries to manufacture its products. Years back, Nike's image suffered accusations involving sweatshops and unethical manufacturing due to difficulties in controlling its contract manufacturers. In the beginning of the 1990s, the sportswear brand came under fire regarding low wages and working conditions in its Indonesian factories. Though Nike lately has successfully improved its reputation and has become the top-selling sportswear brand in the world, it could improve its corporate social responsibility (CSR) standards by ensuring that the policies and practices match.[2] In 2017, Nike took a step backwards, as the International Labor Rights Forum reported that Nike had turned back its commitment to the Workers' Right Consortium, which effectively blocks labor rights experts from independently monitoring Nike's supplier factories (see the website Good On You – https://goodonyou.eco – which offers ratings of fashion brands along aspects of sustainability and ethics). Controlling sustainability aspects has become relevant in all strategic options yet poses a specific challenge in offshore outsourcing or buyer–supplier relationships; see Box 6.4.

> **Box 6.4   Further insights: CSR practices in buyer–supplier relationships**
>
> In a study of large Swedish retailers' management of CSR within their network of supplier relationships, eight best practices were identified: (i) developing a code of conduct (CoC), (ii) requiring first-tier suppliers to deploy practices to follow the CoC, (iii) following up with control of second-tier suppliers' best practices, (iv) having a local presence through a purchasing office in key sourcing markets abroad, (v) regularly conducting site visits of suppliers, (vi) consulting external experts on international sourcing, (vii) deploying supplier audits with involvement of an external party and (viii) publishing sustainability reports. The use of the various practices varies considerably; see Figure 6.7.
>
>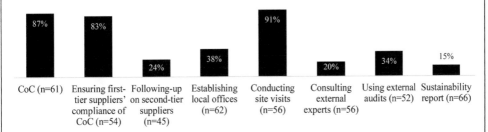
>
> **Figure 6.7**   Eight CSR practices in buyer-supplier relationships'
>
> The development of a CoC (87 percent), requiring first-tier suppliers to deploy practices to follow the CoC (83 percent), and regular site visits (91 percent) are widespread CSR practices. On the other hand, conducting supplier audits with the involvement of an external party (34 percent), controlling second-tier practices (24 percent) and involving external expertise (20 percent) are only implemented to a smaller extent. Only 15 percent of the retailers had published a sustainability report.
>
> The results of the study indicate that many large Swedish retailers did not follow most of the best practices. Discussing differences based on the type of retail sector, the study indicated that the perishable sector (for example, foods) was especially progressive when dealing with CSR issues, while the electronics, optics and office supply sectors lagged behind. Moreover, the study also found a significant, albeit limited impact of firm size and internationalization experience on the retailers' use of best practices in managing CSR within supplier relationships (that is, the bigger and more experienced firms use more CSR best practices).
>
> *Source:* Adapted from Elg and Hultman (2011)

The simplicity of the 2×2 matrix in Figure 6.6 may be criticized for focusing too much on corner solutions; that is, either/or strategies (see Tallman and Mudambi, 2013). More realistically, firms make partial decisions over time regarding the location of and control over the value chain activities, as illustrated in Figure 6.7. It shows that there are several development paths. One development path starts by gradually outsourcing peripheral activities to other external partners in the firms' home country, and then later over time also includes offshoring. Recently, evidence suggests that managers began to reverse the outsourcing and offshoring strategies previously followed; that is, they reshore or return activities from a foreign location

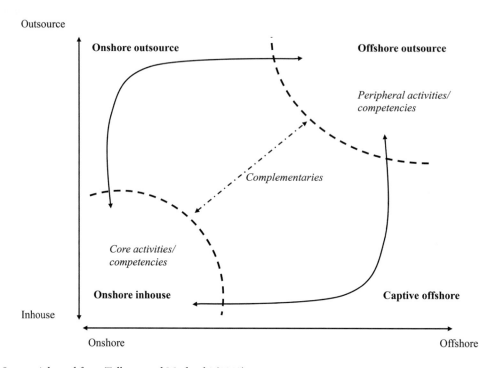

Source: Adapted from Tallman and Mudambi (2013)

Figure 6.8 Value chain control and location development paths

to the country where the activity was originally performed. Studies with managers suggest that 40 percent see a trend towards reshoring and insourcing activities five years after the initial outsourcing or offshoring decision (Kinkel, 2014; Tate et al., 2014). The background is that many firms have realized that managing an increasingly dispersed GVC is more difficult and costly than initially expected. Offshore implementations require substantial coordination and control and therewith costs of transferring knowledge between organizational units that can be prohibitive. Firms engaging in offshoring experience several layers of complexities; that is, task complexities, operational complexities, social complexities and cultural complexities (see Bals et al., 2013; Richter, 2014).

For example, due to cultural and language difficulties and time delays, Dell Inc. decided in 2003 to close its Indian service center, which had been offshored and outsourced. Throughout most of the firm's history, Dell manufactured desktop machines in-house and contracted out the manufacturing of base notebooks. By the late 2000s, Dell's "configure to order" approach of manufacturing (that is, delivering individual PCs configured to customers' specifications) from its US facilities was no longer competitive with high-volume Asian contract manufacturers as PCs became powerful low-cost commodities. Most of the activities performed in Dell's US plants were transferred to contract manufacturers in Asia and Mexico or to Dell's own factories overseas in Malaysia and China – facilities that serve the Asian market and assemble 95 percent of Dell notebooks. For the European, Middle East and African markets,

Dell assembled computers at a facility in Ireland. In 2010, Dell Inc. decided to close the Ireland factory and instead moved assembly manufacturing to a new factory located in the Polish city of Lodz.[3]

6.3 GLOBAL VALUE CHAIN DESIGN AT ECCO A/S VERSUS COMPETITORS

ECCO A/S, based in Denmark, is one of the world's 10 largest shoe manufacturers and is a global market leader in the so-called "comfort shoe" segment. It offers an interesting case due to its specific value chain set-up, as we will illustrate in the following (based on Hansen et al., 2010; Strandskov, 2019). It is family-owned, with the Toosbuy family owning 100 percent of the firm's share capital. ECCO's original slogan "A perfect fit – A simple idea" still applies around 60 years after its inception in 1963. *Design, comfort* and *quality* are the keywords defining ECCO shoes. It manufactures casual classic and sports shoes for men, women and children, as well as clothing and accessories to a lesser extent.

Recently, Steen Borgholm, the CEO of ECCO A/S, celebrated after the publication of the shoe group's annual accounts for 2018. The historically good accounts showed the largest profit ever: approximately EUR 200 million, earned in a highly volatile and competitive global footwear market. "We are very satisfied with the result," said Steen. "We have experienced progress in earnings and have created several changes to ensure that ECCO can continue to be successful in the future. It's hard to say [anything] other than that it's really good when you deliver the best result ever." In 2020, ECCO had a turnover of EUR 1.2 billion and 21,400 employees, of which approximately 600 were employed in Denmark.

Central to the Danish global shoe manufacturer is its "from cow to customer" philosophy, under which the entire process from the development of an idea, product design and production of leather and shoes to marketing, distribution and wholesale operations is fully controlled by the firm (see Figure 6.9). The management strongly believes that keeping all the key activities of the value chain in-house is vital to ensure the quality and standard of shoe production and consequently the final product. As often stated by the founder of ECCO, Karl Toosbuy: "We cannot get the best quality if we don't do it ourselves." Hence, compared to some of its competitors – among them Nike and Timberland – ECCO has taken a rather atypical path, namely to internalize and fully integrate the entire value chain. In contrast to ECCO, its main competitors in the footwear industry have outsourced most activities to subcontractors in low-cost countries that are part of the industry's many GVCs.

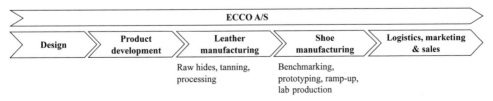

Figure 6.9   ECCO's GVC

ECCO is, thus, one of the few fully vertically integrated shoe manufacturers that manages the entire GVC itself; that is, from tanning hides to designing, manufacturing, marketing and selling shoes in its own stores. Still, ECCO's production takes place at a number of factories around the world, including – in addition to Denmark – Portugal, Slovakia, Indonesia, Thailand, China and Vietnam. ECCO has own tanneries in the Netherlands, Thailand, Indonesia and China, which transform raw hides into high-quality leather. The leather is further processed at ECCO's many shoe factories but is also sold to other firms that use high-quality leather in their production. The leather division, which is headquartered in the Netherlands, sells approximately 33 percent of its leather production to external partners, but the division only accounts for about 7 percent of the consolidated revenue. ECCO's factories in Indonesia, Thailand, Slovakia and China have full-scale production of both "uppers" (shafts) and finished shoes, while the factories in Indonesia and Vietnam primarily manufacture the labor-intensive (that is, wage-heavy) uppers. A factory in Portugal (formerly a full-scale production unit that has been gradually scaled down) is responsible for the production of shoe prototypes.

ECCO started the relocation of major parts of its value chain in the 1970s. Back then ECCO's value chain was broadly grouped into raw materials, tanning, manufacturing, sales and distribution. The relocation of shoe manufacturing started early with the establishment of uppers production in Brazil (back in 1974). Later, other low-cost economies such as Portugal (1984), Indonesia (1991), Thailand (1993), Slovakia (1998), China (2005) and Vietnam (2018) became host countries of full-scale production of uppers and finished shoes. In addition, ECCO owns a global network of tanneries, which transform raw hide into various kinds of high-quality leather for ECCO's factories around the world. Since the end of the 1980s, ECCO has played a pioneering role in the use of automated production techniques, including so-called "direct injection technology"; its robotic production lines can be compared to those of the automotive industry. The automated production process enables ECCO to produce high-quality shoes according to strict specifications. This book's website includes a link to a video that provides insights into the ECCO factory and production process.

The geographical spread of the GVC at ECCO is based on the desire to ensure the best access to the raw materials, to locate the manufacturing and processing of the shoe's components where labor is cheap but of good quality, and to sell the shoes through the firm's own distribution and sales channels. ECCO is just one among many firms that have reconfigured their value chains on a global scale following differences in comparative advantages among countries or regions (for example, in terms of wages, labor supply and quality, taxes and duties, and infrastructure).

ECCO operates R&D and design centers primarily in Denmark; that is, it has not relocated these activities. Many firms, however, are no longer just relocating their labor-intensive activities to save costs but are also relocating knowledge-intensive activities and services with the aim of getting access to highly qualified labor, increasing innovation, performance and learning. ECCO operates its own sales and distribution channels in more than 50 countries, including the United States and in Europe and Australia. Globally, ECCO's shoes are sold in more than 2,200 of the company's own stores, including about 500 franchise-controlled brand stores. Another 14,000 wholesaling stores in 90 countries sell ECCO shoes. ECCO also owns and operates several flagship stores in London, San Francisco, Berlin, Amsterdam and Hamburg, among others. The United States, China, Germany, Russia and Sweden are its largest single markets. About 95 percent of the group's revenue is generated outside Denmark. Its main segment is the 30- to 49-year-old age group and more than 25 million pairs of shoes are sold annually. In the early 2000s, the company expanded its traditional markets with the launch of a sports shoe line, a children's product line and other products to attract younger age groups. Most recently, ECCO is focusing on its own online sales.

Thus, ECCO has with its "from cow to customer" philosophy also followed the smile curve in terms of the geographical location of its value chain. However, it has done this in contrast to, for instance, Nike, by owning and controlling the entire chain. Nike concentrates on design and marketing in key advanced market economies, while outsourcing and closely coordinating the production of standard components through an offshore network of low-cost suppliers. Most important is the ownership of Nike's brand and the intangible assets related to highly creative design processes and marketing activities in both ends of the value chain – stages Nike fully controls.

> **Box 6.5   Further insights: ECCO's code of conduct**
>
> ECCO's CoC was first formulated by its founder, Karl Toosbuy, nearly 30 years ago. It is the firm's "constitution" and all employees and suppliers are familiarized with it. As the world constantly evolves, new legislation is continuously implemented in many countries. In response, ECCO has added several policies to support the CoC that are explained in detail. Yet, overall, the CoC consists of the following 10 commitments:
>
> ## THE 10 COMMITMENTS
>
> 1. ECCO is a guest in each of the countries in which it operates, and respects the local culture.
> 2. ECCO supports, respects and takes a proactive approach to protecting internationally defined human rights.
> 3. ECCO respects equal opportunities and fights discrimination in the workplace.
> 4. ECCO respects the individual's right to religious freedom.
> 5. ECCO respects the right to freedom of association.
> 6. ECCO wishes to provide employees with a workplace free of harassment or abuse and condemns any form of enforced labor.
> 7. ECCO supports the UN Convention on the Rights of the Child.
> 8. ECCO provides training, education and further development of human resources at all levels.
> 9. ECCO aims to be a leader within the environment, health and safety and supports sustainable development.
> 10. ECCO wishes to ensure that it complies with all relevant laws and regulations.
>
> *Source:* CoC from ECCO's firm information

From the above, it appears that ECCO has over time chosen a captive offshore strategy. In addition to ensuring a high and standardized quality in all parts of the value chain, the management of ECCO argues that this highly integrated–dispersed strategy reduces the risk of negative effects (to the brand) of ethically deviant behavior of subcontractors, such as engaging in child labor or poor working conditions. Moreover, it increases the short-term flexibility to react to changing market conditions (tariffs, demand, and so on), reduces supplier risks (for example, missing or late deliveries), protects knowledge that is critical (for example, manufacturing technologies, which is a key determinant of success at ECCO), maximizes scale and scope advantages, and enables reduced storage costs across the value chain. In order to support ECCO's highly integrated value chain strategy, for years the firm has with its CoC been engaged in CSR, long before it became a forefront topic; see Box 6.5.

CHAPTER REVIEW QUESTIONS

1. Explain the difference between a firm's value chain and a global value chain (GVC). Discuss the analytical focus that underlies each of them.
2. Explain the concept of "globalization's second unbundling."
3. Explain the "smiling curve" concept and its relevance to GVC localization.
4. What factors do you think contribute to the "smiling curve" becoming deeper and thereby increase the cross-border value chain dispersion?
5. What are the key dimensions of a GVC configuration?
6. Which factors influence the geographic spread of the value added and the location of value chain activities?
7. Explain the different governance structures of GVCs and the pros and cons of each.
8. What potential value chain strategies can a firm take advantage of? Discuss the pros and cons of each.
9. What are the pros and cons of ECCO's GVC strategy, and what economic and strategic factors should be analyzed to answer the question?
10. How well do you think ECCO's GVC configuration (location, sourcing, integration, and so on) matches the industry drivers of the footwear industry?

NOTES

1. OECD data, available at: https://data.oecd.org/.
2. See Nike Inc.'s 2021 impact report "Breaking Barriers," available at: https://purpose-cms-preprod01.s3.amazonaws.com/wp-content/uploads/2021/04/26225049/FY20_NIKE_Inc_Impact_Report2.pdf.
3. Wikipedia, available at: https://en.wikipedia.org/wiki/History_of_Dell.

REFERENCES

Ali-Yrkkö, J., Rouvinen, P., Seppälä, T., and Ylä-Anttila, P. (2011). Who captures value in global supply chains? Case Nokia N95 Smartphone. *Journal of Industry, Competition and Trade, 11*, 263–278.

Baldwin, R. (2013). Global supply chains: Why they emerged, why they matter, and where they are going. In D. K. Elms and P. Low (Eds), *Global Value Chains in a Changing World* (pp. 13–60). Geneva: WTO Publications.

Bals, L., Ørberg Jensen, P. D., Larsen, M. M., and Pedersen, T. (2013). Exploring layers of complexity in offshoring research and practice. In T. Pedersen, L. Bals, P. D. Ørberg Jensen and M. M. Larsen (Eds), *The Offshoring Challenge* (pp. 1–18). London: Springer.

De Backer, K., and Miroudot, S. (2013). *Mapping Global Value Chains*. Paris: OECD Publishing.

Elg, U., and Hultman, J. (2011). Retailers' management of corporate social responsibility (CSR) in their supplier relationships: Does practice follow best practice? *International Review of Retail, Distribution and Consumer Research, 21*, 445–460.

Fernandez-Stark, K., Bamber, P., and Gereffi, G. (2011). *The Fruit and Vegetables Global Value Chain*. Durham, NC: Center on Globalization, Governance & Competitiveness, Duke University.

Foerstl, K., Kirchoff, J. F., and Bals, L. (2016). Reshoring and insourcing: Drivers and future research directions. *International Journal of Physical Distribution & Logistics Management, 46*, 492–515.

Gereffi, G., and Fernandez-Stark, K. (2016). *Global Value Chain Analysis: A Primer* (2nd ed.). Durham, NC: Center on Globalization, Governance & Competitiveness, Duke University.

Gereffi, G., Humphrey, J., and Sturgeon, T. (2005). The governance of global value chains. *Review of International Political Economy, 12*, 78–104.

Gereffi, G., and Lee, J. (2012). Why the world suddenly cares about global supply chains. *Journal of Supply Chain Management, 48*, 24–32.

Hansen, M. W., Larsen, M. M., Pedersen, T., and Petersen, B. (2010). *Strategies in Emerging Markets: A Case Book on Danish Multinational Corporations in China and India*. Copenhagen: Copenhagen Business School Press.

International Bank for Reconstruction and Development (2017). *Global Value Chain Development Report 2017: Measuring and Analyzing the Impact of GVCs on Economic Development*. Washington, DC: World Bank.

Kano, L., Tsang, E. W. K., and Yeung, H. W.-c. (2020). Global value chains: A review of the multidisciplinary literature. *Journal of International Business Studies, 51*, 577–622.

Kinkel, S. (2014). Future and impact of backshoring: Some conclusions from 15 years of research on German practices. *Journal of Purchasing & Supply Management, 20*, 63–65.

Mudambi, R. (2008). Location, control, and innovation in knowledge-intensive industries. *Journal of Economic Geography, 8*, 699–725.

Porter, M. E. (1985). *Competitive Advantage: Creating and Sustaining Superior Performance*. New York, NY: Free Press.

Richter, N. F. (2014). Information costs in international business: Analyzing the effects of economies of scale, cultural diversity and decentralization. *Management International Review (MIR), 54*, 171–193.

Strandskov, J. (2019). *The ECCO-case: From Cow to Customer* (unpublished teaching case). Odense: Department of Marketing and Management, University of Southern Denmark.

Tallman, S., and Mudambi, S. M. (2013). Offshoring and outsourcing of customer-oriented business processes: An international transaction value model. In T. Pedersen, L. Bals, P. D. Ørberg Jensen and M. M. Larsen (Eds), *The Offshoring Challenge* (pp. 99–122). London: Springer.

Tate, W. L., Ellram, L. M., Schoenherr, T., and Petersen, K. J. (2014). Global competitive conditions driving the manufacturing location decision. *Business Horizons, 57*, 381–390.

UNCTAD (United Nations Conference on Trade and Development) (2020). *World Investment Report 2020: International Production Beyond the Pandemic*. New York, NY: United Nations.

6 CASE STUDY
MAGIC JUICE: EXPANDING THE VALUE CHAIN?

According to Magic Juice's chairman Anton de Vries, acquiring the Spanish juice manufacturer Zumo Saludable holds great prospects. The dream that by 2025 Magic Juice is the market-leading juice bar chain in Europe presupposes – in his opinion – full control of the entire value chain, from growing fruits and vegetables and manufacturing juice products to marketing food and drinking experiences in the juice bars. When purchasing raw materials, Magic Juice has so far used several subcontractors, including Zumo Saludable. The development of prices for fruit and vegetables has over time been highly volatile in the international markets. For Magic Juice it has not always been possible to buy at the right price or the desired quantities of high-quality organically grown ingredients. The dominance of the large retailers and trading houses within the GVC of fruit and vegetables has not improved the situation, as Anton states.

Magic Juice's CEO Dirk de Jong also sees great opportunities in a potential partnership with Zumo Saludable. However, he considers it more from a "consumer to grower" perspective. Magic Juice's customers are more critical and wish to be informed about the origins and processes of procurement, safety levels, production methods, use of genetically modified seeds, application of pesticides and other environmental issues like transportation and carbon footprints. Hence, Dirk considers the potential acquisition of Zumo Saludable as a way to better control the sustainability of the entire supply chain; upstream and downstream. For the customer, absolute traceability in all food matters is very important; that is, how the fruits and vegetables are organically grown, how regulative compliances are being met, how production practices are documented, and so on. Dirk is also fascinated by Starbucks' keen sense of CSR and commitment to sustainability and community welfare. In terms of CSR, "Magic Juice has much to learn," he says.

THE FRUIT AND VEGETABLES GLOBAL VALUE CHAIN

Fernandez-Stark, Bamber and Gereffi (2011) provide some insights into the fruit and vegetable value chain that are important to understand. As with other agri-food systems, the fruit and vegetables industry is increasingly structured around GVC led by food processors, retailers and food service firms. Supermarkets, for example, work with both importers and exporters and seek to control how products are grown and harvested. They wish to ensure that quality and food safety standards are met all along the chain, and this requires vertical coordination.

The fruit and vegetable GVC includes several stages: inputs, processing, production, packing and storage, and distribution and marketing; see Exhibit 6.1. Due to the fragile and perishable nature of the products, a high degree of coordination between the different actors along the chain is required. This ensures that the perishable products reach their destination in good condition. Cold storage units are used throughout the chain to keep the products fresh, and both air and sea freighting supported by the cold chain are key elements to ensure timely delivery.

The first stage of the value chain is the inputs. The most important inputs for production in the horticultural industry are seeds, fertilizers, agrochemicals (for example, pesticides), farm equipment and irrigation equipment. The next stage of the chain is processing. This is typically divided into production for fresh consumption and production for processed fruit and vegetables. In some cases, the fresh fruit and vegetables that are not accepted for sale as fresh products are used as inputs for the processing stage. In other cases, such as orange juice or preserved peaches, a specific variety and grade quality is required, and production occurs separately. The next stage of the value chain is packing and cold storage. This also includes washing, trimming, chopping, mixing and labeling. Once the products are ready for transport, they are blast chilled and placed in cold storage units ready for sale. Packing usually requires EOS due to the high costs of cold storage and other capital investments necessary at this stage; thus, this is usually carried out by large producer-exporter and exporter firms that buy the fresh fruit and vegetables and package, store and export them. Processed fruit and vegetables include dried, frozen and preserved products, as well as juices and pulps. Many of these processes add value to the raw product by increasing the shelf life of the fruit and vegetables. Processing plants purchase fruits and vegetable inputs from the producers, and sell the products under their own brand, as well as under the buyer's brand. The last stage of the value chain before consumption is distribution and marketing. In this final stage, the products are distributed to different channels, including supermarkets, small-scale retailers, wholesalers and food services.

Over the last decades, the structure of the global fruit and vegetables industry has evolved substantially. Strong lead firms have emerged in key markets, which now control shorter, more complex global supply chains, and many of the value-added functions within the industry have shifted from developed to developing countries as the latter have gained expertise. The fruit and vegetables industry operates as a buyer-driven value chain (Fernandez-Stark et al., 2011). These buyers (including firms such as Sainsbury's, Marks & Spencer, Carrefour and Walmart) look for enhanced cost competitiveness, consistency and product differentiation, such as convenient, "ready to eat" products, from their global supply chains. Also, food service firms exert significant influence over the entire value chain and dictate how fruit and vegetables are produced, harvested, transported, processed and stored. Buyer control has been achieved by the introduction of private standards and codes of conduct that govern the characteristics of the product (including quality, size and pesticide use), and the social and environmental conditions of cultivation and post-harvest handling.

CASE EXHIBIT

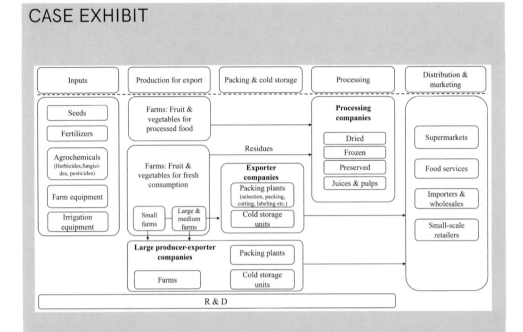

Source: Adapted from Fernandez-Stark et al. (2011)

Exhibit 6.1 The fruit and vegetables global value chain

CASE QUESTIONS

Based on the above, Dirk wonders in which stage(s) of the entire value chain of fruit and vegetable juice the greatest value added is created. He wants to learn more about the advantages and disadvantages of Magic Juice integrating backwards into the production stage of fruit and vegetables, and ultimately needs to answer the question of whether Magic Juice should continue to use independent subcontractors of juice or should own its supply channel. What would you recommend?

7
Designing the MNE organization

Within the last two to three decades, the growth and changing character of international business (IB) has strongly challenged the organizational design of multinational enterprises (MNEs) (see, for example, Kostova, Marano and Tallman, 2016). Before the turn of the millennium, the international environment was more stable and predictable, and a hierarchical system of command, control and compliance was a usable form of organizing. However, the opening of markets in Russia, Eastern Europe, China and other Asian countries; new information technologies; the emergence of e-business models; and global competition, among other things, have contributed to the creation of a global environment that is more "liquid," unpredictable and complex. The emergence of the internet pushes MNE managers to rethink how to best arrange organizational roles, tasks, processes and responsibilities and to design the coordination and control in the firm. The internet and related technologies offer real-time access to local, regional and global information (at low costs), and have closed the old global–local gap as well as the classical discussion about center and periphery. Frontline employees are becoming masters of their local marketplace, and there are far fewer jobs that subsidiary managers cannot do; hence, a finer distribution of authority between headquarters (HQ) and subsidiaries has evolved. Consequently, hierarchical models of organizing MNEs ("lines and boxes") are challenged, and for some MNEs became obsolete and unsuitable. The demand for more sophisticated organizational forms calls for alternative, heterarchical models. These new heterarchical models rely to a lesser extent on formal structures, but instead broaden relationships, expand communications and promote collaboration between and across organizational units of the MNE (see, for example, the transnational or network model).

MNE managers need to design organizations; that is, their structures, processes and culture (see Figure 7.1). These design parameters will influence the functioning of the organizational context – the decision-making processes, the level of information-sharing, the level of teamwork and cooperation, and individual motivations, among other things – which in turn will influence different performance outcomes, such as growth, flexibility, efficiency, speed or innovation. In this chapter, we will discuss the various organizational designs used by MNEs. We begin with classical hierarchical structures, introduce the relevant elements of heterarchical models and discuss the advantages and disadvantages of the models, including industry and firm examples. In the remainder, we will analyze HQ–subsidiary relationships, including coordination and control mechanisms, subsidiary roles and subsidiary mandates. The chapter will close with a discussion of power and conflicts within the MNE and will address how subsidiaries can influence and improve their roles and functions within the MNE.

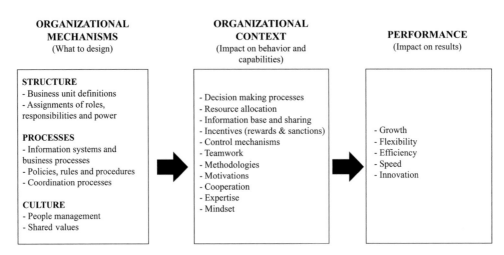

Source: Adapted from Lasserre (2018)

Figure 7.1 Organizational mechanisms, context and performance

7.1 HIERARCHICAL MODELS (TRADITIONAL STRUCTURES)

Designing the organization typically begins with determining the ideal structure for arranging individuals and units to implement the MNE's strategy. Following the idea that "structure follows strategy," the choice of the organizational structure should primarily be based on the firm's overall strategy. This again is a response to the external environmental and industry opportunities and threats, and the MNE's experiences in relation to its markets, customers and competitors. For example, we need to answer questions, such as: Is there a strong demand for global integration of the MNE's businesses or is there rather a requirement to be locally responsive? In the former (that is, forces for global integration), a centralization of the organization is crucial; in the latter (that is, forces for local responsiveness), decentralization is decisive (Richter et al., 2009). Likewise, we need to think about: Which organizational structure is most suitable in relation to our value chain? If it is concentrated in only a few countries, we can implement a structure that enables a high degree of control; if it is dispersed across many countries, we need to ensure a significant degree of coordination.

Making sense of the strategy-structure situation implies several decisions to be made that are related to the *vertical and horizontal differentiation* of the MNE: First, we need to decide who has what authority to make which decision. This basically relates to the centralization versus decentralization of decision-making or to the degree of vertical differentiation. Decisions that are made above the subsidiary level signify centralization, while decisions made at or below that level signify decentralization. A centralized structure concentrates decision-making authority among the top-level executives of the MNE. The arguments for centralization are that key decisions should be made by senior managers at the HQ level who have superior knowledge and broader experiences. Moreover, centralized decision-making ensures that local operations support the MNE's vision and mission, pre-empts a duplication of activities and facilitates coordination. A decentralized structure pushes decision-making authority to those subsidiary managers, product lines or marketing managers that are closer to customers, competitors and other collaborators. As such it is likely to profit from a more thorough knowledge of and insights into local markets than would be provided by senior managers at the HQ level. Furthermore, a decentralized decision-making encourages lower-level managers to innovate and behave entrepreneurially, and improves the loyalty and accountability of frontline employees.

Second, we need to decide which people in which units do which jobs and tasks; or which organizational principles for disaggregating jobs and tasks are implemented: functional, geographical, divisional or mixed principles. This is dealt with in horizontal differentiation. Horizontal differentiation includes: (i) the sets of tasks that should be done; (ii) the division of those tasks among a mix of business units, subsidiaries, departments, teams, jobs and individuals; and (iii) the definition of relationships between various organizational units and the specification of their roles and responsibilities in the overall structure. In relation to relationships, roles and responsibilities, MNEs have traditionally been organized along four traditional structures: the functional structure, the geographic area structure, the division structure and the matrix structure. We will briefly discuss these below. In addition, Figure 7.2 provides an overview of the rationales, advantages and disadvantages of the respective structures, as well as examples of businesses and industries in which they are prevalent.

The functional structure is based on global centralization at the level of key functional activities such as R&D, production, marketing and sales, and most strategic decisions and operational policies within each functional area are made at the HQ level. The employees are grouped by their competencies (knowledge and skills), allowing them to achieve high performance. Most functional strategies and policies of the upstream value chain are globally standardized (that is, R&D, product development, procurement, and manufacturing), while some local adaptation at the downstream part of the value chain is possible upon authorization by the HQ. In general, the heads of the country subsidiaries have the responsibility of ensuring that the unit satisfies the relevant national governmental and legal matters, while the functional managers at the subsidiary level take their instructions from the corporate vice presidents of functions and act at the operational level. A functional structure fits MNEs or business units that operate in single business environments with strong demand for global integration and coordination. Large capital-intensive MNEs within, for example, the extraction and energy industries, basic chemical industries and aircraft industries find a functional structure appealing (see Box 7.1 for practical insights). However, this structure is also efficient for smaller and medium-sized (SME) exporting firms that are too small to have overseas subsidiaries. A functional specialization can take place by separating the export department from the overall sales and marketing department of the SME. Organizing the MNE in different functional units, however, has some limitations. Top-down decision-making reduces motivation and initiative in country subsidiaries, limits flexibility and fosters a bureaucratic and rigid perception of the organization. Moreover, the functional structure constrains cross-functional information- and knowledge-sharing, which can make the organization less innovative and agile.

INTERNATIONAL BUSINESS STRATEGY AND CROSS-CULTURAL MANAGEMENT

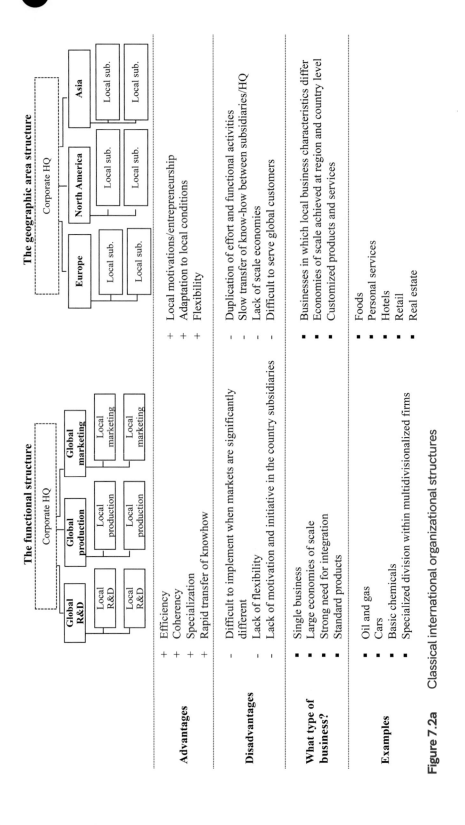

Figure 7.2a Classical international organizational structures

DESIGNING THE MNE ORGANIZATION

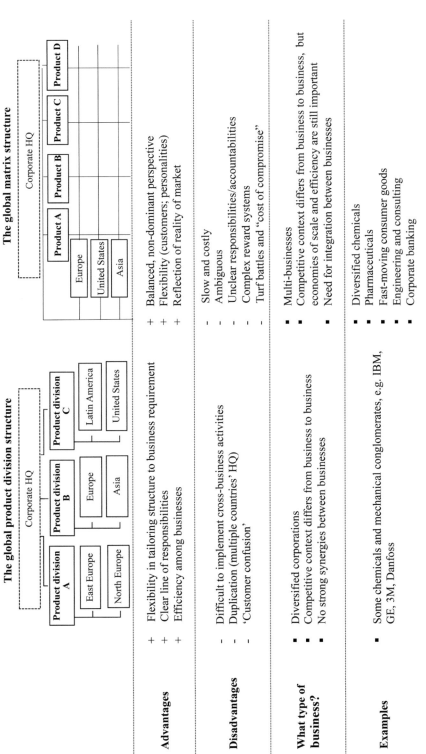

Figure 7.2b   Classical international organizational structures (continued)

> **Box 7.1 Examples: Hierarchical models in MNEs and industries**
>
> Exxon Mobil Corporation is an example of a firm with a focus on functional aspects of organizing. It uses upstream, downstream and chemical as functions that define operating segments. In its Houston HQ, it controls and manages the global upstream value chain that explores for and produces crude oil and natural gas. The downstream value chain is organized based on manufacturing and sales of petroleum products. The chemical segment is organized for the manufacturing and sales of petrochemicals.
>
> The geographical area structure mainly suits industries like food, retail and hospitality, transportation, personal services, real estate and other businesses that need to be near their sources of supply and customers, and need to be local (for example, for deliveries, production and services, or on-site support). For example, International Service System A/S (ISS), headquartered in Denmark, is organized around four major area divisions: Continental Europe, North Europe, Asia and Pacific America, and other countries. ISS is one of the largest service conglomerates in the world and a leading provider of workplace and facility service solutions, with a turnover of DKK 79 billion (EUR 11 billion) and more than 400,000 employees. It is highly decentralized: the 50 country organizations have a high degree of autonomy in terms of bidding on large workplace and facility management contracts, delivering service solutions to key account customers, and staffing and educating the ISS workforce.
>
> IBM's organizational structure is divided into product-type divisions (including cloud and cognitive software, global business services and global technology services), that determine how it can address opportunities in the IT market. In addition, two worldwide organizations are of relevance: the global markets organization that leads country-based IBM operations that serve clients locally, and R&D services. Likewise, the German automobile manufacturer the Daimler Group – headquartered in Stuttgart – is organized with three subunits that follow a product/brand division of responsibilities: Mercedes-Benz AG is responsible for Mercedes-Benz cars and vans, Daimler Truck AG conducts all activities related to Daimler trucks and buses, and Daimler Mobility AG is responsible for all mobility and financial services. This organizational structure was implemented in 2019 to strengthen the group's commitment to brand quality and luxury products, and with the aim of increasing customer focus and organizational agility.
>
> The Swiss food multinational Nestlé is organized according to the matrix structure. It has decentralized decision-making to subordinate branches that enjoy a proportionately high level of independence. Although it still makes major strategy decisions at the HQ level, daily operations are left to the subordinate branches. In addition, it is managed by geographic zones for most of the food and beverage business: Europe, Middle East and North Africa (EMENA), Americas and Asia/Oceania/Sub-Saharan Africa. Exceptions are a few globally managed businesses, including Nespresso and Nestlé Health Science.
> *Sources:* Company websites and information from the media

A self-centered mentality where functional managers pay more attention to their own department and ignore others' interests fosters "silo thinking" and promotes conflicts between functional departments.

The geographic area structure groups activities based on geographic regions and countries, and is based on a worldwide decentralization of decision-making, coordination and control at the level of area divisions and subsidiaries. Geographic structuring is especially important if customer demands, consumer tastes, cultures and institutions, and so on, differ across regions, as it allows for flexibility in product offerings and marketing strategies. Moreover, where different geographies have different needs in terms of resources, staffing and logistics, it makes sense to organize geographically rather than to centralize functions. The geographic area structure is commonly used by MNEs pursuing multi-domestic strategies where decentralization gives local managers more authority to adapt to local environments and circumstances, while the role of HQs is to retain the strategic and financial control of MNE activities. The deep knowledge of local conditions in certain regions supports the area division managers in making decisions; local factors that senior HQ managers may know very little about. For Western MNEs, the prevalence of emerging markets in Asia and Latin America has made the geographic area structure more popular given the sales trends in emerging versus developed markets. The main disadvantage of a geographical organizational structure is the potential duplication of resources, functions and tasks, whereby economies of scale (EOS) advantages are not exploited but lost. This means escalating costs, additional resources, extra staff requirements and an administrative inefficiency. Therefore, it is crucial to find the right balance between the advantages (that is, adaptability and agility) and the disadvantages (that is, inefficiency and resource-demands) of a locally responsive organizational structure. There is also the potential for conflict between local and central management, depending on how much decision-making autonomy is granted to each area division. On the one hand, the HQ may give each region enough autonomy to react to local market conditions, but on the other hand not enough autonomy to independently deviate from the MNE's overall goals. Finally, the geographic structure can be problematic in terms of the overall firm culture, namely if different cultures exist between the various area divisions. It thus requires strong coordination and communication across the geographical area divisions.

The global product division structure is particularly suitable for MNEs who have diversified into several business activities. It divides firms into business units (or divisions) which are in charge of a product or service line (see the examples in Box 7.1). The business units are different in relation to the markets and customers served, competitors are different, as are marketing channels, and logistics vary across the product and service lines. Typically, product divisions work well where products are technical and require specialized knowledge and comprehensive after-service support. Each business/product division manager is responsible for the global performance of the business unit (including all functional and geographically spread activities); she or he formulates the global strategy of the product division and organizes the division in accordance with the units' market and competitive context. Mostly, the design involves two or more tiers: Country subsidiary managers' report to the division heads. The role of the corporate HQ is limited to overall strategic planning, financial control and executive career management. Moreover, the HQ is typically supporting the product divisions by central services, including public relations, business development, legal expertise, and so forth. Due to its flexibility to adapt to the competitive context of each business unit, the product division format is the most widely used structure among MNEs. Moreover, it provides MNEs with the flexibility to support differentiated product groups that share resources, capabilities and competences. The autonomy of each product division, however, means that different subsidiaries from different divisions within the same foreign country often report to different senior managers at the HQ, which can cause coordination problems. As with the geographical area structure, the risk of duplication of resources and functions is also present in the product division structure. Another disadvantage is a potential lack of customer orientation; for instance, when the same customer is approached by salespersons coming from different product divisions.

The global matrix structure differentiates the MNE using two dimensions (see Figure 7.2): often product lines and geography (it could also be by function and geography). In this structure the responsibilities are shared between (here) product divisions and geographic units. As a given business unit is experiencing competing pressures for both local responsiveness (the geographic dimension) and global integration and efficiency (the product dimension), a global matrix structure may be the answer. It combines the efficiency of the product organizational structure with the flexibility of local operations. In the matrix structure, employees commonly report to two managers instead of one. For example, an employee may report to both a product division manager and an area division manager. The product division manager's role is to establish the firm's strategy and policies related to product offerings, manufacturing and inbound logistics. The role of the geographic area manager (for example, the subsidiary manager) is to assist the sales and marketing teams in targeting the products and services to the needs of the local market. Since the matrix structure assigns equal authority to the product and area managers, both must work together to set relationships, and coordinate resources and tasks. Often, a global matrix structure creates cross-national teams for special projects and promotes cross-divisional communication and collaboration. The global matrix structure is complex and difficult to manage, and therefore several disadvantages exist, including: role ambiguity due to dual bosses, unclear responsibilities, cost inefficiencies (high coordinating costs due to too many meetings, committees, and task forces in place), and power struggles about objectives and means. Many MNEs with dual requirements, such as Dow Chemicals, BASF and ABB, have experimented with the global matrix structure with mixed experiences, and the practicality of the organizational form has been questioned from time to time (Burton, Obel and Håkonsson, 2015).

7.2 HETERARCHICAL MODELS: NETWORKS AND TRANSNATIONALS

The main criticism against the hierarchical models is that the formal organizational chart is often a poor representation of how an organization really functions. Organizations represent a set of relationships among individuals, groups and departments with different relationship patterns that prosper within the same formal structure (Bartlett and Ghoshal, 1989). We therefore need to also focus on the patterns of these relationships, including horizontal relations (subsidiary–subsidiary relationships), and the managerial processes of MNEs that are almost omitted in the hierarchical models. Instead of taking a hierarchical top-down view, the perspective should be heterarchical – a notion that was originally introduced by the Swedish IB scholar Gunnar Hedlund. He characterized the MNE as an organization that is actively seeking to exploit firm-specific advantages (FSA) on a global scale using centers with different characteristics that are loosely coupled between units and involve normative control systems (Hedlund, 1986). The idea was further developed by Ghoshal and Bartlett (1990). According to these authors, the hierarchical model institutionalizes organizational boundaries that create rivalry and conflicts between units, induce slow communication, discourage collaboration and bureaucratize decision-making. The idea is that removing these boundaries will position the MNE better towards expanding to a diversity of markets, and involvement with customers, suppliers, distributors and external partners.

Ghoshal and Bartlett (1990) identified the following four models of the MNE: two variants of the multi-domestic firm, namely the multinational model and the international model, which have subsidiaries that are locally oriented and contain most of the value chain; the global model, where value-adding activities are concentrated in the home country to capture global-scale economies; and the transnational model or the transnational solution, which they conceptualized as an internally differentiated network. The first three are "hub and spoke" models with the MNE home country constituting the hub. The transnational model is, in contrast, a highly integrated network of interdependent, differentiated and goal-disparate subsidiaries with their own external stakeholder networks. While the transnational model does not prescribe any specific organizational structure, it recognizes that the MNE is made up of differentiated managerial roles and a few key design parameters; see Figure 7.3.

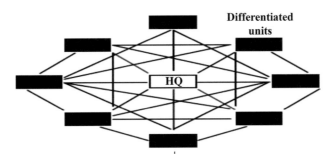

Managerial roles
- *Global managers* act as overall corporate leaders and developers of talent
- *Global business managers* act as strategists, architects of assets distribution, and coordinators of global activities
- *National managers* act as sensors of local opportunities and threats, builders of national resources and contributors to global competitiveness
- *Functional managers* act as specialists and coordinators in sharing resources, activities and "best practices" within their functional area of expertise

Key design features
- *Business units* are part of a *network* characterized by reciprocal dependencies
- Clearly defined and tightly controlled *set of operation systems*
- *Strong interpersonal relationships* among all types of managers
- Establishment of *inter-unit decision forums* (task forces, committees etc. with active participation of global, functional, and national managers)
- *Strong cultural values*
- An organizational culture that *promotes the willingness to share knowledge and to collaborate*

Source: Adapted from Lasserre (2018)

Figure 7.3   The transnational organizational model

The transnational model represents flat organizational structures, with loosely connected networks of self-organizing and self-governing units and individuals. A network structure is anchored by a core unit that arranges roles, relationships and responsibilities in a pattern flow of activities that allocates people, tasks and resources to decentralized projects. Differentiated units (for example, a local marketing subsidiary, an international production center, a regional HQ) are the frontlines of the network. Operationally, cross-partner arrangements share production facilities, distribution and sales centers or service resources (Ghoshal and Bartlett, 1990). The channel of exchange that facilitates the flows of information, goods and money creates linkages between the differentiated and interdependent functional, area and product units. Digital communication tools (for example, video conferencing, social media, e-mail and file-sharing services) support coordination and promote collaboration. For the MNE, this means that functional departments and foreign subsidiaries have a very important strategic role to play. To profit from subsidiaries' access to unique local resources, they often operate with high degrees of freedom, and turn decentralized and informal mechanisms of coordination into an important factor for the success of the MNE.

Since the transnational model does not rely on a formal organizational structure, it is a bit more challenging to find firms that officially represent examples of a transnational network. Authors who tried to operationalize this structure used various ratios. Garbe and Richter (2009) referred to three ratios calculated for the subsidiary network of MNEs: First, the average hierarchical level of subsidiaries in the network (for example, subsidiaries directly owned by the HQ are level 1, second-level subsidiaries are owned by first-level subsidiaries, and so forth). Many hierarchical levels imply that, on average, decision-making power is found on a lower level, which points to decentralization. Second, they used the number of overseas subsidiaries whose immediate parent is not located in the MNE's home country (divided by the total number of subsidiaries). Third, they measured the number of overseas subsidiaries whose immediate parent is located in another (other than their own) foreign country in relation to the total number of subsidiaries. If foreign subsidiaries coordinate the operations of other subsidiaries either in their country or even in another foreign country, sub-organizations are created. The authors then imply that mid-level shares point to transnational structures balancing elements of centralization and decentralization. Using this approach, Garbe and Richter (2009) found that a transnational set-up contributes to good performance among the top 100 most international firms worldwide, though the implementation of the network approach can be a challenge in large MNEs (see below). In addition, the ratios may help to generate a first idea of the formal organizational set-up (see Table 7.1), yet a full understanding of the organizational structures requires a more in-depth qualitative analysis of each firm's network of subsidiaries, and some authors do this by analyzing the roles of subsidiaries in specific MNEs (as we will discuss in an upcoming section).

Table 7.1 Ratios to identify organizational set-ups and firm examples

Firm	Average hierarchical level	Share of subsidiaries with parent outside MNE's home country	Share of subsidiaries whose parent is located in another foreign country	Indication
Nestlé	4.7	0.9	0.3	Rather transnational
Pfizer	1.9	0.5	0.3	Central organization (see average hierarchical level) with transnational elements
General Motors	8.8	0.9	0.3	Decentralized organization
Mitsubishi Corporation	1.3	0.1	0.1	Centralized organization

Source: Based on Garbe and Richter (2009)

Heterarchical models have their advantages and disadvantages. The network perspective enables an understanding of the subsidiary as a node in a network with links to external partners (sub-suppliers, key customers, R&D partners, and so on) and internal actors (other subsidiaries), with greater degrees of freedom but also a greater degree of interdependence better reflecting realities. However, loosely coupled and self-governing units, many internal management committees and task forces, unclear responsibilities, and so on, create organizational complexities and a lack of transparency in heterarchical models. Consequently, a poor implementation of the ideas behind the heterarchical models can lead to sub-optimal decisions on resource allocations, role ambiguities, potential power struggles and cost inefficiencies. Often it has been argued that the format of the network structure works particularly well in small organizations (Birkinshaw and Pedersen, 2009). In large MNEs, "hidden" hierarchies can arise as local subsidiary managers and staff – far from the inner circles of top management – organize based on the reality of their own rules, rewards and sanctions, which can be problematic.

7.3 ORGANIZATIONAL COORDINATION MECHANISMS: CENTRALIZATION, FORMALIZATION AND SOCIALIZATION

The conceptualization of HQ–subsidiary relationships originally had a focus on the formal systems to coordinate and control foreign subsidiaries. The mechanisms of coordination were seen from the perspective of the MNE HQ and focused on how the center controls a portfolio of subsidiaries through top-down directives. Later, the perspective was extended by putting emphasis on the complexities that are associated with managing the internal and external relationships involved and on collaborative mechanisms related to culture and "bottom-up" processes (Birkinshaw and Pedersen, 2009; Kostova et al., 2016). We define a mechanism of coordination as any administrative tool for achieving integration among different units within the organization. All organizations have a certain degree of specialization and differentiation between units, which call for some sort of coordination effort across them. These "mechanisms of organizational coordination" can be divided into three main groups: centralization, formalization and socialization; within each a few sub-groups can be derived (see also Martinez and Jarillo, 1989, and Table 7.2).

Table 7.2 Organizational coordination mechanisms

Coordination mechanisms	Characterization
Centralization	The structural distribution of tasks, decision-making competences and responsibilities between the HQ and subsidiaries: • departmentalization • direct surveillance and controlling of the subsidiary (command management)
Formalization	The use of procedures for creating and maintaining relations and connections between the HQ and subsidiaries (management through instructions and rules): • standardization of business processes (for example, procedures, manuals, plans, routines and policies) • standardization of output measures (that is, performance or results) • standardization of employee skills (that is, job descriptions)
Socialization	Specifies the adjustment process where subsidiary manager(s) acquire the values and attitudes that are attached to her/his job, and the organization that she or he is part of: • definition of norms and values (value management)

Centralization has two sub-mechanisms. The first is the grouping of activities within organizational units (departmentalization), following the principle of labor division. The centralization–decentralization mechanism determines who has the authority to make what decision; that is, whether the locus of decision-making authority lies in the higher or lower level of the organization pyramid. If decisions on subsidiary-level activities are made by executives at the HQ level, the firm has a high degree of centralization. A low degree of centralization – a decentralized structure – in contrast pushes decision-making authority down to the middle managers on the front lines, namely to those running the local subsidiaries.

Formalization includes the use of either formal procedures to create and maintain relations between the HQ and subsidiaries (that is, management through instructions and procedures) or informal lateral or cross-unit relations, and direct and personal communications. Formalization contains three sub-mechanisms: First, the standardization of business practices in the form of procedures, manuals, plans, budgets, routines and policies, or standard practices that are written down in documents with the intention of guiding the activities and actions of organizational units and individuals. Second, formalization can come in the form of a standardization of output measures (such as performance indicators or specific results) that consist of various forms of exercising control, follow-up actions, financial performance evaluation, total quality management evaluations, organizational and personal performance evaluations, and so forth. Third, it can come in the form of a standardization of employee skills; that is, job descriptions, job training and programs, formal courses and other practices of HR management. Informal mechanisms include: direct managerial contacts, informal communications, e-mails and video communication, and all non-written coordination.

Socialization (sometimes referred to as "normative integration") is a mechanism that specifies the adjustment process through which the organizational members acquire the values and attitudes that are attached to the job and/or the organization itself. It involves the learning process of employees to fit their organizational roles: Newcomers learn about the organization and its history, values, jargon, culture and procedures. This process of socialization affects the ways in which employees later apply their skills and abilities to their jobs.

The use of the organizational mechanisms in IB involves several dilemmas and trade-offs. Analyses of MNE organizations have often assumed that HQ–subsidiary relationships are identical for all subsidiaries throughout the firm; however, each relation can be governed by different combinations of the above-mentioned mechanisms depending on the contingencies. In particular, a key question arises in relation to which coordination mechanisms should be applied: Should the MNE HQ manage the foreign subsidiaries in the same way or differently?

To answer this question, it is useful to consider the local context of the subsidiary (see Ghoshal and Nohria, 1989; Nohria and Ghoshal, 1994), which can differ in several ways: One important way is the environmental complexity of the host country in which the subsidiary is located; for instance, the level of technological dynamism and competitive intensity. A highly complex environment at the local subsidiary level is supposed to decrease the efficacy of both centralization and formalization, and increase the efficacy of socialization. Another dimension to consider is the amount of local resources available to the subsidiary. An increase in resources that are possessed on the subsidiary level decreases the efficacy of centralization, but increases the relevance of formalization. Differentiating the local context into these two dimensions – the degree of environmental complexities and the amount of local resources – results in a 2×2 matrix that matches structures with local context (see Figure 7.4).

Following Figure 7.4, we differentiate between four structures (Ghoshal and Nohria, 1989; Nohria and Ghoshal, 1994), which indicate different coordination mechanisms. A hierarchical structure that fits a situation that is characterized by a low degree of environmental complexity and low levels of local subsidiary resources indicates a high level of centralization, and low levels of formalization and socialization. A federative structure fits a situation characterized by low environmental complexity and high local subsidiary resources, and dictates a low level of centralization, a high level of formalization and a low degree of socialization. A clan structure fits a situation

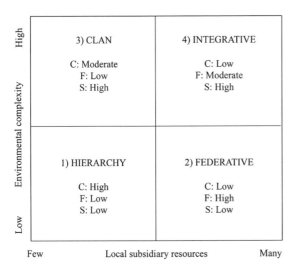

Source: Adapted from Ghoshal and Nohria (1989)

Figure 7.4 Different organizational structures: The importance of the local context

characterized by a high degree of environmental complexity and low local resource levels, and dictates a moderate level of centralization, a low level of formalization and a high degree of socialization. Finally, an integrative structure that fits a situation characterized by a high degree of both environmental complexity and many local resources indicates a low level of centralization, a moderate level of formalization and a high level of socialization. Opting for the right structures or the right coordination mechanisms that fit environmental realities contributes to the performance of the organization (see, for instance, Richter et al., 2019).

Often the local context also differs in terms of the national cultures of the MNE HQ and the subsidiaries. Then, the same mechanisms applied in a foreign subsidiary can be perceived very differently from how they are perceived in the HQ location; assume, for instance, that the HQ is located in a low-power-distance culture whereas the subsidiary's location is characterized by a high power distance. If the MNE has many subsidiaries located in diverse host-country environments with large cultural differences, the management task is further aggravated. To make coordination and communication work across these country units, the organizational socialization process needs to implement a joint understanding of the organizational values and potential differences between locations. This is a task that heavily relies on good management and leadership practices. To support this endeavor, we offer a toolset in Chapter 8 that assists in navigating intercultural coordination. In addition, research indicates that although national cultures are constraining organizational cultures, there is quite some room to differentiate the organizational culture from the national culture. In a conceptual analysis and re-analysis of empirical evidence on the effects of national cultures on organizational cultures, Gerhard (2008) did not find that national culture is a particularly strong constraint on organizational culture. Especially in countries that have a less tight national culture or more individual-level variance among cultural values, organizations have more discretion in choosing whether to localize or standardize organizational culture and related management practices than is suggested by conventional wisdom.

7.4 SUBSIDIARY ROLES AND MANDATES

A subsidiary's role within the MNE organization is formally assigned by the parent company; that is, the subsidiary is given a special mandate by the HQ (Birkinshaw and Hood, 1998). A subsidiary mandate is a business for which it is recognized to have responsibility within the MNE network in terms of serving the market, manufacturing goods, holding technologies or covering functional areas, for example. A subsidiary mandate can be to sell the MNE's products in New Zealand (a sales subsidiary), or to manufacture a line of products to the EU markets (a production subsidiary), or to perform R&D in the Unites States involving access to scientific knowledge from key university institutions (an R&D department). Box 7.2 gives some further examples of concepts used to characterize subsidiary roles.

These subsidiary roles can also be developed and shaped by the subsidiaries; that is, by developing a subsidiary strategy. Obviously, there are constraints to subsidiary strategy-making that are imposed by the HQ and the host environment, yet subsidiary managers have some degree of freedom in putting forward their own agenda or proposals, especially when they are responsible for significant value-adding activities on behalf of the MNE or when they represent an important geographical market.

Table 7.3 Examples: Subsidiary roles

Subsidiary role	Description
World product mandate	"A world product mandate gives the subsidiary global responsibility for a single product line, including development, manufacturing and marketing. This arrangement ensures that high value-added activities are undertaken in the subsidiary, as well as providing subsidiary management with the opportunity to develop and grow the mandate over time." (Birkinshaw, 1996)
Strategic leader	"The role as a strategic leader can be played by a highly competent national subsidiary located in a strategically important market." (Bartlett and Ghoshal, 1986)
Center of excellence	An organizational unit with capabilities that are important sources of value-creation of the firm. These capabilities should be leveraged by the firm and/or disseminated to other parts of the firm (see Frost, Birkinshaw and Ensign, 2002).
Global innovator	"The subsidiary serves as the fountainhead of knowledge for other units. This role has traditionally been played only by the domestic units of export oriented MNCs [multinational corporations]. However, as technological gaps among countries have declined, some foreign subsidiaries have begun turning into major knowledge creators for the entire corporation." (Gupta and Govindarajan, 1991a)
Miniature replica	"A miniature replica business produces and markets some of the parent's product lines or related product lines in the local country." (White and Poynter, 1984)

Over the years, scholars have developed several "subsidiary role typologies" (Birkinshaw and Pedersen, 2009; Enright and Subramanian, 2007). For example, Gupta and Govindarajan (1991b) classify the roles or strategies of subsidiaries into four categories based on the degree of two-way knowledge flows between a subsidiary and the MNE. These are: global innovator (high outflow, low inflow), integrated player (high outflow, high inflow), implementer (low outflow, high inflow) and local innovator (low outflow, low inflow). Hogenbirk and van Kranenburg (2006) propose a framework based on two dimensions, market scope and value-added scope, and categorize the subsidiary roles into four types: local satellites, truncated miniature replicas, export platforms and regional or world mandated hubs. The most well-known typology has, however, been developed by Bartlett and Ghoshal (1986), and is given in Figure 7.5.

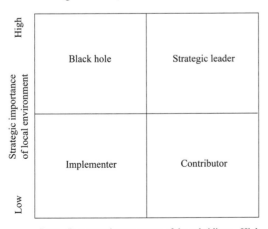

Source: Bartlett and Ghoshal (1986)

Figure 7.5 Typology of subsidiary roles

The typology refers to two dimensions: the strategic importance of the local environment and the competences held by the local subsidiary. These competences can result from transfers received from the MNE network or the subsidiary may have developed these itself. Each subsidiary controls a part of the overall resources of the MNE, yet it is not just defined by the internal resources and capabilities it controls, but also by its access to relevant external resources in specific host-country environments. These two dimensions enable a classification into a 2×2 matrix that provides a simplified conceptualization of the roles of subsidiaries in the MNE network. A subsidiary can hold one of four generic roles: strategic leader, contributor, implementer and black hole.

Strategic-leader subsidiaries typically act as highly competent national subsidiaries in important markets. The markets may be strategically important due to either their size, sophistication of demand or access to important inputs. Strategic-leader subsidiaries are given the formal responsibility to lead in development, manufacturing or marketing, and to transfer their competences to other units of the MNE. Strategic leader subsidiaries are often considered as centers of excellence (COEs) and are profiled as a way of capitalizing on unique resources of certain locations and MNE network integration (see also Frost et al., 2002; Holm and Pedersen, 2000).

A contributor subsidiary operates in a small and strategically less attractive market but has distinctive competences. Typically, contributors represent older and more established subsidiaries that have pooled their resources through a long process of resource accumulation. Often contributors located in smaller, peripheral markets such as Scandinavia or middle-income countries have been acquired by the MNE due to their unique competences. Contributors are important organizational units for the MNE because of their capabilities in specific areas (most often technological competences) and their ability to develop new resources and expertise that can be applied on a local or even global basis.

If the competences of a local subsidiary are low and the market in which it operates has a low (or insignificant) strategic importance, it acts as an implementer. Even if this role does not appear as special, an implementer subsidiary often enables reaping EOS that are of specific relevance (especially in global strategic set-ups). For larger markets in which it is attractive to both manufacture and market products locally, implementer production units can be an effective way to reach local customers. Historically, most national subsidiaries of MNEs have taken an implementer role. In addition, where the market potential is limited and the conditions to conduct local production are less attractive, the chosen entry mode is often a sales subsidiary. The task of a sales subsidiary is to market and sell branded products of the MNE based on the overall strategy, policies and guidelines formulated at the HQ level. For many large food processing and beverage MNEs (for example, Nestlé and Unilever), electronic consumer and professional healthcare MNEs (for example, Philips and Procter & Gamble, or P&G) many of their subsidiaries are implementers. A particular problem that characterizes implementer subsidiaries is a lack of local motivation and engagement, as the subsidiary often has limited autonomy and freedom to conduct its own national strategy (see the example of Merrild Coffee A/S in Box 7.2).

Finally, a subsidiary can be classified as a black hole; however, this is not a desirable strategic position for a subsidiary, following the ideas of Bartlett and Ghoshal (1986). They posit that in important markets a stronger local presence that enables access to and utilization of valuable external resources and capabilities is essential. However, building such a strong local presence in a national environment that is large but in which competitors already possess competitive advantages can be extremely difficult, expensive and time-consuming. In the case of major host-country restrictions or political or cultural barriers, a way to manage one's way out of the black hole situation is to enter a strategic alliance with a local partner.

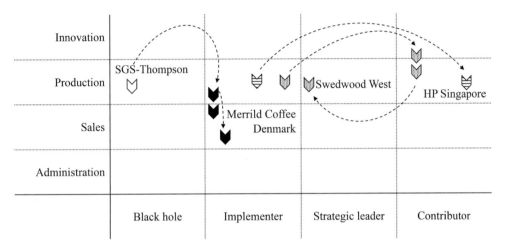

Source: Adapted from Rugman, Verbeke and Yuan (2011)

Figure 7.6 The dynamics of subsidiary roles and the value chain

The above typology of subsidiary roles can be extended by decomposing the value chain specialization of the subsidiaries. This allows for a more detailed analysis of subsidiary roles in terms of innovation, production (including procurement and operations), sales (including marketing, distribution and after-sales services) and administration. In Figure 7.6, we offer an example of such a value chain decomposition: The horizontal axis presents the four subsidiary roles, and the vertical axis presents the value chain activities (here: innovation, production, sales and administration). The resulting grid is used to visualize the examples given in Box 7.2 and shows how some of the strategic roles of subsidiaries have changed over time (for example, HP Singapore and Swedwood West started as implementers; HP Singapore became an important contributor and Swedwood West first moved into the contributor role by covering innovation and production, and later became a strategic leader; Merrild Coffee remained an implementer subsidiary and gradually lost more and more activities).

> **Box 7.2   Examples: MNEs and subsidiaries with different roles**
>
> - *Strategic leader:* The IKEA Group has historically developed close ties with its suppliers and production units. This has gradually led to the establishment of COEs. Three formerly independent Polish furniture producers of cabinets (located in the Poznań area) were suppliers of IKEA. They were acquired in 1992 and became a part of IKEA's production arm, known as Swedwood West. Swedwood West was an inexpensive manufacturer of the Lack table in the beginning, but gradually developed into a significant contributor of innovative production technology that reduced costs, and manufactured more and more products. With the establishment of a new factory in 1999 (in the same area), Swedwood West became a technology leader and COE within the IKEA Group. Relying on close collaborations with suppliers, the Polish unit introduced a new surface treatment method, and a revolutionizing technology for building hollow legs for tables. From 2002 to 2007 IKEA did a massive reduction of its supply base (from over 2,500 to 1,300 direct suppliers), yet Swedwood West remained a key source of supply, and received further responsibilities in terms of increased production and technology development along with the establishment of two new factories in 2005 and 2008. After 2010, it began to drive many global tech transfer projects within the IKEA Group by transferring elements of machinery and product components. By providing people, knowledge and experiences, the competences of Swedwood West were used when IKEA opened new factories around the world, including a large Chinese factory in 2013.
> - *Contributor:* HP Singapore evolved from a low-cost manufacturing unit to a highly competent global contributor subsidiary. Over time, it became a key node in the HP Group's global innovation network in the development of ink-jet cartridges, networking products and printers. From being a home-market initiative, the transformation was systematically pursued by a local entrepreneurial subsidiary manager constantly enquiring about the complementary competences HP Singapore could contribute.
> - *Implementer:* The Danish coffee company Merrild Coffee A/S was founded in 1960 with a full value chain (purchasing beans, coffee roasting, packaging and sales). In 1970, it was taken over by the Dutch coffee group Douwe Egbert, owned by the US MNE Sara Lee. In this transformation, Merrild Coffee was given responsibility for the manufacturing and sale of coffee to the Scandinavian markets. However, launching new coffee variants, formulating brand and marketing strategies, and preparing coffee campaigns and marketing materials were activities centralized in Sara Lee's regional office in Brussels. In 2012, the Sara Lee Group was split into two groups, and the coffee roastery of Merrild was closed. In 2014, Merrild Coffee was sold to Reckitt Benckiser Group PLC, and in 2015 the Italian coffeemaker Lavazza took over the Danish company. Over time, the transformation into a local Scandinavian sales office had negatively affected the motivation of the Danish subsidiary.
> - *Black hole:* A subsidiary that was a black hole at least for a period is SGS-Thomson in China. The Swiss electronics firm opened its Shenzhen factory in 1996. The driving force behind the foreign direct investment (FDI) in the related free trade zone was the expectation that production costs would be very low. At the time, SGS-Thomson had a plant in Malaysia which trained the new employees of the Shenzhen factory. When the Chinese workers recognized that they were paid less for the same work than the Malaysian workers, a strike broke out. As a result, the government of China required better working conditions and increased salaries for the around 3,300 employees. The unit costs of production for the new Shenzhen factory were now 10–20 percent higher compared with the Malaysian plant. A new assembly plant was built in Longgang in 2008, but both plants were closed in 2014.
>
> *Sources:* Baraldi and Ratajczak-Mrozek (2019), Doz and Wilson (2012, pp. 78–79), Rugman et al. (2011).

7.5 POWER AND CONFLICTS WITHIN THE MNE ORGANIZATION

Power and political influence are important ingredients in MNE decisions (Becker-Ritterspach and Dörrenbächer, 2009). Subsidiaries can acquire or create valuable resources for the MNE, even without explicit permission from the HQ. If a subsidiary develops such resources, the HQ will become dependent on the subsidiary to some degree, and a relationship of mutual dependence can evolve. In addition, subsidiaries are likely to depend on each other through the intrafirm division of labor: Some subsidiaries may provide outputs that are inputs for the operations at another subsidiary. Figure 7.7 presents a differentiated MNE network structure of subsidiaries operating in four countries. The portfolio of subsidiaries consists of a COE (in country 1), a subsidiary with a world product mandate (in country 4), a contributor (in country 2) and an implementer sales unit (in country 3). The lines illustrate significant exchanges of inputs, goods, information, and so forth, between the subsidiaries across countries.

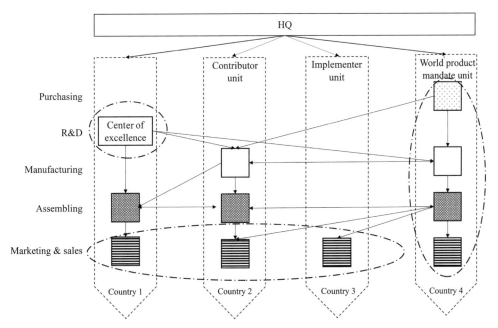

Figure 7.7 An example of an integrated MNE network: Differentiated subsidiary roles and interdependencies

> **Box 7.3 Further insights: Conflicts of interest of key actors in MNEs – main issues**
>
> Relevant actors in intrafirm competition who have the power to impact MNE decisions in their own interests include macro-, meso- and micro-level actors. Macro-level actors such as host-country institutions (that is, local, regional and national governments and NGOs) have an indirect influence on MNE decisions. They attempt to control, influence and regulate the behavior of MNEs to maintain sovereignty, to achieve economic development, to stimulate innovation or to enforce corporate social responsibility (CSR). Also, they aim to attract FDI of MNEs by drawing on a wide repertoire of incentives such as offering tax benefits, subsidies, preferential loans and infrastructure aids.
>
> Meso-level actors are those who operate within the MNE organization and are typically HQ executives and subsidiary managers. They are "political brokers," the chief negotiators and central players in games that evolve around intrafirm competition. There is less research on meso-level actors' goals and interests, especially in relation to the interests and orientations of HQ executives. A few studies indicate that their interests strongly differ based on the sub-organizational or functional backgrounds as well as their nationalities, career paths and aspirations. Expatriate subsidiary managers seem to strongly follow the HQ orientation due to their familiarity with the overall goals, policies and practices of the MNE. Very often they are seen as being most effective in exercising HQ control over the subsidiary. For example, if the HQ decides to close down a subsidiary, it is expected that expatriate managers implement such a policy more effectively than local subsidiary managers that are more closely affiliated with the host-country environment, and therefore will try to resist, modify or delay the HQ decision.
>
> Micro-level actors, such as subsidiary workforces, middle management, works councils or local trade unions, are likewise strongly involved in intrafirm competition. They can be actively involved in initiatives that aim to improve the competitive position of the subsidiary, or passively influence intrafirm competition, by resistance towards imposed measures (for example, strikes).
>
> There are two useful lenses for studying conflicting goals and interests in MNEs: organizational institution theory and agency theory. Organizational institution theory argues that a high degree of institutional distance between the HQ and the subsidiaries causes problems for the MNE in achieving legitimacy, both externally in the host country and internally within the MNE itself. Since it is vital for an MNE to achieve and maintain legitimation in all its environments, it will experience the pressure to adapt to local practices and become isomorphic within the local context. At the same time, an important source of competitive advantage for the MNE is the utilization of organizational resources and capabilities globally. The agent theory focuses on a principal (that is, the HQ) that can ensure that its agents (the subsidiaries) behave in a way that is in accordance with the principal's interest and welfare. A subsidiary actor becomes an agent to two principals: the HQ as the first principal and the subsidiary leader as the second. Due to information asymmetries, potential goal conflicts and the first principal's difficulty in controlling the second principal, agent costs arise from enforcing various control mechanisms (that is, behavioral, output and social controls). The agent theory can thus help to analyze which control mechanisms (or mix of means) are most effective in terms of reducing conflicts in HQ–subsidiary relationships.
>
> *Sources:* Ambos et al. (2019), Becker-Ritterspach and Dörrenbächer (2009), Geppert and Dörrenbächer (2014)

The HQ compares the subsidiaries on their ability to perform certain tasks. This results in relevant subsidiary role decisions (Geppert and Dörrenbächer, 2014). Hence, subsidiaries compete for HQ resources (for example, capital, technology, equipment, specialized human resources, knowledge, information), and play political games to be favored in budgeting and head-count decisions or during the allocation of investments, tasks or mandates. As mandates in MNEs are limited, subsidiary role development becomes a platform for internal competition; subsidiaries engage in intrafirm rivalry for new mandates to develop their role. Subsidiaries also play games vis-à-vis each other despite an underlying premise that subsidiaries must cooperate with one another across their mandates to achieve shared goals of the MNE (Geppert, Becker-Ritterspach and Mudambi, 2016). For example, a production subsidiary is likely to compete for power on technology-related issues (that is, input decisions) with other production subsidiaries. Marketing subsidiaries compete for power on business-related issues such as product design, price policy, and branding and communication policies, and so on. Further conflicts of interest among key actors in MNEs are described in Box 7.3.

Since intrafirm competition between subsidiaries occurs regularly, some subsidiaries obtain a certain degree of bargaining power (that is, future ability to influence or shape the parent's decision-making) at the expense of the parent firm and other subsidiaries (Mudambi, Pedersen and Andersson, 2014). According to Bouquet and Birkinshaw (2008), subsidiary bargaining power increases when (i) the parent firm depends on critical resources located in the subsidiary, (ii) the subsidiary is able to legitimize its existence and (iii) the subsidiary can gain centrality; that is, improve its strategic position within the (internal and external) strategic network of the MNE (see also Andersson, Forsgren and Holm, 2007).

The first determinant of subsidiary bargaining power is the MNE's dependence on a subsidiary's ability to provide critical, non-substitutable resources that enable the overall organization to improve its performance. A subsidiary can, for example, gain power or provide a critical resource through its ability to serve a specific local country customer request for unique products. A critical resource also includes relation-specific competences vis-à-vis key customers, sub-contractors or other partners in the country. Likewise, the capacity of the subsidiary to provide strategic information and knowledge on local competitive developments and the ability to come up with innovative sources of ideas and practices that can be leveraged to other parts of the MNE organization are important.

Second, legitimacy is critical for the MNE to survive in its different contexts. Legitimacy is the perception that the actions of the subsidiary are desirable, proper or appropriate within a system of norms, values, beliefs and definitions (Suchman, 1995). *External* legitimacy refers to how the MNE's operations, decisions and actions are perceived by external stakeholders (that is, host-country stakeholders), while *internal* legitimacy refers to the acceptance/approval by other units within the MNE network. Maintaining external legitimacy is complex given the multiple institutional environments in which MNEs operate (Balogun, Fahy and Vaara, 2019). Often, building local legitimacy in host-country environments relates to CSR aspects, including people-oriented aspects (for example, human rights, philanthropy and safety), environmentally oriented aspects (for example, resource efficiency and emission reduction) and ethical aspects (for example, refraining from deceitful business practices). Internal legitimacy primarily concerns decisions and actions in the internal network. Due to their location (for example, at the periphery of the world), some subsidiaries fail to secure internal legitimacy because they are perceived as only loosely committed to sister subsidiaries or because either their operations are too small or their practices are believed to deviate from the objectives of the parent firm. Simultaneously obtaining external legitimacy and maintaining internal legitimacy is not an easy task. Subsidiaries are situated in dual institutional environments (host- and home-country) and therewith face dual pressures from these environments (that is, strong pressures to adapt to the host country and the home-country environment). The different environments often present different sets of legitimacy rules and norms, especially when there is a large institutional distance between the host and home countries. Even if two nations' institutions are similar, there are always differentiating aspects, including, for example, political and economic systems and cultures.

The third determinant is gaining centrality within the strategic network. The MNE can be seen as a set of linkages among actors that are embedded in two types of networks: the corporate network, which comprises all internal MNE actors (that is, the HQ, division management and the national subsidiaries), and the external network (the host country's customers, suppliers, competitors, R&D partners, local and central government agencies, strategic alliance partners, and so on). Each subsidiary has either strong or weak links to this internal and the external network. Figure 7.8 shows the different levels of influence associated with various combinations of internal and external embeddedness. The lowest sphere of influence comprises a group of subsidiaries labeled local implementers, marketing satellites, or branch plants (Group 1). Typically, these are receptive units given a specific mandate or limited task. They have fewer opportunities to interact with internal and external stakeholders, and therefore their opportunities to develop critical resources over time are constrained (see Andersson et al., 2007; Bouquet and Birkinshaw, 2008).

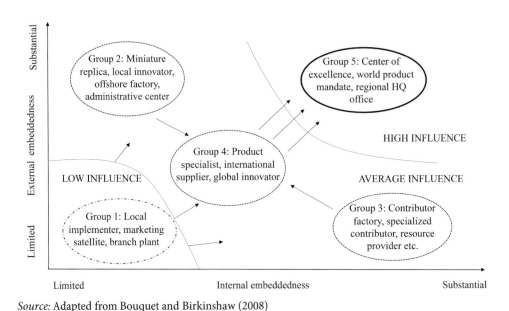

Source: Adapted from Bouquet and Birkinshaw (2008)

Figure 7.8 Types of subsidiaries: MNE centrality and influence

The average sphere of influence consists of three groups of subsidiaries: Group 2 are miniature replicas, local innovators, offshore factories or administrative centers that are at an intermediate stage of development. They are largely autonomous, with a great scope of activities and substantial connections to host-country actors and networks. Group 3 comprises subsidiaries such as contributor factories, buying offices, specialized contributors, and so on, that have developed strong connections to the corporate network but are not strongly connected to local (external) environments. These subsidiaries make important contributions to improving the efficiency of the MNE. Group 4 includes high-performing subsidiaries such as product specialists, global suppliers, global innovators, and so on. They are all in the process of developing strong connections to both internal and the external networks. The highest sphere of influence is found among Group 5 subsidiaries that possess a high degree of both corporate embeddedness and external embeddedness. They assume strategic value-adding roles in the entire MNE system because they fill particularly advanced, knowledge-generating subsidiary mandates. They include world product mandates with full responsibility for single product lines, including R&D, product development, manufacturing and marketing, or they have reached the status of being strategic leaders or COEs in particular fields of expertise. Moreover, they make strong contributions to the development of firm specific advantages for the entire MNE organization at both the HQ and the subsidiary level.

In terms of power and influence, the various groups of subsidiaries may find themselves in different situations. While the subsidiaries in Group 5 must defend their positions and be able to continuously renew themselves to maintain their position, the lower-power subsidiary groups may wish to challenge their status quo and find ways to upgrade their positions or influence within the MNE. Lower-power subsidiaries can use three distinct means to improve their opportunities for influence: First, they can gain control of critical resources by developing new products and technologies, or by bidding for new corporate investments. Second, they can increase their external or internal legitimacy by profile-building with the aim of improving their reputation, image and credibility within the MNE. Third, they can build stronger relationships and increase their centrality in the internal or external network of actors; all three means are closely linked.

7.6 PROCTER & GAMBLE: ORGANIZATIONAL TRANSFORMATION

P&G, the USD 76 billion consumer goods MNE headquartered in the United States, provides a good illustrative example of the challenge of organizing, as it went through several organizational transformations over the years. Until up the Second World War, P&G was active in a single business area (soap), but then diversified into various product categories and into various countries. This expansion process was accompanied by several organizational transformations that can be grouped into different stages that we will describe below (building on, among others, Galbraith, 2010, 2012; Pikorski and Spadini, 2007; and P&G's annual report of 2020, p. 14).

From 1955 to 1987, P&G maintained essentially the same organizational structure: a product division structure. During the rapid development of the consumer goods industry in the 1960s, P&G established a product multidivisional organization that was structured on two dimensions: functions and brands. Each division (that is, foods, toilet goods, soap and detergents) was responsible for R&D, brand management, manufacturing and sales. The functions transferred best practices across many brands and developed leading-edge functional competences. While the product division structure was suitable for handling a large homogenous market such as P&G's home market, the United States, the Western European market with its different cultures, languages and laws was organized in a separate international division headed by a president for overseas operations. At that time the overseas markets accounted for less than a quarter of the total P&G revenues. The country-based international division consisted of several country subsidiaries that were managed by general managers who had the power to adapt P&G technologies, processes and products to the needs of their local markets. Corporate functions were located at the regional HQ in Brussels, while country-specific functions were managed locally.

From around 1987 (to 1995), P&G started to experiment with the matrix structure, comprising categories and functions of its United States operations. In its home market, P&G established category business units, each run by a general manager to whom both brand and functional managers were reporting; see Figure 7.9. In addition to these product divisions, centralized functions were created, such as sales and R&D, that were led by vice presidents. A matrix reporting structure was set up: The managers in the functional line reported directly to the category managers and (as indicated by the dotted line in Figure 7.9) reported to their functional leaders. The adoption of a matrix structure in the United States was aimed at improving functional resource-sharing across business units to achieve EOS and scope in response to intensifying competition (see Pikorski and Spadini, 2007). In the early 1980s, P&G also recognized that the country-based Western European organizational structure was inappropriate due to country-related silo thinking. In addition, the European corporate functions had limited connections to the US operations and the product and brand activities were dissimilar and uncoordinated across the European subsidiaries. This led to a situation in which product innovation and brand extension were considerably slowed down. For example, the Pampers brand which was launched in the United States in the beginning of the 1960s was introduced to the German market in 1973, and not available in France before 1978. Moreover, manufacturing plants in each European country were expensive. Consequently, the European market needed reorganization. P&G decided to create a structure around product categories in Europe, where country managers were replaced by multi-country product-category managers. For instance, a vice president for laundry in Europe was created; the general manager responsible for selling laundry detergents in France then needed to report to this European laundry vice president, who coordinated activities related to the product category all over Europe. The former country managers then became responsible for marketing and sales of the P&G products in their own country.

In 1995, P&G started migrating to a global matrix structure that comprised categories and functions. P&G had expanded into other regions (for example, it was now active in Japan, and in developing countries) and the revenues coming from overseas markets were growing

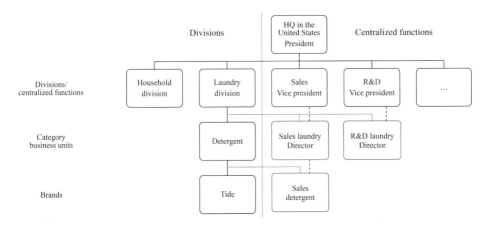

Source: Adapted from Pikorski and Spadini (2007)

Figure 7.9 The US matrix of category and functional business units

considerably and meanwhile accounted for more than one-third of total revenues. Moreover, converging consumer tastes and falling trade and regulatory barriers were making markets more homogenous, opening up opportunities for standardization to exploit EOS and scope on a global basis. First, European country functions were integrated into global functions. Global functional senior vice presidents were established who were responsible for global functions all over the world (see the dotted-line reporting relationship to P&G's global functional senior vice presidents in Figure 7.10). With the aim of better coordinated category and branding strategies, P&G created the positions of global category presidents who reported directly to the CEO. These were responsible for managing the fully globalized R&D function for a given product category. In addition, the country category general managers needed to report to their global category presidents. From 1995, the global matrix structure was run with four regions; that is, North America, Latin America, Europe/Middle East, and Africa and Asia. In the beginning, the global matrix structure created great results (Pikorski and Spadini, 2007): The global functions promoted the pooling of knowledge and transfer of best practices; category management accelerated global product launches (for example, new technologies were quickly injected into the development of several new beauty care brands), and global standardization and integration of all functions allowed for huge economizing benefits (for example, 30 out of 147 manufacturing plants were eliminated).

By the late 1990s, P&G experienced growth problems. While the 1980s demonstrated an average sales growth rate of 8 to 9 percent, sales only grew by 2 to 3 percent in the years 1997 and 1998, for instance. In a fierce competition with other leading consumer goods firms, P&G had lost revenues to US retailers, especially Walmart. Moreover, P&G's global matrix structure exposed several problems: a lack of a proper collaborative culture, too many management levels (13 in total) and profit centers (more than 50 categories), an unbalanced organizational structure (for example, the global functions still retained a high degree of control vis-à-vis the categories and regions), and tensions between regional and product category managers. Around the year 2000, P&G experienced disappointing financial results overall, and increased

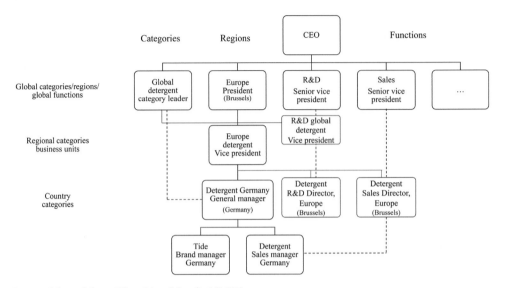

Source: Adapted from Pikorski and Spadini (2007)

Figure 7.10 The global matrix structure, 1995–1998

competition prompted P&G's management to focus stronger on its customer segments. The shift of more buying power to the hands of a few big buyers (for example, Walmart, Target, Tesco) and the move to provide systems or solutions to customers instead of single products forced P&G yet again to organize itself in a new way. Against this background, P&G's management initiated a six-year restructuring plan named "Organization 2005" in 1998. This led to the creation of the front–back hybrid matrix structure in 2005 that was, with several adjustments, in place till 2018 and in major parts beyond, as described below, and is a good illustration of a firm turning its back to more strict hierarchical design principles.

To improve the speed of innovating and globalizing products and processes, the global matrix organization was replaced with several "independent" organizational units, many of them still in place today: Global Business Units (GBUs) with the responsibility for products, brand design and business strategy; Market Development Organizations (MDOs), with the responsibility for geographic markets and key customers; and Global Business Services (GBS), responsible for managing internal processes, were created and all led by a president who reported directly to the CEO. In the new organization, 13 management layers were reduced to seven. The new organizational structure behind these units became known as the front–back hybrid matrix (Galbraith, 2010) because it had two parallel multifunctional line organizations, one focusing on the customer markets (the front end), and a second on products, designated the back end. With the aim to achieve simultaneously a customer focus and/or local responsiveness and global-scale economies, the GBUs constituted the global platforms, while the regional and customer teams (the MDOs) adapted them for their customers (Galbraith, 2012).

These units received some adaptations in recent years; by 2020, P&G's organizational structure consisted of: the GBS and corporate functions (CF), Sector Business Units (SBUs) that replaced the former GBUs (that were structured into the 10 product categories), Selling and

DESIGNING THE MNE ORGANIZATION

Market Operations (SMOs) and Enterprise Markets (EM); see P&G's 2020 annual report. The CF provide firm-level strategy and services, such as accounting, human resource management (HRM), and the like. The GBS offer technology, processes and tools to enable the other units to better understand the business and customer. The SBUs are responsible for developing overall brand strategy, product upgrades and innovations, as well as the supply chain, and have profit responsibility for focus markets (that account for the majority of P&G's sales). The SMOs have the responsibility of developing and implementing go-to-market plans at the local level, and include teams that have a focus on specific retail customers, trade channels and countries. They are organized under six regions: North America; Europe; Latin America; Asia Pacific; India, the Middle East and Africa; and Greater China. The EM were created in 2020 to enable a stronger focus on markets that are important to the future of the firm due to high growth rates. The different units are no longer meant to be independent groups reporting to the CEO, but are envisaged to collaborate, some may say through a four-dimensional matrix organization, or a network that builds on working in teams. While drawing the organizational chart is an almost impossible task, Figure 7.11 assists in understanding the basic idea of the organizational design by using the more classical chart design.

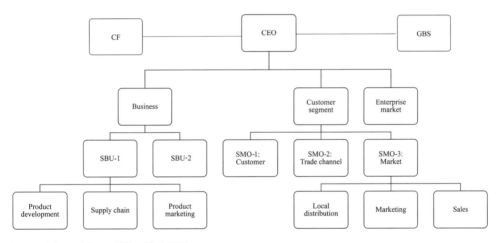

Source: Adapted from Galbraith (2012)

Figure 7.11   Front–back organization with some P&G example units

CHAPTER REVIEW QUESTIONS

1. What are key internal and external factors that influence the organizational structure of MNEs?
2. Identify the major strengths and weaknesses of the global matrix structure.
3. When should MNEs choose a geographical area structure? Explain.
4. Explain the differences between hierarchical and heterarchical models of organizations.
5. Describe the elements of the transnational solution. Why are more and more MNEs using the transnational solution?
6. Discuss the organizational coordination mechanisms (centralization, formalization and socialization) that a Danish MNE can take advantage of in managing its Ukrainian production subsidiary. You may use Hofstede's cultural values for the two countries,[1] or other cultural values that you prefer.
7. Identify the key factors influencing the subsidiary role within the MNE organization.
8. Explain the COE role of a foreign subsidiary.
9. How can subsidiaries improve their bargaining power and their influence within the MNE? Discuss the relevant factors.
10. Please provide examples of critical resources and competences that a foreign subsidiary can build and develop to strengthen its power position within the MNE organization.
11. What is your evaluation of P&G's organizational designs?

NOTE

1. Power distance: Denmark = 18, Ukraine = 92; Individualism: Denmark = 74, Ukraine = 25; Masculinity: Denmark = 16, Ukraine = 27; Uncertainty avoidance: Denmark = 23, Ukraine = 95; Long term orientation: Denmark = 35, Ukraine = 55; Indulgence: Denmark = 70, Ukraine = 18.

REFERENCES

Ambos, B., Kunisch, S., Leicht-Deobald, U., and Steinberg, A. S. (2019). Unravelling agency relations inside the MNC: The roles of socialization, goal conflicts and second principals in headquarters-subsidiary relationships. *Journal of World Business*, 54, 67–81.

Andersson, U., Forsgren, M., and Holm, U. (2007). Balancing subsidiary influence in the federative MNC: A business network view. *Journal of International Business Studies*, 38, 802–818.

Balogun, J., Fahy, K., and Vaara, E. (2019). The interplay between HQ legitimation and subsidiary legitimacy judgments in HQ relocation: A social psychological approach. *Journal of International Business Studies*, 50, 223–249.

Baraldi, E., and Ratajczak-Mrozek, M. (2019). From supplier to center of excellence and beyond: The network position development of a business unit within "IKEA Industry." *Journal of Business Research*, 100, 1–15.

Bartlett, C., and Ghoshal, S. (1986). Tap your subsidiaries for global reach. *Harvard Business Review*, 64, 87–94.

Bartlett, C. A., and Ghoshal, S. (1989). *Managing Across Borders: The Transnational Solution*. Boston, MA: Harvard Business School Press.

Becker-Ritterspach, F., and Dörrenbächer, C. (2009). Intrafirm competition in multinational corporations: Towards a political framework. *Competition & Change*, 13, 199–213.

Birkinshaw, J. (1996). How multinational subsidiary mandates are gained and lost. *Journal of International Business Studies, 27*, 467–495.

Birkinshaw, J., and Hood, N. (1998). Multinational subsidiary development: Capability and charter change in foreign-owned subsidiary companies. *Academy of Management Review, 23*, 773–795.

Birkinshaw, J., and Pedersen, T. (2009). Strategy and management in MNE subsidiaries. In A. M. Rugman (Ed.), *The Oxford Handbook of International Business* (2nd ed.). Oxford: Oxford University Press.

Bouquet, C., and Birkinshaw, J. (2008). Managing power in the multinational corporation: How low-power actors gain influence. *Journal of Management, 34*, 477–508.

Burton, R. M., Obel, B., and Håkonsson, D. D. (2015). How to get the matrix organization to work. *Journal of Organization Design, 4*, 37–45.

Doz, Y. L., and Wilson, K. (2012). *Managing Global Innovation: Frameworks for Integrating Capabilities Around the World*. Boston, MA: Harvard Business Review Press.

Enright, M. J., and Subramanian, V. (2007). An organizing framework for MNC subsidiary typologies. *Management International Review, 47*, 895–924.

Frost, T. S., Birkinshaw, J., and Ensign, P. C. (2002). Centers of excellence in multinational corporations. *Strategic Management Journal, 23*, 997–1018.

Galbraith, J. R. (2010). *The Multi-Dimensional and Reconfigurable Organization*. Los Angeles, CA: Center for Effective Organization.

Galbraith, J. R. (2012). The evolution of enterprise organization designs. *Journal of Organization Design, 1*, 1–13.

Garbe, J.-N., and Richter, N. F. (2009). Causal analysis of the internationalization and performance relationship based on neural networks: Advocating the transnational structure. *Journal of International Management, 15*, 413–431.

Geppert, M., Becker-Ritterspach, F., and Mudambi, R. (2016). Politics and power in multinational companies: Integrating the international business and organization studies perspectives. *Organization Studies, 37*, 1209–1225.

Geppert, M., and Dörrenbächer, C. (2014). Politics and power within multinational corporations: Mainstream studies, emerging critical approaches and suggestions for future research. *International Journal of Management Reviews, 16*, 226–244.

Gerhard, B. (2008). How much does national culture constrain organizational culture? *Management and Organization Review, 5*, 241–259.

Ghoshal, S., and Bartlett, C. (1990). The multinational corporation as an interorganizational network. *Academy of Management Review, 15*, 603–625.

Ghoshal, S., and Nohria, N. (1989). Internal differentiation within multinational corporations. *Strategic Management Journal, 10*, 323–337.

Gupta, A. K., and Govindarajan, V. (1991a). Knowledge flow patterns, subsidiary strategic roles, and strategic control within MNCs. *Academy of Management Proceedings, 1*, 21–25.

Gupta, A. K., and Govindarajan, V. (1991b). Knowledge flows and the structure of control within multinational corporations. *Academy of Management Review, 16*, 768–792.

Hedlund, G. (1986). The hypermodern MNC: A heterarchy? *Human Resource Management, 25*, 9–35.

Hogenbirk, A. E., and van Kranenburg, H. L. (2006). Roles of foreign owned subsidiaries in a small economy. *International Business Review, 15*, 53–67.

Holm, U., and Pedersen, T. (2000). *The Emergence and Impact of MNC Centres of Excellence*. London: Macmillan.

Kostova, T., Marano, V., and Tallman, S. (2016). Headquarters-subsidiary relationships in MNCs: Fifty years of evolving research. *Journal of World Business, 51*, 176–184.

Lasserre, P. (2018). *Global Strategic Management* (4th ed.). London: Palgrave.

Martinez, J., and Jarillo, J. C. (1989). The evolution of research on coordination mechanisms in multinational corporations. *Journal of International Business Studies, 20*, 489–514.

Mudambi, R., Pedersen, T., and Andersson, U. (2014). How subsidiaries gain power in multinational corporations. *Journal of World Business, 49*, 101–113.

Nohria, N., and Ghoshal, S. (1994). Differentiated fit and shared values: Alternatives for managing headquarters-subsidiary relationships. *Strategic Management Journal, 15*, 491–502.

Pikorski, M. J., and Spadini, A. L. (2007). Procter & Gamble: Organization 2005 (A). Harvard Business School Case 707-519, January (revised October 2007). www.hbs.edu/faculty/Pages/item.aspx?num=34016.

Richter, N. F., Wojciechowski, M., and Hansmann, K.-W. (2009). *How international organizational structure decisions affect firm performance*, University of Hamburg: Institute of Industrial Management Working Paper Series, 19, 1–36.

Richter, N. F., Schlaegel, C., Midgley, D. F., and Tressin, T. (2019). Organizational structure characteristics' influences on international purchasing performance in different purchasing locations. *Journal of Purchasing and Supply Management*, 25, 1–25.

Rugman, A. M., Verbeke, A., and Yuan, W. (2011). Re-conceptualizing Bartlett and Ghoshal's classification of national subsidiary roles in the multinational enterprise. *Journal of Management Studies*, 48, 253–277.

Suchman, M. C. (1995). Managing legitimacy: Strategic and institutional approaches. *Academy of Management Review*, 20, 571–610.

White, R., and Poynter, T. (1984). Strategies for foreign-owned subsidiaries in Canada. *Business Quarterly*, 48, 59–69.

7 CASE STUDY
MAGIC JUICE–ZUMO SALUDABLE: HOW TO ORGANIZE THE COMBINATION?

Numerous negotiations throughout 2021 led to an agreement: the private equity fund DCC Capital acquired the Spanish juice producer Zumo Saludable. By January 1, 2022, the plan was to merge the firm with Magic Juice. Two key questions needed to be clarified, namely how to integrate the two partners and how to design the organizational structure of the new firm. As shown in Exhibit 7.1, the two firms consist of several business areas and activities. Together, the two cover more or less a fully fledged value chain within the business of fruit and vegetable juices.

Chairman of the board Anton de Vries sees great prospects in fully integrating the two firms, yet he is in doubt as to what organizational principles should guide the newly merged organization. CEO Dirk de Jong is undecided as to whether the two firms should be run together or independently. Dirk has made many considerations related to how he organized Magic Juice. He has always emphasized that the organization should be flat, without a large hierarchy and without many middle managers. Furthermore, he is of the opinion that business decisions should always be made by people who perform a task and who have in-depth knowledge and insights about the contextual conditions. "Decisions should not be made by managers who are far from the 'front' of the business and far from the customers," he says.

CASE EXHIBIT

Exhibit 7.1 Magic Juice and Zumo Saludable: Business activities and locations

Firm	Business activities	Locations
Magic Juice NV	Juice bar chains	The Netherlands: 19 of its own juice bars
		United Kingdom: 8 bars and 4 franchise bars (Scotland)
		Germany: 18 bars
		France: 2 bars and 5 franchise bars
		Austria: 4 franchise bars
	Online business	Located at the HQ in Amsterdam
	Magic Healthy Food Truck	Located in Düsseldorf, Germany
	Central buying, marketing and sales, legal and HRM	Located at the HQ in Amsterdam
Zumo Saludable SA	Purchasing fruits and vegetables	Located at the HQ in Mataró, Spain
	Production plants	Mataró, Spain
		Maresme, Spain (manufactures 50 percent of the total juice volumes)
	Sales and marketing	Key account management sales (wholesale and retail chains) in Mataró
		Foreign sales subsidiaries in Germany, France, Poland and Japan

CASE QUESTIONS

Several questions needed to be answered during the journey of merging the two firms: What is the right integration approach that takes the two businesses and cultures into account? What is a good organizational structure (a hierarchical versus a heterarchical model)? What guiding principles and mechanisms should characterize the future organization, depending on whether management chooses (a) a single organization (full merger) or b) two separate organizations? DCC Capital requests a proposal for an organizational plan that answers the above questions and moreover provides recommendations on the future roles of subsidiaries that may be established in the countries where Magic Juice and/or Zumo Saludable are located (that is, how these should be managed).

8
Navigating intercultural interactions

Intercultural interaction is at the core of any international business activity. It plays a key role in the exchange of knowledge, the development of business relationships and cooperating with business partners. Successful intercultural interaction is a factor critical to the well-being and performance of individual employees and international teams, and the performance of organizations that are active in international markets. With the rise of international business (IB), global mobility and modern forms of virtual global collaboration, there is a strong need for managers to communicate and to behave effectively in this intercultural environment.

In the first chapter of this book, we introduced key concepts that are of use to understand or measure cultural values on the national level, yet also on the individual level. In the more recent past, two approaches have been developed that in addition to these value frameworks can be of use in becoming successful in intercultural interaction. One approach that is closely related to the cultural value dimensions introduced earlier was proposed by Meyer (2014a): the culture map. She summarized and complemented research on cross-cultural values and condensed it to a framework comprising eight scales that can be used to understand one's own intercultural interaction patterns in relation to other cultures. In developing the framework, she has put the focus on those aspects that have demonstrated strong implications for interpersonal intercultural interaction. The framework assists in successfully navigating the cultural differences faced and will therefore be discussed in more detail. In addition to providing insights on the framework, we will illustrate the use of accompanying toolsets.

A second approach puts the emphasis on intercultural competence. Most scholars define intercultural competence as the capability to function and manage effectively in new cultural contexts (Andresen and Bergdolt, 2017). Intercultural competence can be learned or developed, making it an interesting concept to be understood at the individual level. In addition, understanding the intercultural competence of individuals assists organizations in identifying employees and managers for positions involving intercultural interaction. Hence, it is a concept that is likewise of relevance to HR management in firms. We will in the following introduce key conceptualizations of different forms of intercultural competence, discuss relevant outcomes of intercultural competence and antecedents, and provide insights into a critical reflection on training intercultural competence at a multinational engineering and technology firm.

8.1 THE CULTURE MAP

8.1.1 The dimensions of the culture map

Erin Meyer developed the culture map to assist individuals in navigating the complexity of intercultural situations (see Meyer, 2014a). The map is created using eight dimensions or scales that represent management behaviors with considerable cultural differences in work practices. These dimensions are based on past academic research on culture – you may recognize some similarities to the concepts that we introduced in Chapter 1 – and have been enriched by experiences from consultancy practice with executives. The idea of the map is that it enables managers or individuals who interact with others from abroad to compare their own cultural preferences and viewpoints with the (national) culture of the partner to decode how the relative positioning of the two cultures may influence the daily collaboration. The eight dimensions or scales are provided in Table 8.1.

The communicating scale relates to the question of what represents good communication in a culture. Referring to the ideas of Edward Hall (see, for example, Hall, 1973, 1976), Meyer (2014a) differentiates low-context from high-context communication. In cultures that are low-context, good communication is defined to be precise, simple, explicit and clear. Messages are clearly spelled out, and repetition and putting messages in writing may be useful for clarification purposes. In contrast, good communication in high-context cultures is sophisticated, nuanced and layered. Here, messages are not explicit, but implied. Messages are not put in writing and there is more room to interpret things based on the context. In high-context cultures, in which it is not common to spell out decisions in writing – for instance, after a meeting – doing so can create feelings of distrust. Hence, if individuals who are from both low- and high-context cultures collaborate, this will challenge effective communication. This challenge will even be higher if two individuals who stem from different high-context cultures collaborate: Both use sense-making of more implicit messages, yet based on a different context.

The evaluating scale relates to the definition of constructive feedback, which again differs considerably between cultures. It measures the preference for frank versus diplomatic negative feedback and complements the low- and high-context communication scales. For instance, a culture may be relatively low-context (that is, rather direct), but still prefer a diplomatic expression of criticism. An example is the American culture, which is comparatively low-context yet prefers a rather diplomatic expression of criticism. For smooth daily business, understanding the nuances in evaluation is of high importance. If, for instance, a UK manager suggests that you might think about doing a specific job differently, it is relevant that you decode this message as a diplomatic way of indicating that you should actually do the job differently and it is most probably not just a suggestion.

Several recommendations may be of use to navigate these two dimensions if you are in a management position: The first is to frame your communication style in cultural terms; that is, explain why you communicate in a certain way and acknowledge that this may not necessarily be the best style. Avoid providing negative feedback to someone in front of a group, and remember that positive feedback is a powerful tool. In high-context cultures, blurring the feedback is a strategy; that is, you may give the feedback gradually over a period of time – or,

Table 8.1 Eight dimensions of the culture map

Dimensions	Poles		
Communicating	*Low-context* Good communication is precise, simple and clear; messages are explicit	vs	*High-context* Good communication is sophisticated, nuanced and layered; messages are implicit
Evaluating	*Direct negative feedback* Provided frankly; criticism does not need to be softened and may be given in front of a group	vs	*Indirect negative feedback* Provided diplomatically; wrapped into positive comments and should be given in a one-to-one setting
Persuading	*Principles-first* Develop the theory or concept before presenting a solution/opinion; discussions are approached by conceptual principles	vs	*Applications-first* Start with a solution/opinion and later add concepts to explain; discussions are approached in a practical manner
Leading	*Egalitarian* Low distance with flat structures; communication not bound to hierarchical lines	vs	*Hierarchical* High distance with multi-layered structures; communication should follow the hierarchy
Deciding	*Consensual* Decisions are made in groups through agreement	vs	*Top-down* Decisions are made by the individual, the boss
Trusting	*Task-based* Trust is built through business activities	vs	*Relationship-based* Trust is built through sharing meals, evening drinks and relationship-building
Disagreeing	*Confrontational* Confrontation and disagreement can be positive for the outcome	vs	*Confrontation-avoiding* Confrontation and disagreement will break harmony and are negative
Scheduling	*Linear-time* Projects are sequential, one at a time with a focus on the deadline and schedule	vs	*Flexible-time* Projects are fluid with a focus on adaptability and flexibility

Source: Meyer (2014b)

if this is an option, think about the right context for providing feedback (for example, a coffee shop instead of your office).

The persuading scale relates to the ways in which individuals in a culture are persuaded. The kind of argument that we find persuasive has been found to be rooted in our cultural value system. Building on the work of Richard Nisbett (an American professor of social psychology; see, for instance, Nisbett, 2003), one way to compare countries using this dimension is to assess how individuals in a culture balance holistic versus specific thought patterns. For instance, Western executives tend to break down an argument into specific sequences of distinct components, which is called specific thinking. In contrast, Asian executives tend to demonstrate how different components fit together and form a holistic argument. Hence, if you are managing individuals in a specific culture, you are good to go with detailed instructions and segmented tasks that are distributed among different individuals. In contrast, in holistic cultures, this may not be a good strategy. Instead, here you are advised to motivate others by explaining the big picture and demonstrating how different parts of the job form a holistic whole. Meyer

(2014a) proposed another approach to this dimension, namely to differentiate between deductive or principles-first versus inductive or applications-first. The difference between the two may become most apparent during presentation or negotiation situations. You can invest a lot of time in preparing a presentation to persuade your manager or business partner, but if you do not incorporate the right kind of arguments and logic, you will probably not convince your partner that your solution or proposal is good. Consider an American preparing a presentation to a German management board: The German managers are keen to understand the theoretical concept before adapting it to the practical situation; that is, they like to understand the underlying concepts and assumptions first (principles-first). An American presenter will, however, most probably start with and focus on the solutions and recommendations without dramatizing the parameters or method of analysis too much (applications-first). Hence, the American presenter may fail to convince the audience despite putting a lot of effort into developing a strong presentation that most probably would have convinced an American audience. If you develop an awareness for these aspects and how they influence the persuasiveness of your solutions, you will become more effective in persuading others.

The leading dimension reflects the work introduced earlier by Geert Hofstede, the GLOBE project and the power distance cultural dimension (see Chapter 1). It measures the degree of respect and deference towards individuals with authority and relates to egalitarian cultures (low power distance) versus hierarchical cultures (high power distance). For instance, in Denmark, which is a relatively egalitarian culture, the managing director is called by their first name, team members are invited to voice their opinions in meetings and tasks and decisions are delegated to the team. Using such a leadership style in cultures that are relatively hierarchical, such as Russia, will most probably not be effective. In contrast, leaders behaving this way may be perceived as weak, or even incompetent, as they are not making decisions themselves. Hence, if you are working in a hierarchical culture, the following can be useful recommendations: Communicate with the individual that is on your level hierarchy-wise, and do not skip levels (copy in the boss if you are communicating with someone at a lower level; get permission from an intermediary level before approaching someone from a higher level). In contrast, if you are working in an egalitarian culture, there is no need to bother the boss; you are good to go directly to the person in charge. Copying in the boss, for example into e-mail conversations, is not advised as this may indicate trust issues.

The deciding dimension measures the degree of focus on consensus or the question of whether decisions are built using group agreement. It complements the leading dimension, as a culture can be highly hierarchical and still follow a consensus mindset, as is the case for Japan. In a culture that is relatively consensual, the decision-making may take quite a long time, because everyone is consulted. However, as soon as the decision has been made, its implementation is supposed to be rather fast, because everyone agreed beforehand. That is, the decision made is rather fixed and inflexible. In a culture that is more top-down, specific individuals have the decision-making responsibility, which usually speeds up the process. Hence, in these cultures, decisions are made early in the process. However, these decisions often (have to) demonstrate a higher level of flexibility, as the successive involvement of others and therewith new information may lead to a revision of the decision. Here, implementation is a process of continual revision and usually takes longer. When working in cultures that are more consensual, expect a longer time frame for the decision-making that may involve more exchanges of information. Ensure that you stay involved in the process, avoid pushing for too quick a decision and carefully monitor progress; once the decision is made, changes are hard to implement. In contrast, when working in a top-down culture, do not be disappointed if you are not consulted in decision-making if you are not the decision-maker, and be ready to contribute to the decision afterwards. If you are in the position to make the decision, do it, and do it fast, yet remain flexible in the follow-up process. In a culturally diverse team, it is a good idea to agree upon a decision-making method (that is, specify when decisions are made, with which level of agreement and what kind of revisions are possible later) during the earlier stages of collaborating to avoid later conflicts and frustration.

The dimension of trusting differentiates cognitive trust (resulting from task performance) from affective trust (resulting from relationships). Cognitive trust manifests via tasks that are performed well in the work context. If individuals work well, they demonstrate reliability and gain trust. Affective trust is, in contrast, typical for relationship-based cultures. Here, trust comes from creating affective connections; that is, spending time together, relaxing together, getting to know each other and exchanging personal information. In cultures with a relatively high relevance of relationship-based trust, investing in relationships will save time and effort in the long run. Hence, if you find yourself in a situation in which you wonder why you have to spend so much time dining and socializing with business partners and not just getting down to business, remember that "in many cultures, the relationship is your contract. You can't have one without the other" (Meyer, 2014a: 103).

The dimension of disagreeing relates to the question of whether a little open disagreement is regarded as healthy and potentially productive (for example, as in the American business culture) or not. The scale measures tolerance for open disagreement. In relatively more confrontational cultures, disagreement is interpreted as disapproval of the idea, not of the person; that is, it is fine to attack one's opinion. In cultures that avoid confrontations, disapproving of an idea is, however, interconnected to disapproving of the person, which is why this is to be avoided. While it may be fine to expect discussion of various viewpoints in meetings in confrontational cultures, in cultures that avoid confrontation, meetings are putting a formal stamp on a decision that has most probably been made beforehand. That is, in these cultures disagreement or debate happens before the meeting in an individual setting rather than in front of a group. If you are aiming to encourage debate among individuals in confrontation-avoiding cultures, three approaches are useful to consider: First, this is adapting your communication style by avoiding words that make an opinion sound stronger (such as "absolutely" or "completely"), and by employing softeners (such as "sort of," "slightly," or "partially"). A second approach is using projective techniques, such as third-person techniques; for example, introducing a debate by playing devil's advocate. A third approach applies if you are the boss and thus face the extra challenge that others may not want to confront the boss. Here, it may simply be an idea to skip a meeting to enable more open discussions between relevant peers.

Finally, the eighth dimension is called "scheduling" (and relates to the work by Hall, 1983). It measures the focus that is put on operating in a structured, linear fashion versus being more flexible. It relates to whether cultures are strict in following agendas and timetables or may interpret an agenda or schedule rather as a suggestion. Interestingly, cultures on each pole of the scale perceive the other side as inefficient, either due to too much planning in advance and the inability to react flexibly or due to not following a plan and responding to events in a manner that is perceived as unstructured.

To understand these dimensions further, we recommend watching some of the talks on the framework by Erin Meyer. In addition, to illustrate how countries relate, the authors of this book and invited colleagues from various countries have compiled a sequence of videos that comment on national perspectives using this framework. All videos are linked via the book's website.

8.1.2 The culture map in action

Figure 8.1 provides an example of a culture map between Israel and Russia that was used in a specific management situation of an Israeli manager taking over a management position in Moscow (see Meyer, 2014b).

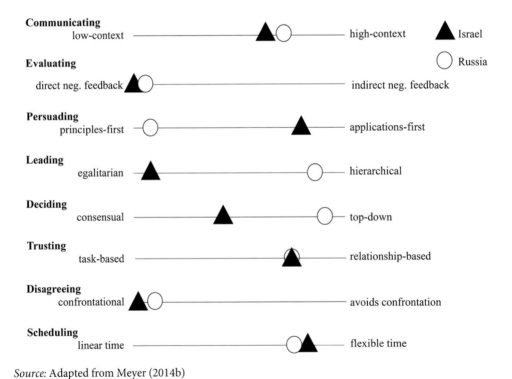

Source: Adapted from Meyer (2014b)

Figure 8.1 A culture map illustrating Israel and Russia

The manager faced several difficulties in managing the Russian team, and used the map to better understand the roots of his management difficulties. The map indicates that there are several similarities between the cultural approaches in Israel and Russia, such as a providing direct negative feedback, a more confrontational mode of disagreement and a preference for a flexible understanding of time. However, there are also several aspects that impose potential challenges to the management situation. For instance, both cultures are rather high-context communicators; as the contexts are different, this aggravates effective communication. Furthermore, while an Israeli manager might be used to an egalitarian leadership style with more consensual decision-making, a Russian team will most probably have a preference for hierarchy and top-down decision-making. The map indicated that many of the practices that the Israeli manager was used to may have been misunderstood and may even have demotivated his Russian team. Visualizing the different dimensions triggered further investigation of critical aspects, and the Israeli manager identified several aspects that were causing problems: among them, his tendency to not use the hierarchical chain in communicating with employees, but directly communicate to all, which was causing high frustration at the level of the middle management.

Hence, creating a culture map for your management challenge can help you understand causes of failure or help you to adjust to the new situation in an appropriate way. In addition, in multicultural teamwork, visualizing cultures using these eight dimensions is helpful to make the collaboration as effective as possible. It is therefore a useful exercise to use the dimensions to identify your own tendencies in relation to others. Figure 8.2 provides an example that can be used for this exercise in a dyadic or team setting. If the map is used with country scores, remember that the position of a country on the scale reflects a national average and not necessarily the cultural perception of each individual in a culture. Hence, if the individual interaction allows, it is recommended that you plot your own individual values into the map.

Individual 1: Mark your own tendency on the scales to the right (if available also mark the midpoint of your culture: ▫), ▪!	**Communicating** low-context	1 2 3 4 5 6 7 8 9 10	high-context
	Evaluating direct neg. feedback	1 2 3 4 5 6 7 8 9 10	indirect neg. feedback
Individual 2: Mark your own tendency on the scales to the right (if available also mark the midpoint of your culture: ○), ●!	**Persuading** principles-first	1 2 3 4 5 6 7 8 9 10	applications-first
	Leading egalitarian	1 2 3 4 5 6 7 8 9 10	hierarchical
	Deciding consensual	1 2 3 4 5 6 7 8 9 10	top-down
	Trusting task-based	1 2 3 4 5 6 7 8 9 10	relationship-based
	Disagreeing confrontational	1 2 3 4 5 6 7 8 9 10	avoids confrontation
	Scheduling linear time	1 2 3 4 5 6 7 8 9 10	flexible time

Figure 8.2 Using the culture map in a team setting

Box 8.1 provides a description of a management situation of a French manager taking over a leadership position in an American subsidiary. To practice the culture map, first read Part I and think about potential causes of the difficulties described. To back up your analyses, feel free to make use of the following national scores for the United States and France (taken from the appendix in Steenkamp, 2017): communicating (low- to high-context) France 66 versus

United States 8, evaluating (direct to indirect negative feedback) France 24 versus United States 50, persuading (principles-first to applications-first) France 10 versus United States 92, leading (egalitarian to hierarchical) France 63 versus United States 39, deciding (consensual to top-down) France 65 versus United States 57, trusting (task- to relationship-based) France 56 versus United States 6, disagreeing (confrontational to avoids confrontation) France 12 versus United States 47, and scheduling (linear- to flexible-time) France 55 versus United States 27.

> **Box 8.1 Exercise: Culture map, Part I**
>
> The American subsidiary of a French furniture producer located in Greensboro, North Carolina, faced considerable challenges to restructure its global value chain (GVC). Financial numbers for the American units were disappointing and a major reorganization of processes was advised. To lead the Greensboro plant and its 3,000 employees, the French manufacturer hired Aude Féjoz, who was expected to implement a huge turnaround (that is, reorganization of value chains and accompanying new sales and marketing strategies).
>
> Aude Féjoz has a solid management education and a long successful career that started in sales at a global cosmetics brand. In addition to working at the Paris HQ, she took several top-level management positions at the brand's UK, Spanish and German offices. She is fluent in English, Spanish and French. She has a fair approach towards employees yet is considered demanding and results-driven. She is expecting a high level of discipline and a structured way of approaching tasks. From her past experiences, she knew that there would be difficulties and resistance to change, yet being demanding and setting very high standards was the best way to motivate the team. These principles worked in the past. Hence, when she was approached with this assignment, she was optimistic and felt well-prepared for the challenge.
>
> After the first six months in Greensboro, the American human resources manager approached her with complaints received from her subordinates. They did not consider her to be doing a good job. Managers felt demotivated and she was perceived as lordly. Several subordinates had already started looking for new jobs, as they were afraid of being laid off. She wondered and carefully reviewed her leadership, and noted the following:
>
> 1. She had put a lot of effort in being available to her middle managers and lower employees and often walked around in the office. She followed an open-door policy, was transparent about her objectives and deliberately shared information. She was sometimes surprised by the openness of people asking her quite personal questions (she found this to be a bit inappropriate).
> 2. There were necessary changes, and this may not be something that everybody likes. She demanded change with regard to approaching and doing things differently – that was why she was in the position. Not everyone agreed with her decisions, but this is impossible anyway.
> 3. She installed a monthly meeting to review the performance of the sales teams that focused on specific KPIs; these reviews were about business. If team members did not achieve goals that were clearly in reach, she stressed that this was not acceptable; she even went to the sources of failure by involving herself in the analysis – she managed to make their employees analyze the problems better, involving a more in-depth evaluation of the situation, including risk and sensitivity analyses. This clearly better

level of detail in reports was hard to achieve; it was often a matter of first disapproving reports and requesting improvements.
4. She was straightforward and provided constructive criticism. She knew from experience that the leader who demands the most will achieve the best results. She intervened directly if things were not going right and was not overly positive about good results. Her idea was to push the team to more than 100 percent, and she knew that her smart and hard-working people could do that.

She could not identify any issues on her side. Could this be a cultural issue? What cultural differences between the United States and France can be the underlying reasons of the above? What would be your recommendations to Aude; how should she behave and what should she do?
Source: The set-up of this exercise and its subsequent parts were inspired by a much more comprehensive case study from Meyer and Gupta (2009)

After developing your own analyses, read Part II in Box 8.2. It provides the analysis of a cross-cultural advisor who may have come to conclusions similar to yours. Feel free to compare your conclusions to the ones of the advisor – maybe your analyses are even better. Finally, you are invited to read Part III in Box 8.3 that describes how Aude Féjoz has navigated the cultural situation. Remember that all of these recommendations and behaviors are individually driven and that there may not be the one and only way forward; that is, you may propose a different behavior than the one implemented by Aude, but still be right.

After reading this section, you may wonder whether it is useful to talk about culture at the national level, following the idea that everybody is different and needs to be approached individually. We believe it is: If you enter every interaction with the mindset that (national) culture does not matter, your own default way of approaching others will most probably be through your own cultural lens. That is, you may fall into the trap of judging or misjudging the other person/people. While you should avoid blindly following assumptions about individual traits based on national cultural values, you still need to understand cultural contexts. "If your business success relies on your ability to work successfully with people from around the world, you need to have an appreciation for cultural differences as well as respect for individual differences. Both are essential" (Meyer, 2014a: 14). This idea of cultural awareness is also part of the concept that we are going to present next, cultural intelligence.

> **Box 8.2   Exercise: Culture map, Part II**
>
> In a meeting with a cross-cultural advisor, Aude discussed the situation.
>
> The advisor used the cultural map as a baseline understanding of the two cultures involved, and evaluated whether Aude's attitudes matched with the French scores and whether the corporate culture at the furniture manufacturer matched with the United States scores. While there were a few differences, none of these were striking, so it was fine to analyze the critical differences building on the national scores.
>
> The advisor identified the key differences along the map's scores and evaluated the key complaints against these dimensions: "lordly behavior," "no good management," "feeling demotivated and having a strong fear of losing the job."
>
> - Persuading (principles-first to applications-first): France 10 versus United States 92, *difference = 82*
> - Communicating (low- to high-context): France 66 versus United States 8, *difference = 58*
> - Trusting (task- to relationship-based): France 56 versus United States 6, *difference = 50*
> - Disagreeing (confrontational to avoids confrontation): France 12 versus United States 47, *difference = 35*
> - Scheduling (linear- to flexible-time): France 55 versus United States 27, *difference = 28*
> - Evaluating (direct to indirect negative feedback): France 24 versus United States 50, *difference = 26*
> - Leading (egalitarian to hierarchical): France 63 versus United States 39, *difference = 24*
> - Deciding (consensual to top-down): France 65 versus United States 57, *difference = 8*
>
> The map indicated that the way Aude made decisions was most probably not causing the problem. Both cultures are used to a rather top-down decision-making process. In addition, the lordly behavior perceived or distrust in job security was most probably not an issue of not engaging enough in relationship-building, as the US colleagues are building trust based on tasks.
>
> Yet the cultural differences point to two issues – one that is related to communication and another to the way that people are persuaded. The French communication is relatively more confrontational, with a direct expression of negative feedback, as practiced by Aude. In addition, her persuasion mechanisms are very different from the team. This became obvious in the sales meetings in which the American team members were presenting KPIs and solutions instead of analyzing underlying mechanisms. The two different approaches to these challenges have induced dissatisfaction on Aude's side and then most probably a strong demotivation on the side of her employees who are not understanding the re-working of their input.
>
> The cultural advisor highlighted that in the United States, managers are trained to use a considerable amount of positive feedback to build self-esteem, encourage initiative and motivate subordinates. Constructive feedback in the US context involves, as a rule of thumb, you providing feedback on three positive aspects for each negative issue that you are going to raise.
>
> The advisor expressed strong doubts that Aude will generate the desired level of motivation for the change by continuing with the low level of positive evaluation of her team; in addition, confronting the team members in the way that she has done may have led to true demotivation and may have triggered their fears of losing their jobs.
>
> Hence, the advisor strongly encouraged thinking about developing a new strategy to lead and approach the team.

> **Box 8.3　　Exercise: Culture map, Part III**
>
> Three years later, Aude finalized the reorganization of the Greensboro unit. She and her team successfully managed the reorganization of the GVC, and successfully repositioned marketing and sales with KPIs going in the right direction. Sitting in her office, she was resuming her way to success and thought about what she has done to turn things around and how everything developed after her meeting with the cross-cultural advisor.
>
> In cooperation with the advisor, she at the time analyzed the options for her to go forward: (i) adapting her style to fit the American team, (ii) making the team adapt to her style, (iii) meeting somewhere in the middle and (iv) continuing with her style; yet in light of the complaints, this last option was not really something to consider further.
>
> Initiating adaptation to her style among 3,000 employees did not seem to be an option either as this takes time and ultimately hinders the success of the turnaround project. Fully adapting her style to the American team was, however, also something that she perceived to be a bit difficult, as habits and styles that she had practiced for decades could not simply be switched off. Yet, how could meeting in the middle be realized?
>
> Here is what she decided to do.
>
> Among the middle managers who reported directly to her and participated in joint sales meetings, she used a meeting-in-the-middle approach by first creating awareness of the cultural differences. She talked to all middle managers in smaller meetings to explain her style and her way of communicating and persuading. In addition, she demonstrated that she understood that there was a misfit between her style and what the team was used to. To resolve the cultural issues quickly, she decided to arrange a small workshop with middle managers and a professional cultural trainer to develop a common base to start good communication with each other. This resolved several of the issues with the middle management rather quickly.
>
> To communicate with the larger group of employees, Aude was engaging in adapting her style to what the employees were used to. To assist this process, she selected two of the middle managers with a high cultural intelligence – a construct that was measured during the meeting with the cultural advisor – to decode her messages to the broader audience. That is, the two managers took the role of consultants, letting Aude know when there was a certain unmet expectation on the side of employees, and evaluated whether the communication that she was about to plan provided the messages in the intended way. In addition, following on from the advice, she started to more strongly express her appreciation for good performance.

8.2　INTERCULTURAL COMPETENCE

8.2.1　The dimensions of intercultural competence

While there is consensus that intercultural competence relates to functioning effectively across cultures, reviewing the literature on the topic reveals more than 50 concepts and related constructs to measure intercultural competence. More broadly, competencies can be assigned to three dimensions, namely personality traits as underlying deep and enduring parts of individuals; attitudes and worldviews that relate to how individuals perceive other cultures; and/or capabilities, including motivations as a cause of performance or behaviors. These dimensions are interrelated and associated with intercultural effectiveness. Leung, Ang and Tan (2014) propose a general framework that demonstrates these relationships. Figure 8.3 presents these associations and provides examples of toolsets that can be used to measure the dimensions of intercultural competence.

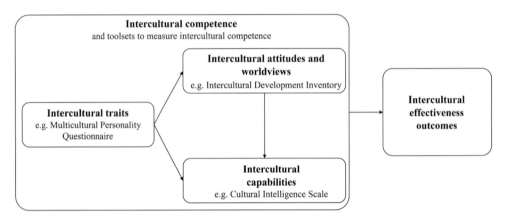

Source: Adapted from Leung et al. (2014)

Figure 8.3 Forms of intercultural competence and related toolsets

Intercultural traits are the most stable among these intercultural competences and are likely to influence both attitudes and worldviews and capabilities. They orient individuals towards certain experiences and are likely to influence the effort that individuals allocate to acquiring intercultural capabilities. The most prominent conceptual framework is called Multicultural Personality and is accompanied by a related questionnaire (Van der Zee and Van Oudenhoven, 2001). In its current form, it involves five dimensions that constitute a multicultural personality, namely cultural empathy, open-mindedness, emotional stability, social initiative and flexibility. Individuals with a high cultural empathy have the ability to empathize with individuals from another culture in terms of their feelings, thoughts and behaviors. Open-mindedness relates to an open mindset towards different individuals, cultural norms and values. Individuals with a high emotional stability remain calm in stressful situations. Individuals with a high social initiative enter interactions in an active way and take initiative in social situations. Finally, individuals with a high flexibility adjust their behavior to the demands of new and uncertain situations. Research indicates that these personality traits are of specific relevance to driving success in intercultural interactions.

Table 8.2 provides the short-form instrument (with 40 items) that aims to measure these five dimensions, the Multicultural Personality Questionnaire (MPQ). Participants are requested to answer whether 40 different statements apply to them ("To what extent do the following statements apply to you") using a five-point scale from 1 = not at all applicable to 5 = totally applicable.

A further concept is the developmental model of intercultural sensitivity that is based on cultural attitudes and worldviews (Hammer, Bennett and Wiseman, 2003). It posits that intercultural competence develops along a continuum with an increasingly complex and sophisticated perception and understanding of culture and the differences between cultures. This development starts with an ethnocentric worldview that is characterized by more simplistic perceptions of cultural differences, and progresses towards an ethnorelative worldview. The ethnorelative worldview involves a complex understanding of cultural differences and in addition the ability to shift between cultural perspectives. The development process follows six stages: Denial, defense and minimization are stages in the ethnocentric worldview in which the cultural perspective is in the focus of the individual. During denial, the individual's own culture is experienced as the only real one, during defense cultural difference is recognized yet their own culture is experienced as the only viable one, and during minimization cultural differences are minimized and elements of their own culture are experienced as universal. Acceptance, adaptation and integration are stages in the ethnorelative worldview in which culture is viewed relative to the (cross-cultural) situation. During acceptance, the individual's own culture is experienced as one of a number of equally complex worldviews. During adaptation the individual adds perspective or shifts their frame of reference towards the other culture. Finally, during integration the individual's self includes two or more cultures with no central culture. Based on this model, the Intercultural Development Inventory (IDI) was developed, and measures the worldviews in the different stages using 60 items.

Finally, in the more recent past researchers have developed the concept of "cultural intelligence" (CQ), which conceptualizes and measures an individual's capability to adapt to or be effective in new cultural contexts. Ang, Van Dyne and Koh (2006) have developed the most popular model of CQ, which involves four dimensions that can be aggregated to overall CQ: cognitive, metacognitive, motivational and behavioral CQ. In addition to the theoretical conceptualization, the authors have developed an instrument that can be used to measure CQ in different situations or for different purposes (for example, self-assessment or employee selection). Researchers who have made use of these measurements have demonstrated that CQ is of relevance to various international business outcomes, such as job performance and team performance (for example, Schlaegel, Richter and Taras, 2021; Yari et al., 2020). As CQ – in contrast to other forms of intelligence – can be learned or developed, being aware of your CQ and that of your team members or collaborators and understanding how it can be developed is useful.

Cognitive CQ reflects the knowledge of norms, values and practices in different cultures, including economic, legal and social systems. A good cognitive CQ enables individuals to understand similarities and differences across cultures. The second dimension is *metacognitive CQ*. It refers to the control of cognition and comprises the processes that individuals use to acquire and understand cultural knowledge, such as planning, monitoring and revising mental models. Hence, a good metacognitive CQ enables individuals to adapt their cultural knowledge during or after cultural interactions. The third dimension is *motivational CQ*. It reflects the energy to learn about and function in cross-cultural situations. Individuals with a high motivational CQ have a high intrinsic interest in cross-cultural interactions and the confidence that they can master intercultural challenges. Hence, a high motivational CQ enables individuals

Table 8.2 Multicultural Personality Questionnaire, short-form

Dimension	Items
Cultural empathy	Pays attention to the emotions of others Is a good listener Senses when others get irritated Gets to know others profoundly Enjoys other people's stories Notices when someone is in trouble Sympathizes with others Sets others at ease
Flexibility	Works according to strict rules Works according to plan Works according to a strict scheme Looks for regularity in life Likes routine Wants predictability Functions best in a familiar setting Has fixed habits
Social initiative	Leaves initiative to others to make contacts Finds it difficult to make contacts Takes initiative Is inclined to speak out Is often the driving force behind things Makes contacts easily Is reserved Takes the lead
Emotional stability	Worries Gets upset easily Is nervous Is apt to feel lonely Keeps calm when things do not go well Is insecure Is under pressure Is not easily hurt
Open-mindedness	Tries out various approaches Is looking for new ways to attain his or her goal Starts a new life easily Likes to imagine solutions to problems Is a trendsetter in societal developments Has a feeling for what is appropriate in a culture Seeks people from different backgrounds Has a broad range of interests

Source: Adapted from Van der Zee et al. (2013)

to enjoy intercultural interaction and to overcome challenging intercultural situations. Finally, *behavioral CQ* is the capability to exhibit a wide and flexible repertoire of verbal and nonverbal behaviors in culturally diverse interactions. Individuals with a high behavioral CQ are able to use the appropriate words, tone, gestures and facial expressions in intercultural interactions.

Cultural intelligence is popular in consulting practice; business leaders and researchers who were involved in its academic development have founded their own institute to transfer

Table 8.3 20-item Cultural Intelligence Scale

Dimensions	Questions
Cognitive CQ	COG1 I know the legal and economic systems of other cultures. COG2 I know the rules (for example, vocabulary, grammar) of other languages. COG3 I know the cultural values and religious beliefs of other cultures. COG4 I know the marriage systems of other cultures. COG5 I know the arts and crafts of other cultures. COG6 I know the rules for expressing nonverbal behaviors in other cultures.
Metacognitive CQ	MC1 I am conscious of the cultural knowledge I use when interacting with people with different cultural backgrounds. MC2 I adjust my cultural knowledge as I interact with people from a culture that is unfamiliar to me. MC3 I am conscious of the cultural knowledge I apply to cross-cultural interactions. MC4 I check the accuracy of my cultural knowledge as I interact with people from different cultures.
Motivational CQ	MOT1 I enjoy interacting with people from different cultures. MOT2 I am confident that I can socialize with locals in a culture that is unfamiliar to me. MOT3 I am sure I can deal with the stresses of adjusting to a culture that is new to me. MOT4 I enjoy living in cultures that are unfamiliar to me. MOT5 I am confident that I can get accustomed to the shopping conditions in a different culture.
Behavioral CQ	BEH1 I change my verbal behavior (for example, accent, tone) when a cross-cultural interaction requires it. BEH2 I use pause and silence differently to suit different cross-cultural situations. BEH3 I vary the rate of my speaking when a cross-cultural situation requires it. BEH4 I change my nonverbal behavior when a cross-cultural situation requires it. BEH5 I alter my facial expressions when a cross-cultural interaction requires it.

Note: The use of this scale is granted to academic researchers for research purposes; if you aim to use the scale for other purposes, permission has to be obtained by contacting cquery@culturalq.com.
Source: Ang et al. (2007)

knowledge to the business practitioner side. There are several helpful videos that introduce the concept with the focus on business practitioners that may be helpful to increase understanding; the relevant links are provided on the book's website. The most common toolset to assess these four dimensions of CQ is the 20-item CQ scale, which is a self-assessment tool (though an extended version of the scale is available too and has recently been tested in the context of expatriation intention; see Richter et al., 2020). Table 8.3 provides an overview of questions that can be used to measure the four dimensions of CQ. The questions can be introduced by text like this: "On a scale from 1 = strongly disagree to 7 = strongly agree, select the response that *best* describes you *as you really are*."

Researchers who have used the scale refer to different scoring systems to generate an overall score. A simple approach to understand the CQ levels using the four dimensions is to calculate an average for each of the dimensions. In a second step, the four averages can again be averaged to an overall CQ score. We have used the scale in several research projects all over the world (involving samples in, for instance, Germany, Denmark, China, the United States, Russia, Turkey and Singapore) among business students, mostly at the master level. In total, we found the following scores that can be used as ballpark benchmark levels to better understand scores generated in your own setting: cognitive CQ of 57 percent (or 4.4 on a seven-point scale), metacognitive CQ of 67 percent (or 5.0 on a seven-point scale), motivational CQ of 72 percent (or 5.3 on a seven-point scale), and behavioral CQ of 63 percent (or 4.8 on a seven-point scale). In total CQ was scored at 65 percent (or 4.9 on a seven-point scale).

In a more qualitative fashion, you can also screen specific candidates, their materials and behavior; for example, in an interview and/or when observing candidates in an assessment center or a more informal meeting. For this purpose, Livermore and Ang (2015) offer a set of questions that can guide your candidate screening or evaluation process; see Box 8.4.

Box 8.4   Further insights: Screening candidates for CQ

Cognitive CQ:

- How does the candidate demonstrate insight into how culture influences her or his decision-making?
- Can she or he describe the basic cultural differences that exist among the cultures where the organization works?
- Does she or he speak another language?
- Can she or he read between the lines of what someone is saying?

Metacognitive CQ:

- How does she or he demonstrate awareness of herself/himself and others?
- How does she or he plan for cross-cultural interactions and work?
- Does she or he check back to see if her or his cross-cultural behavior is effective?

Motivational CQ:

- To what degree does she or he show an interest in different cultures?
- Has she or he sought out opportunities to work with colleagues from different backgrounds?
- What is her or his confidence level like when engaging in cross-cultural situations?

Behavioral CQ:

- Can she or he alter her or his communication for various contexts?
- Does she or he demonstrate flexible negotiation skills?
- To what degree does she or he flex her or his behavior when working with people and projects in different cultural contexts?

Source: Livermore and Ang (2015)

Identifying the CQ of employees who are working with international partners and who are to be invited to international assignments is of relevance as it has several positive implications for various work-related outcomes (see Figure 8.4).

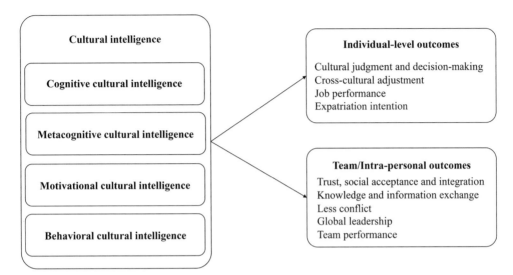

Figure 8.4 Outcomes of cultural intelligence

A higher CQ leads to a better cultural judgment and decision-making and to better adjustment to new international environments. It also has a positive influence on job performance and on the intention of employees to work abroad; that is, to expatriate. Likewise, research has demonstrated that CQ has positive implications for various team or intra-personal outcomes. A higher average CQ in a team that is working in a global (virtual) setting improves the social integration of its team members. That is, team members get along with each other better, have more trust and are willing to work with the same team members again. While this is relevant in itself, it has several relevant implications for other team outcomes, such as knowledge-sharing, the exchange of information, less conflict and ultimately the joint development of strong solutions to practical challenges. Hence, in addition, a higher average team CQ has a positive influence on the performance of the team. This means that it is about selecting the right mix of people for various international tasks. Moreover, there is a specific relevance of CQ among leaders. For instance, in international team projects the leader's CQ has a strong influence on both the social integration of the whole team and the performance of the team. That is, CQ is a relevant determinant of global leadership effectiveness (see, for example, Richter et al., 2021).

8.2.2 Intercultural competence in action

Intercultural competence can be developed or learned. Theories of learning (such as social cognitive theory, situated learning theory and experiential learning theory) indicate that it can be developed by observation, direct experiences or social practice. In the context of the experiential learning theory, Kolb (1976) introduced a four-stage cycle of learning: First, concrete experiences provide a basis for, second, observations and reflections on current knowledge and perspectives. Third, the observations and reflections are transformed into more abstract concepts and/or new knowledge structures. Fourth, the implications of the new concepts are tested in new situations (called active experimentation), which will then trigger another cycle of learning. The learnings generated through this cycle depend on the learning abilities of the individual, which might promote one or more of the stages. Another theory in the context of CQ development is contact theory (Allport, 1954), which assumes that interpersonal contacts can reduce prejudices and thus contribute to a higher intercultural competence.

Following on from the above, these are antecedent factors to intercultural competence that can contribute to a higher intercultural competence among individuals: international experiences (work and non-work), contacts with individuals from abroad or those having a migration background, and foreign language skills. These increase intercultural understanding and knowledge, and improve the ability to question one's own and others' cultural knowledge, values and behaviors. Moreover, often experiences and contacts induce more positive emotions towards the contact partner and increase the motivation to get into further contact. Practicing intercultural interaction furthermore enables a stronger ability to display appropriate behaviors. To actively train your intercultural competence, several guidelines have been outlined. These involve, in short, some key steps that you can use to practice intercultural competence in your daily life (see Box 8.5).

Box 8.5   Further insights: Steps to improve your cultural intelligence

1. Broaden your mind; that is, read foreign newspapers, watch foreign movies, read foreign books.
2. Make use of experiential learning; that is, use the opportunities that pop up to work abroad or to travel to other cultures, and surround yourself with people who stem from other cultures – for instance, engage with expatriate colleagues or become part of a global virtual team project. And do not be afraid to practice a trial-and-error approach in interacting with others.
3. Monitor and adapt future strategies; that is, consciously monitor how you act and react in diverse situations and identify successful and unsuccessful intercultural interactions. Keep a journal of your reflections, which may even be used as a base to discuss the intercultural interactions with a mentor and adapt future strategies accordingly.
4. View interaction from different perspectives; that is, try to view issues from more than your own perspective. Apply a proactive analysis and try to appreciate the differences and similarities between seemingly conflicting perspectives.
5. Practice nonjudgmental observation.

Source: Adapted from Lee and Liao (2015)

To train your intercultural competence, we furthermore recommend the book by Livermore and Ang (2015), which offers a more comprehensive guideline. These colleagues outline several strategies to train your CQ. We highlight and in part adapt several of their ideas in the following.

With regard to cognitive and metacognitive CQ, you may first ask yourself which kind of cultural knowledge or understanding you will need for a certain assignment or collaboration. It is then a good idea to plan ahead and prepare yourself for the assignment or collaboration. Reviewing cultural values and systems is a good idea, and the cultural values introduced in Chapter 1 or the culture map provide a good base to start preparing. Second, it is about creating awareness of the role that your own culture may play in the assignment and collaboration as well as the culture of the others involved. Use the chance to reflect on your cross-cultural interactions and find out why certain interactions ran well while others were more difficult. In this context, it can be a good idea to keep a journal of your intercultural reflections that you can use to check and further develop your cultural knowledge. Overall: Engage in active planning and fill up knowledge gaps; one finding can even be that you will need a cultural guide who bridges some of the cultural differences. Understanding cultural behaviors will also help you to understand if and how you may need to adapt your communication and leadership style.

An interesting facet to be developed is motivational CQ – here it is a lot about being honest with yourself. How strong is your motivation to interact on a cross-cultural basis and what are the aspects that you perceive as inconvenient – are there specific cultures that request more from you than others, and why is this? To increase your motivational CQ you have to experiment; that is, socialize with locals, experience local food, discover the interests of the other culture – generating experiences and affect towards the foreign culture can be of help in increasing your motivational CQ. In addition, some individuals may be motivated by being aware of the external triggers, such as career advancement or a better salary, that are often involved in international assignments.

While the above recommendations are useful, to really see intercultural competence in action there are several exercises that can be done. These assist in increasing your awareness of your own CQ and cultural values and assist in identifying how easily you can navigate a cross-cultural situation. The challenge here is that you cannot learn cross-cultural interaction individually; you need a group or a partner to do so. From the various trainings and simulations offered by authors and trainers, we have compiled several trainings that we found particularly useful in our own practice, and provide the relevant links on the book's website.

8.3 INTERCULTURAL COMPETENCE DEVELOPMENT AT THE BOSCH GROUP

The Bosch Group provides technology and services in four business segments, namely mobility solutions, industrial technology, consumer goods and energy and building technology. In 2020, Bosch reported on its website that it employed about 395,000 associates, owned 440 subsidiaries and regional firms in 60 countries, was active in 129 engineering locations worldwide and achieved a sales volume of EUR 71.5 billion.[1] In its annual report, Bosch lists several of its international activities, among them the locations of its subsidiaries. Table 8.4 gives an overview of the locations of its wholly owned subsidiaries that provides an idea of the intercultural challenges involved in Bosch's organizational network.

For instance, it has 164 subsidiaries located in Europe which are in this region alone diversified across 29 different countries; these are complemented by further 102 in the Asian hemisphere which are again diversified over 13 different countries. Among the 395,000 associates, 262,000 – that is, 66 percent – are employed outside its home location of Germany. More specifically, 29 percent are employed in another European country, 11 percent in the Americas and 27 percent in Asia and what Bosch calls the "rest of the world."

To face the diversity challenge, Bosch developed a comprehensive program to create intercultural competence among all its employees. In the 2000s, it provided a training program that fostered intercultural competence through training centers worldwide (with locations in Brazil, the United States, China, India and Germany) and offered courses to qualify employees for intercultural interaction and promote diversity as one of the firm's values. In 2009, the amount of trainings completed were twice the number of employees. To foster what Bosch called "intercultural development of employees," it created the following guidelines for its HR management: development of managers through experiences from international mobility, promoting the exchange of employees between different locations and hierarchical levels, a policy to accompany expatriates during their stay abroad and when repatriating, language

Table 8.4 Bosch wholly owned subsidiaries worldwide

Region	Subsidiaries	
Europe (except for Germany)	Austria: 6, Belgium: 6, Bulgaria: 2, Croatia: 1, Czech Republic: 6, Denmark: 4, Finland: 3, France: 13, Greece: 2, Hungary: 8, Ireland: 1, Italy: 14, Kazakhstan: 2, Luxembourg: 2, Netherlands: 16, Norway: 3, Poland: 4, Portugal: 5, Romania: 5, Russian Federation: 10, Serbia: 2, Slovakia: 3, Slovenia: 2, Spain: 10, Sweden: 4, Switzerland: 7, Turkey: 5, Ukraine: 4, United Kingdom: 14	164 in total
Americas	Argentina: 3, Brazil: 7, Canada: 4, Chile: 2, Colombia: 2, Costa Rica: 1, Mexico: 11, Panama: 1, Peru: 2, United States: 24	57 in total
Asia	China: 52, India: 8, Indonesia: 2, Israel: 1, Japan: 9, Korea: 3, Malaysia: 8, Philippines: 2, Singapore: 4, Taiwan: 4, Thailand: 4, United Arab Emirates: 3, Vietnam: 2	102 in total
Rest of the world	Australia: 6, Botswana: 1, Egypt: 2, Ghana: 1, Kenya: 1, Morocco: 2, Mozambique: 2, Namibia: 1, New Zealand: 1, South Africa: 11, Zambia: 1	29 in total

Source: Bosch's 2020 annual report

Table 8.5 Intercultural training catalog at Bosch, 2009

Aspect	Courses offered
Intercultural competence	Intercultural management Intercultural competence Successful international presentations Assistance in an intercultural context Listen with the eyes – body language in an international context Cross-cultural negotiation skills for global sourcing English communication skills for international business
Preparation training for expatriates	Intercultural preparation Reflect on and make use of international experiences Qualification training to become a country representative
International virtual teams	Leading international virtual teams Intercultural workshop for virtual teams Coaching for leaders in virtual teams
Leadership in an international context	Intercultural coaching (in German/English/French/Portuguese) International transition workshop (in English/French/Spanish/Portuguese/Italian) International dialog of leadership (in English/French/Spanish/Portuguese/Italian)

Source: Adapted from Barmeyer and Davoine (2011)

training (that is, English, all languages of countries involved in their networks and German for all employees with a different native language), and development of management teams above and beyond national borders (the creation of diversified top and middle management teams) (see Barmeyer and Davoine, 2011).

As a means to support the above guidelines, Bosch offered two major kinds of trainings or development activities: first, professional training and courses to employees and managers, and second, employee exchanges within specific units or groups between locations that also aimed to facilitate knowledge transfer. In its 2009 catalog of trainings and/or courses (see Table 8.5) it listed courses that more specifically targeted intercultural competence, the preparation of its expatriates, trainings for global virtual teamwork and several courses that have a specific focus on leadership in an international environment. In addition it offered courses that targeted the exchange aspect and focused on the following activities: the offer of country or cultural profiles, which provide an overview of cultural practices and further information on countries that are key in the international mobility of the Bosch Group, and an intranet forum with specific country-related information. Second, it developed a network of former expatriates, who gave talks or workshops related to their experiences in specific countries (an initiative later terminated as it did not show the expected results). Third, it fostered meetings and events between repatriates from different countries and formalized the feedback of these groups to specific international advisors and HR managers.

In 2021, the relevance of the more standardized trainings has diminished. Today, Bosch puts a stronger focus on individual (virtual) coaching and workshops that are customized to specific needs (such as the individual training of expatriates in preparation for their assignment). Why is that? With its diversity-oriented personnel recruitment, it perceives that the contact with and respect for other cultures has become the standard rather than the exception. Openness towards new cultures is part of the Bosch diversity thinking, reducing the need for further, more generic training. The idea at Bosch is to further foster an interculturally open approach that stresses cultural sensitivity and goes beyond teaching cultural values. Various big campaigns for diversity aim to position Bosch as an international not a German firm. A growing relevance is also found for trainings that relate to global virtual teamwork; the growing interest in home offices that has accelerated through the Covid-19 pandemic and relates not only to working from home but also to working from various locations all over the world has created new realities and new challenges to be met.

CHAPTER REVIEW QUESTIONS

1. What is the difference between the culture map concept, the idea of cultural values (for example, by Hofstede or GLOBE) and the concept of intercultural competence?
2. Which concept can be of specific use to recruitment situations in MNEs, to analyze cultural conflicts and to train employees in MNEs?
3. Map your own perceptions on the culture map provided in Figure 8.2 (and if possible, contrast it to the national values for your home country provided in Meyer, 2014a, or the appendix of Steenkamp, 2017). What if you were a manager that had to lead a Russian or Israeli workforce?
4. What is your cultural intelligence? Use the questionnaire provided in Table 8.3 and assess your own level of CQ. How do you evaluate your score in contrast to the benchmarks provided?
5. Think about strategies that could help you to develop your CQ further.
6. Why could it be useful for you to develop your CQ, even though you are working in your home country?

NOTE

1. See www.bosch.com/company/.

REFERENCES

Allport, G. W. (1954). *The Nature of Prejudice*. Reading, MA: Addison-Wesley.
Andresen, M., and Bergdolt, F. (2017). A systematic literature review on the definitions of global mindset and cultural intelligence: Merging two different research streams. *International Journal of Human Resource Management*, 28, 170–195.
Ang, S., Van Dyne, L., and Koh, C. (2006). Personality correlated of the four-factor model of cultural intelligence. *Group & Organization Management*, 31, 100–123.
Ang, S., Van Dyne, L., Koh, C., Ng, K.-Y., Templer, K. J., Tay, C., and Chandrasekar, N. A. (2007). Cultural intelligence: Its measurement and effects in cultural judgement and decision making, cultural adaptation and task performance. *Management and Organization Review*, 3, 335–371.
Barmeyer, C., and Davoine, E. (2011). Unternehmenskultur und interkulturelle Personalentwicklung in der internationalen Unternehmung: Das Beispiel Bosch-Gruppe. In J. Zentes, B. Swoboda and D. Morschett (Eds), *Fallstudien zum Internationalen Management* (4th ed., pp. 770–785). Wiesbaden: Gabler.
Bosch (2020). *Shifting Paradigms: Creativity, Technology, Trust – Annual Report 2020*. https://assets.bosch.com/media/global/bosch_group/our_figures/pdf/bosch-annual-report-2020.pdf.
Hall, E. T. (1973). *The Silent Language*. New York, NY: Anchor Books.
Hall, E. T. (1976). *Beyond Culture*. New York, NY: Anchor Books.
Hall, E. T. (1983). *The Dance of Life: The Other Dimension of Time*. New York, NY: Anchor Books.
Hammer, M. R., Bennett, M. J., and Wiseman, R. (2003). Measuring intercultural sensitivity: The Intercultural Development Inventory. *International Journal of Intercultural Relations*, 27, 421–443.
Kolb, D. A. (1976). Management and the learning process. *California Management Review*, 18, 21–31.
Lee, Y.-T., and Liao, Y. (2015). Cultural competence: Why it matters and how you can acquire it. Harvard Business Publishing, September. https://hbsp.harvard.edu/product/IIR145-PDF-ENG.
Leung, K., Ang, S., and Tan, M. L. (2014). Intercultural competence. *Annual Review of Organizational Psychology and Organizational Behavior*, 1, 489–519.
Livermore, D., and Ang, S. (2015). *Leading with Cultural Intelligence: The Real Secret to Success*. Nashville, TN: AMACOM.
Meyer, E. (2014a). *The Culture Map: Breaking Through the Invisible Boundaries of Global Business*. New York, NY: PublicAffairs.
Meyer, E. (2014b). Navigating the cultural minefield: Learn how to work more effectively with people from other cultures. *Harvard Business Review*, May, 119–123.
Meyer, E., and Gupta, S. (2009). Leading across cultures at Michelin. INSEAD Business School. https://publishing.insead.edu/case/leading-across-cultures-michelin-a.
Nisbett, R. E. (2003). *The Geography of Thought: How Asians and Westerners Think Differently … And Why*. New York, NY: Free Press.
Richter, N. F., Martin, J., Hansen, S. V., Taras, V., and Alon, I. (2021). Motivational configurations of cultural intelligence, social integration, and performance in global virtual teams. *Journal of Business Research*, 129, 351–367.
Richter, N. F., Schlaegel, C., van Bakel, M., and Engle, R. (2020). The expanded model of cultural intelligence and its explanatory power in the context of expatriation intention. *European Journal of International Management*, 14, 381–419.
Schlaegel, C., Richter, N. F., and Taras, V. (2021). Cultural intelligence and work-related outcomes: A meta-analytic examination of joint effects and incremental predictive validity. *Journal of World Business*, 56, 1–27.
Steenkamp, J.-B. (2017). *Global Brand Strategy: World-Wise Marketing in the Age of Branding*. London: Palgrave Macmillan.

Van der Zee, K., and Van Oudenhoven, J. P. (2001). The Multicultural Personality Questionnaire: Reliability and validity of self- and other ratings of multicultural effectiveness. *Journal of Research in Personality, 35,* 278–288.

Van der Zee, K. I., Van Oudenhoven, J. P., Ponterotto, J. G., and Fietzer, A. W. (2013). Multicultural Personality Questionnaire: Development of a short form. *Journal of Personality Assessment, 95,* 118–124.

Yari, N., Lankut, E., Alon, I., and Richter, N. F. (2020). Cultural intelligence, global mindset, and cross-cultural competencies: A systematic review using bibliometric methods. *European Journal of International Management, 14,* 210–250.

8 CASE STUDY
INTERCULTURAL COMMUNICATIONS AT MAGIC JUICE: DIFFICULTIES AHEAD?

In the beginning of 2022, COO Joe Garcia is appointed to lead the integration process and to manage the interface between Magic Juice and Zumo Saludable. He will be posted to Zumo Saludable's HQ in Mataró, Spain, for a period of three to six months.

Joe realizes that whatever the mode of integration, there is a critical period in any merger and acquisition (M&A); that is, the transition phase during which the acquiring partner establishes credibility and demonstrates its ability to manage the new firm. At the same time, Joe acknowledges that the M&A integration phase is the most important since it is the major source of failure when not handled properly. As his most important task, Joe wants to create a climate of mutual understanding between the two organizations. For him this means, first and foremost, bridging the cultural gap between the two parties, to reduce the anxiety and uncertainty for employees, suppliers and other stakeholders, and to create a kind of "winning spiral" that reinforces a sense of success and achievement. He also wishes for visible results – quick wins – so that he can convince the board and management of Magic Juice that the acquisition was the right decision. In addition, he also finds it very important to quickly develop a plan for the establishment of a juice bar chain in Spain and Portugal.

Joe sets up an integration team with the aim of assisting him with the difficult transition phase, but also preparing a proposal for the establishment of several juice bars in Spain and Portugal. The integration team involves the top management team, consisting of Dirk de Jong, Anton de Vries and Zumo Saludable CEO Carlos de Lugo. Joe has prepared a plan that specifies the integration team's tasks, obligations and expected results – so-called "terms of reference." He wants to put together an integration team consisting of management representatives for each of the two organizations: three from Magic Juice (all Dutch) and three from Zumo Saludable (all Spanish) as well as himself, an American (with Hispanic ancestors), as a chairman of the team.

Joe is aware that a cross-cultural team can represent several challenges in terms of communication, trust-building, decision-making, collaboration, and so on. In order to be best prepared for the upcoming meetings and integration process and for the sake of avoiding failures due to intercultural differences, he wants to use Meyer's culture map. His idea is that by applying the culture map, he can compare the cultural preferences and viewpoints of his Dutch colleagues with the (national) culture of the Spanish team members to decode how the relative positioning of the two cultures may influence the daily collaboration in the integration team. He is also aware that his own Hispanic American background may influence the team collaboration. Therefore, he searched for the respective scores on the culture map for these three countries (see Exhibit 8.1).

CASE EXHIBIT

Exhibit 8.1 Country scores on the culture map for selected countries

Country	Communicating (low- versus high-context)	Evaluating (direct versus indirect negative feedback)	Persuading (principles-first versus applications-first)	Leading (egalitarian versus hierarchical)	Deciding (consensual versus top-down)	Trusting (trust- versus relationship-based)	Disagreeing (confrontational versus avoiding confrontation)	Scheduling (linear-time versus flexible-time)
Netherlands	20	12	68	10	20	12	22	27
Spain	57	n.a.	18	63	n.a.	61	27	62
United States	8	50	92	39	57	6	47	27

Source: Taken from Steenkamp (2017)

CASE QUESTIONS

Being involved in the preparation of his upcoming challenge, Joe is puzzled with the details to be worked out: What exactly needs to be on the list of tasks and performance requirements in the terms of reference for the integration team? Based on Meyer's culture map, what potential cultural issues can be expected in relation to the teamwork? What can Joe do to overcome the cultural issues that may complicate and disrupt the work in the team? Finally, he wonders whether there are any other (organizational, political, managerial) issues which are not intercultural, but important for him to deal with. Please provide him with an analysis and recommendation.

9
Leading and motivating people in an international environment

The realities of work are increasingly international: multinational enterprises (MNEs) send their employees to different countries to, for instance, manage the business and lead the employees in a foreign subsidiary. People migrate and seek employment in countries that are not their own. Information and communication technologies (ICT) enable digital forms of collaboration around the globe. Hence, leaders and managers increasingly need to deal with the challenges of leading and motivating employees from cultures that are different from their own.

Leadership can be defined as a "process of influencing others to understand and agree about what needs to be done and how to do it, and the process of facilitating individual and collective efforts to accomplish shared goals" (Yukl, 2013: 23). This definition points out that leadership is a social influence process, where individuals with different interests and goals interact. Therewith, cross-cultural leadership where leaders and followers are from different cultural backgrounds becomes a challenge: Culture shapes what is considered good or bad leadership behavior, and thus it also shapes how employees perceive their leaders and how they respond to their leaders' behavior. For example, in cultures with high power distance, children are taught that parents need to be obeyed. When these children are grown, they will more readily accept or even expect autocratic leadership behavior. In contrast, in cultures with less power distance, children are treated as equals in their families, and these children will expect the same when they work in an organization. The acceptance of leaders depends on how much their behavior matches such expectations. If leaders do not correspond to culturally influenced expectations, employees will often react with negative emotions, attitudes and behavior.

The same applies in the context of motivation. Motivation is usually understood as the "processes that account for an individual's intensity, direction, and persistence of effort toward attaining a goal" (Robbins and Judge, 2013: 202). This definition captures various elements. First, motivation is about the achievement of goals. This can be any goal, and each of us has a good idea of what it means to be motivated to achieve something. In an organizational context, managers want to influence individuals in such a way that they contribute to achieving organizational goals. Second, it is important that a person really tries to achieve a goal (intensity), that the efforts are channeled toward a specific outcome (direction) and that a person maintains their efforts as long as it takes to achieve the goal (persistence). Numerous theories have tried to explain how people are motivated and how motivation can be influenced, and we know that people around the globe have different values and motives; thus motivation is unlikely to be universal. Hence, we need to understand specific differences in the motives of people around the globe to effectively motivate individuals in MNEs.

In this chapter we highlight the influence of culture on leadership and motivation. We will first discuss how culture shapes the behaviors and perceptions of leaders and followers. Building on that, we discuss leadership in teams which are geographically spread and cooperate using digital media. Then, we present major motivation theories (that is, Maslow's Hierarchy of Needs, McClelland's Three Motives, equity theory) which have been formulated from a Western perspective, and discuss their applicability in different cultural contexts. We also show that work centrality and work values can have a different importance around the globe and that the influence of situational job characteristics on job satisfaction depends on culture. The chapter concludes with an illustrative example in the context of motivation and leadership of a marketing consultancy.

9.1 LEADERSHIP IN INTERNATIONAL ENVIRONMENTS

9.1.1 Global leadership dimensions and attributes

Leadership styles and attributes are not generalizable across cultures. Similarly, we should be very cautious in applying leadership theories and instruments in different societies. Most of the current leadership theories and instruments were developed and tested in Western countries. Thus, it is likely that they are biased, since researchers have specific mental models about good leadership. Similarly, if these theories are tested in a specific cultural context, it is likely that the results are biased, since respondents share these mental models.

One of the biggest endeavors to study cross-cultural leadership empirically is the GLOBE project (House et al., 2004). In addition to identifying and measuring cultural practices and values (see Chapter 1), the GLOBE researchers also studied which leadership attributes are universally endorsed and which are culturally contingent (see Box 9.1). Their analyses were guided by the culturally endorsed theory of leadership (CLT), which is an extension of implicit leadership theory (ILT). According to the ILT, individuals have specific belief systems (also called "mental models," "schemas" or "stereotypes") about the traits and behaviors that distinguish effective from ineffective leaders. The key argument in CLT is that individuals in a culture have shared belief systems about leadership, which in turn will influence how leaders behave and how followers interpret and respond to this behavior.

> **Box 9.1   Further insights: What is meant by "universal"?**
>
> A main issue in cross-cultural leadership research is the question of whether leadership is universal (or "etic") or contingent ("emic") on culture. However, what is meant by "universal"?
>
> In simple terms we may answer this question by identifying whether leadership phenomena or principles are constant around the globe. For example, if we find participative leadership in every culture, it can be considered a universal leadership phenomenon. Yet, sometimes, general leadership phenomena or principles are the same but there are slight variations across nations and cultures, such as that we find participative leadership across the globe but the amount of participation varies in different cultures. Is this still universal?
>
> From a functionalistic perspective, "universal" can also imply that the relationships between leadership behavior and certain outcomes are constant across different cultures. For example, participative leadership may have a positive effect on job satisfaction across different cultures. Yet, what if there is a similar relationship but the degree of the relationship varies? For instance, participative leadership can be more effective in some cultures than in others.
>
> Finally, "universal" can also imply that leadership theories and instruments can be equally applied across different cultures. The latter is often questioned in cross-cultural leadership research. Most leadership theories and instruments have been developed in Western countries. Since every researcher is socialized in a specific culture, it is highly likely that these theories and instruments are biased. Cross-culturally designed theories and instruments try to avoid such a bias in order to be applicable in an international environment (Bass, 1997).

This is illustrated in Figure 9.1. Together with individual dispositions and demographics (for example, age, personality, capabilities) and other contextual variables (for example, the organizational environment), culture shapes the perceptions and behaviors of leaders and followers. Culture also influences key outcomes of leader behavior, like employee performance, motivation, engagement and job satisfaction. These outcomes in turn impact on subsequent perceptions and behaviors.

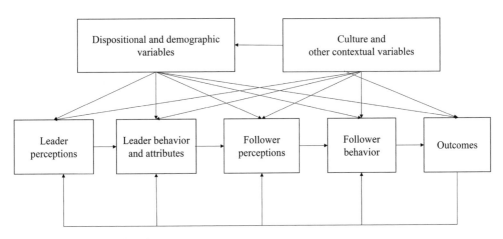

Source: Herd and Lowe (2020)

Figure 9.1   A dyadic model of leadership and cultural processes

Table 9.1 Leadership dimensions and attributes

Leadership dimensions		
Global leadership dimensions	Primary leadership dimensions	Leadership attributes
I. Charismatic/ value-based leadership	Charismatic 1: Visionary	Foresight, prepared, anticipatory, plans ahead
	Charismatic 2: Inspirational	Enthusiastic, positive, morale booster, motive arouser
	Charismatic 3: Self-sacrificial	Risk taker, self-sacrificial, convincing
	Integrity	Honest, sincere, just, trustworthy
	Decisive	Willful, decisive, logical, intuitive
	Performance-oriented	Improvement-oriented, excellence-oriented, performance-oriented
II. Team-oriented leadership	Team 1: Collaborative team orientation	Group-oriented, collaborative, loyal, consultative
	Team 2: Team integrator	Communicative, team builder, informed, integrator
	Diplomatic	Diplomatic, worldly, win–win problem solver, effective bargainer
	Malevolent (reverse scored)	Hostile, dishonest, vindictive, irritable
	Administratively competent	Orderly, administratively skilled, organized, good administrator
III. Participative leadership	Nonparticipative (reverse scored)	Autocratic, dictatorial, bossy, elitist
	Autocratic (reverse scored)	Individually oriented, non-delegator, micromanager, non-egalitarian
IV. Humane-oriented leadership	Modesty	Modest, self-effacing, patient
	Humane orientation	Generous, compassionate
V. Autonomous leadership	Autonomous	Individualistic, independent, autonomous, unique
VI. Self-protective leadership	Self-centered	Self-centered, non-participative, loner, asocial
	Status conscious	Status conscious, class conscious
	Internally competitive	Secretive, normative, intragroup competitor
	Face-saver	Indirect, avoids negatives, evasive
	Bureaucratic	Habitual, procedural, ritualistic, formal

Source: House et al. (2014)

Following this conceptual thinking, the GLOBE researchers elaborated the Leader Attributes and Behavior Questionnaire that was used to identify universally desirable and culturally contingent leadership attributes and behaviors. This instrument contains more than 100 items on a wide variety of leader attributes and behaviors, to be rated from 1, indicating that the behavior or characteristic "greatly inhibits a person from being an outstanding leader," to 7, indicating that they "contribute greatly to a person being an outstanding leader." The project involves several waves of data collection (2004, 2014 and 2020), with the 2020 survey still running at the time that this book is written (currently with 57,000 managers interviewed by 527 country co-investigators in 172 countries). The GLOBE researchers identified six "global leadership" dimensions involving further so-called "primary leadership" dimensions (see Table 9.1).

The six global leadership dimensions are defined as follows (Dorfman, Hanges and Brodbeck, 2004; House et al., 2014): Charismatic/value-based leadership refers to the ability to inspire, to motivate and to encourage high performance based on a foundation of core values. Team-oriented leadership stresses effective team-building and the pursuit of a common goal. Participative leadership reflects the degree to which leaders involve others when they make decisions. Humane-oriented leadership comprises supportive and considerate leadership as well as compassion and generosity. Autonomous leadership refers to independent and individualistic leadership attributes. Self-protective leadership focuses on ensuring the safety and security of the individual and group through status enhancement and face-saving.

Some of these global dimensions reflect leadership styles that are widely discussed in the Western-oriented leadership literature. In particular, charismatic/value-based leadership, team-oriented leadership and participative leadership – yet also humane orientation, which closely resembles supportive leadership – are well-known leadership constructs in the Western hemisphere. However, there are two dimensions that are typically less discussed in the extant literature: autonomous leadership, which refers to an independent and individualistic aspect of leadership, and self-protective leadership, which refers to aspects such as face-saving and status consciousness that are important in some non-Western cultures; for instance, in China and Japan.

Universally positive leadership attributes

Trustworthy	Effective bargainer
Dynamic	Motive arouser
Decisive	Win–win problem solver
Intelligent	Positive
Dependable	Foresight
Plans ahead	Just
Excellence oriented	Communicative
Team builder	Motivational
Encouraging	Coordinator
Confidence builder	Administratively skilled
Informed	
Honest	

Universally negative leadership attributes

- Nonexplicit
- Dictatorial
- Loner
- Ruthless
- Asocial
- Egocentric
- Irritable
- Noncooperative

Source: Adapted from Dorfman et al. (2004)

Figure 9.2 Universally desirable and undesirable attributes

A central question addressed by GLOBE was whether there are leadership attributes and behaviors that are universally endorsed or refuted. The results showed that 22 of the surveyed attributes are universally desirable and eight are universally undesirable (see Figure 9.2). Universally desirable attributes are, for example, trustworthiness, honesty and the ability to motivate and encourage. Universally undesirable attributes are, for example, egocentric, dictatorial and ruthless behaviors. The universally desirable attributes correspond to four primary leadership dimensions, namely performance orientation, being visionary, being inspirational and having integrity. The universally undesirable attributes correspond to one primary dimension, namely being malevolent. Thus, an ideal leader, independent of culture, should be able to inspire others, develop a vision and encourage high performance, while behaving in an integrative and benevolent way.

At the time of writing, the GLOBE 2020 project was ongoing.[1] The new survey contains further leadership styles, like ethical leadership. Topics such as business ethics and sustainability have gained relevance in strategic management. Leaders play a significant role in the ethical guidance of a firm's employees, which is why authors have developed the concept of ethical leadership. Although there is not much research yet on the cultural impact on ethical leadership, we believe it is of key importance considering the relevance of business ethics in international business. Box 9.2 provides further insights on the concept of ethical leadership.

Box 9.2   Further insights: Ethical leadership

Brown, Treviño and Harrison (2005) were among the first to conceptualize ethical leadership, and defined it as the "demonstration of normatively appropriate conduct through personal actions and interpersonal relationships, and the promotion of such conduct to followers through two-way communication, reinforcement, and decision-making."

In addition to conceptualizing ethical leadership, they developed a measurement concept that has recently been used more and more. They measure ethical leadership with the following 10 statements on an agreement scale from 1 (strongly disagree) to 5 (strongly agree): (i) listens to what employees have to say, (ii) disciplines employees who violate ethical standards, (iii) conducts his/her personal life in an ethical manner, (iv) has the best interests of employees in mind, (v) makes fair and balanced decisions, (vi) can be trusted, (vii) discusses business ethics or values with employees, (viii) sets an example of how to do things the right way in terms of ethics, (ix) defines success not just by results but also the way that they are obtained, and (x) when making decisions, asks, "What is the right thing to do?"

In various studies, the authors demonstrate that their measurement scale can be used to predict important employee outcomes, such as the perceived effectiveness of leaders, the job satisfaction and dedication of employees following the leader and the willingness of employees to report problems to the management level. Furthermore, they demonstrate that ethical leadership is related to aspects that are involved in other leadership dimensions, such as honesty, trust, interactional fairness and charismatic leadership.

9.1.2 Cultural values and clusters as predictors of leadership expectations

A key assumption of cross-cultural leadership research is that the mental models and perceptions about leadership are influenced by culture. In particular, the CLT (House et al., 2004) highlights that individuals from different cultures have different views on the attributes and behaviors of effective leaders. Indeed, the GLOBE findings support this assumption. For each of the six global leadership dimensions there are several significant relationships with GLOBE's cultural dimensions (see Table 9.2). For example, a humane-oriented leadership is highly desirable in societies that have a high orientation towards performance, a high humane orientation, high uncertainty avoidance, a high future orientation and high assertiveness. A participative leadership is preferred in societies with high performance orientation, humane orientation and gender egalitarianism, but it is not preferred in societies that value power distance, have a high uncertainty avoidance and assertiveness. The influence of the cultural dimensions on preferred leadership styles differs. Some influence all global leadership dimensions (for example, performance orientation) while others have a rather low influence

Table 9.2 Associations between cultural dimensions and global leadership dimensions

	Global leadership dimensions					
Cultural dimensions (values)	Charismatic/ value-based leadership	Team-oriented leadership	Participative leadership	Humane-oriented leadership	Autonomous leadership	Self-protective leadership
Power distance	--		--			++
Institutional collectivism					--	
In-group collectivism	++	++				-
Gender egalitarianism	++		++			--
Assertiveness			-	++		
Uncertainty avoidance		++	--	++		++
Future orientation	+	+		+		
Performance orientation	++	+	++	+	++	-
Humane orientation	+	+	++	++	--	

Note: + indicates a positive hypothesized relationship; ++ indicates a positive hypothesis and results that support the hypothesis; - indicates a negative hypothesized relationship; -- indicates a negative hypothesis and results that support the hypothesis. For a description of the cultural dimensions, see Chapter 1.
Source: House et al. (2014)

Table 9.3 Ranking of global leadership dimensions in cultural clusters

Charismatic/ value-based leadership	Team-oriented leadership	Participative leadership	Humane-oriented leadership	Autonomous leadership	Self-protective leadership
Higher	*Higher*	*Higher*	*Higher*	*Higher*	*Higher*
Anglo Latin America Southern Asia Germanic Europe Nordic Europe	Latin America	Germanic Europe Nordic Europe Anglo	Southern Asia Sub-Saharan Africa Anglo	Eastern Europe Germanic Europe Confucian Asia Southern Asia Nordic Europe Anglo Middle East Latin Europe Sub-Saharan Africa Latin America	Southern Asia Middle East Confucian Asia Eastern Europe
Sub-Saharan Africa Latin Europe Eastern Europe Confucian Asia	Eastern Europe Southern Asia Nordic Europe Anglo Latin Europe Sub-Saharan Africa Germanic Europe Confucian Asia	Latin America Latin Europe Sub-Saharan Africa	Confucian Asia Latin America Middle East Eastern Europe Germanic Europe		Latin America Sub-Saharan Africa Latin Europe
Middle East	Middle East	Eastern Europe Southern Asia Confucian Asia Middle East	Latin Europe Nordic Europe		Anglo Germanic Europe Nordic Europe
Lower	*Lower*	*Lower*	*Lower*	*Lower*	*Lower*

Note: The placement of each cultural cluster indicates the relative rank of this cluster compared with other clusters with regard to the size of the absolute scores on this dimension.
Source: Dorfman et al. (2004)

(assertiveness, institutional collectivism). In sum, the GLOBE results confirm that the preferred leadership styles vary in accordance with cultural values.

Cultural dimensions interact in influencing the mental models of leadership (see also the cultural archetypes approach in Chapter 1). To demonstrate the influence of cultural values on the preferred leadership styles, we look at the relative importance of the global leadership dimensions in cultural clusters (see Table 9.3). For example, in Germanic Europe, Nordic Europe and the Anglo cluster, following a participative leadership style is much more important in being effective as compared to Eastern Europe, Southern Asia, Confucian Asia and the Middle East.

9.1.3 Keys for successful leadership in international environments: Expectation–behavior fit

In the previous sections we have portrayed the influence of cultural values on the expectations of good (and bad) leadership, and learned that some of these expectations are universal whereas others are culturally contingent. Now we want to go a step forward and consider how the fit between these expectations and the actual behavior of leaders influences their effectiveness. Our implicit assumption so far was that leaders will be more effective if they adapt to the specific expectations of followers. In other words, leaders in a foreign country will be more successful if they lead in a manner that is consistent with the local culture. Likewise, leaders in international teams will be more effective if they are able to consider the different cultural values and satisfy the leadership expectations of the different team members.

The GLOBE researchers also addressed this question by surveying and interviewing more than 1,000 CEOs and 5,000 top management direct reports of these CEOs in 24 countries (for full details see Dorfman et al., 2012; House et al., 2014). Figures 9.3 and 9.4 show the results regarding leadership expectations and behaviors in the United States and Germany. In both countries we see that the actual behavior of CEOs largely corresponds to the leadership expectations. These findings are in line with the CLT: Cultures shape the preferred leadership styles, and leaders tend to behave in accordance with these expectations.

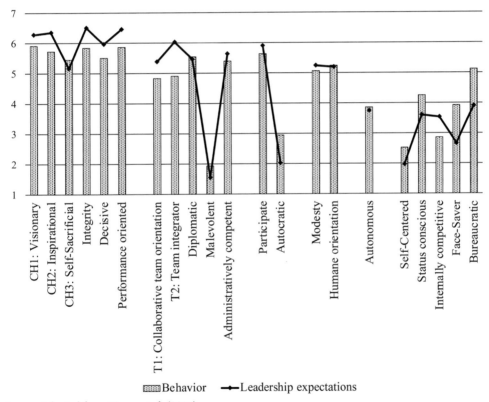

Source: Adapted from House et al. (2014)

Figure 9.3 Leadership expectations and CEO behavior in the United States

In addition, the GLOBE findings demonstrate that the fit, or the extent to which the behavior of leaders is consistent with the cultural expectations, has a positive impact on the effectiveness of leaders (House et al., 2014). Indeed, leaders who correspond to the expected leadership style are able to achieve higher levels of effort and commitment among their subordinates. These positive outcomes can be explained by favorable perceptions and evaluations by subordinates: If leaders behave in a manner consistent with the expectations of followers, followers will respond in a positive way.

INTERNATIONAL BUSINESS STRATEGY AND CROSS-CULTURAL MANAGEMENT

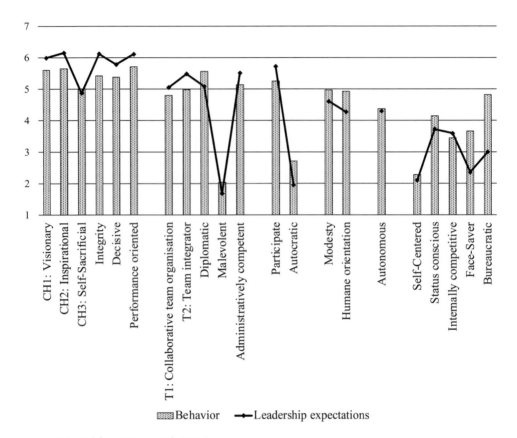

Source: Adapted from House et al. (2014)

Figure 9.4 Leadership expectations and CEO behavior in Germany

> **Box 9.3   Exercise: Discover leadership expectations and CEO behaviors**
>
> We invite you to go online and discover the leadership expectations and CEO behaviors in other countries via the GLOBE website (the relevant links are provided on the book's website). Pick your home country and a country that you would consider to have a quite different culture. For these two cultures, answer the following questions:
>
> - What are the key differences in leadership expectations and CEO behaviors?
> - Which differences would you need to keep in mind when working there or leading a team there?
> - Can you also find similarities?

The key to successful leadership in an international environment is that leaders behave in a manner that is consistent with the leadership expectations in a specific culture. Dorfman et al. (2012) summarized this finding by rephrasing the cliché "When in Rome do as the Romans do" into "Roman leaders lead in a manner expected in Rome." Since the fit between expected leadership behavior and actual leadership behavior leads to positive outcomes, we posit: "Roman leaders damn well best do what they are expected to do if they want to be successful."

However, it is not always easy to adapt. Similarly, leaders of international teams are not always able to treat everyone according to her or his individual expectations. In such instances, leaders can rely on the common grounds; that is, the leadership attributes that are universally considered as good. Accordingly, we use a new maxim: "When in Rome and you do not know what to do, exhibit leadership that is universally desirable." According to the GLOBE project, this includes inspiring others, developing a vision and encouraging high performance, while behaving in an integrative and benevolent way. While this is a desirable common ground, realizing such behavior is easier said than done.

9.2 LEADERSHIP IN GLOBAL VIRTUAL TEAMS

9.2.1 The challenge of leading global virtual teams

A particular challenge in today's world is leading a global virtual team (GVT). GVTs consist of individuals from different countries and cultures who use ICT (for example, e-mail, videoconferencing, e-collaboration tools) to achieve a common goal. In the last few years, we have observed an increasing diffusion of such teams, and not just as a result of the Covid-19 pandemic.

The diversity involved in GVTs can have beneficial yet also malevolent impacts on the well-being of the team members and the team's performance (Jimenez et al., 2017; Taras et al., 2019). According to similarity-attraction and social categorization theories (Tajfel, 1981), individuals categorize themselves into groups of similar members that they favor, and categorize others as outsiders. What follows is that diversity creates faultlines, aggravates social processes and negatively impacts performance (see also Box 9.4 for drawbacks of GVTs).

> **Box 9.4   Further insights: Drawbacks that limit the effectiveness of virtual teams**
>
> In a survey among executives of major organizations around the world, 89 percent of the respondents stated that they work on a virtual team and that their virtual teams typically include at least two cultures (RW3 CultureWizard, 2018). The interviewed executives identified several drawbacks that limit the effectiveness of virtual teams. The top challenges are:
>
> - Working across different time zones (88 percent)
> - Understanding the full context of what people communicate (86 percent)
> - Managing or resolving conflict (86 percent)
> - Building relationships (86 percent)
> - Establishing trust (81 percent)
> - Understanding different accents (80 percent)
> - Timeliness and responsiveness (80 percent)
> - Pace of decision-making (79 percent)
> - Discussing problems and challenges (78 percent)
> - Unfamiliar leadership style (77 percent)

In contrast, according to information-processing theory, diversity broadens the range of perspectives and increases the information-processing capacity of GVTs. What follows is improved problem-solving and higher creativity (Ancona and Caldwell, 1992). For instance, the cultural diversity of the teams can help them to better understand global markets and be more effective with international customers. Moreover, it can contribute to better solving the specific challenges that come with cross-national endeavors. A key to unlock the benefits and to mitigate the challenges involved in GVTs is good leadership. Hence, we will discuss the key strategies to effectively manage and lead GVTs.

We draw attention to three particular impediments in GVTs that leaders need to be aware of or bridge as they have a specific impact on the effectiveness of these teams (Steers and Osland, 2020): First, GVTs lack mutual knowledge and context. The members of GVTs are still embedded in their local contexts; that is, they live in different time zones, work in different offices and have different access to information. Often, we tend to ignore these differences in the virtual setting, which can create misunderstandings or conflicts. For example, there might be good reasons that people are coming too late to a meeting or do not answer an e-mail, but we might not know that the wet season has started in a specific region, causing traffic jams, or that there is a local holiday. Furthermore, cultural differences are harder to be recognized. When we are in a different country, we are constantly reminded of being in a different culture, as we hear different languages, see people with different clothes, smell different food, and so on. However, this does not apply to a virtual meeting. Here we tend to forget that our partners are from different countries, and we might not realize that we are in a cross-cultural situation.

Second, leaders have to pay attention to not over-relying on technology. Using ICT daily, we know that sometimes messages are not delivered, attachments might be missing and calls can have a lousy quality or get interrupted, especially when cooperating with countries that provide differing quality levels of ICT. Hence, good leaders need to develop a good sense of using the right tools for the virtual collaboration, so that working together on the same document does not become messy.

Third, GVTs lose useful details due to missing nonverbal communication. Body language and facial expressions are an important part of communication and often help us to better understand a message. In addition, when using written communication we often tend to simplify our messages in order to save time and energy. Hence, leaders need to pay specific attention to decode the messages conveyed by team members. That is, they need to develop strategies on when to use which medium to cover relevant details of nonverbal communication (to the extent possible using virtual tools) and understand the message correctly.

9.2.2 Keys for successful leadership in global virtual teams

To effectively lead GVTs, it is important first to know which processes influence the performance of virtual teams, second to understand how structural characteristics affect these processes, and third to know which leadership behavior and team practices help teams to achieve high-quality processes in the light of given structural characteristics (see Figure 9.5).

LEADING AND MOTIVATING PEOPLE IN AN INTERNATIONAL ENVIRONMENT

Source: Jonsen, Maznevski and Davison (2012)

Figure 9.5 Global virtual team performance

Key processes that make a difference between high- and low-performing GVTs are communication, collaboration, conflict management and task management (Jonsen et al., 2012). One of the greatest challenges of global virtual teamwork is effective communication, since communication is often asynchronous and lacks richness and social presence. Leaders can increase the effectiveness of communication by providing the right technology. Table 9.4 provides some virtual collaboration options depending on the task and the number of people involved. The effectiveness of communication is, however, not only influenced by the decision about the right technology. Leaders should also ensure that the team members know how to use the technology. In addition, they should establish communication norms, actively provide information and encourage others to do the same (Steers and Osland, 2020).

Collaboration can be accomplished through high-quality relationships which are characterized by trust, mutual respect and a shared identity. Such relationships are important in every team, but they are of special importance in teams that do not regularly meet face to face. In order to achieve such relationships, team members need to get to know each other. This can be facilitated by scheduling online meetings that have the explicit goal of sharing personal information. Examples of such meetings are virtual lunch breaks, virtual after-work parties or online game nights. In addition, periodic face-to-face meetings should be organized. Both measures increase team members' awareness of the different contexts in which their colleagues are working. They also help to build trust and to avoid conflicts and categorization into subgroups. Finally, tasks need to be carefully managed in order to ensure high performance. In a face-to-face team, tasks, roles and interaction norms are often implicitly negotiated while team members interact with each other (Jonsen et al., 2012). In a virtual team, there are limited opportunities to do so. Accordingly, team members should ensure that processes are well structured and roles are clearly defined (for example, by using project management tools, such as Scoro, Jira or Asana).

Table 9.4 Virtual collaborative options in the absence of a face-to-face meeting

Task	Number of people	Virtual collaborative options
Review a document	Two	Option 1: Document is shared by e-mail, then reviewed by phone call. Option 2: Software (for example, Lotus Sametime) allows both participants to view and edit the document in real time online while on a phone call. Participants can pass control of the document back and forth.
	Three or more	Option 1: Document is shared by e-mail, then reviewed by conference call. Option 2: Software allows all participants to view and edit the document in real time online while on a conference call. Participants can pass control of the document around to all participants.
Reach consensus on a pressing issue	Two	Option 1: Phone call. Option 2: Desktop videoconferencing.
	Three or more	Option 1: Conference call. Option 2: Conference room videoconferencing. Option 3: Desktop videoconferencing.
Group brainstorm session, with some members working remotely (for example, capturing ideas on sticky notes to be integrated later)	Three or more	*If anonymity is not an issue:* Option 1: Conference call or videoconferencing with one person playing the role of facilitator (to ensure that remote participants are able to participate) and one person as scribe (to write down the remote members' contributions). *If anonymity is desired:* Option 1: Remote participants can e-mail their comments to the facilitator, who can write them on sticky notes and add them to the local group's work. Option 2: Each remote participant can be assigned a "buddy" in the local room and can call, e-mail or send an instant message with comments. The buddy writes down the remote person's input, adds it to his or her own, and posts it with the rest of the group's. Option 3: A software program can be used with all participants at computer workstations. Input is captured and compiled but not attributed.

Source: Bradley (2008)

The described processes are influenced by several structural characteristics. The key issues here are to select tasks that are appropriate for virtual teamwork, organize an adequate physical distribution of team members and identify the right people. Not every task can be accomplished virtually, and managers need to decide which tasks can be achieved by virtual teams. A general rule of thumb is that the necessity of communication increases with the complexity of tasks and the level of decision processes (Steers and Osland, 2020). If the need for communication achieves a critical level, managers might opt for on-site teams instead of virtual teams. The geographical distribution of virtual teams also affects how virtual teams are working together. For example, teams that cover many different time zones need to rely more on asynchronous information compared to teams that work in the same time zone. Furthermore, since working in virtual teams is often challenging, team leaders need to select people with the right knowledge, skills and abilities.

In addition to the role leaders play within the discussed processes and structural characteristics, literature provides several best practices in terms of leadership behavior and team practices that can help GVTs to be more effective. Key issues are to (i) communicate thoughtfully – that is, to communicate in the right ways and in the right amount; (ii) manage differences

– for example, by providing intercultural training in order to increase mutual understanding; (iii) build a rhythm, by structuring interaction over time in such a way that there are regular virtual and face-to-face meetings; (iv) empower the team, by giving team members autonomy and responsibility; (v) support high performance – for example, by providing necessary trainings and by setting clear expectations and measurable goals; (vi) structure the processes – for example, by developing milestones; (vii) facilitate strong relationships, by allowing team members to get to know each other, and (viii) develop and communicate a vision, by articulating a shared goal for the team that provides meaning for all team members.

The last aspect, to develop and communicate a clear vision, is one of the most significant aspects of leadership (Steers and Osland, 2020). A strong vision increases commitment and motivation to work towards a common goal. It also reduces the attention to team differences and therewith reduces conflicts and discrimination among team members (Lauring and Jonasson, 2018). Furthermore, it allows for more autonomy and empowerment of the team members: If everyone understands and shares the team's goals, the team members can trust more that each one of them acts in a way so that these goals will be achieved. This is vital for GVTs.

It should be clear by now that leading a GVT is not without challenges. However, it can also be highly satisfying to work with people around the globe. To get a glimpse into leadership practice, and learn more about leading an international team, go to the book's website and listen to the podcast with Valeria Loreti, Delivery Manager Motorsport at Shell and head of an international team that develops fuel and oils for Shell's Innovation Partner Scuderia Ferrari.

9.3 MOTIVATION IN AN INTERNATIONAL ENVIRONMENT

Motivation related to work is of crucial importance for the success of organizations, but also the well-being of employees. It influences job decisions, and affects what skills employees develop and how individuals behave during work. The question of motivation has a long history, and numerous theoretical developments and empirical studies have influenced our understanding of motivation. From a cross-cultural perspective it is, however, questionable if motivation theories or the findings of these studies are generalizable to people in different countries. In the following, we will therefore introduce major motivation theories and discuss their applicability in an international environment. We also discuss international differences in work centrality and work values as well as the relative influence of work and employment conditions on job satisfaction across cultures.

9.3.1 Theories to understand motivation: Maslow, McClelland and equity theory

The "hierarchy of needs" theory, which goes back to Abraham Maslow, an American psychologist (Maslow, 1943, 1954), is one of the most popular but also most controversial approaches in motivation research and practice. According to this theory, the needs of individuals can be categorized into five hierarchically arranged classes (see Figure 9.6, left side). On the lowest level of the hierarchy are basic "physiological needs" like food, water, air, sleep and shelter. These basic needs are – according to Maslow – the strongest of all needs, and individuals will always drive to satisfy these needs first. Organizations can address physiological needs, for example, by providing wages that allow employees to cover the costs of living or by providing sufficient recreational and regeneration breaks during working hours. On the next level of the hierarchy we find "safety needs," which include the desire for a predictable, secure, stable and structured environment. In the working context this especially refers to health and safety programs, job security and retirement plans. "Belonging needs" include desires for affiliation, acceptance and affection by other people. These needs can be satisfied by social interaction at the workplace and a good working atmosphere. "Esteem needs" cover needs for self-affirmation and self-esteem, but also respect and esteem from others (for example, status, prestige). Organizations can address these needs through feedback, bonuses and promotion. On the highest level in the hierarchy we find "self-actualization needs." They refer to the human desire to seek personal growth, to make the best of one's potential and to reach self-fulfillment. In the context of work motivation, this can, for instance, be achieved by giving individuals autonomy and challenges.

A central assumption in Maslow's hierarchy of needs is that hierarchically higher needs are only activated when the hierarchically lower needs are satisfied. Maslow also distinguishes between "deficiency needs" and "growth needs." The first four levels (that is, physiological, safety, social and esteem needs) represent deficiency needs that can fully be satisfied. The top level (that is, self-actualization needs) represents growth needs which can never really be satisfied.

A key critique of Maslow's hierarchy of needs is that it is only applicable to a specific cultural context (for further critique see, for example, Petri and Govern, 2013). Geert Hofstede, for example, questioned the broader applicability of the theory by stating that "the ordering of needs in Maslow's hierarchy represents a value choice – Maslow's value choice" (Hofstede, 1984: 396). He points out that Maslow used his very own perspective to describe the motivation of others, and this perspective reflects mid-twentieth century US middle-class values. Accordingly, individualistic values, in particular self-actualization and autonomy, are found on the top level. In contrast, values that are dominant in collectivist cultures, such as "harmony" or "family support," are not considered in the hierarchy. Thus, from a cross-culture perspective Maslow's theory might not reflect the whole spectrum of potential needs, and the ordering of the needs might be different in different cultures.

Nevis (1983), for example, suggested that a Chinese hierarchy of needs would be very different: Ranging from the lowest to the highest, it would have four levels, namely (i) belonging, (ii) physiological, (iii) safety and (iv) self-actualization in the service of society (Figure 9.6, right side). There are several major differences between Maslow's and the Chinese need hierarchies. First, belonging needs are placed on completely different levels; since belonging and affiliation to a group and society are crucial in a collectivist culture, belonging needs are considered the most basic needs in China. Second, esteem needs are not included in the Chinese hierarchy. According to Nevis, self-esteem is not a universal need; it is a product of Western culture and typical for individualistic cultures. Third, even though self-actualization is placed on the top

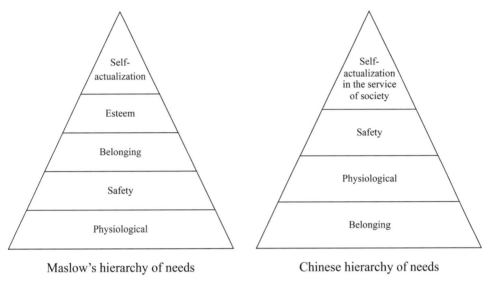

Source: Nevis (1983)

Figure 9.6   Need hierarchies

level of each hierarchy, it has a different meaning. Self-actualization in Maslow's hierarchy of needs implies the self-fulfillment of the individual as a personal goal. In China, however, self-actualization is considered a duty to society and a moral imperative in terms of "My country needs me to do my best."

Box 9.5   Further insights: Universal human needs

The cross-cultural applicability of Maslow's approach has always been questioned, and the empirical support is inconclusive. However, lately we find a renewed interest in the idea of universal human needs (Vansteenkiste, Ryan and Soenens, 2020). This revival is, in particular, triggered by proponents of the Basic Psychological Need Theory (BPNT), a central mini-theory within the broader framework of Self-determination Theory (Ryan and Deci, 2017).

BPTN has several criteria that must be fulfilled for a need to be included in the list of basic psychological needs. One of these criteria concerns the universal nature of basic needs; according to that idea, basic psychological needs are relevant for all individuals, regardless of differences in socio-demographic characteristics, personality or cultural background. Until now, three needs have formally been identified as basic psychological needs: the needs for autonomy, competence and relatedness. The need for autonomy refers to an individual's desire to experience ownership of their behavior and to act with a sense of volition. The need for competence denotes the desire to be able to master events, achieve expected outcomes and manage challenges. The need for relatedness denotes the human striving for close, meaningful and supportive relationships and the desire to achieve a sense of bonding and belongingness. Many studies and meta-analyses have confirmed that the satisfaction of those needs is crucial for motivation and well-being across cultures.

A different approach to conceptualize human needs has been proposed by McClelland (1961). McClelland stated that we all, independent of our gender, age or culture, have three different motives: a need for achievement, a need for affiliation and a need for power. The need for achievement lets people strive for performance and perfection. Individuals with a high need for achievement try to accomplish or even exceed a self-imposed standard of quality and performance. They are unmotivated if an activity is not challenging or does not offer enough personal responsibility or if there is hardly any feedback. The need for affiliation is the urge for personal contact, belonging, and friendly and harmonious relationships with other people. The need for power is the desire to be strong and to control others. Individuals with a high need for power try to enhance their influence and authority. Competition motivates them and they aspire to reputation and status.

In contrast to Maslow, McClelland did not believe that these three needs are activated in a specific order, nor did he believe that individuals share these needs in a similar fashion. One of the three motives will be a dominant motivator, depending on personality, life experience or culture. A decisive aspect here is that McClelland assumes that motives can be learned during the life course. Thus, cultural values and norms, which are shared and transmitted from one generation to another, should have an impact on the relative importance of these three motives within a society. The most obvious hypotheses are that performance orientation, humane orientation and power distance – cultural dimensions which were partially derived from McClelland's motives in the GLOBE study – have a positive influence on the need for achievement, the need for affiliation and the need for power, respectively. However, even if these assumptions seem obvious, the results are currently mixed. For example, the GLOBE study did not find a higher need for achievement in cultures with a high performance orientation (Javidan, 2004). Yet, in one of the most comprehensive studies, with 17,358 managers in 24 countries, Van Emmerik et al. (2010) found that performance orientation is significantly related to the need for achievement, and that humane orientation is significantly related to the need for affiliation. However, they found a significant negative relationship between power distance and the need for power, which contradicts the general assumption.

McClelland's theory has been widely applied in leadership, management and cross-cultural studies. A particular stream of research has also addressed the role and importance of high achievement needs for the overall economic development of a country. McClelland assumed that a high need for achievement, which is characteristic of Western societies, is key to economic success. However, the empirical support for this claim was also limited. The basic critique is again the ethnocentric perspective of this assumption: the American McClelland has chosen a typical Anglo value to be a universal recipe for economic success. However, while achievement is usually measured in financial terms in the American culture, other cultures define achievement differently (for example, in terms of affiliation in Japan). Moreover, even the word "achievement" is difficult to translate into some languages (Hofstede, Hofstede and Minkov, 2010).

Another approach to motivation builds on the desire for fairness of individuals. Employees always compare their contributions (for example, education, experience, effort) to an organization with the organizational rewards received (all monetary and non-monetary benefits like pay, career, recognition); and they will be motivated and stay in the organization as long as this input–output ratio is in their favor. Equity theory (Adams, 1965) expands this general assumption by including social comparison. Analyzing one's own input–output ratio is often difficult because there is no clear reference point. Do I get enough money for the work I do? Do I deserve to be promoted? Should I work harder? In order to answer these questions employees usually compare their own input–output ratio with the input–output ratio of others. The relevant other maybe a direct colleague, a friend from university or an acquaintance working in another company. Yet, the reference can also be made to the employee's own input–output ratio in different situations (for example, in a former job). Equity theory emphasizes that every imbalance in this comparison leads to a perception of unfairness and creates a psychological tension that influences the motivation of employees. They will, for example, show more effort if they perceive that others perform better for the same money. Or they will be unhappy and try to leave the organization if they feel unfairly treated.

Equity theory received strong support in Western countries. There is, however, some doubt about its applicability in an international environment. First, the equity principle often guides the perception of fairness in Western countries, especially in a business context. However, there are other principles of (distributive) fairness like equality (everyone should be rewarded equally independent of the effort or performance) and need (resources should be allocated according to people's needs). The relative importance of these principles might be culture-bound. For example, employees in Asia and the Middle East apparently are more willing to accept inequity (for example, related to gender-based pay differences) in order to preserve societal harmony (Sanchez-Runde and Steers, 2020).

A second issue refers to the culture dependence of the model's components – that is, the input, the output, the choice of a referent other and the reaction to a perceived state of imbalance (Fadil et al., 2005). Figure 9.7 shows how individualism and collectivism, which are often used as the major dimension of cultural variability between Western and Eastern cultures, might influence each of these components. It becomes apparent that equity theory can also be applied to non-Western, collectivistic cultures, but the specifics of these cultures should always be considered.

INTERNATIONAL BUSINESS STRATEGY AND CROSS-CULTURAL MANAGEMENT

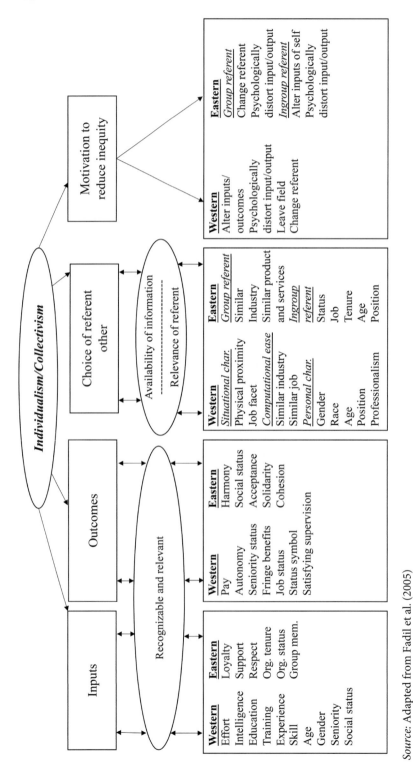

Source: Adapted from Fadil et al. (2005)

Figure 9.7 The culturally sensitive equity model

9.3.2 Work centrality and work values around the globe

A further way to study work motivation is to analyze international differences in "work centrality" and "work values" (Sanchez-Runde and Steers, 2020). Work centrality refers to the importance of work as compared to other domains in an individual's life (for example, leisure, family) and provides a general tendency about the motivation to work. Work values refer to the importance of specific work and employment conditions. They are usually defined as desirable end-states (for example, high pay or job security) or desirable behaviors (for example, working independently, doing a job that is useful to society). Since work values signify what people want out of work, they are important for the evaluation of the workplace, the attitudes towards specific workplace situations and the behavioral responses.

Work values are formed through socialization, which in turn is influenced by historical and cultural factors. Therefore, work values are relatively stable. They are "relatively" stable since the situation and experiences at the workplace can influence the importance of work values during the life course (Hauff and Kirchner, 2014). Moreover, it is assumed that changes in the structure of the workforce (for example, entering of new generations, larger participation of women) will influence the general importance of different work values (Brinck, Hauff and Kirchner, 2020). Thus, the evaluation of work and employment conditions and therewith the question of what makes a job good or bad changes over time.

Cross-national differences in work centrality and work values have been analyzed in numerous empirical studies (for example, Gesthuizen, Kovarek and Rapp, 2019; Hauff and Kirchner, 2015). In Table 9.5 we demonstrate the differences in work centrality and work values in selected countries. Work centrality is measured with two items, namely the (dis)agreement with the statements "A job is just a way of earning money – no more" and "I would enjoy having a paid job even if I did not need the money." If individuals disagree with the first statement and agree with the second, work centrality is high. The results show that work centrality is, for example, relatively high in Norway, Denmark and Australia. In contrast, we find rather low values in South Africa and Russia.

Work values are distinguished between extrinsic, intrinsic and social/altruistic work values. The results in Table 9.5 show that all of these work values are on average rather important (given that the lowest average is 3.91 for "Contact with other people" on a scale from 1 (not important at all) to 5 (very important). However, we identify several differences in the relative importance. A relatively high importance of extrinsic work values (including aspects like job security, high income and advancement opportunities) is found in Mexico, Poland, South Africa and the Philippines, for example. Denmark and Switzerland are examples with a relatively low importance of extrinsic values. Intrinsic work values (including aspects like an interesting job or being able to work independently) are comparatively more important in Germany and Switzerland, but less important in China, Japan and Russia. Finally, social/altruistic work values (including aspects like contact with other people, a job that allows one to help other people and a job that is useful to society) are of particular relevance in Chile and Mexico. A relatively lower importance is found in Japan and Hungary.

Such differences in work centrality and work values interact with cultural characteristics but also with other economic and political settings in a country. For example, the relatively low importance of extrinsic work values in Denmark and Switzerland might be a result of the already high wages and the strong welfare state. If these aspects are not guaranteed in a country (like Mexico, Poland, South Africa and the Philippines) they might become more important.

Table 9.5 Work centrality and work values around the globe

	Work centrality		Extrinsic work values			Intrinsic work values		Social/altruistic work values		
Country	Job is a way of earning money – no more	Enjoy a paid job even if money not needed	Job security	High income	Opportunities for advancement	An interesting job	Work independently	Contact with other people	Job that allows to help other people	Job that is useful to society
Australia	2.29	**3.71**	4.52	3.67	3.92	**4.45**	3.85	3.78	3.92	3.97
Chile	3.03	*2.98*	4.54	4.30	**4.38**	4.33	4.10	**4.21**	**4.33**	**4.36**
China	**3.47**	3.66	*4.33*	4.25	**3.86**	3.80	3.67	3.74	3.85	4.05
Denmark	*2.43*	**3.89**	4.15	*3.55*	*3.35*	**4.51**	4.19	4.05	3.90	*3.84*
France	2.72	3.38	**4.55**	3.92	3.93	**4.69**	3.66	**4.11**	*3.72*	3.86
Germany	2.69	**3.73**	4.52	3.82	*3.76*	**4.47**	4.24	**4.13**	3.82	3.86
Great Britain/ United Kingdom	2.67	3.64	4.51	3.68	4.02	4.38	*3.80*	3.79	3.88	3.88
Hungary	3.43	*2.99*	4.52	4.26	*3.77*	*3.95*	3.82	*3.65*	*3.68*	3.86
India	**3.93**	3.62	*4.39*	4.26	4.21	*4.13*	3.93	3.75	3.95	3.95
Israel	2.67	3.67	4.46	4.14	4.23	4.39	3.96	4.05	4.19	4.19
Japan	3.00	3.55	*4.17*	3.92	*2.97*	3.88	*2.92*	*3.60*	*3.60*	*3.76*
Mexico	3.28	3.58	**4.67**	4.45	**4.55**	4.37	**4.19**	**4.14**	**4.29**	**4.32**
Norway	*1.90*	**3.92**	4.41	*3.57*	*3.44*	4.40	3.97	3.89	*3.76*	*3.76*
Philippines	**3.82**	3.56	4.49	4.42	**4.42**	4.28	**4.27**	3.98	**4.21**	**4.27**
Poland	3.21	3.44	**4.62**	4.44	4.04	4.37	4.06	3.76	3.92	3.92
Russia	**3.52**	*2.80*	*4.39*	4.52	3.85	*4.14*	3.71	*3.44*	*3.70*	3.90
South Africa	**3.44**	*3.12*	4.51	4.35	4.37	4.29	3.99	3.94	4.16	4.21
Spain	2.81	*3.18*	**4.74**	4.12	4.23	4.38	4.19	3.92	**4.27**	**4.34**
Switzerland	*2.44*	**3.81**	4.52	*3.51*	*3.72*	**4.60**	4.25	**4.20**	4.04	4.06
United States	2.65	3.62	**4.69**	4.03	**4.40**	4.42	3.99	3.74	**4.23**	**4.32**
Total	2.99	3.49	4.51	4.08	3.94	4.34	3.94	3.91	3.99	4.03

Note: Italics: lower 25 percent (25 percent quartile), bold: upper 25 percent (75 percent quartile), values range from 1 (strongly disagree/not important at all) to 5 (strongly agree/very important).
Source: Data from International Social Survey Program Research Group (2017), own calculation

9.3.3 Determinants of job satisfaction across cultures

A further possibility to think about motivational differences around the globe is to analyze the relevance of different job characteristics for job satisfaction in different cultural clusters that an MNE is active in. By evaluating the relevance of different work and employment conditions (that is, their importance) for job satisfaction and contrasting it to how employees perceive these determinants (that is, the performance of the MNE regarding these work and employment conditions), MNEs can understand the motivation of their employees and identify ways to improve it.

Multiple work and employment conditions are potentially relevant for job satisfaction. The most comprehensive list of relevant job characteristics is presented by Warr (2007), which includes the following aspects: (i) opportunity for personal control (employee discretion, autonomy, self-determination), (ii) opportunity for skills use (skills utilization, opportunities for learning), (iii) externally generated goals (job demands, workload, work–family conflict), (iv) variety (in job content and location), (v) environmental clarity (information about the future, required behavior), (vi) contact with others (quantity and quality of interactions), (vii) availability of money (income level), (viii) physical security (absence of danger, good working conditions), (ix) valued social position (status in society, task significance), (x) supportive supervision (leader consideration, supportive management), (xi) career outlook (job security, opportunities for promotion, advancement) and (xii) equity (fairness in one's employment relationship, morality in an employer's relationship with society).

As cultural values prevalent in a nation predispose how its members value different job characteristics, these job characteristics are of different relevance for job satisfaction in different countries (Hauff, Richter and Tressin, 2015). When we compare the relative influence of different job characteristics on job satisfaction, we can see some overlaps, but also considerable differences (see Figure 9.8). The most important drivers of satisfaction are an interesting job and good relationships between management and subordinates, across almost all nations. Nonetheless, there are several country specifics. For employees from the Philippines, for instance, low workload is most important, which is also a relevant driver in Australia, New Zealand, Germany and Finland. For workers from the United States, Switzerland, France and Sweden, good relationships with colleagues are among the top drivers of job satisfaction, in contrast to all other nations. Income is among the top three drivers in Taiwan, yet it is not a significant antecedent of job satisfaction in countries such as Sweden or Spain, among others.

In an organizational setting we recommend that managers identify what matters to motivate their employees in different international units. Table 9.6 offers example statements that can be used to assess how employees perceive their work and employment conditions. Managers should, however, always think about the work and employment conditions that might matter to their employees. Indeed, typically surveys on job characteristics and job satisfaction (and related facets, such as commitment, engagement and turnover intention) involve between 30 and 50 different questions to operationalize the various characteristics (for example, Meyerding, 2015) and may in addition put a focus on measuring the quality of leader–member relationships (for example, Graen and Uhl-Bien, 1995). Next to the perception of the work and employment conditions, managers should also assess the importance of these characteristics.

Top driver = +++ Second driver = ++ Third driver = + Other drivers = * Nonsignificant	Income	Advancement	Job security	Interesting job	Independent work	Qualification possibilities	Opportunities for skills use	Low workload	Good relationships with management	Good relationships with colleagues	Opportunities to help others	Usefulness to society	Work & family compatibility
New Zealand		*		+++				+	++			*	
Australia	*	*	*	+++		*		+	++				
Great Britain	*		*	+++					++		*		+
United States	*	*	*	+++		*		*	++	+			
Canada	*	*		+++	*			*	++				+
Israel	*			+++	*	++		*	+		*	*	*
Germany	*			+++	*			+	++				*
Switzerland	*			+++			*			+		*	++
France	*	*		+++	*	*	*	*	++	+			
Spain		*		+++		*	*	*	++		*	*	+
Finland	*		*	+++				+	++		*		
Sweden		*		+++		*		*	++	+		*	*
Hungary				+++		+			++		*		
Japan				++		+		*	+++				
Taiwan	+		*	++			*	*	+++				*
Philippines							+++						

Source: Hauff and Richter (2015)

Figure 9.8 Influence of situational job characteristics on job satisfaction in selected countries

They can do this by asking their employees about the importance of these characteristics in addition to their agreement on these characteristics (see Table 9.6). If managers are familiar with advanced statistical procedures, they can also use a regression-based method to identify the importance of these characteristics for an outcome, such as job satisfaction. That is, they use a regression with the job characteristics as independent and the overall job satisfaction (for example, measured by asking how satisfied employees are on a scale from 1 (completely dissatisfied) to 5 (completely satisfied) as independent variables.

In a next step managers identify how they perform on the characteristics which are of high relevance to their employees. For a better interpretation of the importance and performance scores, they can also plot them in a matrix like in Figure 9.9. To draw a cut-off line between low and high performance, managers can use the middle rating (that is, a 3 on a five-point scale), the average of all performance scores from their survey or external benchmarks, or set a specific target that they aim to achieve. They can opt for a similar procedure for the importance scores. If managers are using a regression-based approach, they can, for example, use the mean of the coefficients as a cut-off.

In the top-right cell of Figure 9.9, you will then find the work and employment conditions that are very important for job satisfaction and which already have high levels of performance. The message here is to keep up the good work. In our example, this applies for independent work, income levels and the relationships with managers. The top-left cell will contain work and employment conditions that have a low importance for job satisfaction but a high performance. In this case, you should carefully reconsider if the respective resources are needed.

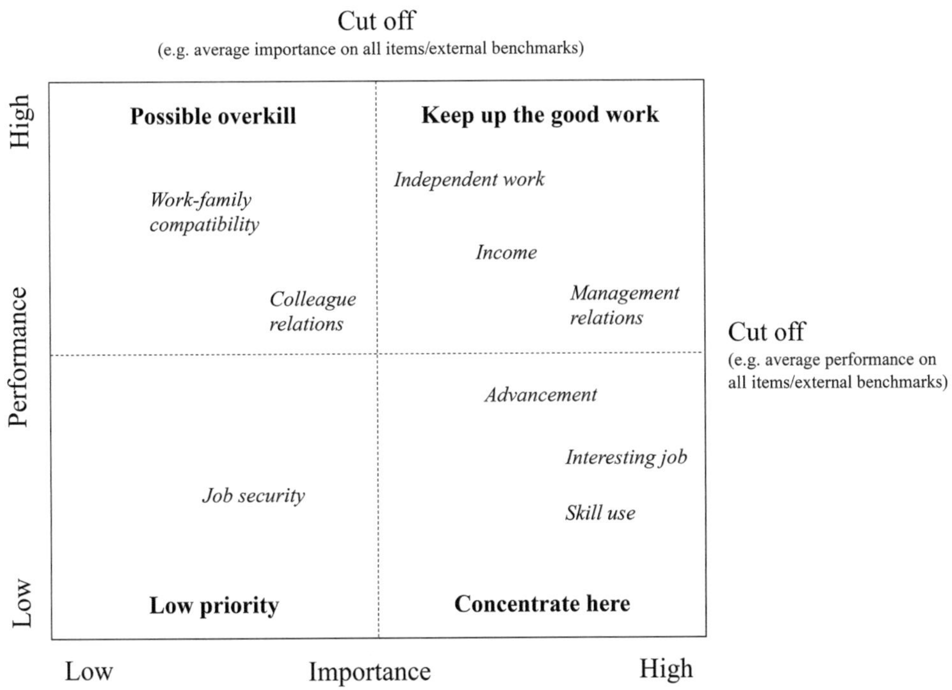

LEADING AND MOTIVATING PEOPLE IN AN INTERNATIONAL ENVIRONMENT

Cut off
(e.g. average importance on all items/external benchmarks)

	Possible overkill	**Keep up the good work**
High	*Work-family compatibility*	*Independent work*
	Colleague relations	*Income*
		Management relations
	Low priority	**Concentrate here**
		Advancement
		Interesting job
	Job security	*Skill use*
Low		
	Low — Importance — High	

Cut off
(e.g. average performance on all items/external benchmarks)

Figure 9.9 Importance and performance matrix

Table 9.6 Example items to assess work and employment conditions

Job characteristic	Question (performance measurement)	Question (importance measurement)
	To what extent do you agree or disagree with each of the following statements? Please use a scale from 1 = strongly disagree to 5 = strongly agree.	How important is it for you personally that … Please use a scale from 1 = not important at all to 5 = very important.
Income	My income is high.	… your income is high.
Advancement	My opportunities for advancement are high.	… your opportunities for advancement are high.
Job security	My job is secure.	… your job is secure.
Interesting job	My job is interesting.	… your job is interesting.
Independent work	I can work independently.	… you can work independently.
Opportunities for skill use	I can make adequate use of my skills.	… you can make adequate use of your skills.
Good relationships with management	My manager helps and supports me.	… your manager helps and supports you.
Good relationships with colleagues	My colleagues help and support me.	… your colleagues help and support you.
Work–family compatibility	I have enough time to get my job done.	… you have enough time to get your job done.

In our example you may wonder whether you should continue investing in the compatibility between work and family. In the bottom-left cell you will find work and employment conditions of low importance and low performance. There is no real need for specific improvements, as these conditions are not of relevance to the employees. In the bottom-right cell you will encounter all work and employment conditions that are very important for job satisfaction, but have rather low performance levels. Accordingly, you should focus your actions here to increase job satisfaction. In our illustrative example, you will need to think about strategies to improve career opportunities, the use of skills among employees and ways to generate a better interest in the jobs performed by employees.

9.4 EMPLOYEE ENGAGEMENT AT A MARKETING CONSULTANCY

In the following, we refer to an illustrative example in the context of motivation and leadership of a marketing consultancy – we call it the FIRM – that is based in Europe and has around 9,000 employees worldwide. The FIRM performs a yearly global online survey that aims to identify the strengths and weaknesses of individual organizational units worldwide with regard to employee motivation and leadership performance, among other issues. More specifically, the FIRM (i) measures the engagement and satisfaction of its employees and (ii) identifies the facets of the job that contribute to the engagement and satisfaction of its employees. For consultancies, human resources are often the key resources providing a sustainable competitive advantage, and have relatively more relevance than in firms that profit from specific manufacturing technologies or machinery. Thus, employees' motivation and contribution to the performance and strategic objectives of the firm are of utmost importance.

The online survey covers around nine different questions to understand the level of engagement and satisfaction among employees worldwide. Table 9.7 provides examples of questions integrated. In addition, the survey involves around 40 questions on the aspects that determine or drive the engagement and satisfaction of employees. These are structured along five categories: (i) characteristics of the job, (ii) the leadership of the direct manager, (iii) the top management team, (iv) the team and (v) opportunities for career development (see Table 9.7). In addition to these five categories, local organizational units have the opportunity to add specific categories that they deem to be of specific relevance in their national surroundings. That is, the idea of the survey is to apply a set of questions that have worldwide applicability or are of relevance in all markets, so that the performance on these facets is of relevance in all markets and allows a worldwide benchmarking among local organizational units.

All questions are implemented in the form of a scale from 1 (strong disagreement) to 5 (full agreement). To report the findings on each of the questions and on the different categories, the results are transformed to a point system, the idea being that this improves the understandability of the reporting. A strong agreement (that is, a 5 on the five-point scale) provides 100 points, and 75 points are assigned to a partial agreement, 50 to a neither/nor, 25 to a disagreement and zero to a strong disagreement (see Table 9.7). The results of the survey are reported to all employees, and the management team reflects on measures taken to improve potential

Table 9.7 Core items used to measure engagement, satisfaction and their drivers

Category	Question (examples)	Scale/points
Overall constructs to be explained		1 = strongly disagree: 0 points
Engagement	At my work I feel full of energy. I am enthusiastic about my job. Time flies when I am working.	2 = disagree: 25 points
Satisfaction	All in all, I am satisfied with my job.	3 = neither agree nor disagree: 50 points
Drivers/determinants		4 = agree: 75 points
Characteristics of my job	My job is interesting. In my job, I can make adequate use of my skills.	5 = strongly agree: 100 points
My leader	My leader behaves in a manner that is respectful and appreciative. My leader gives meaningful feedback that helps to improve my performance. I respect my leader.	
The top management team	The top management team of my local FIRM keeps me informed about business issues and about how well my organization is doing. The top management team of my local FIRM has a convincing strategy for a successful future of our unit.	
My team	We respect each other in our team. In our team, we help and support each other.	
My career	There are plans for my future career development.	

weaknesses identified. In addition to the results that are specific to the local unit, a worldwide benchmark is added to identify the strengths and weaknesses in each local organization. Each local organization receives a dashboard after the survey that summarizes the results; the benchmark is presented in the form of illustrating the values achieved by the bottom 30 percent of local organizational units and the top 30 percent of local units. Figure 9.10 presents an example of such a dashboard for one of the local units of FIRM.

The results for this local unit indicate that the employees demonstrate a rather low engagement but are nonetheless quite satisfied with their jobs. To understand the reasons for the low engagement, the firm is then evaluating the scores on the drivers or determinants. On some of the drivers the unit performs among the top 30 percent. The characteristics of the job seem to be no issue in this local unit, and the team atmosphere seems to be very good. On other drivers, however, the unit has only average performance, namely with regard to leadership and the career. In addition, there is a low performance that is revealed for the top management team since employees do not seem to feel well informed about the future and current development, and have doubts on the future strategic positioning of their local unit. Thus, the top management team at FIRM needs to evaluate whether it has a communicative issue with this local unit and needs to check if the local strategy implemented is best in light of national market requirements. Hence, such a project not only identifies issues that relate to key human resources or leadership aspects, but may also point to strategic issues in the firm. In addition to the dashboard, a full report is provided to enable an in-depth evaluation using single questions and sub-facets within each of the categories.

Overall, participation rates of the survey at FIRM range from 79 to 86 percent among all employees every year, which is a very good percentage. More important than asking many

INTERNATIONAL BUSINESS STRATEGY AND CROSS-CULTURAL MANAGEMENT

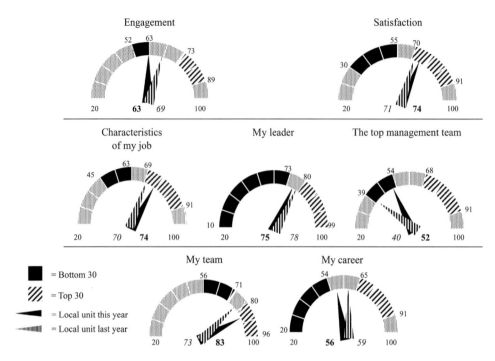

Figure 9.10 Employee engagement and satisfaction dashboard

employees is ensuring that all kinds of employees are represented in the survey, so as to not have a blind spot in a specific group of employees or a specific region. Good participation rates in the long term depend strongly on the follow-up procedures of these surveys. That is, informing staff about the findings, developing relevant means to tackle weaknesses identified and implementing the most relevant ones as a follow-up to the survey. Thus, results need to lead to action.

CHAPTER REVIEW QUESTIONS

1. The GLOBE study has provided a comprehensive analysis of leadership attributes which are universally endorsed and which are culturally contingent. What are the implications of the results for cross-cultural leadership?
2. GVTs are multicultural in composition and virtual in action. What are the challenges resulting from this?
3. Which factors influence the performance of GVTs? What issues should be considered?
4. Compare and contrast Maslow's needs hierarchy theory with McClelland's three motives. Are there any similarities? What are the key differences?
5. Equity theory highlights the importance of justice and fairness. How does culture influence justice and fairness?
6. What are work values? Why are they important?
7. Job satisfaction can be influenced by many factors. What are the key challenges if leaders want to increase the satisfaction of their followers?

NOTE

1. Since the results of the new survey were not yet available while writing this chapter, the presented results are based on the previous survey.

REFERENCES

Adams, J. S. (1965). Inequity in social exchange. In L. Berkowitz (Ed.), *Advances in Experimental Social Psychology* (2nd ed., pp. 267–299). San Diego, CA: Academic Press.

Ancona, D. G., and Caldwell, D. F. (1992). Demography and design: Predictors of new product team performance. *Organization Science*, 3, 321–341.

Bass, B. M. (1997). Does the transactional-transformational leadership paradigm transcend organizational and national boundaries? *American Psychologist*, 52, 130–139.

Bradley, L. (2008). The technology that supports virtual team collaboration. In J. Nemiro, M. Beyerlein, L. Bradley and S. Beyerlein (Eds.), *The Handbook of High-Performance Virtual Teams: A Toolkit for Collaborating Across Boundaries* (pp. 331–344). San Francisco, CA: Jossey-Bass.

Brinck, K. L., Hauff, S., and Kirchner, S. (2020). Is there a new meaning of work? The how and why of a change in altruistic work values in Germany between 1989 and 2016. *Management Revue*, 31, 167–187.

Brown, M. E., Treviño, L. K., and Harrison, D. A. (2005). Ethical leadership: A social learning perspective for construct development and testing. *Organizational Behavior and Human Decision Processes*, 97, 117–134.

Dorfman, P., Hanges, P. J., and Brodbeck, F. C. (2004). Leadership and cultural variation: The identification of culturally endorsed leadership profiles. In R. J. House, P. J. Hanges, M. Javidan, P. W. Dorfman and V. Gupta (Eds), *Culture, Leadership, and Organizations: The GLOBE Study of 62 Societies* (pp. 669–716). Thousand Oaks, CA: SAGE.

Dorfman, P., Javidan, M., Hanges, P., Dastmalchian, A., and House, R. (2012). GLOBE: A twenty year journey into the intriguing world of culture and leadership. *Journal of World Business*, 47, 504–518.

Fadil, P. A., Williams, R. J., Limpaphayom, W., and Smatt, C. (2005). Equity or equality? A conceptual examination of the influence of individualism/collectivism on the cross-cultural application of equity theory. *Cross Cultural Management*, 12, 17–35.

Gesthuizen, M., Kovarek, D., and Rapp, C. (2019). Extrinsic and intrinsic work values: Findings on equivalence in different cultural contexts. *Annals of the American Academy of Political and Social Science*, 682, 60–83.

Graen, G. B., and Uhl-Bien, M. (1995). Relationship-based approach to leadership: Development of leader-member exchange (LMX) theory of leadership over 25 years: Applying a multi-level multi-domain perspective. *Leadership Quarterly*, 6, 219–247.

Hamel, G., and Zanini, M. (2020). *Humanocracy: Creating Organizations as Amazing as the People Inside Them*. Boston, MA: Harvard Business Review Press [Audiobook version – Prince Frederick, MD: Recorded Books].

Hauff, S., and Kirchner, S. (2014). Changes in workplace situation and work values: Relations and dynamics within different employment regimes. *Management Revue*, 25, 27–49.

Hauff, S., and Kirchner, S. (2015). Identifying work value patterns: Cross-national comparison and historical dynamics. *International Journal of Manpower*, 36, 151–168.

Hauff, S., and Richter, N. F. (2015). Power distance and its moderating role in the relationship between situational job characteristics and job satisfaction: An empirical analysis using different cultural measures. *Cross Cultural Management*, 22, 68–89.

Hauff, S., Richter, N. F., and Tressin, T. (2015). Situational job characteristics and job satisfaction: The moderating role of national culture. *International Business Review*, 24, 710–723.

Herd, A. and Lowe, K. (2020). Cross-Cultural Comparative Leadership Studies and A Critical Look to the Future. In B. Szkudlarek, L. Romani, D. Caprar, J. Osland (Eds.), *The SAGE Handbook of Contemporary Cross-Cultural Management* (pp. 357–374). Los Angeles: SAGE.

Hofstede, G. (1984). The cultural relativity of the quality of life concept. *Academy of Management Review*, 9, 389–398.

Hofstede, G., Hofstede, G. J., and Minkov, M. (2010). *Cultures and Organizations: Software of the Mind – Intercultural Cooperation and Its Importance for Survival* (3rd ed.). New York, NY: McGraw-Hill.

House, R. J., Dorfman, P. W., Javidan, M., Hanges, P. J., and Sully de Luque, Mary F. (2014). *Strategic Leadership Across Cultures: The GLOBE Study of CEO Leadership Behavior and Effectiveness in 24 Countries*. Thousand Oaks, CA: SAGE.

House, R. J., Hanges, P. J., Javidan, M., Dorfman, P. W., and Gupta, V. (Eds) (2004). *Culture, Leadership, and Organizations: The GLOBE Study of 62 Societies*. Thousand Oaks, CA: SAGE.

International Social Survey Program Research Group (2017). International Social Survey Programme: Work Orientations IV – ISSP 2015. GESIS Data Archive, Cologne. ZA6770 Data File Version 2.1.0.

Javidan, M. (2004). Performance orientation. In R. J. House, P. J. Hanges, M. Javidan, P. W. Dorfman and V. Gupta (Eds), *Culture, Leadership, and Organizations: The GLOBE Study of 62 Societies* (pp. 239–281). Thousand Oaks, CA: SAGE.

Jimenez, A., Boehe, D. M., Taras, V., and Caprar, D. V. (2017). Working across boundaries: Current and future perspectives on global virtual teams. *Journal of International Management*, 23, 341–349.

Jonsen, K., Maznevski, M., and Davison, S. C. (2012). Global virtual team dynamics and effectiveness. In G. K. Stahl, I. Björkman and S. Morris (Eds), *Handbook of Research in International Human Resource Management* (pp. 363–392). Cheltenham, UK and Northampton, MA, USA: Edward Elgar Publishing.

Lauring, J., and Jonasson, C. (2018). Can leadership compensate for deficient inclusiveness in global virtual teams? *Human Resource Management Journal*, 28, 392–409.

Maslow, A. H. (1943). A theory of human motivation. *Psychological Review*, 50, 370–396.

Maslow, A. H. (1954). *Motivation and Personality*. New York, NY: Harper & Row.

McClelland, D. C. (1961). *The Achieving Society*. New York, NY: Van Nostrand.

Meyerding, S. G. H. (2015). Job characteristics and job satisfaction: A test of Warr's vitamin model in German horticulture. *Psychologist-Manager Journal*, 18, 86–107.

Nevis, E. C. (1983). Using an American perspective in understanding another culture: Toward a hierarchy of needs for the People's Republic of China. *Journal of Applied Behavioral Science*, 19, 249–264.

Petri, H. L., and Govern, J. M. (2013). *Motivation: Theory, Research, and Application* (6th ed.). Belmont, CA: Wadsworth/Cengage Learning.

Robbins, S. P., and Judge, T. A. (2013). *Organizational Behavior* (15th ed.). Harlow: Pearson.

RW3 CultureWizard (2018). *2018 Trends in High-Performing Global Virtual Teams*. https://content.ebulletins.com/hubfs/C1/Culture%20Wizard/LL-2018%20Trends%20in%20Global%20VTs%20Draft%2012%20and%20a%20half.pdf.

Ryan, R. M., and Deci, E. L. (2017). *Self-Determination Theory: Basic Psychological Needs in Motivation, Development, and Wellness*. New York, NY: Guilford.

Sanchez-Runde, C. J., and Steers, R. M. (2020). Culture, context, and work motivation. In B. Szkudlarek, L. Romani, D. Caprar and J. Osland (Eds), *The SAGE Handbook of Contemporary Cross-Cultural Management* (pp. 289–312). Thousand Oaks, CA: SAGE.

Steers, R. M., and Osland, J. S. (2020). *Management Across Cultures: Challenges, Strategies, and Skills* (4th ed.). Cambridge: Cambridge University Press.

Tajfel, H. (1981). *Human Groups and Social Categories: Studies in Social Psychology*. Cambridge: Cambridge University Press.

Taras, V., Baack, D., Caprar, D., Dow, D., Froese, F., Jimenez, A., and Magnusson, P. (2019). Diverse effects of diversity: Disaggregating effects of diversity in global virtual teams. *Journal of International Management*, 25, 100689.

Van Emmerik, H., Gardner, W. L., Wendt, H., and Fischer, D. (2010). Associations of culture and personality with McClelland's motives: A cross-cultural study of managers in 24 countries. *Group & Organization Management*, 35, 329–367.

Vansteenkiste, M., Ryan, R. M., and Soenens, B. (2020). Basic psychological need theory: Advancements, critical themes, and future directions. *Motivation and Emotion*, 44, 1–31.

Warr, P. B. (2007). *Work, Happiness, and Unhappiness*. Mahwah, NJ: Lawrence Erlbaum Associates.

Yukl, G. A. (2013). *Leadership in Organizations* (8th ed.). Harlow: Pearson.

9 CASE STUDY
MAGIC JUICE: TOWARDS SELF-MANAGEMENT?

The year 2022 was a very busy but positive one. The merger with Zumo Saludable has been successful and the first stores in Spain and Portugal were opened. During the Christmas holidays, Dirk de Jong listened to the audiobook *Humanocracy: Creating Organizations as Amazing as the People Inside Them*, co-authored by Gary Hamel and Michelle Zanini (2020). The book provides thought-provoking examples from business practice on developing an organization culture equipped for the challenges of the future. The book is mainly about how to move a traditional bureaucracy towards a "self-management" model. Dirk has often heard from other business leaders that self-management principles can hardly be applied in their organizations. Statements such as "It works only for small organizations" and "It will never work with low-skilled workers" are some of the most-heard arguments.

Dirk was always attracted to the thoughts behind self-managing organizations. Some time ago, he also participated in Gary Hamel's management course at the London Business School, "Reboot Your Company for the Age of Upheaval." Here he became aware of the American firm Morning Star Company, which for years – and with great success – has practiced "self-management" (see Exhibit 9.1). Dirk thinks that "self-management" does not mean "no management," and radical decentralization is not anarchy. He expresses this by saying that "Self-management is not doing whatever you want, it's about being part of determining what to do."

Back in the office, Dirk tries to convince others of his ideas. He wants a passionate, agile and fluid organization with a leadership that suits this. He wants to avoid an overload of bureaucracy and slowness as well as fear of change. He is of the opinion that management often stands in the way with too many policies, procedures and rules. "Magic Juice is synonymous with the employees and their personalities; those who are at the forefront and servicing the customers," he says.

Chairman Anton de Vries is somewhat skeptical and reticent about Dirk's ideas about self-management. Anton acknowledges that the initiatives Dirk has launched for his juice chain – among other things, giving the individual employees responsibility, competence and freedom – have worked. However, he is more doubtful that they will still be working after the expansion and all the restructuring processes in the last few years. Moreover, he asks, "Will the principles of self-management be transferable at all across countries?"

CASE EXHIBIT

Exhibit 9.1 Principles/conditions of self-management at Morning Star

The US-based company Morning Star, headquartered in California, is known for its unique form of organization: It is entirely self-managing. Founded by Chris Rufer in 1970, Morning Star is today the world largest tomato processor, with a total revenue close to USD 1 billion. The firm has 600 permanent employees and an additional 4,000 seasonal workers who join the organization during the 100-day harvesting season. Morning Star is a company where:

- No one has a boss.
- Employees negotiate responsibilities with their peers.
- Everyone can spend the firm's money.
- Everyone is responsible for acquiring the tools needed to do her or his work.
- There are no titles or promotions.
- Compensation decisions are peer-based.

Self-management in Morning Star is based on several conditions and principles:

Condition 1: The right mindset

To ensure the right mindset in relation to self-management, Morning Star is relying on two basic principles:

- All interaction should be voluntary: With no bosses, no titles and no structural hierarchy, the firm's prime principle is that all interactions should be voluntary. Each colleague has the same set of rights as any other colleague. No colleague can force another colleague to do something they do not want to do.
- Honor your commitments: If colleagues do not honor commitments they have to other colleagues, self-management is doomed to fail; see also condition 3.

Condition 2: A collective of mission statements

While most firms today focus on having a clear mission statement, Morning Star does it rather uniquely. At the highest level, Morning Star has its mission statement: "To produce tomato products and services which consistently achieve the quality and service expectations of our customers in a cost effective, environmentally responsible way." One level down, Morning Star also has mission statements at the departmental level. For example, the mission statement for the Morning Star Tomato Kitchens is: "To be a full-service tomato ingredient supplier providing unequivocally superior services and supply chain solutions to specialty, and geographically unique customers." One level further down, each employee has her or his own personal mission statement. This means that every employee has a clear idea of how she or he contributes to the purpose of the organization. Besides that, it keeps people's jobs fluent. There is no strict job description, but there is a personal mission (that is, as the business changes, so does the job).

Condition 3: The Colleague Letter of Understanding (CLOU)

The CLOU is a document that details an employees' personal commercial mission and all the commitments they have made with employees who are affected by their work. At the start of every year each employee negotiates a CLOU and the corresponding commitments with the colleagues that are affected by her or his work. Most employees have about 10 CLOU colleagues with whom they negotiate commitments. Each CLOU specifies the commitments between two employees, deliverables, goals and performance metrics. The CLOU is used throughout the rest of the year to hold each other accountable for the agreed-upon commitments.

Condition 4: A clear process to resolve conflicts

Whenever a conflict, disagreement or problem arises, the employees must solve it themselves. For those employees who are facing a conflict, they have to start talking to each other to try to solve it. No complaining about it to others is allowed. If needed, a confidential ombudsman or panel of different people with various perspectives can be consulted and involved. If the conflict – quite exceptionally – is not resolved, the firm's founder can be involved.

Condition 5: A trusted leader

A trusted and highly respected leader must be in place.

Source: Adapted from https://corporate-rebels.com/morning-star/

CASE QUESTIONS

Dirk is really passionate about his ideas, but after his talks with Anton he started to wonder whether Magic Juice is ready to apply self-management principles and conditions like Morning Star. A first step, he thought, should be to get a better overview of the status of leadership performance and employee motivation in each of the countries Magic Juice is active in. Building on that, he could better assess whether it is possible to transfer the ideas of self-management to every country in Magic Juice's network. What would be your recommendations to Dirk about implementing the right leadership and motivational incentives in Magic Juice's network? Provide specific ideas for the overall organization and potentially relevant adaptions for the different countries. How do the concepts of work centrality and work values influence the potential implementation of Dirk's ideas in Magic Juice's country network?

10
Building an effective international workforce

Human resource management (HRM) can be defined as "a strategic approach to managing employment relations which emphasizes that leveraging people's capabilities and commitment is critical to achieving sustainable competitive advantage or superior public services. This is accomplished through a distinctive set of integrated employment policies, programs and practices, embedded in an organizational and societal context" (Bratton and Gold, 2012: 7). This definition acknowledges the increased importance of people and the potential capacity that employees have to add value in a highly competitive economy. Moreover, this definition highlights that HRM refers to multiple activities that need to be internally aligned and coherent to the specific (international) context.

In an international context, HRM becomes more complex compared to a domestic context (Dowling, Festing and Engle, 2017). HR managers working in an international environment need to take a broader view since they need to design and administer HRM practices for more than one national group (for example, expatriates, host-country nationals, international migrants) who also have a higher mobility (for example, expatriates who are assigned to different countries). A key success factor is the acknowledgment and appreciation of cultural differences and the implied variety of values, practices and routines.

In this chapter, we examine the influence of national culture on key instruments of international HRM. Our focus is on the design of international recruitment and selection, training and development, and compensation as well as performance management. The reader will be familiarized with these HRM practices and the question of how they should be adapted to fit specific cultures. We will further discuss how international migrants can be best integrated into the local workforce. The integration of international migrants into the local labor markets involves great opportunities, but also great challenges. We will therefore discuss how organizations can facilitate the integration of international migrants and therewith contribute to employee well-being and organizational performance.

10.1　RECRUITMENT AND SELECTION

10.1.1　Recruitment approaches

Staffing in an international environment provides more options compared to staffing in a domestic environment. For example, to fill a position in a subsidiary, multinational enterprises (MNEs) can send employees from the parent organization ("expatriates"), and/or can hire employees from the host country or from third countries. Likewise, if positions at the HQ need to be filled, organizations can recruit locally, but they can also use employees from subsidiaries (who are commonly called "inpatriates") and recruit globally. Building on the works of Perlmutter (Heenan and Perlmutter, 1979; Perlmutter, 1969), we distinguish four recruitment approaches: ethnocentric, polycentric, geocentric and regiocentric. Each approach has its own advantages and disadvantages, which are summarized in Table 10.1.

Table 10.1 Key advantages and disadvantages of recruiting approaches

Approach	Advantages	Disadvantages
Home-country nationals	Familiarity with the MNE, its culture, strategy and policies Enhanced capability to implement corporate objectives and policies in the new subsidiary Better control and coordination of international activities Possession of specific knowledge, skills and expertise Home-country nationals can gain international experience	Can impose an inappropriate HQ style Often, high salary, benefits Relocation costs and other barriers (for example, work permit) Adaptation (employee's own and/or their family's) may take a long time Job satisfaction and motivation of host-country employees can decrease due to salary differences and limited career opportunities
Host-country nationals	No relocation and other costs Mostly lower salaries and benefits No adjustment problems (for example, language) Knowledge of the local environment (for example, laws, customs, culture) Established relations with local customers and community Increased job satisfaction and motivation of host-country employees Continuity in staffing	Lack of familiarity with HQ Organizational control and coordination impeded Possible language and cultural problems with HQ Home-country nationals have limited opportunities to gain experience outside their own country Limited possibilities for the corporate HQ to gain insights into the foreign markets
Third-country nationals	Hiring the best candidates around the globe Possibility to establish a global talent pool Salary and benefits may be lower compared to home-country nationals Third-country nationals may be more familiar with the host country than home-country nationals	Relocation costs and other barriers (for example, work permit) Adaptation (employee's own and/or their family's) may take a long time Limited acceptance of third-country nationals among host-country nationals

Source: Adapted from Dowling et al. (2017), Fatehi and Choi (2019)

The ethnocentric or home-country approach implies that key positions in the HQ and the subsidiaries will be filled with home-country employees. The home-country approach is often observed in the early stages of internationalization, based on the idea that it may reduce the risks associated with the foreign business. If an MNE acquires a new firm in a foreign country, sending home-country executives can help to implement corporate objectives and policies in the new subsidiary. Furthermore, home-country employees may be needed if local employees do not have the necessary competencies. A home-country approach is, however, not without disadvantages. Employing expatriate managers may have a negative influence on host-country employees' job satisfaction and motivation since expatriate managers often receive a much higher salary and limit the promotion opportunities for host-country nationals (Michailova et al., 2017). Expatriates themselves also need to adapt to the host country and they may lack the necessary experience and knowledge of how to behave in a foreign economy and culture. Finally, since there is not an infinite number of managers who can be sent abroad, such an approach is limited if MNEs want to further expand their foreign activities (Muratbekova-Touron, 2008).

The polycentric approach puts emphasis on the host country. The guiding idea is that regional specifics require local insights and management. Thus, expatriate managers are seldom transferred to foreign subsidiaries. Applying a polycentric approach can reduce some of the limitations of the home-country approach: Giving host-country nationals more responsibility and autonomy increases their satisfaction and motivation, which reduces turnover and provides more continuity in staffing. Host-country employees are often also less expensive than expatriates, which reduces personnel costs. Moreover, host-country nationals do not have adjustment problems (for example, language barriers) and do not need expensive cross-cultural training. A key shortcoming of the polycentric approach is its limited ability to bridge the gap between the corporate HQ and its subsidiaries. Since there is no (or limited) exchange of human resources, differences in terms of orientation and corporate values are likely to persist. Furthermore, home-country nationals have limited opportunities to gain experience outside their own country. Importantly, corporate HQs gain limited insights into foreign markets, which may have negative effects on their strategic decisions.

Using a geocentric approach implies a global perspective characterized by the belief that top employees can come from any background and culture (Fatehi and Choi, 2019). Thus, recruitment decisions are based less on nationality but focus on knowledge, skills, abilities and performance. A geocentric approach enables MNEs to establish a global talent pool that contributes to a shared orientation throughout the global organization. Even though this approach seems appropriate in a globalized world, it also has its challenges: Employees need to adapt to new environments and the employment of international talents may be expensive and aggravated through migration policies.

Finally, the regiocentric approach represents a "Think global and act local" philosophy. Employees are recruited from a wider pool, which is, however, narrower as compared to the geocentric approach. Employees may move outside their home country, but they usually stay within specific regions like Europe, North America and South America (Dowling et al., 2017). The regiocentric approach facilitates staff transfers and allows MNEs to better address the needs of specific regions and cultures. On the downside, it can, similar to the polycentric approach, produce federalism on a regional scale, which prevents a true global perspective.

10.1.2 Selection tools

There is a wide range of established instruments for the selection of applicants in corporate practice. According to LinkedIn's (2018) Global Recruiting Trends Survey, which interviewed 9,000 recruiters and hiring managers from 39 countries, the most common instruments are structured interviews, behavioral interviews, screening by phone, interview panels and case

BUILDING AN EFFECTIVE INTERNATIONAL WORKFORCE 293

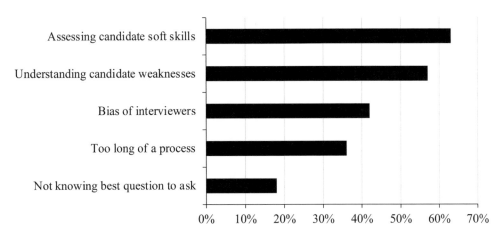

Source: Adapted from LinkedIn (2018)

Figure 10.1 Limitations of traditional interviews

study/work assignments. These instruments are generally considered effective. However, these traditional techniques have not been without critique. In the LinkedIn survey, respondents stated that traditional interviews, for example, fail in assessing a candidate's soft skills or in understanding candidates' weaknesses. Respondents also noted that interviews can be biased, that the process can be too long or that interviewers do not know which question to ask (see Figure 10.1).

Besides these limitations, we should also take into account that cross-cultural differences might lead to misunderstanding because interview questions and the specific interview situation might be interpreted differently. To avoid such misunderstandings, Table 10.2 provides several examples of critical interview questions and situations and recommendations on how to deal with them. For more examples and suggestions, see Kühlmann and Heinz (2017).

Table 10.2 Critical interview questions, situations and how to deal with them

Situation	Example of question/behavior	Notes	Suggestions
Asking for the candidate's strengths and weaknesses	"Can you tell me your greatest strengths and major weaknesses?"	In some cultures, talking about strength and weakness will evoke unpleasant situations as the interviewee is forced to "lose face" and self-praise is regarded as inappropriate.	Rephrase the question. Do not ask for strengths and weaknesses, but try to get this information indirectly; for example, "How would others describe you as an employee?" or "Could you tell me three things which you would like to improve in your work in the future?"
Asking about leisure-time activities	"What do you do in your leisure time?"	In some cultures, it is not usual to talk about one's private life. Interviewees are expected to concentrate on work tasks and professional skills.	If you want to know more about a candidate, explain to her or him why you ask this question; for example, your organization is interested in a good work–life balance.

Situation	Example of question/behavior	Notes	Suggestions
Asking for opinions and values	"What do you expect your supervisor to be?"	To assess others' behavior and to criticize authorities is not appropriate in some cultures. For example, people might think that they are not allowed to ask for the characteristics of a good leader.	Avoid direct questions. Ask indirect questions in a more subjunctive way; for example, "If you were a supervisor, what would be your most important characteristics?"
Interpretation of behavior	Eye contact, body language	Nonverbal communication can be very different between cultures. For example, in some cultures, eye contact is a sign of honesty, confidence and interest. In other cultures, eye contact as regarded as disrespectful.	Analyze your interpretation of nonverbal communication for cultural differences. Ask yourself if the behavior really reflects uncertainty, for example, or if the behavior might be based on the candidate's cultural norms.
Asking for questions	"Do you have any questions to ask me?"	In Western countries, interviewees are usually asked if they have any questions. In Western countries, questions are regarded as an indication of interest, initiative and good preparation. However, in Asian countries, for example, direct questions might be regarded as impolite and disrespectful.	Prepare for the specific interviewee and her or his cultural background. Keep in mind that "deviant" behavior might be caused by cultural differences.

Source: Kühlmann and Heinz (2017)

Given the limitations of traditional interviews, and technological developments, new tools are emerging that improve the selection of employees. Examples of these new tools are online soft skills assessments, job auditions, meetings in casual settings, virtual reality assessments and video interviews (see Figure 10.2). With online soft skills assessments, organizations screen candidates for their abilities related to communication, learning, teamwork and the like. Job auditions are scenarios that allow organizations to observe candidates while they perform real work (sometimes even paid work). For example, a software developer may be asked to write a particular code, or a marketer may be asked to present a strategy proposal. For casual interviews, recruiters invite candidates for coffee or lunch, for example. In such an informal setting, recruiters hope to get an exclusive look into a candidate's character. With virtual reality, organizations use 3-D environments to test a candidate's abilities. Finally, video interviews emerged as a convenient tool to easily interview candidates around the globe. While the latter has its key advantage in bridging geographic distance, the first four new tools are promising since they are less biased and give a more realistic snapshot of a candidate's personality; and the candidates can get a better understanding of the organization and the job.

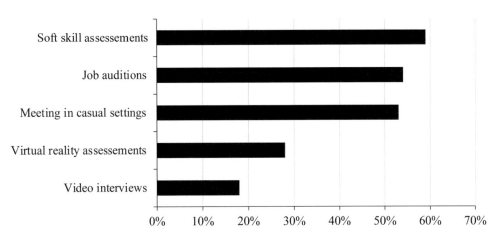

Source: Adapted from LinkedIn (2018)

Figure 10.2   Most useful interviewing innovations

When using selection tools globally, we need to ask whether these tools are equally accepted and effective across cultures. Researchers have often speculated that societal cultural values influence the acceptance and usage of selection tests. For example, it is assumed that organizations in cultures with a high performance orientation will more likely use tests that elicit performance-related behavior, or that organizations in high-uncertainty-avoidance cultures will use a comparatively greater variety of assessment tools. However, in a large study in 23 countries with more than 1,000 HR professionals, Ryan et al. (2017) find little evidence that cultural values are related to selection practices. Their results indicate that selection practices are generalizable across cultures. Still, we need to be cautious when applying tests in different countries: Not every selection tool is automatically culturally transportable. Dong and Dumas (2020), for example, show that personality assessments across cultures do not demonstrate (full scalar) measurement invariance; that is, the questions used are not equally applicable across cultures (see also Box 10.1). In addition, the implementation of assessment tools also depends on other contextual factors, like legal differences, union or work council objections, and the availability of technology. Thus, selection tools are still not easily transferable from one culture to another.

> **Box 10.1 Further insights: Measurement invariance across cultures**
>
> When we use a specific instrument like a personality test in different countries, we need to ask whether the instrument always works in the same way; more specifically, whether respondents from different cultures interpret the same measure (for example, an answer in a personality test like "I see myself as someone who is generally trusting") in a similar way. This is highly relevant for selection decisions, but also in cross-cultural research. Only if there is measurement invariance can we really compare the answers from respondents from different cultural backgrounds.
>
> In order to test measurement invariance, researchers usually use a statistical technique called "multigroup confirmatory factor analysis." The analysis typically includes three sequential steps. In a first step, the configural invariance is tested. This test shows whether the overall factor structure (that is, the number of factors and the items corresponding to each factor) is equal across different groups. Next, the metric invariance is tested to determine whether the factor loadings are equivalent across different groups. The third step is to test for scalar invariance. This serves to examine whether the item intercepts are equivalent across groups, which implies that people in one group do not systematically give higher or lower answers compared to another group. For more information about measurement invariance see, for example, Davidov et al. (2014).

10.1.3 Selection criteria for international assignments

A critical task in international recruitment is the selection of expatriates. Expatriates represent the HQ and its strategy, values and policies. Often, the success of international operations depends on the quality of the assigned expatriate managers. But what qualities should expatriate managers possess? Which criteria should be used when selecting expatriate managers? There is no straightforward answer to these questions since the selection decisions need to consider the characteristics of the MNE (strategy, culture, HRM philosophy, internationalization stage), the characteristics of the subsidiary (ownership, role), the characteristics of the host country (culture, language) and the specifics of the position to be filled (job description, duration). Research has, however, analyzed and discussed several criteria that are critical for the success of international assignments. These include job-related factors, personality traits, intercultural competencies, motives and desires, language skills, and the family situation of the expatriate manager (Waxin and Brewster, 2020).

Job-related factors involve the knowledge, skills or abilities that are necessary to do a specific job. Basic technological, administrative and managerial skills are essential qualities of an expatriate manager and often have priority when making selection decisions. Since expatriates are usually employees who already work for the MNE, past performance evaluations can be used to assess if a candidate has the required skills. However, firms should consider that past performance in the home country might not be a perfect or even good predictor of success in a foreign environment. Therefore, technological, administrative and managerial skills should not be the only criteria for deciding which manager should be sent to an international endeavor (Ott and Michailova, 2016).

Several personality characteristics have been associated with a better cross-cultural adjustment and job performance of expatriate managers. In particular, it is widely agreed that the big five personality traits (that is, high extraversion, conscientiousness, agreeableness, openness and emotional stability) cause proactive behavior that helps one to adapt within a new and unfamiliar environment, to better connect with foreign people and to be more effective (Harari et al., 2018). Further predictors of expatriate adaptation and job performance are, for example, attributes like creativity, flexibility and stress resistance (see, for example, Andresen and Margenfeld, 2015; Waxin, Brewster and Ashill, 2019).

Apart from having the right job-related knowledge, skills or abilities and specific personality traits, expatriates require intercultural competencies (see Chapter 8). Intercultural competencies broadly describe an individual's ability to function effectively across cultures (Leung, Ang and Tan, 2014). That is, expatriate managers with intercultural competence have the ability to think and act in a way that fits the intercultural challenge of the assignment. Research has demonstrated the relevance of intercultural competence for several outcomes of relevance in the expatriation process, such as adjustment and job performance (see Schlaegel, Richter and Taras, 2021). Several personal characteristics have been identified as intercultural competencies, and researchers have introduced various intercultural competence models (Leung et al., 2014). The personal characteristics identified in previous research include (i) intercultural traits (for example, open-mindedness, tolerance of ambiguity, quest for adventure), (ii) intercultural attitudes and worldviews (that is, the ways in which individuals perceive other cultures or information from outside their own culture) and (iii) intercultural capabilities (for example, knowledge of other cultures/countries; metacognitive, motivational and behavioral cultural intelligence). Influential examples of intercultural competence models are the multicultural personality model (Van der Zee and Van Oudenhoven, 2000) and the cultural intelligence model (Earley and Ang, 2003) (see Chapter 8 for further details and examples of measurement instruments).

Motives and desires refer to the question of why employees seek an international assignment. Some individuals possess a genuine interest in foreign countries and cultures and are thus predestined for a position abroad. Others might look for an adventure or just see an opportunity to earn more money or to make a necessary step forward in their careers. Even if all of these perspectives are legitimate, we can say that an individual who is more intrinsically motivated is likely to adapt more quickly and to be more successful.

Language skills are often considered an important criterion for the selection of an expatriate manager. The importance of speaking the local language is, however, disputed (Ott and Michailova, 2016). While some see the proficiency in the host-country language as absolutely necessary and vital for expatriate performance, others consider the fluency in the corporate language as more important. It certainly depends on the specific circumstances in the organization and the host country; in some country and firm environments, speaking English could work quite well for the expatriate. Either way, speaking the local language can help expatriates to build relationships inside and outside of the workplace, and to adjust to the host country (see also the findings in Schlaegel et al., 2021).

The family situation of expatriates is a factor that is often overlooked, though it is absolutely crucial for the success of the international assignment. The spouse/partner and children of an expatriate are largely affected by an international assignment. In short-term assignments, the family may not consider also moving to a foreign country, but long-distance relationships may be difficult for expatriates and their families. If the spouse/partner and the children are also moving, the responsibility for settling the family usually lies with the spouse/partner, who does not have a social network in the new country. Likewise, children have to interrupt their education, and need to get used to a new school and find new friends. These are some examples of the many challenges that come along with international assignments. The inability of a spouse/partner and children to face these challenges and to adapt to the new circumstances can affect the performance of the expatriate and can result in a premature ending of the international assignment (Waxin and Brewster, 2020).

While the above are the key criteria of relevance, other factors can also be relevant for the selection of expatriates, such as gender, age, education, experience, and physical and mental health (Ott and Michailova, 2016; Waxin and Brewster, 2020).

10.2 TRAINING AND DEVELOPMENT

In Chapter 8 we highlighted how soft skills like intercultural competence are crucial to compete successfully in international markets, and we introduced suggestions on how these competences can be trained. Such trainings can be included in broader pre-department training programs, in which employees who are to be sent to a foreign country receive information about the country's economy, its culture and the role they are expected to assume during the international assignment. International and intercultural training and development is, however, not limited to employees who are sent to a foreign country. When MNEs set up a subsidiary in a foreign country and also in the aftermath of international mergers and acquisitions, they often need to offer training to employees.

If organizations decide to send employees to a foreign country, pre-departure training is key for a successful integration and a good performance by these employees. Essential components of these training initiatives are cross-cultural trainings (including language courses), preliminary visits, assistance with practical day-to-day matters and security briefings (Dowling et al., 2017).

The objective of cross-cultural trainings is to familiarize employees (and if required their spouse/partner and children) with a foreign culture to facilitate adjustment and increase the likelihood that foreign assignments will be successful. More specifically, cross-cultural trainings aim to (i) teach how to learn and acquire information about another culture, (ii) enable expatriates to make isomorphic attributions (that is, to make the same judgments regarding behavior as do host nationals), (iii) enable expatriates to handle disconfirmed expectations and effectively cope with the stressors encountered while on the foreign assignment, (iv) aid expatriates to develop positive relationships with host nationals and (v) help expatriates to accomplish work-related tasks (Littrell et al., 2006).

Cross-cultural trainings can be done in very different ways, and organizations need to decide how to design an appropriate program. The length and depth of the training program as well as the decision of the right training method should depend on, among other factors, the length of the stay, the degree of interpersonal interaction with host nationals, the degree of cultural novelty and the position of the expatriate in the organization's hierarchy. We follow Mendenhall and Oddou (1986) and distinguish three basic cross-cultural training approaches (see Figure 10.3). If the foreign assignment is short and the expected level of interaction low, an information-giving approach that can take less than a week will suffice. Examples are area and cultural briefings, the use of films or books, the use of interpreters and "survival-level" language training. If a foreign assignment is of intermediate length (that is, two to 12 months), and if the expatriate is expected to have a moderate interaction with host-country nationals, the length and rigor of training activities should be increased and affective approaches should be followed. Examples are cultural assimilator training, role playing, critical-incident training, case studies, stress-reduction training and moderate language training. Finally, if the foreign assignment is long-term, and thus the expected degree of interaction high, training activities should follow an impression approach with extensive in-depth trainings. Examples are assessment centers, field experiences, simulations, sensitivity trainings and extensive language trainings.

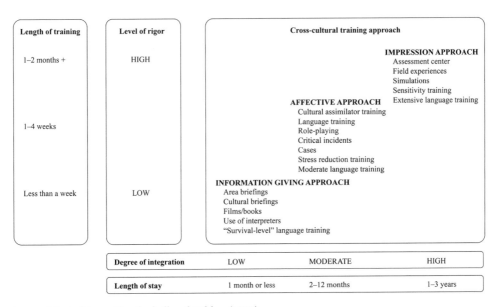

Source: Adapted from Mendenhall and Oddou (1986)

Figure 10.3 Cross-cultural training approaches

Regardless of the training method chosen, we should pay attention to the following key factors for the success of the cross-cultural training (Bennett, Aston and Colquhoun, 2000): The first is a thorough needs assessment of the employee (and her or his spouse/partner and children) prior to the training, since needs are different depending on the assignment objectives and the employee's responsibilities, knowledge, skills and past international experience. Second, the content of the training should meet the identified needs (see also Table 10.3). Trainings should include culture-specific content (that is, in-depth content related to the culture concerned) and culture-general content (that is, general information on the culture and cultural differences). Third, the design and methodologies of the training should be adapted to the needs and learning style of the employee. The training methods should be complementary, including didactic and experiential approaches. In general, a deductive approach to cross-cultural learning should be preferred, since inductive approaches with generalizations about "dos and don'ts" are often of limited value. A "learning to learn" approach is most effective since it produces more sustainable outcomes: Cultural training is of limited duration and cannot cover all aspects of a foreign culture; therefore, it is important that employees know how to continue their cultural learning after finishing the training program. Fourth, the duration and timing of the training should also be aligned with the needs. If necessary, trainings should be continued after arrival in the destination country. Fifth, selecting the right trainers and training team is key: Cross-cultural training should be delivered by specialists and country experts. Trainers need to perform in different roles, including coach, educator, facilitator, counselor, moderator and cultural role model for the participants. Accordingly, they need a broad set of competences, and extensive international experience. Finally, a quality assurance system should be implemented. In order to ensure a high quality, cross-cultural trainings should include program evaluations, debriefings of the members of the training team, written documentation by the trainer, regular meetings between the organization and the training team or a representative of the training firm, and ongoing trainer performance management. Table 10.3 provides some guidance on methods that address specific desired outcomes and on how they can be evaluated.

Table 10.3 Desired training outcomes, suggested methods and evaluation activities

Desired outcomes	Training methods and activities	Evaluation activities
Knowledge (facts and information) *Learner will understand*	Readings, songs, lectures, brainstorming, TV, radio, audiotapes, videos, computer, programmed instruction, debates, panels, interviews, galleries, field trips	Written exams, oral exams, application in other training activities
Skills (manual, thinking, planning, and so on) *Learner will be able to do something*	Demonstration or instructions followed by practice with feedback to correct mistakes; role playing, in-basket exercises, drills, games, coaching, case studies, worksheets, simulations	Observation on the job, in practice or during role play using an observation checklist
Attitudes *Learner will adopt new values, perspectives*	Discussion, role plays, role modeling, values-clarification exercises, films and videos, case studies, critical incidents, debates, games, self-analysis, feedback, simulations, field trips	Indirectly, by observing behaviors, such as interpersonal relations, approaches to problems, choices of activities

Source: Fowler and Yamaguchi (2020)

Cross-cultural trainings can be accompanied with pre-assignment visits (Dowling et al., 2017). This enables a better impression of the situation in the foreign country and the organizational unit, and therewith a more informed decision about accepting the international assignment. Importantly, such visits should be relevant and realistic: They should give detailed insights into the intended position as well as the living situation in the foreign country. A sugar-coated tourist experience will only lead to disappointment after the expatriate agrees to the assignment.

In a survey on global assignment policies and practices, the consultancy KPMG (2019) reports that 45 percent of the participating organizations use pre-assignment visits as a core policy for international assignments. The remaining organizations use pre-assignment visits for selected assignees (16 percent) or at the discretion of the organization (27 percent), and only 13 percent of the organizations do not provide pre-assignment visits. The goals and quantity of the pre-assignment visits are, however, diverse: 18 percent of organization provide one trip to determine whether the assignee will accept the assignment, 35 percent provide one trip to find housing and/or schools once the assignment has been accepted, 34 percent provide one trip for one of these goals and only 6 percent provide two trips.

Another useful component of training programs is the assistance with practical day-to-day matters. This includes various forms of support before and during the assignments. Pre-departure practical support can include, for example, assistance with official papers and visas, shipping an assignee's goods to the host country and providing interim accommodation or furniture storage in the home country. On-assignment practical support can include, for example, administrative support in finding and negotiating accommodation, opening a bank account, and filling in tax and official administration forms.

Finally, security briefings might be needed if employees are to be sent to countries with an increased security risk. The personal safety of expatriates can be threatened in various ways, due to, for example, hostile political environments (terrorism, kidnapping, hijacking, and war), natural disasters, disease or accidents. In KPMG's (2019) survey, 51 percent of the organizations provide some sort of security briefing either as a core policy or for selected assignees, countries or projects. Forty-eight percent of the organizations state that they have contracted with a third-party service provider for emergency evacuations/assistance during crises, and 34 percent state that they have a global (not location-specific) plan in place.

In practice, we usually find a mix of different approaches and tools depending on the specific circumstances and needs. For example, Boeing, one of the world's largest aerospace companies, uses a wide range of trainings, including online modules, afternoon seminars, cultural orientation sessions and one-on-one trainings, to increase cultural sensitivity and to prepare expatriates and their family members before they move to a foreign country. The company also offers "lunch and learn" cultural talks and diversity conferences for leaders twice a year. Employees from outside the United States can also participate in a rotation program that allows them to work for nine to 18 months in the United States. SAP, the market leader in enterprise application software, follows a similar strategy. As part of the company's diversity program, all employees can participate in classroom-based trainings and/or interactive instructions to become more culturally aware. Employees can access online cultural briefings if they are planning a business trip in a foreign country. For long-term assignments, employees receive customized trainings depending on the destination and their specific needs. Thereby, SAP relies on internal and external trainers (Chebium, 2015).

In addition to the training of employees who are to be sent to a foreign country, international operations often require training for host-country employees. After acquiring a subsidiary in a foreign country, an international merger or an equity joint venture, organizations are advised to provide local employees with an introduction and orientation program. These should familiarize them with the organization's overall purpose and mission, its strategies and its management policies and philosophies, as well as its culture norms and values.

Beyond these aspects, host-country employees might need further job-specific training. Several issues should be considered (Fatehi and Choi, 2019). First, many countries face a shortage of skilled professionals, which implies high competition for skills and talents. Thus, organizations should not only think about training but also about implementing measures to increase the commitment of their employees (for example, through career development). Second, successful home-country trainings may require modifications to make them fit the needs of the foreign country. Cultural factors can affect the acceptance and success of training. For example, a trainer from a specific ethnic group or religion might be rejected by another ethnic group or religion. Trainers also need to demonstrate intercultural competence and be able to adapt their approach to the group of employees trained. While a frank confession of personal limitations or knowledge gaps may be appreciated in most Western cultures, it is not in others. Furthermore, while employees from Western cultures often expect an active learning approach that allows participation and exchange of personal opinions, employees from other cultures may be more comfortable with passive learning.

10.3 COMPENSATION

Organizations can use a great variety of financial and non-financial rewards to attract, motivate and retain employees. In Chapter 9 we have already emphasized that non-financial rewards like job design, job security or career opportunities need to be aligned to the specific cultural context. In the following, we will focus on financial rewards. We will outline the key components of compensation and point to the specifics related to an international environment. We will also discuss different approaches for compensating international employees.

10.3.1 Compensation components in an international context

The key components of compensation are base salary, variable or performance-based pay, indirect financial rewards and taxes. The base salary is usually the largest part of the financial reward and is mostly provided to employees at regular time intervals (for example, weekly or monthly). Base salary rates depend on a variety of factors, including individual characteristics (for example, education, level of skills), organizational factors (for example, level of the job, organizational culture), supply and demand on the labor market, and the geographic area. The base salary represents the minimum amount of pay that can be expected in return for work performed. While some countries (for example, Australia, Canada, France, Germany, Japan, the United Kingdom, the United States) have legislation ensuring a minimum base salary (known as the "minimum wage"), most countries do not. The question of which base salary is necessary to afford a living depends on the living costs, which vary considerably around the globe (see Figure 10.4).

The calculation of living costs around the globe is not easy since the issue of which aspects of life should be considered is a point for discussion. The Swiss bank UBS, for example, uses the "Big Mac Index," which indicates the time span that an average employee needs to work to earn enough money to buy a Big Mac in her or his country. We would like to invite you to pause and reflect a bit; that is, please use some time to think about further approaches and costs that should be considered before you continue reading.

Variable pay is contingent on performance. Performance-based pay systems tie pay to the contributions of the individual, the team or the collective (Gerhart and Weller, 2019). They can be results- or behavior-oriented as well as short- or long-term-oriented. Examples of

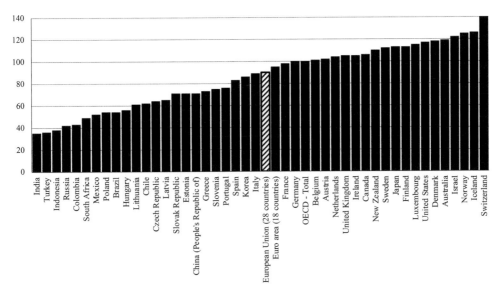

Source: Adapted from Organisation for Economic Co-operation and Development (OECD; 2021)

Figure 10.4 Price level indices 2021

performance-based pay are merit pay, bonuses, profit-sharing and stock options. Research suggests that culture influences the preference for performance-based pay as well as its effectiveness. Scott et al. (2015), for example, found that nationality plays an important role for the preference of individual pay variability and the opportunity for collective bonuses. Prince, Prince and Kabst (2020) found that the relevance of profit-sharing for performance is stronger in cultures with a high performance orientation, high in-group collectivism and low uncertainty avoidance.

Indirect financial rewards represent a range of benefits, services and allowances that are offered to employees. These typically involve benefits and services, such as different types of deferred income (for example, health care plans, retirement plans) and perquisites (for example, paid time off, company car, club memberships). National practices and regulations related to benefits and services vary considerably, especially in relation to medical coverage benefits, social security and retirement plans. This heterogeneity is a challenge for the HR departments in MNEs. In addition, employees can receive payments for specific purposes, called allowances. Allowances are particularly relevant in the context of expatriation remuneration since they represent an expensive feature of expatriate compensation packages. The most common allowances for expatriates are cost-of-living allowance (to compensate for potential differences in expenditures between the home and host country), housing allowance (to maintain the home-country living standard), home leave allowance (to cover trips to the home country), education allowance (for example, for children), and relocation allowance (for example, for shipping, moving and storage costs) (Dowling et al., 2017).

Another component of income are taxes. Taxation is also not an easy issue for MNEs since regulations differ considerably across countries. This becomes particularly challenging during international assignments since expatriates may have two tax bills: one for the host country and one for the home country. MNEs usually deal with this issue by paying the extra tax burden in the host country.

10.3.2 Approaches for compensating international employees

MNEs have a number of options regarding how to compensate their expatriates. We outline three main options and their strengths and weaknesses (see Table 10.4 and Bonache and Stirpe, 2012). The first approach is the "host-country approach" (also called the "going rate approach" or "localization approach"). With this approach, the salary of the expatriate is comparable to the salaries of local nationals. A key advantage of this approach is that it creates equity between expatriates and local employees as well as between expatriates from different countries. Furthermore, such an approach can help to reduce costs if the pay level in the host country is lower compared to the home country. If the latter is the case, the host-country approach has the disadvantage of being less attractive for expatriates and does not stimulate international mobility.

The second approach is the "home-country approach" (also called the "balance sheet approach"). The basic objective is that the expatriate does not lose by agreeing to an international assignment. Therefore, the expatriate receives the home-country salary plus extra benefits and allowances. Such an approach makes international assignments more attractive and ensures equity among expatriates who are sent to different locations. However, it creates higher costs and disparities between expatriates and local employees as well as between expatriates from different nationalities working in the same location.

The third approach is the "global approach," in which the compensation of expatriates is regulated uniformly across countries. This is particularly interesting for MNEs who assign employees from different countries of origin and who expect their expatriates to move to more than one foreign country. It can increase the attractiveness of international assignments and creates equity between expatriates in different locations. In addition, it is also fair with respect to other expatriates from different nationalities in the same location. The disadvantages of this approach are the related costs, the discrepancies between expatriates and local employees, and the potential problems related to expatriates' re-entry into the home country.

Table 10.4 Compensation approaches and impact on compensation objectives

Objectives of an international compensation system	Approach		
	Host-country	Home-country	Global
1. To attract personnel for the international assignment	-	+	+
2. To be cost-effective	+	-	-
3. To be fair …			
… with respect to local employees	+	-	-
… with respect to other expatriates from different nationalities in the same location	+	-	+
… with respect to other expatriates in another location	-	+	+
4. To facilitate re-entry	-	+	-

Note: + = positive impact; - = negative impact.
Source: Bonache and Stirpe (2012)

BUILDING AN EFFECTIVE INTERNATIONAL WORKFORCE

	1-6 months	1-12 months	13 months – 5 years	
	Short-Term Assignment (STA)	**Short-Term Expat (STX)**	**Long-Term Expat (LTX)**	**National Condition Expat (NCX)**
Headcount	Home	Host	Host	Host
Salary	Home salary + STA allowance + housing	Host salary = Home Salary + Living (=STA) Allowance + Housing; On gross basis OR market salary if better	Expatriate balance sheet as basis; Subsequent salary development according to host salary review process	Local salary
Benefits	– Family not considered – Home trip allowance	– Family not considered – Home trip allowance	BENEFIT PACKAGES > 18 Months = Full 13-18 Months = Basic	– One time allowances – Health insurance – No LTX benefits
Processes	Remains in home country processes	Very simplified: – No salary review – Performance bonus built into salary – Goal: return position pre-defined	Salary review in host	Salary review in host

Source: Bosch

Figure 10.5 The international assignment policy at Bosch

10.3.3 International assignment policy at Bosch

The Bosch Group is a leading global supplier of technology and services. Its operations are divided into four business sectors: mobility solutions, industrial technology, consumer goods, and energy and building technology. As mentioned in Chapter 8, in 2020, the company generated sales of EUR 71.5 billion and employed almost 400,000 associates worldwide. The Bosch Group comprises Robert Bosch GmbH and its 440 subsidiary and regional companies in 60 countries. Accordingly, international assignments are a key element of the HR policy.

In the past, the Bosch Group followed a classical home-country (net) approach, which is well suited for expatriates from high-cost locations. Due to the increasing internationalization of the expat group (today, about 60 percent of expatriates come from countries other than Germany), Bosch switched to an integration (gross) approach in 2019. In addition to a "classic" salary build-up, following the home-country principle, this approach allows a best-of comparison with the gross salary in the host country and thus does serve expatriates from all countries. Expatriates are integrated into the compensation processes of the host country during their stay abroad. Expatriate benefits such as home trips, partner support, and so on, are structured as lump sums, where possible.

Bosch relies on a small number of assignment models, which are primarily defined by the length of stay. Figure 10.5 illustrates the key features of Bosch's international assignment policy.

10.4 PERFORMANCE MANAGEMENT

Performance management is a "continuous process of identifying, measuring, and developing the performance of individuals and teams and aligning performance with the strategic goals of the organization" (Aguinis, 2019: 1). It is one of the crucial processes that determine the success of MNEs, and every international organization has a specific type of performance management system. In the following we will discuss how culture can influence these systems. Building on that, we introduce the concept of high-performance work practices as a holistic approach to foster employee performance.

10.4.1 Cross-cultural perspectives on performance management

Performance management systems are pervasive worldwide. As culture influences the design, implementation and ultimately effectiveness of these systems, we need to consider several issues (Cho and Payne, 2016). First, culture influences the importance and therefore the frequency of performance appraisals in organizations. For example, cultures with a high performance orientation put more emphasis on performance management than cultures with a low performance orientation. Second, culture influences the purpose or goals of performance management and therefore the practices that are implemented. Performance appraisals can serve multiple goals. They can, for instance, aim to stimulate communication, give feedback, identify avenues for development or simply provide data in order to judge employees. Third, culture influences the way feedback is given and received. For example, Asian cultures try to avoid criticism and direct confrontation in performance feedback. Fourth, culture can lead to discrepancies between raters, which impacts all sources of performance feedback. Self-ratings are influenced, as culture leads to fundamental differences in self-perceptions. For example, collectivism leads to more modest self-ratings as compared to valuing individualism. In supervisor ratings, culture influences the relevance of specific performance criteria. For example, managers in collectivistic cultures put more emphasis on relational aspects (such as helping other colleagues) when deciding about a bonus. Finally, culture influences peer and subordinate ratings. In collectivistic cultures, employees focus more on giving positive feedback for their coworkers. Similarly, subordinates in high-power-distance cultures are more reluctant to give negative feedback of their supervisor.

In light of these issues, it seems evident that performance management systems should always be customized to the local context. However, we present five universal principles, as identified in Aguinis et al. (2012), that lead to effective performance management regardless of the cultural context. These are: congruence between job descriptions and organizational goals, training regarding performance management, measurement of performance based on behaviors and results at the individual and collective levels, delivering performance feedback using a strengths-based approach and allocating rewards that are meaningful (see Table 10.5).

Table 10.5 Performance management universals and their implementation in different cultural contexts

Performance management universal	Illustrative cultural context	Recommendations for practice
1. Congruence between job descriptions and organizational goals	High uncertainty avoidance	Create and maintain job descriptions that are highly specific and clear
	Low power distance	Encourage employees to be active participants in the process of creating job descriptions
2. Training regarding performance management	High individualism (that is, low collectivism)	Provide individual-based training
	High uncertainty avoidance	Provide highly standardized and structured on- and off-the-job training
	High gender egalitarianism (that is, low masculinity)	Provide training programs that contain opportunities for interpersonal interactions among training participants
	Low power distance	Provide training programs that promote active trainee participation
3. Measurement of performance based on results and behaviors at the individual and collective levels	High individualism (that is, low collectivism)	Emphasize individual over collective (for example, team, department) performance (but measure both)
4. Delivering performance feedback using a strengths-based approach	High power distance	Encourage supervisors to deliver performance feedback (rather than peers or subordinates)
	High collectivism (that is, low individualism)	Use non-confrontational and indirect language, preferably in informal settings
5. Allocating rewards that are meaningful	High collectivism (that is, low individualism)	Avoid large levels of inequality in rewards across individual performers holding a similar position in the organizational hierarchy
	High uncertainty avoidance	Provide a very clear and detailed description of what types of behaviors and results at the individual and collective levels will lead to which intangible and tangible rewards

Source: Aguinis et al. (2012)

The first universal principle suggests that job descriptions (of job duties, knowledge and skills needed) which form the basis for performance management should always be aligned with the organizational goals. The second principle points out that an effective performance management system requires adequate training of raters and ratees (for example, to reduce the bias during the rating process). The third principle refers to the measurement of performance. According to this principle, performance evaluations should always consider the behaviors and results at the individual and the collective (for example, team) level. The fourth principle indicates that performance feedback should always be given using a strength-based approach. This implies identifying employees' strengths, providing positive feedback on how these strengths can be used to achieve organizational goals, and asking employees to build on and further develop these strengths. The fifth principle suggests that, regardless of the cultural context in question, rewards should always be meaningful for the individuals who receive them.

Building on these universal principles, Aguinis et al. (2012) argue that organizations should think globally but act locally: Thus, although these principles are cross-cultural invariant, organizations should implement them differently depending on their specific context. Table 10.4 illustrates recommendations on how to implement these principles in different cultural contexts.

10.4.2 High-performance work practices

Research in strategic HRM focuses on the analysis of bundles or configurations of HRM practices when examining HRM's effects on individual and organizational performance. A key assumption is that firms use different HRM practices that do not function in isolation. Instead, it is often argued that the alignment of different HRM practices in HRM systems should exert synergistic effects that go beyond the effects of the single HRM practices. Researchers in this field often argue that certain sets of HRM practices contribute to increasing individual and thus organizational performance, regardless of the specific context. One of the most prominent approaches is the concept of high-performance work practices (HPWPs) (Appelbaum et al., 2000; Huselid, 1995). Even though there is no generally accepted understanding on the HRM practices that are HPWPs, most researchers use the ability, motivation, opportunity (AMO) framework, according to which HRM practices should contribute to employees having the necessary abilities, being highly motivated and also having the opportunity to use their abilities and motivation accordingly (Hauff et al., 2021). Key HPWPs are intensive recruitment and regular training to enhance abilities; performance assessment, profit-sharing, career prospects and job security to increase motivation; and diversified work, autonomy and participation as means to increase opportunities (see Table 10.6). Abilities, motivation and the opportunities to use them are basic challenges of HRM, which must be solved globally. Following this line of reasoning, firms should be urged to use HPWPs without restriction to increase the performance of all their employees independent from the context.

Table 10.6 High-performance work practices

Domain	HPWPs	Measures
Ability-enhancing HPWP	Comprehensive recruitment/selection	The recruitment/selection process for these employees is comprehensive.
	Continuous training	There is continuous training for these employees.
Motivation-enhancing HPWP	Profit-based pay	Compensation/rewards for these employees are based on the firm's profits.
	Extensive benefits	Compensation/rewards for these employees include an extensive benefits package.
	Clear career paths	These employees have clear career paths in the organization.
	Job security	These employees have long-term perspectives.
Opportunity-enhancing HPWP	Task variety	These employees perform jobs that include a wide variety of tasks.
	Semi-autonomous work groups	These employees work in semi-autonomous work groups.
	Empowerment	These employees perform jobs that empower them to make decisions.
	Information-sharing	Superiors and employees engage in intensive information exchange.

Source: Hauff, Alewell and Hansen (2018)

Numerous studies have provided substantial evidence for positive relationships between HPWPs and different types of organizational performance measures (Jiang and Messersmith, 2018). The universalistic perspective is, however, not without critique. Authors from the contingency perspective (Jackson, Schuler and Jiang, 2014) and the contextual perspective (Brewster, 1999) contend that HRM practices' effectiveness depends on the internal environment (for example, the firm's strategy, general HRM philosophy, size, technology and qualification structure) and external environment (for example, sector, labor market, institutions, culture). Regarding the influence of culture, we may wonder whether HPWPs are equally effective in different cultures, in particular because HPWPs represent a Western concept. In order to test this assumption, Rabl et al. (2014) consolidated insights from different studies and analyzed 156 effect sizes from 35,767 firms/establishments in 29 countries. They found that HPWPs were positively related to performance in each country, regardless of its culture. Thus, HPWPs might indeed be best practices that can serve as a global standard of management practice. However, the authors also found that the strength of the relationship between HPWPs and the performance of employees varied between countries (that is, they found a moderating effect): The influence of HPWPs on performance was higher in countries high in power distance, high in collectivism and low in performance orientation. Thus, even though there are overall positive effects, culture is still important to understand why HPWPs work better in some countries than in others.

10.5 INTEGRATION OF INTERNATIONAL MIGRANTS

While our previous focus has largely been on expatriates and host-country employees, we now flip the focus and draw our attention to international migrants. International migrants represent a particular group of global workers who initiate their own mobility (in contrast to expatriates who are sent by an organization) and intend to stay in a foreign country for an indefinite period of time. Typically, international migrants move to another country either because of personal or family reasons (for example, to live and work in a more developed country, to be united with a spouse) or because they are forced to by specific circumstances (for example, because of violence, conflict, persecution or environmental changes and disaster). The latter group of international migrants is usually referred to as "refugees" or "displaced persons." While they represent a rather small fraction of all migrants, they often capture specific (public) attention.

In recent years, we have observed a considerable increase in international migration. In 2019, the number of international migrants reached 272 million (3.5 percent of the world's population), compared to 174 million in 2000. The majority, namely 74 percent, of all international migrants were of working age (that is, between 20 and 64 years) (International Organization for Migration, or IOM, 2020). In addition to the increased importance of international migration, we observe a growing interest in research on the individual-, organizational- and societal-level antecedents of acculturation, coping and integration success of migrants, and several business practices initiatives that aim to successfully integrate migrants into their organizations (see Box 10.2; for more useful links to background information and organizational activities, visit the book's website).

Box 10.2   Exercise: Organizational initiatives in the migration context

Helping international migrants can be considered a part of organizational social responsibility, but it also helps organizations to achieve their goals. The Tent Partnership for Refugees currently represents a network of 140 major firms like SAP, Volkswagen and Accenture that are committed to integrating refugees.

Go online and discover this network and its initiatives (the relevant links are provided on the book's website). Try to answer the following questions:

- Why should, according to the Tent Partnership, organizations support refugees?
- What are key areas in which to support refugees?
- Which specific guidelines are provided?

International migrants face various challenges when coming to and working in a foreign country, starting with legal barriers and administrative difficulties in obtaining visas and work permits. Compared to expatriates, they do not get assistance from an organization and do not have a secured job in the host country. In contrast, they have to find a job on their own, which can be a lengthy and costly process. In addition, professional credentials and qualifications may not be recognized, which leads to underemployment and precarious job situations. Finally, international migrants might not be acknowledged and supported by local colleagues and managers, but subject to discrimination and unequal treatment. Mastering this challenge is of relevance to the migrants, but successful integration outcomes also contribute to organizational objectives such as making best use of the available knowledge and abilities, and benefit society (for example, less brain-wastage).

Integration success is a multidimensional construct and refers to multiple outcomes. Following Hajro et al. (2019), these outcomes can be classified as subjective or objective outcomes, which can be observed in either the personal/family life domain or the workplace/career domain (see Table 10.7). Integration success implies a higher well-being of international migrants in terms of, for example, life satisfaction, job satisfaction or health. Likewise, it implies positive outcomes for organizations in terms of, for example, higher engagement, commitment and job performance.

Table 10.7 Dimensions of integration success of international migrants

	Subjective	Objective
Personal/family life domain	Life satisfaction Subjective well-being Family satisfaction Desire to repatriate Deviant behaviors Identity uncertainty	Physical health Mental health Development of social networks Host-country embeddedness
Workplace/career domain	Organizational commitment Subjective career success (for example, job/career satisfaction) Work engagement Capital mobilization Professional identity reaffirmation	Job performance Objective career success (for example, salary, promotions) Entrepreneurial success Social integration

Source: Hajro et al. (2019)

Building on the strategic HRM literature and the concept of well-being-oriented HRM, we developed a broad perspective on how firms can contribute to the integration of international migrants (Hauff and Richter, 2021). The concept of well-being-oriented HRM stems from Guest (2017) and has been introduced as a critique of the predominant, performance-oriented perspective on HRM (that is, HPWPs discussed above). It includes five subsets of HRM practices that are explicitly designed to promote employee well-being. The first subset, investing in employees, aims to enhance employee capabilities; for instance, through training and development, mentoring and career support. The second subset, engaging work, focuses on job design and includes motivational job characteristics such as autonomy, work variety and the provision of feedback. The third subset, positive social and physical environment, includes HRM practices aimed at prioritizing employee safety, avoiding workplace violence (for example, harassment, bullying) and discrimination, promoting equal opportunities, ensuring fair rewards and providing employment security. The fourth subset, voice, includes extensive two-way communication, the existence of representative-participation mechanisms (for example, work councils or committees representing employees) and opportunities to express individual opinions. The fifth subset, organizational support, includes participative and supportive management, as well as practices that facilitate employee involvement and flexible working arrangements.

We customized the framework to the migration context in order to provide a holistic understanding of the role of HRM for the integration of international migrants (Hauff and Richter, 2021; see Table 10.8).

Table 10.8 HRM practices that foster the integration of international migrants

HRM practices based on Guest (2017)	Measures In my organization …
Investing in employees	
Recruitment and selection	… recruiting and selection processes favor cultural diversity (for example, in job postings, anonymous application documents, acceptance and consideration of foreign qualifications).
Induction/integration	… an orientation program for newcomers is offered to learn about the company.
Training and development	… all new employees with an international background receive cross-cultural training. … all new employees with an international background receive specific training adapted to their needs (for example, language courses).
Mentoring and career support	… mentoring is used to support the integration of employees with an international background.
Providing engaging work	
Jobs designed to provide autonomy and challenge	… I am allowed to make a lot of job decisions on my own. … my job involves an adequate level of challenge and diversity to keep my work interesting.
Information provision and feedback	… I am kept informed about business issues and about how well my organization is doing. … I am given meaningful feedback regarding my performance at least once a year.
Skill utilization	… it is ensured that I can make adequate use of my skills and abilities.
Positive environment	
Equal opportunities/diversity management	… a diversity-friendly work environment is maintained.
Zero tolerance for bullying and harassment	… it is made clear that cultural differences must be respected.
Required and optional social interaction	… it is standard to work in teams composed of people with different nationalities. … social events are regularly organized (for example, staff excursions and parties) to improve social interaction between all employees.
Fair collective rewards/high basic pay	… fair pay for all employees regardless of their nationality is provided.
Employment security/ employability	… job security is almost guaranteed to all employees regardless of their nationality.
Voice	
Extensive two-way communication	… it is ensured that the opinions and input of employees from different cultural backgrounds are heard.
Employee surveys	… periodic employee surveys giving voice to all employees are conducted.
Collective representation	… there is a works council or a similar committee that represents employees' interests regardless of their nationality.
Organizational support	
Participative/supportive management	… my direct supervisor behaves in a manner which is thoughtful of my personal needs. … my direct supervisor sees that the interests of employees are given due consideration.
Developmental performance management	… there are plans for my future career development. … the promotion process is fair for all employees.
Flexible and family-friendly work arrangements	… the work schedule is adapted to the needs of workers of different nationalities (for example, consideration of religious holidays). … employee off-work situations (family, school, and so on) are considered when making work schedules.
Non-work-related support	… assistance with legal matters and paperwork is offered. … family support (for example, in choosing schools, language courses for family members) is offered.

Source: Hauff and Richter (2021)

```
         Providing engaging work
         ┌─────────────────────┐
         │ - Create jobs that  │
         │   offer challenge   │
         │   and diversity     │
Positive environment            │            Organizational support
         │ - Enable an         │
         │   adequate use of   │
┌─────────────────────┐         │         ┌─────────────────────┐
│ - Diversity-friendly│  employee skills   │ - Develop career    │
│   environment       │   and abilities    │   plans and fair    │
│ - Fair pay          │ - Inform about the │   promotion         │
│   regardless of     │   organization and │   processes         │
│   nationality       │   provide feedback │ - Consider          │
│ - Organize social   │                    │   employee needs    │
│   events to improve │                    │   (e.g. in work     │
│   interaction       │                    │   schedules)        │
│                     │                    │ - Assist in legal   │
│                     │                    │   matters           │
```

Figure 10.6 HRM practices that promote integration success of international migrants

To understand the relevance of the sets of HR practices involved, we did a large-scale survey with international migrants living and working in Germany. The results of our analysis show that an HRM strategy that applies a well-being-oriented HRM perspective is indeed of high value to improve the cross-cultural adjustment and organizational commitment of international migrants, and ultimately leads to a good performance of the migrant workforce. Looking at all three outcomes together, Figure 10.6 presents the top three sets of HR practices that contribute to integration success.

However, not all HRM practices and subsets of HRM practices are equally important for all integration outcomes. To improve the cross-cultural adjustment of international migrants – for example, their adjustment to the working conditions in the new country – managers are well advised to focus on a positive environment, in particular by establishing a diversity-friendly work environment, offering fair pay regardless of nationality and organizing social events to improve social interaction. To enhance the commitment of international migrants to the organizations, managers should offer organizational support to migrant workers, including a supervisor who is thoughtful of the personal needs of employees, a fair promotion process, plans for future career development, assistance with legal matters and the consideration of employees' off-work situations when making schedules. Finally, managers should also ensure that work is engaging, to increase commitment. The most relevant practices here are the adequate use of skills and abilities and an adequate level of challenge and diversity, followed by being informed about the organization and the business, and the provision of feedback (Hauff and Richter, 2021).

We invite HR managers in firms with international workforces to make use of these HR practices to foster positive integration outcomes. Alternatively, we recommend evaluating the organization's performance on the relevant HR practices; for instance, by using the items proposed in Table 10.8 in HR surveys.

CHAPTER REVIEW QUESTIONS

1. Outline the four international recruitment approaches and discuss their advantages and disadvantages.
2. A wide range of instruments has become established in corporate practice for the selection of applicants. Which are the main instruments? Which instruments would you consider most effective?
3. What are the main selection criteria for international assignments?
4. Cross-cultural trainings can be done in very different ways, and organizations need to decide how to design an appropriate program. Which basic approaches can be distinguished?
5. What are the essential components of pre-departure training?
6. What are the key factors for the success of cross-cultural trainings?
7. Which issues should be considered during training of host-country employees?
8. Outline the key components of compensation and discuss some specifics that are related to an international environment.
9. What are the three main options for compensating international employees? Which advantages and disadvantages are associated with each of them?
10. Discuss the principle of "thinking globally but acting locally" during performance management.
11. Discuss the concept of high-performance work practices and its applicability in different international contexts.
12. Which HRM practices can foster the integration of international migrants?

REFERENCES

Aguinis, H. (2019). *Performance Management* (4th ed.). Chicago, IL: Chicago Business Press.

Aguinis, H., Joo, H., and Gottfredson, R. K. (2012). Performance management universals: Think globally and act locally. *Business Horizons, 55,* 385–392.

Andresen, M., and Margenfeld, J. (2015). International relocation mobility readiness and its antecedents. *Journal of Managerial Psychology, 30,* 234–249.

Appelbaum, E., Bailey, T., Berg, P., and Kalleberg, A. L. (2000). *Manufacturing Advantage: Why High-Performance Work Systems Pay Off.* Ithaca, NY: Cornell Univ. Press.

Bennett, R., Aston, A., and Colquhoun, T. (2000). Cross-cultural training: A critical step in ensuring the success of international assignments. *Human Resource Management, 39,* 239–250.

Bonache, J., and Stirpe, L. (2012). Compensating global employees. In G. K. Stahl, I. Björkman and S. Morris (Eds), *Handbook of Research in International Human Resource Management* (pp. 162–182). Cheltenham, UK and Northampton, MA, USA: Edward Elgar Publishing.

Bratton, J., and Gold, J. (2012). *Human Resource Management: Theory and Practice* (5th ed.). New York, NY: Palgrave Macmillan.

Brewster, C. (1999). Strategic human resource management: The value of different paradigms. *Management International Review, 39,* 45–64.

Chebium, R. (2015). How to create an effective cross-cultural training program. www.shrm.org/hr-today/news/hr-magazine/pages/010215-cross-cultural-training.aspx.

Cho, I., and Payne, S. C. (2016). Other important questions: When, how, and why do cultural values influence performance management? *Industrial and Organizational Psychology, 9,* 343–350.

Davidov, E., Meuleman, B., Cieciuch, J., Schmidt, P., and Billiet, J. (2014). Measurement equivalence in cross-national research. *Annual Review of Sociology, 40,* 55–75.

Dong, Y., and Dumas, D. (2020). Are personality measures valid for different populations? A systematic review of measurement invariance across cultures, gender, and age. *Personality and Individual Differences, 160,* 109956.

Dowling, P. J., Festing, M., and Engle, A. D. (2017). *International Human Resource Management* (7th ed.). Andover: Cengage Learning.

Earley, P. C., and Ang, S. (2003). *Cultural Intelligence: Individual Interactions Across Cultures.* Palo Alto, CA: Stanford University Press.

Fatehi, K., and Choi, J. (2019). *International Business Management: Succeeding in a Culturally Diverse World* (2nd ed.). Cham: Springer International.

Fowler, S. M., and Yamaguchi, M. (2020). An analysis of methods for intercultural training. In D. Landis and D. P. S. Bhawuk (Eds), *Handbook of Intercultural Training* (Vol. 74, pp. 192–257). Cambridge: Cambridge University Press.

Gerhart, B., and Weller, I. (2019). Compensation. In A. Wilkinson, N. Bacon, S. A. Snell and D. Lepak (Eds.), *The SAGE Handbook of Human Resource Management* (pp. 210–237). Los Angeles, CA: SAGE.

Guest, D. E. (2017). Human resource management and employee well-being: Towards a new analytic framework. *Human Resource Management Journal, 27,* 22–38.

Hajro, A., Stahl, G., Clegg, C., and Lazarova, M. B. (2019). Acculturation, coping and integration success of international skilled migrants: An integrative review and multi-level framework. *Human Resource Management Journal, 29,* 328–352.

Harari, M. B., Reaves, A. C., Beane, D. A., Laginess, A. J., and Viswesvaran, C. (2018). Personality and expatriate adjustment: A meta-analysis. *Journal of Occupational and Organizational Psychology, 91,* 486–517.

Hauff, S., Alewell, D., and Hansen, N. K. (2018). Further exploring the links between high performance work practices and firm performance. A multiple-mediation model in the German context. *German Journal of Human Resource Management, 32,* 5–26.

Hauff, S., Guerci, M., Dul, J., and Rhee, H. (2021). Exploring necessary conditions in HRM research: Fundamental issues and methodological implications. *Human Resource Management Journal, 31,* 18–36.

Hauff, S., and Richter, N. F. (2021). Successfully integrating migrants into the workplace. Paper presented at AIB 2021 Online Conference.

Heenan, D. A., and Perlmutter, H. V. (1979). *Multinational Organizational Development: A Social Architectural Perspective*. Boston, MA: Addison-Wesley.

Huselid, M. A. (1995). The impact of human resource management practices on turnover, productivity, and corporate financial performance. *Academy of Management Journal, 38*, 635–672.

International Organization for Migration (2020). *World Migration Report 2020*. https://publications.iom.int/system/files/pdf/wmr_2020.pdf.

Jackson, S. E., Schuler, R. S., and Jiang, K. (2014). An aspirational framework for strategic human resource management. *Academy of Management Annals, 8*, 1–56.

Jiang, K., and Messersmith, J. (2018). On the shoulders of giants: A meta-review of strategic human resource management. *International Journal of Human Resource Management, 29*, 6–33.

KPMG (2019). *Global Assignment Policies and Practices Survey: 2019 Results*. https://assets.kpmg/content/dam/kpmg/xx/pdf/2019/10/2019-gapp-survey-report-web.pdf.

Kühlmann, T. M., and Heinz, R. (2017). *Managing Cultural Diversity in Small and Medium-Sized Organizations*. Wiesbaden: Springer.

Leung, K., Ang, S., and Tan, M. L. (2014). Intercultural competence. *Annual Review of Organizational Psychology and Organizational Behavior, 1*, 489–519.

LinkedIn (2018). *Global Recruiting Trends 2018*. https://business.linkedin.com/content/dam/me/business/en-us/talent-solutions/resources/pdfs/linkedin-global-recruiting-trends-2018-en-us2.pdf.

Littrell, L. N., Salas, E., Hess, K. P., Paley, M., and Riedel, S. (2006). Expatriate preparation: A critical analysis of 25 years of cross-cultural training research. *Human Resource Development Review, 5*, 355–388.

Mendenhall, M., and Oddou, G. (1986). Acculturation profiles of expatriate managers: Implications for cross-cultural training programs. *Columbia Journal of World Business, 21*, 73–79.

Michailova, S., Piekkari, R., Storgaard, M., and Tienari, J. (2017). Rethinking ethnocentrism in international business research. *Global Strategy Journal, 7*, 335–353.

Muratbekova-Touron, M. (2008). From an ethnocentric to a geocentric approach to IHRM. *Cross Cultural Management: An International Journal, 15*, 335–352.

OECD (2021). Price level indices (indicator). www.oecd-ilibrary.org/economics/price-level-indices/indicator/english_c0266784-en.

Ott, D. L., and Michailova, S. (2016). Expatriate selection: A historical overview and criteria for decision-making. In Y. Guo, H. G. Rammal and P. J. Dowling (Eds), *International Business and Management, Vol. 32: Global Talent Management and Staffing in MNEs* (pp. 1–24). Bingley: Emerald.

Perlmutter, H. V. (1969). The tortuous evolution of the multinational corporation. *Columbia Journal of World Business, 4*, 9–18.

Prince, N. R., Prince, J. B., and Kabst, R. (2020). National culture and incentives: Are incentive practices always good? *Journal of World Business, 55*, 101075.

Rabl, T., Jayasinghe, M., Gerhart, B., and Kühlmann, T. M. (2014). A meta-analysis of country differences in the high-performance work system–business performance relationship: The roles of national culture and managerial discretion. *Journal of Applied Psychology, 99*, 1011–1041.

Ryan, A. M., Reeder, M. C., Golubovich, J., Grand, J., Inceoglu, I., Bartram, D., Derous, E., Nikolaou, I., and Yao, X. (2017). Culture and testing practices: Is the world flat? *Applied Psychology, 66*, 434–467.

Schlaegel, C., Richter, N. F., and Taras, V. (2021). Cultural intelligence and work-related outcomes: A meta-analytic examination of joint effects and incremental predictive validity. *Journal of World Business, 56*, 1–27.

Scott, D., Brown, M., Shields, J., Long, R. J., Antoni, C. H., Beck-Krala, E. J., Lucia-Casademunt, A. M., and Perkins, S. J. (2015). A global study of pay preferences and employee characteristics. *Compensation & Benefits Review, 47*, 60–70.

Van der Zee, K. I., and Van Oudenhoven, J. P. (2000). The multicultural personality questionnaire: A multidimensional instrument of multicultural effectiveness. *European Journal of Personality, 14*, 291–309.

Waxin, M.-F., and Brewster, C. (2020). The recruitment, selection and preparation of expatriates. In J. Bonache, C. Brewster and F. J. Froese (Eds), *Global Mobility and the Management of Expatriates* (pp. 31–57). Cambridge: Cambridge University Press.

Waxin, M.-F., Brewster, C., and Ashill, N. (2019). Expatriate time to proficiency: Individual antecedents and the moderating effect of home country. *Journal of Global Mobility: The Home of Expatriate Management Research, 7,* 300–318.

10 CASE STUDY
MAGIC JUICE: TOWARDS AN HRM STRATEGY

Dirk always knew that people are key to the success of his organization. However, so far Magic Juice has followed a rather informal approach to HRM without overarching HR policies and guidelines. For example, Dirk and Sofie have largely recruited corporate and juice bar managers themselves, while the bar managers have completed the recruitment of their employees. Similarly, Magic Juice has to a lesser extent worked on training and development as well as performance management. After the merger with Zumo Saludable and the opening of the first stores in Spain and Portugal, Dirk wants Magic Juice to work in a more dedicated and professional way on HRM.

In order to get a first idea on how to approach this, Dirk opened his laptop and typed the words "HRM strategy" into Google. Quickly, he came across the concept of HPWPs, which immediately aroused his interest. He liked this approach in particular because it fitted with Magic Juice's overall business philosophy and his idea of the self-management model: Employee responsibility and engagement are considered a crucial part of HPWPs to increase performance. With his first ideas in mind, he approached Liv Bakker, who handles the personnel files, contracts and payrolls at Magic Juice. Dirk told Liv about his ideas and that he is fascinated by the concept of HPWPs. At the end of their discussion, he asked Liv to create a first draft of an HRM policy that elucidates general principles for the HRM practices related to employees' ability, motivation and opportunities.

At first, Liv was very enthusiastic. For some time, she had not really felt fulfilled by her administrative tasks, and the prospect of a more responsible and influential role felt very exciting. However, after a while she started to wonder whether it is possible to have an HRM strategy that fits for every country the company operates in. Liv knows that rules and regulations are different in every country, and that people in different countries expect different things. Furthermore, she wondered how much she should go into detail. Even though she could think of some principles that may guide the HRM activities in every country, she thought that the implementation of these principles should probably be different depending on the local context.

CASE QUESTIONS

As a first step, Liv wants to formulate possible HRM principles based on the HPWPs concept. Building on that, she wants to analyze whether these principles can represent standardized guidelines for all countries where the firm operates. In order to do that, she thinks, it may also be good to select at least one HRM practice in each of the AMO domains and discuss how the principles regarding these practices need to be implemented differently depending on the needs and requirements of individual countries. Quickly, she writes down the following key terms: "training as ability-enhancing practice," "performance appraisal as motivation-enhancing practice," and "involvement as opportunity-enhancing practice." These are the practices she wants to analyze in detail. While Liv thinks about how to proceed, Dirk opens the door and says, "Liv, can you also think about how to ensure that our franchise outlets are guided by our HRM strategy?" Liv's head is buzzing. Can you help her?

INDEX

ability, motivation, opportunity (AMO) framework 308
"acquisition" 75
affective trust 235
agri-food industry 186
Aguinis, H. 307, 308
Ali-Yrkko, J. 176
alternative forms of exporting 64
AMO framework *see* ability, motivation, opportunity (AMO) framework
Andersen, P. H. 45
Ang, S. 242, 243, 246, 249
Asian cultures 306
asset-based valuation 105
asset specificity 89
autocratic institutions 6
autonomous leadership 261

balanced scorecard 157, 159
Bartlett, C. A. 207, 213, 214
Basic Psychological Need Theory (BPNT) 273
behavioral CQ 244, 246
"belonging needs" 272
Bestseller Fashion Group China Ltd 91, 92
"Big Mac Index" 302
Birkinshaw, J. 219
body language 268
Borgholm, Steen 191
Bosch diversity thinking 252
Boston Consulting Group 4, 31
bottom-up or expansive international market selection 35–41
Bouquet, C. 219
BPNT *see* Basic Psychological Need Theory (BPNT)
brand equity 89
Brown, C. L. 33
Brown, M. E. 262
business model canvas 146
"business model canvas" 145
business-to-business industries 65
business-to-business markets 64
buyer–seller relationships 78
buyer–supplier relationships, CSR practices in 189

CAGE framework 37–9
capital investment (CAPEX) 102
captive governance 185
captive offshore strategy 188, 193
case study
    competitors 54–5
    entry mode(s) 95
    European food service market 53
    fruit and vegetable juice market 52–3
    juice/smoothie bar stores in selected countries 56–7
    Magic Juice 22–4, 95, 124–8, 167–9, 196–7, 229, 255, 287, 318
    selected market indicators for selected countries 55
cash-and-carry concept 44
cash-deal scenario 107
cash *versus* stock deals in M&A 107
category and functional business units 223
cause–effect relationships 140
Cavusgil, S. T. 33
centers of excellence (COEs) 214
centralization–decentralization mechanism 210
centralized decision-making 200
charismatic/value-based leadership 261
Chinese fashion retail market 91
Chinese hierarchy of needs 272
civil law systems 72
classical international organizational structures 202, 203
CLOU *see* Colleague Letter of Understanding (CLOU)
CLT *see* culturally endorsed theory of leadership (CLT)
codesharing arrangement 74
COEs *see* centers of excellence (COEs)
cognitive CQ 243, 246
cognitive trust 235
Colleague Letter of Understanding (CLOU) 289
collectivistic cultures 307
"comfort shoe" segment 191
commitment-trust theory 65
comparable valuation 105
compensation components in international context 302–4
competitive marketplace 73
competitive markets 84
conceptual thinking 260
"configure to order" approach 190
consensual decision-making 237

constructive feedback, definition of 232
contemporary strategy concept 141
contracting modes 65–9
contract manufacturing 65–6
contract production 65
contractual arrangements 63
contractual entry modes 70
cooperative entry modes 86
cooperative marketing agreements 73
corporate network 220
corporate social responsibility (CSR) 188, 218
    practices in buyer–supplier relationships 189
correlation coefficient between indicators 30
Corruption Perceptions Index 28
cost-leadership strategy 133
country-based international division 222
country markets 31, 47
"country ranking pipeline" 44
CQ *see* cultural intelligence (CQ)
"creeping expropriation" 85
critical interview questions 293–4
cross-cultural leadership research 257, 259, 263
cross-cultural learning 300
cross-cultural training approaches 298–300
cross-national differences 277
CSR *see* corporate social responsibility (CSR)
cultural archetypes and individual cultural value
    patterns 17–19
cultural classification schemes 11
cultural clustering 16, 17
    global leadership dimensions in 264
cultural dimensions
    and global leadership dimensions 263
    in Hofstede and GLOBE 14
cultural dissimilarities 1
cultural distance 86
cultural diversity of teams 268
cultural integration 96, 113–16
cultural intelligence (CQ) 243, 244, 247, 297
Cultural Intelligence Scale 245
culturally endorsed theory of leadership (CLT)
    258, 263
culturally sensitive equity model 276
cultural novelty 299
cultural scores for selected countries 15
cultural similarities and dissimilarities 11
cultural training 300
cultural values 263–4
    at individual level, measuring 19
    surveys 16
culture-general content 299

culture map
    in action 236–9
    dimensions of 232–6
    eight dimensions of 233
culture-specific content 299
Cummings, J. L. 100
"customer needs" 141
customer needs and viable segments 140–144
customer value map 145

Danish Industrialization Fund for Developing
    Countries 91
decision-making method 235
decision-making process 60
decision-making responsibility 234
defensive alliances 73
defensive foreign divestment 88
defensive voluntary divestment 89
de-internationalization 88
"*de novo* investment" 75
Dietsch, Johannes 102
differentiated subsidiary roles and
    interdependencies 217
digital business models 174
digital communication tools 208
direct exporting 64
"direct injection technology" 192
discriminatory costs 35
dispersion 178
diversity-oriented personnel recruitment 252
Dong, Y. 295
Dorfman, P. 266
downstream activities 176
Dumas, D. 295
Dutch–Danish partnership 77

ECCO's code of conduct 193
"eclectic framework" 79
Economic Freedom Index 8
"economic quality" 3
economic risks 84
economies of scale (EOS) 27, 149
economies of scope 27
effective communication strategy 117
effective international workforce 306–9
    approaches for compensating international
        employees 304
    compensation components in international
        context 302–4
    integration of international migrants
        310–314

INDEX

international assignment policy at Bosch 306
   performance management 306–9
   recruitment approaches 290–292
   selection criteria for international
      assignments 296–8
   selection tools 292–5
   training and development 298–302
effective performance management 307
efficiency-seeking firms 27
efficiency-seeking motives 60
egalitarian leadership style 237
EMC *see* export management company (EMC)
emerging market 4, 5, 9, 29, 39, 83, 164, 181, 205
Emmerik, Van 274
employee engagement and satisfaction dashboard 284
entry mode decision 77, 82
   analytical framework to guide 77–87
   complexity of 60–63
entry-mode-related decision criteria 79
entry modes 61
   case study 95
   choice 78–9
   considerations 82
   contractual 70
   cooperative 86
   decision trade-offs 62
   in fashion retailing 89–92
   foreign 87
   high-commitment 63, 84
   international 59
   investment-heavy 80
   low-commitment 63, 84
   lower-control 90
environmental complexity 212
EOS *see* economies of scale (EOS)
equity joint ventures 72
equity modes 61, 63, 69–77, 88
   establishment modes 75–7
   international markets 69–77
   ownership modes 70–73
equity theory 275
"esteem needs" 272
ethical leadership 262
ethnocentric or home-country approach 291
Euclidean distance (ED) metric 39, 40
European brewing industry 77
European car manufacturer 103
European corporate functions 222
European food service market 53
exporter–agency relationships 88

export intermediaries 63
export management company (EMC) 64
export modes 63–5
external legitimacy 219
external network 220

face-to-face meeting 270
facial expressions 268
fashion retailing, entry modes in 89–92
faster execution 71
FDI *see* foreign direct investment (FDI)
Fejoz, Aude 238, 239
financial capability 90
financial incentives 86
Fireman, Paul 118
FIRM 282, 283
firm-level strategy and services 225
firm's own sales subsidiary, foreign intermediaries *versus* 65
firm-specific advantages (FSAs) 78, 207
fiscal incentives 86
fixed-share deal 107
fixed-value deal 107
"flexible replication" 162
"focused cost leadership" 133
"focused differentiation strategy" 133
food and food services, megatrends in 170–171
food service management contracts 69
forced divestiture 85
foreign-based intermediaries 64
foreign direct investment (FDI) 3, 28, 60, 69, 183, 216
foreign entry modes 87
foreign intermediaries *versus* firm's own sales subsidiary 65
foreign markets 80–83
   commitment 88
   exit 87–9
   reductions and divestments 88
foreign-operation learning costs 88
foreign subsidiaries 70
formalization 210
formal organizational set-up 208
formal *versus* informal institutions 6
form of payment 106–8
fractionalization 178
franchisor–franchisee relationships 67–8
free-market system 4
Friis, Dan 92
front–back hybrid matrix 224
front–back organization 225

fruit and vegetable juice market 52–3
fruit and vegetables global value chain 196–8
fruit juice market profiles 172
FSAs *see* firm-specific advantages (FSAs)

Garbe, J.-N. 208
Gaston-Breton, C. 28
GBS *see* Global Business Services (GBS)
GBUs *see* Global Business Units (GBUs)
GDP *see* gross domestic product (GDP)
geographical distribution and governance 182–3
geographical organizational structure 205
geographic structuring 205
Gerhard, B. 212
German market 6
Ghemawat, P. 37
Ghoshal, S. 207, 213, 214
global assignment policies and practices 300
Global Business Services (GBS) 224, 225
Global Business Units (GBUs) 224
Global Competitiveness Index 9, 12
global consumption database 2
globalization and unbundling, stages of 179
global leadership dimensions
    and attributes 258–62
    in cultural clusters 264
    cultural dimensions and 263
global matrix structure 206, 224
global product division structure 205
global product standardization 150
Global Recruiting Trends Survey 292
global value chain (GVC) 238
    design at ECCO A/S *versus* competitors 191–4
    elements of value chain and value added 174–7
    and smiling curve 177–82
    strategic options to configure value chain 186–91
    typology of 184
    value chain strategies 182–5
global virtual team (GVT) 267–71
GLOBE framework 13–16, 20, 262
"go global" policy 83
Govindarajan, V. 213
gradual learning process 75
Greenfield investments *versus* acquisitions 75–7
gross domestic product (GDP) 2, 28, 84
Guest, D. E. 311
Gugler, P. 151
Gupta, A. K. 213

GVC *see* global value chain (GVC)
GVT *see* global virtual team (GVT)

Hainer, Herbert 118, 120
Hajro, A. 311
hard services 82
Harrison, D. A. 262
Haspelagh, P. 111, 113, 114
Hedlund, Gunnar 206
Heineken–Carlsberg alliance 76
Herfindahl–Hirschman Index (HHI) 32, 33
Heritage Foundation 8
HHI *see* Herfindahl–Hirschman Index (HHI)
hierarchical governance 185
hierarchical models in MNEs and industries 204
"hierarchy of needs" theory 271
hierarchy of strategic statements 131
high-commitment entry modes 63, 84
high-performance work practices (HPWPs) 308–9
high-performing subsidiaries 221
high transaction costs 78
Hofstede, Geert 13–16, 20, 234, 272
Hofstede Insights 14
Hofstede model 40
Hogenbirk, A. E. 213
Holmberg, S. R. 100
home-country approach 292, 304
home-country environment 83
home-country factors 83
home-country government policies 83
"host-country approach" 304
host-country factors 83–7
hotel management contracts 69
hotel services 82
HPWPs *see* high-performance work practices (HPWPs)
HQ–subsidiary relationships 209, 211
HRM *see* human resource management (HRM)
"hub and spoke" models 207
humane-oriented leadership 261, 263
human resource management (HRM) 116, 290

IB *see* international business (IB)
ICT *see* information and communication technologies (ICT)
IDI *see* Intercultural Development Inventory (IDI)
ILT *see* implicit leadership theory (ILT)
IMF *see* International Monetary Fund (IMF)
implicit leadership theory (ILT) 258

INDEX

IMS *see* international market selection (IMS)
incremental internationalization-process model 35
incremental market-entry process 60
"independent" organizational units 224
Indian Tata Group 28
indirect exporting 64
indirect financial rewards 303
"individualism *versus* collectivism" 13
individualistic cultures 13
individualistic values 272
individual organizational units 282
information and communication technologies (ICT) 2, 9, 179, 257, 268
information-processing capacity of GVTs 268
information-processing theory 268
in-group collectivism 13
institutional collectivism 13
institutional theory 6, 79
intangible resources 136
integrated MNE network 217
integration
    approaches 111–13
    cultural 96, 113–16
    of international migrants 310–314
    success of international migrants 311
integration-responsiveness (IR) framework 149, 150, 153
intercultural competencies 231, 241–9, 297, 298
    in action 248–9
    development at Bosch Group 250–252
    dimensions of 241–7
    models 297
Intercultural Development Inventory (IDI) 243
"intercultural development of employees" 250
intercultural interactions 231
    culture map 232–41
    intercultural competence 241–9
    intercultural competence development at Bosch Group 250–252
intercultural sensitivity, developmental model of 243
intercultural training catalog 251
intercultural traits 242
interdependent activities 176
internal firm factors 79–82
internal legitimacy 219
"internal process perspective" 158
internal retail organization 92
international assignments 296–8
    policy at Bosch 305, 306

international business (IB) 129, 199, 231
    literature 35
    opportunities 147
    strategy 1
international employees, approaches for compensating 304
international entry mode 59
international environment 257
    employee engagement at a marketing consultancy 282–4
    in global virtual teams 267–71
    leadership in 258–67
    motivation in 271–82
international fashion industry 89
International Federation of Robotics 2
internationalization
    costs 35
    motives 26–8
International Labor Rights Forum 188
international markets 1, 59, 129
    analytical framework to guide entry mode decision 77–87
    analyzing formal context 2–9
    analyzing informal context 11–19
    complexity of entry mode decision 60–63
    developing global or local positioning 140–152
    entry mode changes over time and foreign market exit 87–9
    entry modes in fashion retailing 89–92
    equity modes 69–77
    international business (IB) 129
    monitoring strategic success 153–61
    non-equity modes 63–9
    pillars of Global Competitiveness Index 10–11
    schools of thought in strategy 130
    strategic analyses 134–40
    strategic positioning and strategy at IKEA 161–4
    strategy statements 130–133
international market selection (IMS)
    bottom-up or expansive international market selection 35–41
    selection at Metro Group 42–5
    toolset 45–9
    top-down or restricted international market selection 26–34
international migrants 290, 310–314
international migration 9, 310
International Monetary Fund (IMF) 2, 84

international opportunities 1
international strategy 129, 161
international team projects 247
internet/digitalization effects 148
inter-organizational cooperative arrangements 73
inter-organizational relationships 73
interviewing innovations 295
intrinsic work values 277
investment-heavy entry modes 80
investment-heavy entry process 60
"inward FDI performance index" 3
IR framework *see* integration-responsiveness (IR) framework

Jemison, W. 111, 113, 114
job-related factors 296
job satisfaction
    across cultures, determinants of 279–82
    situational job characteristics on 280
"jobs to be done" analyses 143, 145
joint ventures/strategic alliances 70–73
juice/smoothie bar stores in selected countries 56–7

Kabst, R. 303
Kamprad, Ingvar 162
key performance indicators (KPIs) 157
Kogut, B. 40
Koh, C. 243
Kolb, D. A. 248
KPIs *see* key performance indicators (KPIs)

language skills 297
large capital-intensive MNEs 201
Lasserre, P. 152
leadership
    and cultural processes 259
    dimensions and attributes 260
leadership expectations
    and CEO behavior in Germany 266
    and CEO behavior in the United States 265
leadership styles 261
    in cultures 234
    egalitarian 237
"learning to learn" approach 300
legal counseling 116
Leung, K. 242
"levels of aggregation" 176
liabilities of foreignness (LoF) 35–7
licensing 81
    agreement 66

Livermore, D. 246, 249
LoF *see* liabilities of foreignness (LoF)
long-term or future-oriented cultures 13
Lord, A. W. 33
low-commitment entry modes 63, 84
lower-commitment modes 79, 80
lower-commitment operation mode 89
lower-control entry mode 90
lower-power subsidiary groups 221

Maastricht Treaty 84
macroeconomic stability 84
macro-segmentation of countries 31
Malekzadeh, A. R. 114
management agreement 69
management contract 68, 69
"management of distance" 35
market attractiveness 84
Market Development Organizations (MDOs) 224
market entry, timing of 43
market governance 185
marketing-oriented method of selling 67
marketing practice and research 144
marketing subsidiaries 219
market-seeking motives 27, 60
market selection 27, 32, 52, 83, 87
markets with partner 96
    Adidas and Reebok 118–22
    best practices to integrate partners 116–17
    cultural integration 113–15
    integration approaches 111–13
    negotiations 108–11
    paying right price 101–8
    selecting right partner 97–100
Martin, O. M. 28
M&As *see* mergers and acquisitions (M&As)
"masculinity *versus* femininity" 13
Maslow, Abraham 271–2
matrix structure 206, 222
McClelland, D. C. 274
MDOs *see* Market Development Organizations (MDOs)
measurement invariance across cultures 296
"mechanisms of organizational coordination" 210
Mendenhall, M. 299
mergers and acquisitions (M&As) 60, 96, 105
    cash *versus* stock deals in 107
meso-level actors 218
metacognitive CQ 243, 246
Meyer, Erin 231–3, 236
micro-political risks 85

migration 9, 170, 248, 310, 311
mission statements, collective of 288
MNEs *see* multinational enterprises (MNEs)
mobile handset industry 181
modular governance 185
Morschett, D. 87
motivational CQ 243, 246, 249
motivation in international environment 271–82
MPQ *see* Multicultural Personality Questionnaire (MPQ)
Multicultural Personality Questionnaire (MPQ) 242, 244
"multigroup confirmatory factor analysis" 296
multinational enterprises (MNEs) 1, 62, 130, 146, 174, 181, 199, 257, 304
    centrality and influence 220
    conflicts of interest of key actors in 218
    hierarchical models 200–206
    networks and transnationals 206–9
    organizational coordination mechanisms 209–12
    power and conflicts within 217–21
    Procter & Gamble (P&G) 221–5
    regional or global strategies of 151
    and subsidiaries 216
    subsidiary roles and mandates 212–15
Musk, Elon 8

Nahavandi, A. 114
national cultural scores 15
national cultures, clustering 16
national market requirements 283
national practices and regulations 303
national subsidiaries of MNEs 214
need hierarchies 273
negotiations 108–11
"net exports" 3
net present value (NPV)
    of cash flows 101
    estimations 104
networks
    corporate 220
    external 220
    integrated MNE 217
    and transnationals 206–9
Nevis, E. C. 272
Nisbett, Richard 233
non-binding document 110
non-equity modes 61, 63–9, 80, 88
    contracting modes 65–9
    export modes 63–5

non-equity ventures 80
non-substitutable resources 219
non-tariff barriers 86
NPV *see* net present value (NPV)

Oddou, G. 299
OECD *see* Organisation for Economic Co-operation and Development (OECD)
offensive alliances 73
offshore outsource strategy 188
"offshoring" 187
Olejnik, E. 87
OLI framework 79
on-assignment practical support 301
online cultural briefings 301
online soft skills assessments 294
onshore in-house strategy 187
open-mindedness 242
operational risk-sharing 106
Organisation for Economic Co-operation and Development (OECD) 2, 9, 180
"Organization 2005" 224
organizational coordination mechanisms 209–12
organizational (culture) fit 99, 212
organizational initiatives in migration context 310
organizational institution theory 218
organizational set-ups and firm 209
organizational socialization process 212
organizational structures 99, 112, 137, 200, 207, 211, 222, 224
    classical international 202, 203
    formal 208
    geographical 205
    IBM's 204
    product 206
    unbalanced 223
Osterwalder, Alexander 146
outsourcing 2, 178, 186–90, 193
overseas fashion retailing 90
ownership modes 70–73

parent–subsidiary relationship level 37
Paris Agreement of 2016 8
participative leadership 261, 263
"partnering-related factors of success" 100
partner scoring 101
partner selection process 96, 115
partner-selection process 115
partnership agreement/letter of intent 111
partnership opportunities 98
performance appraisals 306

performance-based pay systems 302, 303
performance management 306–9
    cross-cultural perspectives on 306–8
    effective 307
    effective international workforce 306–9
    high-performance work practices (HPWPs) 308–9
    systems 307
performance-related behavior 295
political institutions 6
political risks, types of 85
political stability 84
polycentric approach 292
Porter, M. E. 174, 175
Porter's five forces 135
portfolio analyses 28–34, 39
post-partnering phase 96
power distance index 14
PPP level *see* purchasing power parity (PPP) level
pre- and post-partnering stage 97
pre-departure practical support 301
"primary leadership" dimensions 261
Prince, J. B. 303
Prince, N. R. 303
producer-driven GVCs 178
production subsidiary 219
product-related factors 80
project management approach 116
purchasing power parity (PPP) level 29

quality assurance system 300

Rabl, T. 309
RBV 78, 79, 89
recruitment
    approaches 290–292
    decisions 292
    diversity-oriented personnel 252
regional economic powerhouses 3
regional industries 151
regional or global strategies of MNEs 151
regional strategy 152
regression-based method 280
regulatory institutions 6
relational governance 185
relationship-based trust 235
relationship-marketing literature 65
research and development (R&D) capabilities 137
research-intensive firms 181
resource-commitment process 36, 61
resource-seeking motives 27, 60

return on investment (ROI) 70
Revson, Charles 141
Richter, N. F. 17, 208
risk-related aspects 100
Robinson Country Intelligence Index 33, 34
Robinson Country Risk assessment 33
ROI *see* return on investment (ROI)
Ronen, S. 16
Rosa, B. 151
Rugman, A. M. 150, 151
rule of thumb 32, 134, 270
"rules of the game" 79
Ryan, A. M. 295

"safety needs" 272
Sakarya, S. 39
Scott, D. 303
Scottish & Newcastle, acquisition of 76
screening candidates for CQ 246
security briefings 301
selection
    criteria for international assignments 296–8
    at Metro Group 42–5
    tools 292–5
self-actualization 272, 273
self-centered mentality 204
self-determination theory 273
self-management, principles/conditions of 288–9
self-protective leadership 261
Selling and Market Operations (SMOs) 225
set-up costs 88
Sharma, P. 18
Shenkar, O. 16
short-term assignments 298
similarity-attraction theories 267
Singh, H. 40
situational job characteristics on job satisfaction 280
small and medium-sized firms (SMEs) 63, 201
SMEs *see* small and medium-sized firms (SMEs)
"smile of value creation" 181
"smiling curve" 177–82
SMOs *see* Selling and Market Operations (SMOs)
social categorization theories 267
socialization 211
soft services 82
Stamminger, Erich 120
stock-deal scenario 107
Strandskov, J. 45
strategic alliances 61, 73
    in airline industry 74

INDEX

strategic analyses 134–40
strategic and organizational (cultural) fit, assessment of 100
strategic-asset-seeking motives 27, 60
strategic-leader subsidiaries 214
strategic management literature 28
strategic partnerships 96
strategic statements, hierarchy of 131
strategy-development process 132
strategy development toolset 149
strength-based approach 308
strengths, weaknesses, opportunities and threats (SWOT) 138, 139
subsidiary-level activities 210
subsidiary roles
    development 219
    and mandates 212–15
"subsidiary role typologies" 213
Sustainable Development Goals of the UN 8
switching costs 87–8
Swoboda, B. 87
SWOT *see* strengths, weaknesses, opportunities and threats (SWOT)

Tan, M. L. 242
tangible resources 136
Taras, V. 15
"task-specific factors of success" 100
taxation 303
TCA *see* transaction cost theory (TCA)
team-oriented leadership 261
technology-intensive firm 81
Testament of a Furniture Dealer 162
"Think global and act local" philosophy 292
too-rapid entry process 60
Toosbuy, Karl 191
top-down decision-making 201
top management statements 113
"traditional" codeshared itinerary 74
traditional interviews, limitations of 293
traditional marketing 141
traditional statistics 2
training and development 298–302
transaction costs 81, 88
transaction cost theory (TCA) 78–81, 88
transaction-cost thinking 84
transition management structure 113
transnational organizational model 207
transnational strategy 150
Trevino, L. K. 262

typical pitfalls in negotiations 110

"uncertainty avoidance" 13
unfavorable industry environment 83
United Nations' (UN's) Sustainable Development Goals 8
universal human needs 273
universally desirable and undesirable attributes 261, 262
Uppsala internationalization process model 36
Uppsala model of internationalization 78
upstream activities 175–6

valuation methods 101–6
value added in value chain 180
value-adding activities 207
value chain configurations 186–91
value chain control and location development paths 190
value chain strategies 182–5
value propositions
    developing 144–6
    integrating 146–52
Van Dyne, L. 243
van Kranenburg, H. L. 213
variable pay 302
Verbeke, A. 151
vertical integration strategy 187
virtual collaborative options 270
voluntary foreign market reduction 88
VRIO framework 136–9, 144, 146
"VUCA characteristics" 1

WACC *see* weighted average cost of capital (WACC)
Warr, P. B. 279
WEF *see* World Economic Forum (WEF)
weighted average cost of capital (WACC) 101
wholly owned subsidiaries (WOS) 62, 70–73, 81, 86, 88, 89
work centrality 277–8
Workers' Right Consortium 188
work values 277–8
World Bank 8, 69
World Economic Forum (WEF) 9
World Governance Indicators 6, 41
    of selected countries 7
World trade and FDI indicators 5
WOS *see* wholly owned subsidiaries (WOS)
written communication 268